From the Rivers to the Sea

From

the Rivers to the Sea

The United States Navy in Vietnam

Commander R. L. Schreadley, USN (Ret.)

Naval Institute Press
Annapolis, Maryland

Copyright © 1992 by the United States Naval Institute
Annapolis, Maryland

Library of Congress Cataloging-in-Publication Data
Schreadley, R. L. (Richard L.)
    From the rivers to the sea : the United States Navy in Vietnam /
R.L. Schreadley.
        p.   cm.
Includes bibliographical references (p.   ) and index.
ISBN 0-87021-772-0 (alk. paper)
1. Vietnamese Conflict, 1961–1975—Naval operations, American.
    2. United States. Navy—History—Vietnamese Conflict, 1961–1975.
I. Title.
DS558.7.S37   1982   91-16668
                                                                        CIP

Printed in the United States of America on acid-free paper ∞

9   8   7   6   5   4   3   2

First printing

All photographs not otherwise credited are official U.S. Navy.

The line drawings are by Bill Thompson.

The maps were drawn by Bill Clipson.

There were nights on the river, away from the cities and the towns, when the stars seemed close enough to touch. In a Swift boat or a PBR, drifting with the current or with engines barely idling, it was easy to forget the war and the enemy who waited for you at the next bend of the river.

Sometimes your reverie was broken by the flash and rumble of artillery—or was it simply heat lightning?—miles away. Sometimes a Cobra gunship appeared from nowhere to lash a village, or the environs of a village, with twin tongues of fire. At other times, it was the sudden chatter of automatic weapons or the whoosh of a rocket directed at your boat that ended the dreaming.

And then you wondered, what the hell am I doing here? What the hell is the navy doing here?

Contents

List of Maps

Preface

When one examines the history of Vietnam, he is struck by its resemblance to a Greek tragedy. In Greek tragedy, and in some of Shakespeare's plays, it seems as though everyone is murdered or betrayed, the best of intentions fall by the wayside, and the entire plot eventually collapses in gloom and doom. The vicissitudes of Vietnamese history unfortunately bear a resemblance to these woeful tales.

—Bernard B. Fall, from a lecture delivered at the Naval War College, Newport, R.I., on 28 September 1966.

One must wonder what Bernard Fall would have said had he lived to see not just Dien Bien Phu, but the dénouement of America's war in Vietnam—the evacuation by helicopter of the last Americans from the roof of the U.S. Embassy in Saigon, the ragtag armada of Vietnamese Navy ships and craft fleeing from the rivers to the sea loaded with panic-stricken refugees, the tanks of Communist North Vietnam rumbling through the streets of South Vietnam's capital to batter down the gates of the presidential palace. In one of the war's great ironies, Fall was killed on 21 February 1967 while accompanying a patrol of U.S. Marines along Vietnam's Route 1, a coastal road he immortalized in his writing as the "Street Without Joy."

There is indeed the essence of Greek tragedy in Vietnamese history, and more particularly in America's involvement in the 30-year war (1945–75) which led, first, to the elimination of French colonial rule in Indochina and, second, to unification of Vietnam under Communist control.

It is frequently said that hubris was the "fatal flaw" in the American character that led the nation recklessly into a second (after Korea) land war in Asia in the short span of a single generation, and few would dispute the presence of tragic figures, themselves fatally flawed, in the American *dramatis personae* of the Vietnam War: Presidents Kennedy, Johnson, and Nixon; Generals Maxwell Taylor and William C. Westmoreland; Admiral Elmo R. Zumwalt, Jr., to name but a few. Some would include in that pantheon every one of the 2,700,000 American soldiers and sailors who fought the "thankless" war in Vietnam in demoralizing circumstances that denied them not only the actuality, but, for many, even the anticipation of victory.

Greek tragedy? Yes, most definitely. Vietnam was America's Trojan War, though with an outcome entirely different from that enjoyed by the ancient Greek expeditionary force that succeeded, ultimately, in toppling the "topless towers of Ilium."

The towers that all the might of the U.S. military could not topple in Vietnam, I suggest, were those erected not by the Viet Cong or by the North Vietnamese Army, but by civilian managers of the war—in the Pentagon, the State Department, and the White House. My research convinces me absolutely that our political leadership never suffered from a lack of sound military advice, only from a lack of political will to follow it. We could have won in Vietnam, we could have saved the long-suffering Vietnamese people from the scourge of communism, but we could not do it the hard way, the way prescribed by those Admiral Thomas H. Moorer once described to me as being "educated beyond their competence."

It is my purpose in the pages that follow to tell, in brief and with as much detachment as I can muster, the U.S. Navy's story in Vietnam. I was given a unique opportunity to observe and document much of that story during my assignment "in-country." In the summer of 1969, fresh from two years of postgraduate work at the Fletcher School of Law and Diplomacy, I reported for duty on the staff of Commander Naval Forces Vietnam (COMNAVFORV). The principal job given me by the then commander, Vice Admiral Elmo R. Zumwalt, Jr., was to write a history of the naval war to that time.

I had blanket travel orders to go wherever I wished in South Vietnam, and in the course of my assignment I visited navy installations from Cua Viet in the north to Sea Float in the south, and from An Thoi in the west to Cat Lo in the east. I went on patrol in virtually every type of naval craft employed in the coastal waters and rivers of Vietnam. I flew with the Sea Wolves (navy UH-1B helicopters) and with the Black Ponies (OV-10 fixed-wing aircraft).

I wrote to the officers then commanding, and to those who had commanded, the major task organizations in NAVFORV, soliciting their thoughts on the conduct of the naval war, their "lessons learned." I collected and read, voraciously, all the end-of-tour reports I could put my hands on. These reports, written by naval advisors just prior to departure from Vietnam, were and are a rich mine of information.

I took a special interest in the navy's "ACTOV" program—the accelerated turnover of U.S. Navy assets to the Vietnamese. It was, I concluded at the time, proceeding much too rapidly to have any meaningful chance of success. The United States was bailing out of the war, and the navy was leading the way. Disaster loomed for those we ostensibly were trying to help, and we were placing in extreme peril the advisors who would be among the last to leave. My assessment and my warnings led to a memorable (for me) confrontation with Admiral Zumwalt just prior to his being named Chief of Naval Operations.

"If history proves you right," I said (misquoting Abraham Lincoln), "it won't matter what anybody says about you. If it proves you wrong, ten angels swearing you were right won't make the least bit of difference." This was a terribly brash thing for a junior commander to say to a vice admiral, and I knew I had angered him. Such was my admiration for him, however, that I felt compelled to tell him what he did not want to hear.

My 500-page manuscript, "The Naval War in Vietnam," was never published nor was the much longer "Compendium of Lessons Learned" I put together in the same period. Reviewing them, years later, I agree with the decision to chunk them into the memory hole. They needed better editing and a better sense of proportion than I was then able to give them. They were too pessimistic for the times. Later they would seem less so.

I ended my history manuscript with the following short paragraph, which I still like:

"The great green fleet of the Delta, the brave PBRs, the Swift boats, and the Brown Water sailor himself will soon belong to the past. Only the rivers and the memories will remain."

The chief of staff, Captain (later Vice Admiral) Emmett Tidd, penciled in the margin, "No! There must be more than that left—i.e., a viable VNN."

Unfortunately, there wasn't.

Three articles culled from the history were published in the Naval Institute *Proceedings* and *Naval Review* in 1970 and 1971. (Since these were written on "company time," I donated what I was paid to the Vietnamese Navy's Helping Hand Foundation, a fund established to improve the lot of the Vietnamese sailor and his family. Lord knows, they needed it.) Perversely, I included my "pessimistic" ending in the long *Naval Review* piece.

In late 1972, I returned to Vietnamese waters as the commanding officer of USS *Blakely* (DE 1072). When the Paris accords ending U.S. participation in the war were signed, my ship was in the northern Tonkin Gulf. The cruise was uneventful except for the introduction it gave me to the famous Tonkin Gulf "ghosts," and the firsthand look I had at the absolutely grim condition of Pacific Fleet ships and crews kept too long and too indefinitely at sea. Many of them (not mine!) were then paying the price rather than reaping the intended benefits of a blizzard of "Z-Grams" unleashed by the then CNO, my old boss, Admiral Zumwalt.

In 1973 I retired from the navy after 25 years of enlisted and commissioned service. I went to work for the Charleston, S.C., daily newspapers, rising in a few years to become editor of the *Evening*

Post and, a few years after that, executive editor of both the *Post* and the morning *News and Courier*. My experiences in Vietnam were not forgotten, and never could be, but it seemed most unlikely that I would ever write about them again.

And then one day in May 1987, I received a letter from the Naval Institute Press asking if I would consider writing a one-volume history of the U.S. Navy in Vietnam. I had reviewed a few manuscripts for the Naval Institute over the years, and in 1986 Frank Uhlig reprinted my 1971 *Naval Review* article in his book, *Vietnam, The Naval Story*. Next, the *Proceedings* dug out of its trunk and published a piece of mine on Vietnam it had bought and then put aside seventeen years before. Somehow or other, with no real effort on my part, I had achieved status as a supposed authority on the navy in Vietnam. I knew this was mostly fanciful, but given encouragement by employers and mentors at the Charleston newspapers, I agreed to undertake the task if given sufficient time to complete it.

My book is not meant to be the last word on the navy in Vietnam. The definitive, multivolume history of the naval war, *The United States Navy and the Vietnam Conflict*, is being compiled and written by the Naval Historical Center. The first two volumes of this work, which carry the story of the war to 1965, already have been published. I commend them to those particularly interested in the navy's early involvement in Vietnam. I myself look forward to reading later volumes in the series. The men and women of the Naval Historical Center, especially current Director of Naval History Dean C. Allard and Edward J. Marolda, co-author of Volume II of NHC's history, have been most helpful and supportive of my research for this book.

The Naval Historical Center's and the Naval Institute's extensive oral history collections are valuable sources of information and personal reflections on the war. I have made much use of them in putting together my account.

I am particularly indebted to Lieutenant Commander Forrest L. Edwards, NAVFORV force historian in 1969–70, who, a dozen or so years ago, perhaps anticipating I would one day write this book, gave me his personal collection of oral histories recorded during our extensive travels together in Vietnam. He may be pleased to know that his tapes and all the material I squirreled away from that period are now where they belong—in the archives of the Naval Historical Center.

I owe thanks also to Admiral Thomas H. Moorer and General William C. Westmoreland, both of whom very generously consented to lengthy, taped interviews. Scores of navy shipmates have shared their experiences in Vietnam with me, and they, too, have helped me round out the story.

If I learned one thing in my second career as a newspaper editor, it is that an editor, perhaps above all others, needs someone else to edit his work. Those at the Naval Institute Press who have worked with me have helped keep me on track. Where I have strayed, the fault is entirely mine.

The illustrations and line drawings that appear in this book are the work of Bill Thompson, a talented artist, a former marine who saw combat in Vietnam, and whose contributions to my written work, both here and for many years at the Charleston newspapers, are immeasurable.

Finally, I wish to thank my navy wife—I shall always think of her as that—who encouraged and, occasionally, nagged me to complete this work, a work I hope will be accepted as a sincere tribute to the navy men and women who served their country in its longest and most controversial war.

Abbreviations

ACTOV	Accelerated Turnover to the Vietnamese
ACTOVCOM	Accelerated Turnover to the Vietnamese (Communications)
ACTOVLOG	Accelerated Turnover to the Vietnamese (Logistics)
ACTOVOPS	Accelerated Turnover to the Vietnamese (Operations)
ACTOVRAD	Accelerated Turnover to the Vietnamese (Radar)
AH	Hospital Ship
AKA	Attack Cargo Ship
AN	Net Layer
AO	Area of Operations
APA	Attack Transport Ship
APB	Self-Propelled Barracks Ship
APD	High-Speed Transport Ship
APL	Non-Self-Propelled Barracks Ship
ARG	Amphibious Ready Group
ARL	Landing Craft Repair Ship
ARVN	Army of Vietnam
ASAP	As Soon As Possible
ASPB	Assault Support and Patrol Boat
ASW	Antisubmarine Warfare
ATC	Armored Troop Carrier
ATSB	Advance Tactical Support Base

AV	Seaplane Tender
BB	Battleship
BEQ	Bachelor Enlisted Quarters
BOQ	Bachelor Officers Quarters
BUSHIPS	Bureau of Ships
CAG	Chief Advisory Group/Commander Air Group
CCB	Command and Control Boat
CENTO	Central Treaty Organization
CG	Coastal Group/Commanding General
CHINFO	Chief of Naval Information
CHNAVADVGRP	Chief Naval Advisory Group
CIA	Central Intelligence Agency
CIDG	Civilian Irregular Defense Group
CINC	Commander in Chief
CINCPAC	Commander in Chief Pacifie
CINCPACFLT	Commander in Chief Pacific Fleet
CO	Commanding Officer
COMNAVFORV	Commander Naval Forces Vietnam
COMNAVSUPPACT	Commander Naval Support Activity
COMPHIBPAC	Commander Amphibious Force Pacific
COMUSMACV	Commander U.S. Military Assistance Command Vietnam
COMSEVENTHFLT	Commander Seventh Fleet
CNO	Chief of Naval Operations
CRB	Cam Ranh Bay
CSC	Coastal Surveillance Center
CTF	Commander Task Force
CTG	Commander Task Group
CTU	Commander Task Unit
CTZ	Corps Tactical Zone
CV	Aircraft Carrier
CVA	Attack Aircraft Carrier
CVAN	Attack Aircraft Carrier (Nuclear Powered)
CVS	Aircraft Carrier (Antisubmarine)
CZ	Coastal Zone
DAO	Defense Attaché Office
DD	Destroyer
DE	Destroyer Escort
DER	Radar Picket Escort Ship
DEROS	Date Eligible to Return from Overseas

DMZ	Demilitarized Zone
DOD	Department of Defense
DRV	Democratic Republic of Vietnam (North Vietnam)
EOD	Explosive Ordnance Disposal
FWMAF	Free World Military Assistance Force
FRAM	Fleet Rehabilitation and Modernization
GDA	Ground Damage Assessment
GVN	Government of Vietnam (South Vietnam)
H&I	Harassment and Interdiction
HSA	Headquarters Support Activity
HSAS	Headquarters Support Activity Saigon
ICC	International Control Commission
ISA	International Security Affairs
JCO	Jackpot Control Officer
JGS	Joint General Staff (Vietnamese)
KCS	Kit Carson Scout
KIA	Killed in Action
KKK	Khmer Kampuchea Krom
LAFT	Light Attack Fire Team
LCI	Landing Craft, Infantry
LCM	Landing Craft, Mechanized
LCPL	Landing Craft, Personnel, Large
LCT	Landing Craft, Tank
LCU	Landing Craft, Utility
LCVP	Landing Craft, Vehicle, Personnel
LDNN	Lien Doc Nguoi Nhia (Vietnamese Navy SEALs)
LHFT	Light Helicopter Fire Team
LLDB	Luc Luong Dac Biet (Vietnamese Special Forces)
LOC	Line of Communications
LPH	Amphibious Assault Ship
LSD	Landing Ship, Dock
LSIL	Landing Ship, Infantry, Large
LSM	Landing Ship, Medium
LSM(H)	Hospital Ship (Vietnamese)
LSMR	Inshore Fire Support Ship
LSSL	Landing Support Ship, Large
LST	Landing Ship, Tank
MAAG	Military Assistance and Advisory Group

MACV	Military Assistance Command Vietnam
MAF	Marine Amphibious Force
MATSB	Mobile Advance Tactical Support Base
MEDCAP	Medical Civic Action Program
MILCON	Military Construction
MIUW	Mobile Inshore Undersea Warfare
MLMS	Minesweeping Launch
MOAT	Mobile Operational Advisory Team
MOOSE	"Move Out of Saigon, Expeditiously"
MP	Military Police
MPC	Military Payment Certificate
MRB	Mobile Riverine Base
MRF	Mobile Riverine Force
MSB	Minesweeping Boat
MSC	Minesweeper Coastal / Military Sealift Command
MSF	Mobile Strike Force (Montagnards)
MSL	Minesweeping Launch
MSM	Minesweeper, River
MSO	Minesweeper, Ocean
MSTS	Military Sea Transportation Service
NAG	Naval Advisory Group
NATO	North Atlantic Treaty Organization
NAU	Naval Advisory Unit
NAVCAT	Naval Construction Assistance Team
NAVFORV	Naval Forces Vietnam
NAVSUPPACT	Naval Support Activity
NCO	Noncommissioned Officer
NGFS	Naval Gunfire Support
NHC	Naval Historical Center
NILO	Naval Intelligence Liaison Officer
NITZ	Northern I Corps Tactical Zone
NOC	Naval Operations Center
NSA	Naval Support Activity
NSC	Naval Supply Center
NTC	Naval Training Center
NVA	North Vietnamese Army
NVN	North Vietnam
OASD	Office of Assistant Secretary of Defense
OCS	Officer Candidate School

OINC	Officer in Charge
OOD	Officer of the Deck
OPLAN	Operation Plan
ORI	Operational Readiness Inspection
PACOM	Pacific Command
PACV	Patrol Air Cushion Vehicle
PA&E	Pacific Architects and Engineers
PBR	Patrol Boat, River
PC	Submarine Chaser
PCE	Patrol Craft, Escort
PCF	Patrol Craft, Fast (Swift Boat)
PF	Provisional Force
PGM	Motor Gunboat
PMS	Planned Maintenance System
PO	Petty Officer
POL	Petroleum, Oil, Lubricants
POW	Prisoner of War
PRU	Provincial Reconnaissance Unit
PSYOPS	Psychological Operations
PT	Motor Torpedo Boat
PTF	Fast Patrol Boat
RAC	Riverine Assault Craft
RAF	Riverine Assault Force
RAG	River Assault Group
RAGREP	River Assault Group Report
RAID	River Assault and Interdiction Division
RAS	Riverine Assault Squadron
RD	Revolutionary Development
RF	Regional Force
RID	River Interdiction Division
RIVDIV	River Division
RIVSUPRON	Riverine Support Squadron
RIVRON	River Squadron
RPG	Rocket Propelled Grenade
R&R	Rest and Recreation
RSSZ	Rung Sat Special Zone
RTC	Recruit Training Center
RVN	Republic of Vietnam (South Vietnam)
RVNAF	Republic of Vietnam Armed Forces
SAC	Strategic Air Command

SAM	Surface-to-Air Missile
SCATTOR	Small Craft Assets, Training and Turnover of Resources
SEAL	Sea, Air and Land (U.S. Navy special forces)
Sea Lords	Southeast Asia Lake, Ocean, River, and Delta Strategy
SEATO	Southeast Asia Treaty Organization
SECDEF	Secretary of Defense
SERVPAC	Service Force Pacific
SSB	Swimmer Support Boat
SVN	South Vietnam
STCAN/FOM	French-built, 36-foot river patrol boat
TOC	Tactical Operations Center
UDT	Underwater Demolition Team
USA	U.S. Army
USAF	U.S. Air Force
USAHAC	U.S. Army Headquarters Activity Command
USAID	U.S. Agency for International Development
USCG	U.S. Coast Guard
USCGC	U.S. Coast Guard Cutter
USO	United Services Organization
VC	Viet Cong (Vietnamese Communist)
VCI	Viet Cong Infrastructure
VECTOR	Vietnamese Engineering Capability, Training of Ratings
VNAF	Vietnamese Armed Forces/Vietnamese Air Force
VNMC	Vietnamese Marine Corps
VNN	Vietnamese Navy
VNNSY	Vietnamese Naval Shipyard
WBGP	Waterborne Guard Post
WESTPAC	Western Pacific
WHEC	U.S. Coast Guard High-Endurance Cutter
WIA	Wounded in Action
WLV	Lightship
WP	White Phosphorus
WPB	U.S. Coast Guard 82-foot Cutter
XO	Executive Officer
YFU	Harbor Craft, Utility
YOG	Gasoline Barge, Self-Propelled
YRBM	Repair, Berthing, and Messing Barge
YTB	Harbor Tug, Large

From the Rivers to the Sea

1

From Earliest Times to the Indochina War

What is past is prologue. Study the past.

—Pedestal inscription, north entrance to the National Archives, Washington, D.C.

I n the beginning there were mighty rivers rushing to the sea. Silt-laden, fed by the snows and pelting rains of inner Asia, they built much of the land that came to be known as Vietnam.

Bordered on the north by China, and on the west by Laos and Cambodia (Kampuchea), Vietnam curves for a distance of 1,435 miles along the shores of the South China Sea. At its broadest, near the 21st parallel, it stretches four hundred miles from the Laotian border to the Gulf of Tonkin. Near the 17th parallel, it narrows to a mere thirty miles. In total land area it is approximately the size of California.

A range of mountains, the Annamites, forms the country's spine, running from the Chinese border in the northwest through Vietnam's narrow waist to a region of low hills fifty miles north of Saigon. The mountains and upland plateaus are thinly populated, and the eth-nically distinct tribal people who live there, considered "savages" by the Vietnamese, were called "montagnards" by the French, a term adopted later by the Americans.

Vietnam's climate is tropical and its weather is governed by mon-soonal winds that, in summer, blow out of the southwest, bringing heavy rains to the southern part of the country. The winter mon-soons, from the northeast, give the northern part of Vietnam its rainy season. Between April and November, Saigon, or as it is now offi-cially called, Ho Chi Minh City, receives about 80 inches of rain. Hanoi, in the north, has an annual rainfall of about 72 inches, with most of that falling between October and May.

The winds, the rains, the overcast, and the heavy seas that ac-company the winter monsoon in the Gulf of Tonkin restricted the U.S. Navy's air operations over North Vietnam throughout the war. The summer monsoon similarly made life miserable for those en-gaged in coastal operations in the Gulf of Thailand and in the South China Sea.

It is likely that Vietnam's earliest inhabitants came by way of the rivers and the sea—from China, from India, and from the Indonesian islands that lie to the south. Its ancient and modern links with peoples of the rivers and the seas are nowhere so well illustrated as in the tombs lining the banks of the Perfume River near Hue: They are built in the shape of the basket boats with rounded hulls one still sees occasionally in this part of the world.

Those who settled the land constructed an intricate system of dikes and canals in the river deltas, particularly those formed by the Red River in the north and the Mekong in the south. With incredible labor they converted the wetlands of Vietnam into one of the richest agricultural regions in the world. One of the saddest and most telling sights of the Vietnam War in the late 1960s was the sacked rice cluttering the wharfs of Saigon—most of it shipped across the Pacific from Texas and Louisiana. The "ricebowl of Asia" no longer could feed itself, so devastating had been the effects of Viet Cong terror, U.S. bombing and defoliation, and, not least of all, misguided efforts by the Saigon government to control and pacify its rural population.

Vietnam's rivers and canals served another purpose: They substituted for highways and roads in low-lying parts of the country where it was next to impossible to travel and transport goods by land. And they became, inevitably, invasion routes for conquerors and would-be conquerors throughout recorded history.

For more than a thousand years (111 B.C. to A.D. 934), Tonkin and Annam, the northern and central parts of Vietnam, were ruled by China, and to this day a marked antipathy exists between the Vietnamese and Chinese peoples. Ho Chi Minh's celebrated and oft-quoted remarks concerning cooperative efforts with the French in 1946 to end Nationalist China's occupation of northern Vietnam illustrate an attitude that has survived the centuries:

"You fools!" he thundered to critics within his own party. "Don't you realize what it means if the Chinese remain? Don't you remember your history? The last time the Chinese came, they stayed a thousand years. The French are foreigners. They are weak. Colonialism is dying. The white man is finished in Asia. But if the Chinese stay now, they will never go. As for me, I prefer to sniff French shit for five years than eat Chinese shit for the rest of my life."[1]

Vietnamese of Chinese extraction, who were, by and large, the shopkeepers and entrepreneurs of "pre-liberation" South Vietnam, made up a disproportionately large share of the boat people who braved long odds to escape their Communist masters after the fall of Saigon in 1975.

Though China's direct rule of Tonkin and Annam was ended by a successful rebellion in 934, a political relationship of sorts continued well into the nineteenth century. China, as the dominant power, collected tribute from her neighbors to the south, and in return shielded them during much of this period from outside invaders.

Late in the thirteenth century, however, the Mongols of Kublai Khan invaded Annam from the sea and moved north by land to occupy Hanoi and much of Tonkin before being defeated in a great battle in the Red River Valley. The Vietnamese commander in this

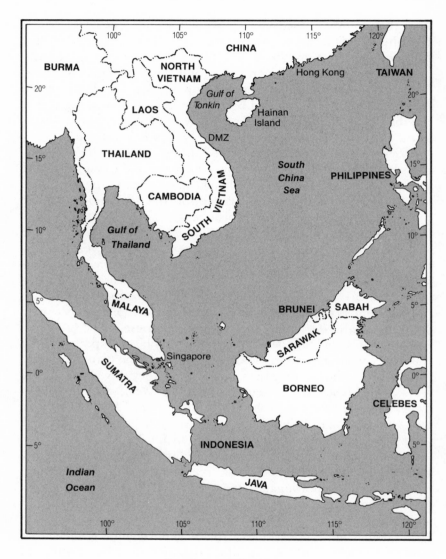

Southeast Asia, 1960

battle was Tran Hung Dao, whose statue still glowers over the Saigon waterfront. His name was invoked and attached to a series of South Vietnamese Navy operations in 1968 and thereafter—Tran Hung Dao I, Tran Hung Dao II, III, IV, etc.

Cambodia and Vietnam also share a history of ethnic dislike rooted in long-ago battles over territory and commercial advantage. For hundreds of years the border between the two has been unstable, and it was not at all surprising that in 1978 the Socialist Republic of Vietnam would turn its army west against an age-old enemy. The Cambodians, ironically employing guerrilla tactics perfected by the Vietnamese in their successful wars against the French and the Americans, proved to be more than the Socialist Republic could digest, however. In September 1989, Vietnam withdrew its army, leaving behind a political and social quagmire fraught with renewed peril for the Cambodian people.

In 1535 the first Europeans arrived in Vietnam. Portuguese traders established a post 15 miles south of Tourane (present day Danang). They were soon followed by missionaries spreading the gospel far and near. Hundreds of thousands of Vietnamese were converted to the Roman Catholic faith. Buddhism, however, remained the country's dominant religion.

In 1633, Dutch merchants appeared on the scene, and not long thereafter they were joined by the first of many Frenchmen who would seek souls and personal fortune in the ancient kingdom.

The first U.S. Navy ship to visit Vietnam anchored off Tourane on 1 January 1833. The sloop of war *Peacock* was on a mission to promote commerce with countries in the region. In May 1845, the U.S. frigate *Constitution* paid a visit to the same port and soon became embroiled in a diplomatic controversy involving a French bishop then being held prisoner at the royal court in Hue. The *Constitution*'s commanding officer, Captain John Percival, put a landing party ashore and seized five hostages in an attempt to secure the bishop's release. It is not clear if the tactic worked. The bishop was, however, later released to the custody of a French naval officer and transported out of the country. The United States government then apologized for Percival's action.

In view of later developments, it is ironic that the U.S. Navy's first involvement in Vietnamese affairs was in pursuit of French interests.

In 1858 the Emperor Napoleon III sent a squadron of thirteen ships and more than two thousand men to secure the port of Tourane and bring an end to bloody persecution of Vietnam's Christian community. The French Asiatic Squadron, augmented by a small force provided by Spanish authorities in the Philippines, took the port and then sailed south to occupy Saigon, the principal entrepôt for Vietnam's lucrative rice trade. France called the southern region of Vietnam "Cochinchina," a corruption of an old Portuguese name, to distinguish its new conquest from still nominally independent Tonkin and Annam. The period of French dominance in Vietnam dates from this expedition.

In 1863, Cambodia became a French protectorate. In 1895, Laos, which had been a Chinese tributary, was added to the French sphere.

Throughout its campaign to consolidate power in Indochina, France made extensive use of rivers and canals to transport men and material to otherwise inaccessible areas. French gunboats and armed river craft were forerunners of the "brown water" navies it and the United States would deploy in Vietnam almost a hundred years later.

By the beginning of the twentieth century, France had in place a colonial administration, almost entirely staffed by its own nationals, that ruled Vietnam with a firm and sometimes brutal hand. Its officials administered summary justice by way of the firing squad and the guillotine. It monopolized the production and distribution of key commodities, including alcohol and opium. It encouraged, as a source of revenue, the consumption of both.

The society France created in Vietnam was not unlike the plantation society of America's pre–Civil War South—elegant and cultured on the surface, but squalid and festering underneath.

In February 1989, I met a French woman in Saigon who, with her husband, was making her first visit there since 1946. (I was making my first since 1970.) Her father had owned a rubber plantation in Vietnam before World War II. She was born in Saigon and educated in private schools there and in France.

"We would spend eighteen months out here," she said, "and then we would go home to Paris for six months. You can't imagine how beautiful things were here in the 1930s—the parties, the dances, the flowers. But it's all changed now. It's 'Gone With the Wind' written all over again. I didn't want to come back, but my husband insisted. Oh, it was nice to see my old school again. I sat at the same desk I sat at as a child. But I'll never come back here again. There are too many memories!"

Too many memories and, it is safe to say, too much blood. When her family left Vietnam for good, the time of troubles for the French already had begun. Some of their best friends, she said, were killed and mutilated by the Viet Minh. Some, she said, were tied to boards and sawed in half.

The French, who ruled Vietnam for almost a century, never succeeded in extinguishing the spark of Vietnamese nationalism, a spark that World War I and an American president's rhetoric helped blow into a burning ember. In an address to the U.S. Congress on 8 January 1918, Woodrow Wilson spelled out America's war aims:

"What we demand in this war," he said, "is nothing peculiar to ourselves. It is that the world be made fit and safe to live in; and particularly that it be made safe for every peace-loving nation which, like our own, wishes to live its own life, determine its own institutions, be assured of justice and fair dealing by the other peoples of the world as against force and selfish aggression."[2]

In this same speech, Wilson listed his "Fourteen Points," the fifth of which most certainly had special meaning for Indochinese nationalists. The American president called for nothing less than "a free, open-minded, and absolutely impartial adjustment of all colonial claims, based upon a strict observance of the principle that in determining all such questions of sovereignty the interests of the population concerned must have equal weight with the equitable claims of the government whose title is to be determined."

Wilsonian ideals paled in the glitter of Versailles, and with them faded the hope for an early negotiated settlement of the Indochina question. America's allies in the "war to end all wars" had no intention whatsoever of applying the Fourteen Points to their own colonial possessions.

Resistance to French rule in Indochina between the two world wars became increasingly identified with the growth of international communism. The leader of the movement in Vietnam was a man of many aliases, but the one by which he was best known is Ho Chi Minh—"He Who Enlightens."

Born in 1890 in northern Annam, he received his early education at a French school in Hue. For two years he sailed as a messboy on a French merchant ship. He lived for a time in London and in Paris where he associated with various left-wing groups. He may have visited the United States.

In 1919 he was one of those who petitioned the Versailles Peace Conference on behalf of the peoples of Indochina. Rebuffed, he joined the French Communist party, which sent him to Moscow for training at the "University of the Toilers of the East." In 1924, in Canton, China, he organized the Vietnamese Nationalist Movement, and in 1930 he founded the Indochinese Communist party.

In the decade leading to World War II, he led demonstrations and participated in riots against French rule in Indochina, spent time in a Hong Kong prison hospital, and traveled once more to Moscow, where he studied at the Lenin Institute. In 1941 he returned to Vietnam and founded yet another revolutionary group, the "Viet Nam Doc Lap Dong Minh Hoi" (League for the Independence of Vietnam), better known in its abbreviated form as the Viet Minh. Leadership of this organization was drawn principally from the Indochinese Communist party. Ho Chi Minh took the title of secretary general.

Throughout World War II, the Viet Minh, with some help and encouragement from the Allied powers, organized popular resistance to the military occupation forces of Japan and Vietnam's nominal rulers: Vichy France and the hereditary Emperor Bao Dai. In 1940, Japan had demanded and received the assent of French authorities to the landing of its troops in Indochina, thus securing for itself a rich storehouse of critical raw materials and a strategic base for further expansion in South Asia.

Japan's partnership with the French in Indochina lasted until 5 March 1945 when, fearing imminent Allied landings and doubtful of French intentions should an attack occur, Japan formally and brutally completed its occupation, disarming, interning and, where necessary, killing those who resisted.

Ho Chi Minh seized this opportunity to establish "national liberation committees" in all parts of Vietnam. When, on 13 August 1945, Japan surrendered to the Allies, the Viet Minh Central Committee quickly formed a provisional government headed by Ho Chi Minh. The "Vietnam People's Army," led by a former school teacher, Vo Nguyen Giap, marched into Hanoi and occupied key government buildings.

Pressured by the Viet Minh, Bao Dai abdicated, urging his countrymen to rally behind Ho Chi Minh in the cause of national liberation. This gave basis to Ho's later claim that he had received, from the emperor's very hands, the "mandate of heaven."

On 2 September 1945, before a cheering throng in Hanoi, Ho Chi Minh presented a "Declaration of Independence," closely modeled on that of the United States, and proclaimed the Democratic Republic of Vietnam with himself as provisional president.

"During and throughout the last 80 years," he said, "the French imperialists, abusing the principles of 'freedom, equality and fraternity,' have violated the integrity of our ancestral land and oppressed our countrymen. Their deeds run counter to the ideals of humanity and justice. . . .

"They have built more prisons than schools. They have callously ill-treated our compatriots. They have drowned our revolutions in blood. . . .

"A people which has so stubbornly opposed the French domination for more than 80 years, a people who, during these last years, so doggedly ranged itself and fought on the Allied side against fascism, such a people has the right to be free, such a people must be independent.

"For these reasons, we, members of the Provisional Government of the Democratic Republic of Vietnam, solemnly declare to the world:

"Vietnam has the right to be free and independent. The people of Vietnam decide to mobilize all their spiritual and material forces and to sacrifice their lives and property in order to safeguard their right to liberty and independence."[3]

Ho Chi Minh, his forces equipped with a remarkable hodgepodge of French, Chinese, Japanese, and American weapons, moved quickly to consolidate his position—but not quickly enough. Within weeks, Allied occupation forces, British in the south and Chinese in the north, arrived to accept the Japanese surrender. And not far behind were the French.

The disposition of Allied forces had been decided at the Potsdam Conference in July 1945. The British were given responsibility for military operations in the southern part of Indochina, and the Chinese were assigned similar responsibility in the northern part. When Japan, reeling from the atomic bombing of Hiroshima and Nagasaki, suddenly and unconditionally surrendered, the task of disarming Japanese troops in Indochina fell naturally to Britain and China. France, itself newly liberated, hastily organized a military expedition to put down the would-be liberators of Vietnam, the Viet Minh, and let it be known that it intended to reassert its colonial claims in Indochina.

U.S. policy, so far as it was then formulated, was neither to assist nor hinder France in its efforts to restore authority in Indochina.

President Franklin D. Roosevelt, as was well known, had been no admirer of French colonial rule. His successor, President Harry S. Truman, presumably had had things of more pressing importance on his mind at Potsdam. For the time being, then, the United States left to others the prickly question of how to deal with the French in Indochina. As events would prove, this was a huge and costly mistake.

Britain welcomed cooperation from the French in restoring order in its occupation zone and promised that as soon as France proved capable of governing, it would withdraw its troops. On 1 January 1946, therefore, France assumed sole responsibility for civil and military functions south of the 16th parallel (just below Danang), with the exception of those having to do with the repatriation of the Japanese.

In the north, where the Viet Minh were more firmly entrenched and Chiang Kai-shek less disposed to welcome the return of the French, the situation was more complex. A Chinese army group, some two hundred thousand strong, had been deployed to disarm the Japanese. Anti-Communist as well as anti-French, this occupation force, rapacious in the extreme, looked as if it might have come to stay.

Ho Chi Minh tried to placate the Chinese commander, even to the extent of formally disbanding the Indochinese Communist party. He soon came to realize that the French were less of a threat to his independence movement than were the Chinese, and on 6 March 1946 he signed a preliminary agreement with France permitting the reintroduction of French troops in the northern part of the country. Pertinent parts of the agreement read as follows:

"The French Government recognizes the Republic of Vietnam as a free state, with its own government, parliament, army and finances, belonging to the Indochinese Federation and to the French Union.

"Concerning the reunification of [Tonkin, Annam, and Cochinchina] . . . the French Government undertakes to carry out the decisions of the population consulted by referendum.

"The Government of Vietnam declares itself ready to receive the French army amicably when, in conformance with international agreements, it relieves the Chinese troops. . . ."[4]

Ho Chi Minh's agreement was premature. Political upheavals in the north of China soon led to withdrawal of most of China's occupying force. Chinese Communists under Mao Tse-tung, with the support and encouragement of the Soviet Union, had resumed their war of "liberation" against the rule of Chiang Kai-shek.

With the U.S. Navy providing sealift, China's armies in Vietnam were transported to new and more dangerous fronts many hundreds of miles to the north. And with Ho Chi Minh's apparent blessing, French forces were poised to take their place.

Thus was the stage set for a new war in Vietnam that would last nearly thirty years, a war that eventually would engulf the United States and take the lives of fifty-eight thousand American men and women.

2

The Indochina War, 1946–54

Truck convoys valiantly crossed streams, mountains and forests; drivers spent scores of sleepless nights, in defiance of difficulties and dangers, to bring food and ammunition to the front, to permit the army to annihilate the enemy.

Thousands of bicycles from the towns also carried food and ammunition to the front.

Hundreds of sampans of all sizes, hundreds of thousands of bamboo rafts crossed rapids and cascades to supply the front.

Day and night, hundreds of thousands of porters and young volunteers crossed passes and forded rivers in spite of enemy planes and delayed-action bombs.

Near the firing line, supply operations had to be carried out in the shortest possible time. Cooking, medical work, transport, etc., were carried on right in the trenches, under enemy bombing and crossfire.

Such was the situation at Dien Bien Phu. . . .

—General Vo Nguyen Giap, *People's War, People's Army*

In late 1945 and early 1946, as the British and Chinese occupation forces withdrew from their respective zones in the south and north of Vietnam, they left near chaos behind. Ho Chi Minh, representing the strongest, but not the only nationalist movement, had declared the independence of all Vietnam. His provisional government had been recognized, grudgingly, by France, but the all-important question of unifying the three parts or "ky" of Vietnam—Tonkin, Annam, and Cochinchina—had not been resolved.

In exchange for recognition, and as a ploy to encourage a more rapid departure of Chinese troops, Ho Chi Minh had agreed, on 6 March 1946, to "amicable" deployment of French forces in the north. Some 21,700 French troops were then already embarked in twenty-eight ships and craft headed north. Many of the vessels and much of the military equipment in this expeditionary force had been supplied by the United States through the World War II lend-lease program.

On 7 March the French force entered Haiphong. The day before, perhaps due to a failure in communications, Chinese coastal artillery had taken the expedition under fire, resulting in twenty-four French dead and one hundred wounded.

For a time, the French command and the Viet Minh maintained an uneasy truce. But on 30 May, apparently acting without specific instructions from Paris, France's high commissioner for Indochina, Vice Admiral Georges Thierry d'Argenlieu, gave "interim" recognition to the "Republic of Cochinchina." Even though this recognition was made contingent on a favorable referendum by the people of Cochinchina and ratification by the French Union, Ho Chi Minh saw it as a clear violation of the agreement France had signed with him.

In a climate of growing bitterness and intrigue, and with terrorist acts, including political assassination, spreading in all parts of Vietnam, negotiations between Ho's Democratic Republic of Vietnam and France resumed on 6 July 1946 at Fontainebleau, outside Paris. The DRV delegation was headed by Ho Chi Minh. Of Cochinchina he exclaimed, "It is Vietnamese soil. It is the flesh of our flesh, the blood of our blood."[1] There was more than mere sentiment in this outburst. The rice paddies, the rubber plantations, and the timber of Cochinchina were of crucial importance to the DRV's future as an economic entity.

The Fontainebleau negotiations ended in failure, and in Vietnam clashes between the French and the Viet Minh grew in both frequency and intensity.

In October, France assumed control of the customs service in

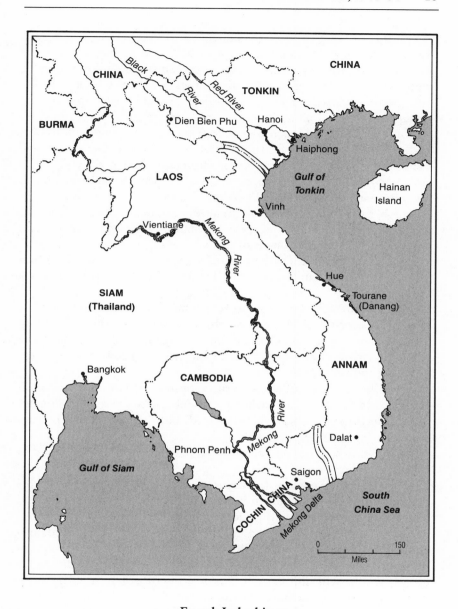

French Indochina

Haiphong, vowing to stop the smuggling of arms through the port. This act also was intended to dry up a principal source of the funds fueling the insurgency. Most of the arms then supplied the insurgents were purchased from private dealers, many of them Chinese. In the aftermath of World War II, the region was awash in war supplies, and entrepôts existed in almost every major port.

In November, a French patrol craft seized a Chinese junk loaded with munitions destined for the Viet Minh. It was one of France's few successful intercepts of large arms shipments, and it touched off a violent confrontation in the port. The Viet Minh, in true French revolutionary fashion, erected barricades in the streets, and on 23 November the French delivered an ultimatum demanding evacuation of certain parts of Haiphong. The ultimatum went unanswered, and a naval and air bombardment of the city commenced, followed by an assault on the ground. Civilian casualties were heavy. The Viet Minh said twenty thousand died; the French said no more than six thousand.

In December the fighting spread to Hanoi. Ho Chi Minh issued a virtual declaration of war against the "French colonialists." Fighting broke out in all parts of Vietnam, and though the Viet Minh and the "People's Army" were forced out of the cities and into the country-side, their power was not broken.

Ho Chi Minh, rebuffed in his attempt to negotiate a settlement in Paris, knew he could not achieve a quick victory over the French. France, in turn, should have recognized, but did not, that it had no hope of winning a long war.

Viet Minh strategy was clearly stated in a pamphlet distributed in Hanoi in 1947:

"To protract the war is the key to victory. . . . The more we fight, the more united our people at home will be, and the more the world democratic movement will support us from the outside. On the other hand, the more the enemy fights, the more the anti-war and demo-cratic movement in France will check his hands; the revolutionary movement in the French colonies will oblige the enemy to divide his forces; and he will find himself in a position of isolation in the inter-national arena. To achieve all these results, the war must be pro-longed, and we must have time. Time works for us—time will be our best strategist, if we are determined to pursue the resistance war to the end. . . ."[2]

With France essentially controlling the cities and towns, and the Viet Minh the countryside, the "war of resistance" settled into a pattern that later would become all too familiar to Americans in Vietnam. On the Communist side, it involved hit-and-run attacks on French military outposts, ambush of patrols and supply columns, assassination of "collaborators," disruption of essential public services, and psychological warfare waged in both Vietnam and France.

France sought to take command of roads and waterways, denying their use to the enemy while ensuring its own lines of communication. By adding new bases and new strongpoints within easy reach of a secure logistic network, it hoped to spread its power gradually into areas controlled by the Communists, much as an oil slick spreads over water. The strategy indeed has been given that name, the "oil slick," by a generation of political and military writers. Unfortunately, the French and many others failed to take into account another characteristic of an oil slick—while it may spread far and wide, it is neither very deep nor lasting.

Final phases of the French strategy, "pacification" of the people and creation of an effective indigenous military force to assist in the prosecution of the war, never really got off the ground and perhaps never could have, given the legacy of French colonialism in Vietnam. It is hardly surprising that Ho Chi Minh, who vowed to liberate Vietnam from hated French rule, had a greater claim to the loyalty and affection of the people than any of the generals and admirals sent from France to oppose him.

On 8 March 1949, responding to pressure from the United States to find a non-Communist solution to the problem of independence for Vietnam, France signed an agreement, the Elysée Accords, with the deposed Emperor Bao Dai, calling on him to head a government that would rule over a united Vietnam, a Vietnam incorporating not only Tonkin and Annam, but France's short-lived Republic of Cochinchina as well. Under the terms of the agreement, France would retain direct control over the armed forces, foreign relations, and state finances. So restricted was this granting of "independence" that few Vietnamese nationalists rallied behind it. Even the emperor expressed little enthusiasm for it, saying that "what they call a Bao Dai solution turns out to be just a French solution."[3] Nevertheless, on 14 June 1949, France formally proclaimed the State of Vietnam with Bao Dai as its head. The move was generally welcomed by the United States.

Ho Chi Minh did not welcome it at all, and early in 1950 he persuaded the Soviet Union and the People's Republic of China to recognize the regime he headed, the Democratic Republic of Vietnam. The war in Vietnam thus became more than ever a focal point in the Cold War, a test of wills between East and West. The issue of French colonialism versus Vietnamese nationalism, particularly insofar as the United States was concerned, henceforth would be of only secondary importance.

In late July 1950, the United States dispatched a joint State-Defense survey mission to Indochina. One of its objectives was to determine what kind of military assistance, and how much, the French needed to prosecute their war successfully. The senior military officer on this mission was Major General Graves B. Erskine, USMC, and the naval officers attached were Captain Mervin Halstead and Commander Ralph J. Michels. They recommended that, there being no threat to the French from the sea, the naval aid program should support a buildup of river and coastal forces. Specific recommendations included: (1) the provision of modern, radar-equipped patrol aircraft; (2) the transfer of a variety of small ships and craft to extend offshore patrols into coastal waters and rivers; and (3) the establishment of adequate repair and logistic facilities. With little modification, these early recommendations shaped the broad direction of the naval assistance program in Vietnam for the next fourteen years.

On 3 August 1950, the U.S. Military Assistance Advisory Group (MAAG) Indochina was formed in Saigon. It consisted of thirty-five officers and men, the vanguard of an American military presence that would grow to more than half a million. Commander John B. Howland headed a seven-man navy section. The MAAG's primary function at this time was to process French requests for U.S. military equipment and to expedite its delivery.

The assignment of military advisors marked a significant change in U.S. policy, a change triggered by two cataclysmic events elsewhere in Asia—the conquest of Mainland China by the armies of Mao Tse-tung, a conquest completed on 1 October 1949, and the 25 June 1950 invasion of South Korea by Communist North Korea.

These events, reinforced by other troubling developments in Europe and the Middle East, gave rise in Washington to a specter, the specter of monolithic communism everywhere on the march. No matter that cracks already were appearing in the supposed monolith, a strategy had to be developed to deal with it. The one finally adopted was called "containment," a term coined in the context of international relations by George F. Kennan in 1947. Kennan, a distinguished foreign service officer, was assigned to the National War College at the time.

In a celebrated article, "The Sources of Soviet Conduct," published in the magazine *Foreign Affairs* and signed anonymously as "X," Kennan had suggested a strategy for dealing not with a perceived military threat from the Soviet Union, but with what he considered the much more dangerous ideological-political one. Further, his concern was directed to threats faced by Western Europe and Japan, not Third World countries where, in his view, vital U.S. national interests were not then at stake.[4]

The theory of containment evolved, however, into a strategy that called for drawing an imaginary line around the Communist world, a line patrolled and defended as necessary by the armed forces of the United States and its allies in three overlapping treaty organizations (NATO, CENTO, and SEATO) in Europe and Asia. The Communist threat would be opposed in every country lying outside that line, for were it not, the reasoning went, the free nations of the world would fall like a stack of "dominoes."

Shortly after the outbreak of war in Korea, President Truman signed legislation authorizing $15 million in military assistance to the French in Indochina. More than $2.5 billion would follow, a sum greater than the total of Marshall Plan aid given France for reconstruction after World War II.

American military aid would come none too soon, for the French were reeling from a series of coordinated attacks directed at their increasingly isolated outposts. Lao Ky, 150 miles northwest of Hanoi, where the Red River crosses the border from Communist China, had fallen in February 1950. With arms, including artillery, now flowing freely down that river to the People's Army, General Giap embarked on a new phase of the war. He called it "mobile warfare," which he defined as concentrating troops in such a way that "relatively big forces are regrouped and operating on a relatively vast battlefield, attacking the enemy where he is relatively exposed, with a view to annihilating enemy manpower, advancing very deeply then withdrawing very swiftly. . . ."[5]

French mobility in the war relied heavily on naval forces. At peak strength, these included some three hundred amphibious ships and craft, seventy-five patrol vessels and minesweepers, two cruisers and two small aircraft carriers.

Overall command was exercised by Commander French Naval Forces Far East, who was himself directly subordinate to the theater commander, Commander in Chief Armed Forces Indochina. Under the senior naval commander was the officer actually responsible for naval operations in Indochina, Commander Naval Division Far East. His forces were divided into three area commands—North, Central, and South. The area commands were in turn divided into river, coastal, and sea forces.

The principal operational unit of the river force was the *division navale d'assault* or, as commonly abbreviated, the *dinassault*. Ships and craft assigned to the typical *dinassault* included these: landing support ship, large (LSSL); landing ship infantry, large (LSIL); landing craft infantry (LCI); landing craft mechanized (LCM); landing craft tank (LCT); landing craft utility (LCU); landing craft vehicle, personnel (LCVP); and a French-built, 36-foot, steel-hulled river patrol boat, the STCAN/FOM or "Stay-can." The letter designation for the latter stands for *Services Technique des Constructions et Armes Navales/France Outre Mer.*[6]

The landing ships and craft were all U.S.-furnished from leftover World War II stock, and these were modified for river warfare by the addition of protective armor, heavy automatic weapons, and improved crew accommodations. The French "monitor" (a converted LCM), for example, was armored and ordinarily carried one 40-mm and two 20-mm cannons, a .50-caliber machine gun and an 81-mm mortar.

Each *dinassault* had its own permanently assigned marine landing force, which was augmented by army troops for large operations. The total personnel strength of the typical *dinassault,* including the landing force, was about eight hundred men. At war's end, six were operational, and three each normally were assigned in the Red River and Mekong River deltas. Those in the south were nominally part of the Vietnamese Navy (established in 1952), but were commanded by French officers.

Highly versatile and wide-ranging, the *dinassault* gave the French a capability for amphibious operations both on the coast and far inland on the great river systems of Indochina. The largest such operation occurred in 1952 and involved more than thirty thousand men.

As would prove true in later U.S. Navy river operations in Vietnam, the principal threats to river forces were ambushes and mines. Various countermeasures were taken, but with only marginal success. Scouting aircraft were assigned to search out potential ambush sites ahead of advancing *dinassault* columns, but dense vegetation normally made these undetectable from the air. Attempts were made to destroy suspected ambush sites with automatic weapons fire ("hosing down" the area, Americans would later call it) and with LCM-mounted flame throwers (early versions of the U.S. Navy's "Zippo" boats).

The Viet Minh mine threat against boats under way came from moored or bottom mines command-detonated from concealed positions on river and canal banks. These mines were often jury-rigged and primitive in design, but nonetheless effective. In the absence of positive control of the land areas immediately adjacent to waterways, minesweeping, never a simple nor a safe task, took on added dimensions of difficulty and danger. Attempts were made to vector unmanned minesweeping craft, but this exceeded the range of what was then technically feasible in narrow and restricted waters. Years later, similar efforts by the U.S. Navy would not be successful either. In the end, reliance had to be placed on the oldest sweep known to mine warfare—the chain or grapnel bottom drag. This required the towing craft, usually an LCM, to pass near both banks in the waterways swept, in order to snag or cut the firing leads attached to controlled mines, or engage the cables holding moored mines in place. Minesweepers were thus placed in double jeopardy: they were vulnerable to ambush at extremely close range, and, particularly in narrow streams, they were themselves subject to destruction by mines their sweep tactics required to be passed close aboard.

Moored or anchored river craft were also subject to mine damage. Enemy "sappers," swimmers who approached the boats underwater or under cover of darkness, tied off small mines to anchor chains or screws. Timed charges were sometimes attached directly to the hulls of boats. Contact mines on small rafts were floated into anchorages and moorings. Maintaining a vigilant watch, periodically starting up engines and turning over screws, and randomly throwing grenades into the water were the best countermeasures available against this threat.

For rather obscure reasons, the Viet Minh did not, apparently, employ mines in the coastal waters of Indochina, despite the success achieved by Communist miners in Korea. It is possible they chose not to do so because of the importance these waters had for their own logistics. More likely, they simply lacked the resources for an open-sea mining campaign. Had they been able to mount one, both the French and the Americans would have been hard-pressed to counter it.

French coastal patrols had to contend with basically two kinds of enemy supply operations. The first involved the shipment of war materials from sources outside Indochina—after 1949, primarily Communist China. The second took the form of transshipment of men and material from one Communist post to another within the coastal regions of Vietnam. In checking the first, the French were reasonably successful, especially after the arrival of U.S.-furnished patrol planes. In controlling the second, they were considerably less so. There were simply not enough naval ships and craft assigned to patrol, effectively, the long and heavily indented coastline. There may not have been enough in the entire world.

Large sections of the coast remained in Viet Minh control throughout the war, and other sections were fought over repeatedly. Under these circumstances it was relatively easy for Communist logistic craft to lose themselves in the tens of thousands of junks, sampans, and small fishing boats that frequented these waters.

Later, during the American phase of the war, curfews were established off many fishing ports in what was then South Vietnam. In 1969, I spent some nights riding Swift boats on patrol along the central coast, and I remember well the sound of many hundreds of small outboard motors revving up in the predawn hours and, not long after, as the curfew expired, a galaxy of lights moving out to sea. To think that either the French or the Americans could do more than simply harass enemy supply operations along a disputed strip of coastline borders on the absurd.

Over the years, the operators of the Communist seaborne supply chain became highly skilled in deception and in using to full advantage the natural cover afforded by offshore islands, jutting headlands, and monsoon rains. Their tactics included surf-line movement (the running of small boats closely parallel to a breaking surf in order to minimize the chances of visual or radar detection); the use of advance scouting junks to establish the location, routine, and degree of alertness of patrols; the deliberate sinking of weapons-laden craft in sheltered coves for later salvage and onward shipment. Well-packaged and well-preserved, guns and ammunition retrieved from shallow depths were none the worse for wear when delivered into the hands of intended users.

Seagoing vessels of trawler size or larger commonly followed routes that took them well out to sea beyond the area of highest detection probability, then due north or south to the latitude of the infiltration point for a direct, perpendicular run to the coast, taking

full advantage of the phases of the moon and local patterns of innocent traffic. Once in Communist China's hands (after 1949), Hainan
Island became a favorite point of departure for these runs. The
amount of cargo even a small ship could deliver often made the risk of
detection acceptable.

Throughout the Indochina War, French sea forces were used to
supplement and strengthen the coastal patrol. In addition, fleet units
provided gunfire support for amphibious operations and for French
garrisons in isolated coastal outposts. Carrier aircraft ranged far inland in tactical support of the army.

Despite constant urging by the United States to expand the combat capability and role of non-Communist Vietnamese forces, the war
ended with the Vietnamese Navy operating only one LSIL, one LCU,
and some thirty smaller amphibious craft. Further, a French officer
commanded the Vietnamese Navy.

In the Vietnamese Army the situation was much the same.
Though half-hearted attempts were made, beginning in 1952, to
"Vietnamize" the war (the French called it *jaunissement* or "yellow-
ing"), credible leadership never developed within the Vietnamese military. In part this can be explained by France's long-time policy of
discouraging Vietnamese initiative, and in part by Viet Minh intimidation or murder of those who might have aspired to positions of
leadership under the French. It was a problem that would plague
American efforts in Vietnam as well.

In the spring of 1953, General Raul Salan, then commanding the
French Expeditionary Force, proposed a new strategy he hoped
would reverse the fortunes of war for France. His plan was to train
and assign Vietnamese soldiers to posts in the relatively secure Red
River Delta. French troops relieved of garrison duty would then form
a mobile strike force that would carry the battle to the Viet Minh in
their strongholds in the north and west.

In April 1953, Salan was relieved by General Henri Navarre, who
expanded the strategy to include the establishment of a secure base
far behind Viet Minh lines, a base from which French troops could
harass the enemy's rear. The site chosen was a small village near the
Laotian border. Its name was Dien Bien Phu.

On 20 November, French paratroopers occupied the village,
which sat in a valley 11 miles long and 5 miles wide, surrounded by
low mountains and hills. Navarre and the colorful officer he placed in
command at Dien Bien Phu, Colonel Christian de Castries, moved

quickly to create what they thought would be an impregnable fortress. A garrison thirteen thousand strong defended the base and its small airstrip. Significantly, the only means of reinforcing and supplying the garrison was by air. Dien Bien Phu was far removed from secure water or land lines of communication.

Within three months, fifty thousand Communist troops were in the hills overlooking the French base. Perhaps as many as twenty thousand more were strung out in a line of supply that ran all the way to China. General Giap deployed thirty-three infantry battalions, six artillery regiments, a regiment of engineers, and one hundred or more artillery pieces that were, with incredible labor, dragged through jungle, across streams, and up steep mountain trails to where, well dug in, they could be brought to bear on French positions in the valley below.

Giap maintained a conventional siege until 13 March 1954 when, his forces at last assembled, he began the fateful battle. It would end on 7 May when the shattered remnants of the French garrison surrendered. Frantic diplomatic efforts to persuade the United States to intervene militarily to save Dien Bien Phu failed—narrowly. Possible measures considered, had a decision been taken to intervene, included the use of "small" nuclear weapons.

Dien Bien Phu has been called one of the decisive battles in world history. Insofar as a French presence in Indochina was concerned, the battle was indeed decisive. After Dien Bien Phu there was simply no French stomach left to continue the war. On 20 July 1954, at Geneva, three separate cease-fire agreements were signed by the French and the Viet Minh, one each for Vietnam, Laos, and Cambodia.

The Geneva Conference failed to produce a political settlement in Indochina, and the "Final Declaration" of 21 July was not signed by any of the parties represented: the United States, the Soviet Union, Britain, France, and China (the "Big Five" of World War II); the State of Vietnam (South); the Democratic Republic of Vietnam (North); Laos; and Cambodia.

The cease-fire agreements called for the withdrawal of foreign troops, both French and Viet Minh, from Laos and Cambodia. A military demarcation line was drawn at the 17th parallel in Vietnam. A narrow demilitarized zone (DMZ) was established on either side of the line. A staged withdrawal of French military forces from north of the DMZ was to be completed within three hundred days. Similarly,

Viet Minh forces south of the DMZ were to regroup in the north. Civilians were free to move in either direction during the regroupment period.

The drawing of the military demarcation line at the 17th parallel resulted from a compromise proposed by the Soviet Union. France and the State of Vietnam wanted the 18th parallel, the latitude of the historic "Gate of Annam." The DRV wanted the 16th parallel, which would have given it the old imperial capital at Hue and the port city of Danang.

The military demarcation line was not intended to serve as a political boundary between a Communist North Vietnam and a non-Communist South, though that is exactly how many South Vietnamese and Americans came to view it. Pending elections in both north and south to unify the country, the Viet Minh were to administer the north, and the State of Vietnam (Bao Dai) and France were jointly to administer the south. The elections were to be held within two years—again the result of a Soviet proposed compromise. Ho Chi Minh had wanted them held earlier.

An International Control Commission with Canada, India, and Poland as its members was to oversee the cease-fire. No arms and munitions, and no new foreign military personnel, were to be introduced into either North or South Vietnam, though "war materials, arms and munitions which have been destroyed, damaged, worn out or used up after the cessation of hostilities" could be replaced. This would provide a loophole big enough to drive the largest of tanks and trucks through in the years leading up to direct U.S. military intervention.

On 21 July 1954, President Dwight D. Eisenhower said he was "glad" agreement had been reached in Geneva to stop the bloodshed. He continued:

"The United States has not been a belligerent in the war. The primary responsibility for the settlement in Indochina rested with those nations which participated in the fighting. . . . Accordingly, the United States has not itself been a party to or bound by the decisions taken by the conference, but it is our hope that it will lead to the establishment of peace consistent with the rights and the needs of the countries concerned. The agreement contains features which we do not like, but a great deal depends on how they work in practice.

"The United States . . . in compliance with the obligations and principles contained in Article 2 of the United Nations Charter . . .

will not use force to disturb the settlement. We also say that any renewal of Communist aggression would be viewed by us as a matter of grave concern. . . ."[7]

The next day, Ho Chi Minh issued his own statement:

"At the Geneva Conference, thanks to the struggle of our delegation and to the assistance of the two delegations of the USSR and the People's Republic of China, we have scored a great victory; the French Government has recognized the independence, sovereignty, unity and territorial integrity of our country and accepted to withdraw French armed forces from our land. . . .

"To carry out the cease-fire, it is necessary to regroup the armed forces of the two sides into two separate zones, that is to readjust the military areas.

"The readjustment of the military areas is a temporary and transitional measure to realize the armistice, restore peace and progress toward national reunification by means of general elections. [It] . . . does not mean by any way a partition of our country nor a division of powers. . . ."[8]

Dating its start from the French shelling of Haiphong in November 1946, and its end with the signing of the Geneva cease-fire agreements, the Indochina War lasted seven years and seven months, more than twice as long as the Korean War. French Union forces suffered more than 172,000 casualties, including 45,000 dead.

3

The Advisory
Period, 1954–64

Advice can get you in more trouble than a gun can.

—Will Rogers, 1933

At Geneva, France agreed to "regroup" its armed forces south of the demilitarized zone within three hundred days. The Viet Minh, in turn, were to regroup north of that line. Civilians desiring to move from one regroupment zone to the other were to be allowed to do so within the same time frame.

In the north, warnings were scrawled on the walls of public buildings, and leaflets were distributed urging the people to flee. Catholic priests advised their flocks to abandon ancestral homes and fields and seek sanctuary in the south. The streets of the two principal evacuation centers, Hanoi and Haiphong, were soon choked with masses of desperate people.

The near panic that seized large segments of the population in the north was not without cause. Some of it was inspired by the work of a U.S. psychological warfare team headed by Colonel Edward G. Lansdale. Some resulted from actions taken by the Viet Minh themselves. Months before, on 4 December 1953, the Communists had published an "Agrarian Reform Law," spelling out what could be expected when the French departed. It read, in part:

"Land and property belonging to the French colonialists or other imperialist aggressors will be confiscated in their entirety.

"As for the properties of traitors or reactionary landlords or despots, their land, their draught animals, farm implements, surplus food stock and surplus housing will be confiscated in whole or in part according to the gravity of their crimes.

"That part of the above-mentioned properties which is not confiscated will be subject to requisition without compensation. . . .

"All debts owed to the landlords by the working peasantry as well as by various strata of the poor population in the countryside are cancelled. . . ."[1]

The law promised to strip away, for the benefit of the state, almost all wealth from the hands of individuals. A better formula for economic disaster could hardly be imagined, nor a greater incentive for those who could escape south with even a small part of their property to do so.

The heaviest fighting of the war had occurred in the north, and most of the French Expeditionary Force and almost all of its heavy equipment were located there when the war ended. Though the French were allowed three hundred days to complete their evacuation, they had to move within fifteen, eighty, and one hundred days, respectively, inside three progressively smaller perimeters centered on Haiphong. This staged withdrawal was meant to allow for an orderly transition from French to Communist authority in the north.

U.S. assistance was sought by both France and by the State of Vietnam's new prime minister, Ngo Dinh Diem. Diem had been appointed to his post by Bao Dai in June 1954.

On 5 August, utilizing all available ships and aircraft, France began the movement of troops, refugees, and equipment south. Two days later, the U.S. Navy weighed in.

Rear Admiral Lorenzo S. Sabin, Commander Amphibious Force, Western Pacific (Task Force 90), was assigned responsibility for aiding the exodus by sea from the north. The operation was given the code name "Passage to Freedom."

Operating initially with five attack transports (APAs), two attack cargo ships (AKAs), two landing ships dock (LSDs), two high-speed transports (APDs), and four landing ships tank (LSTs), Sabin's task force grew in the first three months of the operation to more than one hundred U.S. Navy and Military Sea Transportation Service (MSTS) ships and craft.

The attack transport *Menard* (APA 201) carried the first load of refugees south. She departed the waters off Haiphong on 17 August 1954 with 1,900 passengers and arrived in Saigon three days later.

U.S. ships engaged in the operation ordinarily anchored off the coast near Haiphong and received passengers and cargo from landing craft that either loaded over the beach or from piers inside the crowded port. Ports of debarkation in the south, in addition to the principal one, Saigon, included Danang, Nha Trang, and Vung Tau (Cap St. Jacques).

Limitations imposed at Geneva on the number of foreign military personnel allowed ashore in Vietnam hampered the navy throughout Passage to Freedom. With few exceptions, these limitations were strictly observed. MAAG Indochina, then about five hundred strong, rotated personnel north to coordinate movement from the beach, but serious bottlenecks still occurred. The processing of refugees was handled entirely by the French.

Many of the refugees required medical treatment, and sanitation at the camps in both north and south was a matter of great concern. Within the limits of its resources, the navy sent doctors, nurses, and corpsmen to alleviate the suffering and the squalor. One of those assigned was Lieutenant (j.g.) Thomas Dooley, who later achieved renown, and gave his life, while working in a jungle hospital in Laos.

Passage to Freedom included a major logistics operation to support the ships and craft engaged in the evacuation. An afloat force commanded by Rear Admiral Roy A. Gano, Commander Service Squadron Three, provided food, fuel, and other supplies to navy and MSTS ships in the South China Sea, thus eliminating the necessity of diverting them to Subic Bay in the Philippines.

When Passage to Freedom ended on 18 May 1955, at the end of the three-hundred-day regroupment period, more than 310,000 people, 69,000 tons of cargo and 8,000 vehicles had been carried south by U.S. ships. Evacuees transported by the U.S. Navy included 18,000 French and non-Communist Vietnamese troops, along with much of their equipment. The navy hospital ship *Haven* (AH 12) took some seven hundred sick and wounded French soldiers directly to Metropolitan France.

An estimated five hundred thousand additional refugees from the north were transported by the French, made their way overland, or traveled by sea in junks or small fishing boats. Fewer than one hundred thousand, a figure that included Viet Minh troops, chose to make the journey in the opposite direction. Most of these took the overland route, though some few may also have made the trip in small boats.

This "balloting by feet" was acutely embarrassing to the Communists, and during the latter part of the regroupment period many would-be refugees from the north were discouraged or prevented from leaving. Once refugees reached Haiphong, however, the Viet Minh made no overt effort to dissuade them.

Propaganda attacks were mounted, charging exploitation and mistreatment of refugees in the south. Some of these charges, unfortunately, were true. Many, perhaps most, of those moving south were Catholics, and there were thousands of ethnic Chinese in the refugee ranks. Their sudden appearance in the south, under French sponsorship, was not always welcomed by southerners who feared being displaced by the new arrivals.

"There was a big difference between the people in the South and Vietnamese in the North," Captain James D. Collette recalled in a taped interview on 15 December 1970. "The southerners were much more lethargic, I think, because of the awful heat in the South. . . . The northerners were much more industrious. They also looked a little different, more like Chinese. It was easy to tell a northerner."[2]

Captain Collette headed the Navy Section, MAAG Indochina from March 1954 to May 1955. His observation that North Vietnamese were more "industrious" than their cousins in the south would be echoed many times by Americans serving in Vietnam as they searched for explanations for their failure as advisors to inspire southerners adequately in the cause of their country's defense.

It is likely that, in general, northerners who followed the French south were better educated, wealthier, and more motivated to preserve or enhance their social status than the largely rural population in the south. Disproportionately, they did rise to positions of leadership. This thesis does not explain, however, how Communist North Vietnam motivated those who remained in the north to fight so long and so tenaciously. More likely than not, nationalism, more so than communism, was the ideology that fired the spirit of both the People's Army in the north, and the Viet Cong in the south. For them, Vietnam was and always had been one country, not two.

Passage to Freedom was the first large-scale U.S. Navy operation in Vietnam. It won much good will and high praise for the United States at the very time South Vietnamese authorities were expressing thorough disillusionment with France. The door was open, therefore, for Americans to displace the French as principal advisors to the government in Saigon. Much to their later grief, Americans rushed through that door, paying little heed to the dangers that lay ahead.

Among the pledges made by a war-weary France at Geneva was that its expeditionary force would be removed from all of Vietnam when and if the "Government of Vietnam" requested it. The State of Vietnam, recognized by France as the legitimate authority in the south, was then headed by Emperor Bao Dai, who found the French Riviera more to his liking than troubled Vietnam. His long-time associate and newly elevated prime minister, Ngo Dinh Diem, announced on 7 July 1955 that a referendum would be held in October to permit the people to choose between Bao Dai and himself as president of a new republic.

Diem was an ascetic who only recently had returned from a religious retreat at a Benedictine monastery in Belgium. Before that, he passed two years at a Maryknoll seminary in the United States. Ardently anti-Communist, he was considered by American officials to be the better candidate by far.

Shortly before the referendum, which Diem won handily (too handily, some observers complained), Diem informed the U.S. government that he would ask France to withdraw its troops by March 1956. He said that he considered the continued presence of French troops in the south to be one of the "principal Communist assets."[3]

In this assessment Diem most likely was correct. Vietnamese hatred of the French, in the south as well as the north, ran broad and deep, as the following personal aside may serve to show:

There was in Saigon, on Hai Ba Trung Street, a large cemetery that contained the graves of hundreds of Foreign Legionnaires and monuments to the fallen (*Mort Pour La France*) in France's colonial wars in Indochina. In 1969, when I first visited the cemetery, the legionnaires' crosses were being scraped systematically into forlorn piles along the edges of the cemetery to make room for above-ground Vietnamese tombs. Grave space was then at a premium in the city.

I remember the old cemetery well, and one legionnaire's grave in particular. It stood out from all the rest in a weed-infested corner as yet untouched. Fresh flowers adorned it. A cross fashioned out of white pebbles had been laid out on the grave, a cross I imagined might have been made, pebble by pebble, over many hundreds of visits. The brass plate affixed to the cross had been shined to the point where it was very difficult to make out the name of the young *legionnaire de deuxième classe* buried there in 1940.

I often wondered who took care of that grave, half-hoping that one day I would see an aging Vietnamese woman bent over it to deposit one more pebble. That at least was my romantic notion, and on a return visit to Saigon in 1989 I went back to the cemetery on Hai Ba Trung Street to see if the legionnaire's grave had been spared.

More correctly, I should say I went back to where the cemetery had been. No trace of it remained. All the tombs and monuments, Vietnamese as well as French, all the crosses, all the symbolic broken columns, all the stones were gone. The site was then a bleak and lonely park. On the day I visited it I saw a few old women sweeping gravel paths, and one young couple holding hands on a park bench.

I made inquiries and I was told that, after the fall of Saigon in 1975, notices were posted saying that anyone who wanted to move graves from the old cemetery could do so. A few were moved, and the rest were still there, unseen and, apparently, unmourned.

I have to think that hatred of the French and those associated with *L'ancien régime* had at least something to do with the desecration of the cemetery.

On 26 October 1955, after the promised referendum, Ngo Dinh Diem proclaimed the Republic of Vietnam with himself as president. He claimed 98.2 percent of the vote. His American advisors had urged him to accept a more believable 60 or 70 percent, but he overruled them.[4]

The lack of political freedom in the north, Diem said, made it impossible to hold the nationwide elections promised at Geneva, elections that were to unite North and South Vietnam under one democratically chosen government. None of the Geneva guarantors made an issue of it, and Ho Chi Minh had his hands full trying to correct the "mistakes" of his Agrarian Reform Law, mistakes that had taken tens of thousands of lives in the north, triggering a full-blown revolt that had to be put down by the People's Army.

The July 1956 deadline for holding elections passed without incident, and a Vietnam permanently divided at the 17th parallel seemed more and more the likely outcome.

France, meanwhile, was mired in yet another colonial war, this one closer to home. Troops were needed to battle insurgents in Algeria. This tended to speed up the French withdrawal from Vietnam and hastened the substitution of American advisors for French. The floodgates of American aid opened wide, and hundreds of millions of dollars were spent to build up Diem, whom President Eisenhower hailed as the "miracle man of Asia."

There was indeed something of the miraculous in Diem's, and his family's, consolidation of power in South Vietnam. Attempted coups were put down, the private armies of the Cao Dai and Hoa Hao religious sects were largely disbanded, and the criminal Binh Xuyen gang, which controlled drugs and prostitution in the capital, was defeated in a memorable "Battle of Saigon" in the spring of 1955. Diem's power spread through most of the country, with the significant exception of the Plain of Reeds, parts of the Ca Mau Peninsula, and the Rung Sat ("Forest of Assassins") southeast of Saigon. These would remain principal bases of operation for Communist insurgents throughout the war.

In August 1955, while still serving as prime minister, Diem appointed a personal friend and confidant, Lieutenant Commander Le Quang My, to the important post of naval deputy to the Armed Forces General Staff. One of My's very first acts was to order the removal of French officers from Vietnamese Navy (VNN) Headquarters. Though the French participated with the Americans for a time in a joint training mission, it was clear that from that moment the U.S. Navy had assumed the major responsibility for assisting and advising the VNN. The last French advisors departed in May 1957.

At the beginning of the American period, the VNN had a fleet of some one hundred landing craft modified for river warfare, two LSMs, two PCEs (patrol craft, escort), and three MSCs (coastal minesweepers). Virtually all of these originally had been transferred to the French through the American naval aid program. The personnel strength of the VNN stood at about nineteen hundred officers and men.

The years of French tutelage had failed, utterly, to develop within the VNN those qualities of leadership and responsibility without which no navy can fill a respectable role in its country's defense. This circumstance, clearly recognized at the time, posed a serious challenge to the American naval advisory effort. It became one of those problems that are agonized over, much talked about, and never solved.

Until 1960, the VNN experienced a period of modest growth and modernization, assisted by a Navy Section of MAAG that in July of that year had increased to sixty officers and men. There were then two major operational commands in the VNN—the River Force and the Sea Force. The former was organized into six river assault groups (RAGs). These were patterned after the old French *dinassaults,* but with two significant differences: they no longer had a permanently assigned landing force, and operational control had been surrendered to Vietnamese Army (ARVN) corps commanders who, not overly enamored with amphibious warfare, used the RAGs almost exclusively in logistic support of encamped ground forces.

Not having a landing force kept the RAG from carrying out, except on a rare, ad hoc basis, the most important part of its combat mission—the quick insertion and fire support of troops in an area of enemy activity. ARVN officers, despite the demonstrated effectiveness of the RAGs when used in this fashion, remained remarkably reluctant to commit troops in river assault operations. This situation would prevail even during the height of direct U.S. military participation in the war.

In numbers of ships and craft assigned, the River Force in 1960 was virtually unchanged from what it had been in 1955. Certain increases had been made in the Sea Force, always the preferred, if least effective, part of the VNN, and overall personnel strength had grown to about thirty-five hundred.

The insurgency in South Vietnam, relatively dormant for the preceding five years, began to assume serious proportions in late

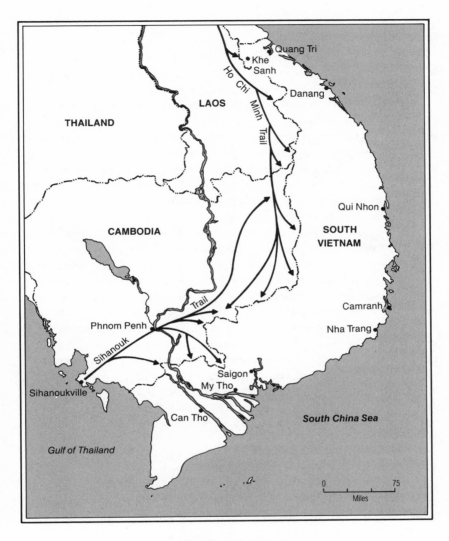

Land Infiltration Routes

1959. Admiral Harry D. Felt, Commander in Chief Pacific (CINCPAC), recommended in April 1960 that the navy assume a larger role in Vietnam.[5] Additional equipment was transferred to the VNN, and stepped-up training of both Vietnamese officers and enlisted men began, some of it in the United States.

In May 1961, President John F. Kennedy announced an expansion of the military assistance program for Vietnam, including large increases in the paramilitary Junk Force that then operated some eighty sailing junks on counter-infiltration patrols near the 17th parallel. In June, Admiral Arleigh Burke, Chief of Naval Operations (CNO), cited an urgent need for the U.S. Navy to prepare to assume naval responsibilities in restricted waters and rivers. That summer, the first SEAL (sea, air, and land) teams were formed.

In spite of increased U.S. assistance, the situation in South Vietnam continued to deteriorate. Naval advisors complained that their advice frequently was not taken, that effective use of new equipment and military supplies was hamstrung by incompetent and/or corrupt Vietnamese officers. Many of their charges were true, but, in fairness, Vietnamese "counterparts" (the VNN officers being advised) were veterans or at least survivors of what was already a very long war, a war that had seen one Western power, France, defeated. It is hardly surprising that the new American advisors, often young and totally inexperienced in counterinsurgency warfare, were sometimes viewed as temporary nuisances to be endured because of the money and material their country provided, rather than as helpful friends and consultants. The short tours normally served by advisors only aggravated the situation.

The chronically inferior political position of the VNN in the Vietnamese General Staff organization made it almost totally subservient to ARVN and to commanders who were often ignorant of navy capabilities. River assault groups seldom went on combat missions. There was a general reluctance in the Sea Force to maintain active patrols. Morale flagged. How much of this can be traced to General Staff indifference, and how much to rank-and-file uncertainty concerning the political and social issues in the war is a subject ripe for speculation. Few would deny today that, in general, leadership in South Vietnam's military was an enduring problem a parade of U.S. advisors seemingly could do little to solve.

In December 1961, U.S. air, sea, and ground units began to play a limited role in Vietnamese operations. In that month, U.S. Navy ocean minesweepers (MSOs) joined VNN ships in patrols near the

17th parallel in the South China Sea. The MSOs were not permitted to intercept suspected infiltrators, but used their radar to assist VNN units. Late in February 1962, U.S. Navy destroyer escorts (DEs) were assigned similar duties in the Gulf of Thailand.

The results of these patrols, which might be considered precursors of later Market Time operations, cast doubt on the existence of large-scale infiltration of Communist troops and supplies by sea. Of the thousands of "suspicious" craft that were stopped and inspected, there were no confirmed infiltrators from North Vietnam across the 17th parallel, and only six persons were apprehended coming from Cambodia.[6] The DEs were withdrawn from the Gulf of Thailand on 26 May 1962, and the MSO patrol was suspended on 1 August.

The use North Vietnam made of the sea to reinforce and supply insurgents in the south would always be a matter of some controversy. As will be shown in a later discussion of Market Time operations, the amount of material actually intercepted was very small compared to the patrol effort expended, not to mention the disruption caused to innocent coastal traffic and fishing. An argument could be made, and frequently was, that the mere existence of the coastal patrol forced North Vietnam to rely on costlier (in terms of time and manpower) overland infiltration routes through Laos and Cambodia. For whatever reason, the pattern established early in the war saw Communist arms shipped into North Vietnamese ports, principally Haiphong, and the "neutral" Cambodian port of Sihanoukville for transshipment by land to hundreds of remote locations along the virtually open South Vietnamese borders with Laos and Cambodia.

In November 1961 there were sixty-nine U.S. Navy advisors in Vietnam. By the following April there were 292. Advisors were assigned to the Sea, River, and Junk forces, to the Naval Shipyard and to VNN Headquarters in Saigon.

In recognition of the expanding U.S. role, the Military Assistance Command Vietnam (MACV) was established in February 1962, and the Headquarters Support Activity Saigon (HSAS), a U.S. Navy command, was commissioned on 1 July.

HSAS provided all essential logistics and "housekeeping" services for U.S. personnel in Saigon and, to a lesser extent, for those assigned elsewhere in Vietnam. It managed the port of Saigon and oversaw the offloading and warehousing of supplies. It ran some twenty-nine hotels for bachelor officers and enlisted men. It was responsible for messes, clubs, exchanges, medical facilities, motor pools, etc. It took care of pay accounts, delivered the U.S. mail, operated a bus and taxi system, furnished fire and police protection. It brought in touring USO groups, ran a golf course, a library. It employed thousands of Vietnamese civilians. Small wonder that its commanding officer carried the unofficial title of "mayor of Saigon." Captain Malcolm Friedman established the command. He was relieved in June 1964 by Captain Archie C. Kuntz.

Much to the regret of U.S. Navy personnel assigned in Saigon, HSAS would be replaced by the U.S. Army Headquarters Activity Command (USAHAC) in 1966.

The large increase in the U.S. military assistance effort that occurred in 1962 had been initiated as a result of an October 1961 visit to Vietnam by President Kennedy's special military assistant, General Maxwell D. Taylor. As Taylor observed, the insurgency was then growing at an alarming pace, and more U.S. aid was needed to keep the Diem regime afloat.

Following Taylor's visit, "Project Beef-up" was announced, a program that authorized more men, more money, and more material for the Vietnamese military. For the VNN, already suffering from a lack of trained officers and petty officers, this meant more ships and boats—3 PCEs, 3 LSTs, 3 PGMs (motor gunboats), 16 LCMs, 16 LCVPs, 12 MLMS's (minesweeping launches), and 240 small swimmer support boats for VNN SEALs (LDNN). The LDNN (*Lien Doc Nguoi Nhia*—literally, "soldiers who fight under the sea") were trained for underwater demolition work and initially were used primarily in beach surveys, merchant-ship hull inspections, and similar kinds of work.

In addition, plans were made to expand the Vietnamese Junk Force to 644 motorized junks, in order to strengthen offshore patrols against Communist infiltration by sea, the existence of which, as already mentioned, was a subject of some doubt. There was a romantic quality associated with the Junk Force, at least among those who didn't have to serve in it, and this perhaps had something to do with the decision to enlarge it. Not a few "junkies" had *Sat Cong* ("Kill Communists") tattooed on their chests. There was little evidence to suggest, however, that this struck much terror in the hearts of the Viet Cong.

In a move intended to improve the performance of the South Vietnamese Civil Guard, 136 LCVPs were transferred to it from U.S. Navy stock. The Civil Guard performed police and regulatory functions on the rivers of Vietnam.

General Taylor's report to the president stopped short of recommending the assignment of U.S. combat forces in Vietnam, though just barely. Taylor urged a "limited partnership" with the Vietnamese military and, while acknowledging that "only the Vietnamese can defeat the Viet Cong," he said that "at all levels Americans must, as friends and partners—not as arms length advisors—show them how the job must be done—not tell them or do it for them."[7]

How to apply this don't-tell-them, don't-do-it-for-them, but-show-them technique was, apparently, left to the imagination and ingenuity of the American advisor in the field.

The hazards of a larger American presence in Vietnam were recognized by at least one senior U.S. commander. Admiral Harry D. Felt, CINCPAC, perhaps responding to the Taylor report, warned that U.S. intervention could provoke an outcry against "white colonialism throughout the world, prompt Communist countermeasures on a like scale, result in a long-term deployment, and ultimately engage U.S. personnel in combat."[8] His warning was ignored, as were others.

U.S. military and economic aid to South Vietnam in 1961 totaled more than $200 million, and at year's end there were more than 3,200 U.S. military personnel in Vietnam. Fourteen had been killed in action.

On 12 January 1962 the U.S. Air Force began "Operation Ranch Hand." Flying specially configured C-123 aircraft, U.S. personnel, over the next nine years, would spray eighteen million gallons of herbicide over parts of Vietnam and Laos, in an attempt to deny natural cover and food to enemy troops.

The program originated with a joint State-Defense proposal in September 1961, and an initial plan drawn up by the U.S. Combat Development and Test Center called for defoliating an incredible 31,250 square miles of jungle, 1,125 square miles of mangrove swamp, and 312.5 square miles of manioc grove—an area equivalent to almost half the total land area of South Vietnam! The herbicide program would reach its peak in 1967 when more than 1.6 million acres were sprayed, 85 percent of it for defoliation and 15 percent for crop denial.[9] After 1965, the principal defoliant used was called "Agent Orange" (from the color of the containers in which it was shipped). It was later found to have carcinogenic properties.

Some Ranch Hand crews adopted the jocular motto, "Remember, only you can prevent a forest." They did their work remarkably well.

Admiral Harry D. Felt

The banks of rivers that were sprayed were often completely denuded of living vegetation. The Long Tau, Saigon's main shipping channel, was a scene of utter desolation when I first saw it in 1969. The land on either side, stretching back many hundreds of yards, was blackened and bare, as if it had been swept by a raging fire.

In the spring of 1970, after U.S. and Vietnamese forces crossed into Cambodia, I traveled by boat up the Mekong as far as the Neak Luong ferry crossing. My notes from this journey compare the land on the Vietnamese and Cambodian sides of the border, respectively, to Dorothy's Kansas and the Land of Oz in the classic film *The Wizard of Oz*—the former black and white, the latter emerald green. The difference was startling.

The last Ranch Hand mission was flown on 7 January 1971, and later that month the Defense Department ordered the termination of all herbicide spraying operations by U.S. forces in Vietnam. In April 1975, President Gerald Ford renounced first use of herbicides in future wars.

In March 1962, the Diem government launched its ill-fated "strategic hamlet" program. Its stated purpose was to protect South Vietnam's rural population from Viet Cong attack. Hundreds of thousands of Vietnamese peasants were forced to abandon their homes and move inside government stockades. Later in the year, Diem would claim that more than four million people, a third of the population, were in strategic hamlets and therefore "pacified." It was neither the first nor the last time Americans would be dazzled by statistics in Vietnam.

In 1962, U.S. helicopter pilots began ferrying Vietnamese troops into combat, and on 4 February the first U.S. helicopter was shot down. U.S. Special Forces, the "Green Berets," were becoming a part of the American folklore.

On the first of his many trips to Vietnam, Secretary of Defense Robert S. McNamara told the press that he was favorably impressed by what he saw. On 11 May he announced that "every quantitative measurement . . . shows that we are winning the war."

Later in the year, however, Senate Majority Leader Mike Mansfield returned from a fact-finding mission in Vietnam and told the president that, in his view, the more than $2 billion the United States had invested in Vietnam since 1955 had been wasted. He sharply criticized Diem, saying that his failure to share power lay at the heart of the insurgency problem.

Diem responded with more statistics: 4,077 strategic hamlets completed out of a projected total of 11,182; 39 percent of the population pacified.

At the beginning of 1963 there were eleven thousand American servicemen in Vietnam. One hundred and nine had been killed or wounded in the preceding year. In 1963 these numbers would increase to 16,500 in country, and 489 killed or wounded.

Despite the growing violence, the mood of the Kennedy administration, heading into a re-election campaign, was upbeat. Secretary McNamara announced that one thousand American servicemen would be withdrawn from Vietnam before the end of the year. The actual situation, however, was deteriorating badly.

In May 1963, Buddhists celebrating the birthday of Gautama Buddha were fired upon by government forces in Hue. Nine persons were killed, including seven children and one woman. The government troops were commanded by a Catholic deputy province chief. Diem blamed the incident on the Viet Cong. The killings ushered in a long summer of Buddhist protest and rioting.

On 11 June a Buddhist monk burned himself to death on a busy Saigon street. The scene was captured on camera, and the film was flashed to a shocked world. Other public acts of self-immolation followed, and Diem's powerful sister-in-law, Madame Nhu (the Western press dubbed her the "Dragon Lady"), derided the burnings as "barbecues," touching off a wave of indignation and revulsion within and without Vietnam. In a climate of near social chaos, the Communist insurgency gained ground, despite increased American aid.

On 2 November, with at the very least the tacit approval of the Kennedy administration (the new U.S. ambassador, Henry Cabot Lodge, seems to have actively encouraged it), Diem was overthrown in a coup led by senior Vietnamese Army officers. The president and his brother, Ngo Dinh Nhu, thought by many to be a gray eminence behind the throne, escaped from the palace by way of a secret tunnel. The two brothers sought sanctuary in St. Francis Xavier Church in Cholon, Saigon's Chinese quarter. There they were persuaded to surrender, perhaps by a promise of safe conduct out of the country. Apparently on the orders of the coup leader, General Duong Van "Big" Minh, the president and his brother were shot to death by ARVN officers, one of whom was General Minh's bodyguard, while being driven in an armored personnel carrier to army headquarters.

The only other senior officer of the Diem government killed in the coup was the commander of the Vietnamese Navy, Captain Ho Tan

Quyen, a Diem loyalist who declined to participate in the overthrow of the president.

General William C. Westmoreland, who in June 1964 would become Commander U.S. Military Assistance Command Vietnam (COMUSMACV), says in his memoirs that the Diem assassination was a "pivotal event: however negative or even neutral the American role, the United States had played a part in the internal governmental affairs of South Vietnam. That inevitably contributed to a feeling of obligation among American officials in Washington."[10]

In a discussion with me in April 1989, Westmoreland expanded on that theme. "Up until Diem's murder," he said, "the United States could have departed Vietnam with honor. After that, there was no turning away."

As 1963 drew to a close, there were 742 U.S. Navy advisors in Vietnam. The Vietnamese Navy had grown to a force that included 258 ships and craft. The personnel strength of the VNN was 6,200 officers and men. Of these, 2,000 served in the Sea Force, 1,200 in the River Force, and 2,600 in the shore establishment. The remainder were assigned to the Junk Force, which consisted of 632 junks and 3,700 civilian crew members.

The River Force at this time was organized into eight major commands. There were six river assault groups, two based in Saigon and one each in My Tho, Vinh Long, Can Tho, and Long Xuyen. Each RAG had one LCM command boat, one monitor, five armored LCMs, eight armored LCVPs, and four STCANs. A river transportation escort group of four LCMs, eight LCVPs, and eighteen STCANs was assigned to escort shipping into and out of the port of Saigon. Finally, a logistics group of seven LCUs supported outlying bases.

Given the gravity of the military situation, the performance of the VNN was far from satisfactory. The average employment of available (not in overhaul, not in upkeep, not in training) Sea Force and River Force units was roughly 50 percent. The Junk Force put only an average 40 percent of its available junks at sea on any given day. Advisors reported that even these statistics gave an inflated impression of force utilization, since units frequently were only "administratively" employed. "Combat patrols" often consisted of short trips to and from anchorage. The Junk Force was notorious for "gundecking" (falsifying) operational reports.

In 1963, patrols off the coasts of South Vietnam searched a reported 135,911 craft and 388,725 people, of whom only 6 were thought to be infiltrators.[11] These figures could be, and were, interpreted in two ways: Either they showed that sea infiltration was not, in this period, a serious problem, or they demonstrated a remarkable lack of effectiveness in the patrol effort.

Captain Phillip H. Bucklew, one of the officers sent by CINCPAC to provide an outside assessment of the situation, found the mood of in-country U.S. Navy officers grim. They "were out there not as advisors," he said, "hell, they were out there as missionaries. . . . They were the most frustrated men I think I ever encountered in the military, these people out in the field."[12]

The frustration had only begun. The U.S. Navy stood on the brink of active, full-scale participation in South Vietnam's war for survival, a war that navy was at best only marginally prepared to fight in the manner dictated by its civilian leadership.

4

The Readiness of the Navy for Limited War

Without an adversary, prowess shrivels. We see how great and efficient it really is only when it shows by endurance what it is capable of.

—Lucius Annaeus Seneca (c. 4 B.C.–A.D. 65)

At the end of World War II, the United States Navy was the greatest sea power the world had ever known. More than one hundred thousand ships and craft and eighty thousand naval aircraft had powered the fleet in its mighty and decisive thrusts across the Atlantic and Pacific oceans.

In the euphoria of victory, and in the false belief that its sole possession of the atomic bomb would guarantee the peace, America demobilized its armed forces with reckless speed. The onset of the Cold War and the Soviet Union's early breaking of the U.S. nuclear monopoly slowed the process somewhat, but the postwar years were marked by declining military budgets and a sharp curtailment of U.S. readiness in general, and the navy's in particular, to fight a conventional war.

Much of the fleet that had fought and won the Battle of the Atlantic and, on the other side of the globe, brought Imperial Japan to its knees, was either scrapped or placed in rusting reserve. Those units that remained active were inadequately manned and supported.

In 1950, the perceived weakness of U.S. forces in the Pacific no doubt played a major part in Communist North Korea's decision to invade the non-Communist South. (Secretary of State Dean Acheson's policy statement on 12 January 1950 in which he delineated a U.S. defensive perimeter in the Pacific running from "the Aleutians to Japan . . . to the Ryukyus to the Philippine Islands"—a perimeter excluding the Korean peninsula—is also thought to have influenced North Korea's decision.)

The Korean War was fought by a Pacific Fleet strengthened immeasurably by mobilization of the Naval Reserve and by "borrowed" assets from the Atlantic Fleet. I myself was in a draft of five hundred enlisted reservists who reported aboard the carrier *Leyte* (CV 32) in August 1950. The *Leyte* had just made a hurried return from deployment in the Mediterranean. At an adjacent berth in Norfolk, Virginia, the battleship *Missouri* (BB 64) had its ship's force augmented by a similar draft of recalled reservists. These two ships and others then sailed for the Western Pacific, there to reinforce a badly stretched Seventh Fleet. Within a few months, Task Force 77 in the Sea of Japan included four aircraft carriers, two battleships, and numerous cruisers and destroyers. It was one of the last great gatherings of World War II warships and a sight I shall never forget.

The relative ease with which the navy built up its forces in the Pacific was deceptive. Many of the recalled reservists were well-

trained veterans of World War II; many of the ships that were reacti-
vated from the reserve fleet were virtually new when laid up and
required little in the way of major overhaul and modernization. And
while the navy's, and the nation's, attention was focused on a "police
action" in far-off Asia, America's vital interests in Europe, the Middle
East, and elsewhere were placed at risk. This was a situation that
would be repeated when the United States became involved in
Vietnam.

The fighting in Korea came to an inconclusive and frustrating end
in 1953. The failure of U.N. forces, overwhelmingly American, to
achieve victory had a profound psychological effect on Asians and
Americans alike. America no longer seemed invincible. It had shown
itself willing to accept something less than total victory on the
battlefield.

President Dwight D. Eisenhower, who had campaigned on a
promise to "go to Korea" and end that unpopular war, adopted a new
strategy for deterring and, if necessary, fighting communism. The
new strategy relied heavily on nuclear weapons. To make the threat of
"massive retaliation" credible, large investments were made in a
"triad" of strategic nuclear weapons: land-based intercontinental bal-
listic missiles, manned bombers, and a fleet of new and revolutionary
nuclear-powered ballistic-missile submarines called Polaris. The first
of these submarines became operational in 1959. Prior to that time,
carrier-based planes gave the navy its nuclear punch.

The lion's share of a diminished defense budget was thus devoted
to deterring "big wars." The decision to stand aloof from the agony of
France at Dien Bien Phu was seen as compelling evidence of America's
reluctance to engage in new "small wars," particularly those on the
mainland of Asia.

The navy received only about a fourth of a defense budget that
averaged roughly $40 billion in Eisenhower's second term, and much
of that was spent on the Polaris submarine program. By 1960, the
fleet had been reduced to 812 ships, and many of these were getting
old. "Block obsolescence" was setting in, and the Fleet Rehabilitation
and Modernization (FRAM) program, begun in 1959, delayed it only
a little. At the end of the Eisenhower years, four out of five navy ships
were of World War II vintage and fast approaching the end of a
normal service life.

In 1959, 72 percent of the ships visited by the Board of Inspection
and Survey were found to be in unsatisfactory material condition,

Robert S. McNamara

and the Commander in Chief Pacific, Admiral Felt, warned bluntly that "the United States has no sustaining power in the Pacific for conventional war."[1]

President John F. Kennedy entered office with a ringing promise to "pay any price, bear any burden, meet any hardship, support any friend, oppose any foe, to assure the survival and success of liberty."[2] These were words that would haunt his successor in the White House, Lyndon B. Johnson, when the price and the burden in Vietnam began to soar.

President John F. Kennedy

Though Kennedy had campaigned on the issue of an alleged "missile gap" that, he said, gave the Soviet Union a numerical edge over the United States in nuclear weapons, his administration, as Eisenhower's before him, made a dramatic and fundamental change in the nation's defense strategy. No longer would the nation's defense rest primarily on the threat of "massive retaliation" (how could it, if the missile gap was real?), but on a new strategy of "flexible response." Henceforth, the United States would be prepared to defend its interests with conventional as well as nuclear arms. This meant greater attention to the nation's readiness to fight small wars, and increased spending for defense.

The new strategy was suggested, in part, by Kennedy's reading of General Maxwell D. Taylor's book, *The Uncertain Trumpet*. Taylor would become Kennedy's principal military advisor, chairman of the Joint Chiefs of Staff in 1962–64, and President Johnson's first ambassador to South Vietnam.

The navy's share of the additional $6 billion Kennedy added to the defense budget in his first months in office amounted to more than $2.7 billion. Navy and Marine Corps personnel ceilings were raised, sealift was improved, marginally, by reactivating several transports, and new amphibious ship construction was authorized.

Secretary of Defense Robert S. McNamara, former president of the Ford Motor Company and a devotee of the management technique known as "systems analysis," promised to run the sprawling defense establishment more like a business. He recruited a corps of bright young managers and academics who, through their whirlwind reshaping of old Pentagon ways, soon became known as McNamara's "Whiz Kids."

Vice Admiral Gerald E. Miller, an early inside observer and critic of McNamara's methods, describes in his reminiscences one of the monumental battles waged between the navy and McNamara—the one fought over the F-111B aircraft. It illustrates a McNamara mindset that later would influence greatly the conduct of the Vietnam War.

"He was never wrong," Miller recalled. "He never fought an airplane, never designed an airplane, never built an airplane, never managed an aircraft company or anything similar. But all of a sudden he's got this great proposition on the F-111, and he can't be wrong because he's McNamara. . . . It's a good example of what happens . . . when you let the civilians get out of the policy and into the details of running the organization. They get into areas where they do not have the competence, or the long-term responsibility, and where they do not belong. They get impressed with the power and fascinated with the business. They like to run it. It's fun. They enjoy it, and the next thing you know, we have ourselves in a real kettle of fish. . . ."[3]

McNamara's attempt to force the F-111B down the navy's throat was defeated, narrowly, in Congress. A young rear admiral, not an aviator, went to the wire arguing the systems analysis case for the aircraft. A protégé of Secretary of the Navy Paul Nitze, the admiral's name was Elmo R. Zumwalt, Jr.

The degree to which systems analysis could be, and was, manipulated to support preconceived notions is suggested in the following excerpt from Admiral Alfred G. Ward's memoirs. (Ward was deputy chief of naval operations in 1963–65.)

"Let me tell you a personal experience. I was in the room one time when Secretary Nitze asked his aide, who was at that time Zumwalt, if he could prove the value of a result that was being discussed—and I think it was the cost of a weapons system—by systems analysis. Zumwalt turned to him and said, 'Mr. Secretary, I can prove anything you tell me to prove by using systems analysis.' "[4]

The Department of Defense, created by act of Congress in 1949, went through several reorganizations in the years leading to the Vietnam War. The clean lines of authority that in World War II ran from the commander in the field, through the army and navy chains of command and the respective service secretaries, to the president were severed and rerouted, and rerouted again, always in the interest of "efficiency" and elimination of wasteful "interservice rivalry." The secretary of defense was given immense power over the uniformed services, and the role of the service secretaries was diminished. A huge bureaucracy formed around the office of the secretary of defense, a bureaucracy staffed in general by political appointees with little or no working knowledge of the military.

Admiral Ward describes what this led to in the McNamara era:

". . . Major decisions were made by people pretty far down the line. As you undoubtedly know, the secretary of defense has a deputy and many assistant secretaries of defense, and each of the assistant secretaries of defense has a deputy assistant secretary of defense, and under Mr. McNamara these were a large number. Frequently, these would be young engineers or young people who had not much experience in building ships or in managing large programs, but they had tremendous power, and they had the power by virtue of the systems analysis process in many cases. They would use these techniques in order to prove a point, and frequently would have more influence with the secretary than would, say, the chief of the Navy or the joint chiefs of staff."[5]

The "people pretty far down the line" Admiral Ward refers to were of course not only civilians. An elite corps of young uniformed officers, aides, and military assistants to the assistant secretaries, and the deputy assistant secretaries, exercised authority and influence far beyond that commensurate with their rank and seniority. They share the burden for many decisions in Vietnam that, in retrospect, made little if any military or strategic sense.

An early McNamara decision with long-range implications for the navy concerned the transport of men and material. Airlift, McNamara said, would be the primary means of transporting troops and light equipment in response to overseas crises, because it was faster. Sealift would be relied upon to move heavy equipment and bulk supplies. The navy viewed this with some misgiving, believing that military airlift clearly was incapable of carrying the numbers of men and the amount of light cargo even a moderate-size operation would require. Indeed, at the height of the Vietnam War, most U.S. military personnel flew from the United States to Vietnam in chartered civilian jetliners—in my case, a canary-yellow DC-8. This was but one of many anomalies in this strange war.

Another McNamara idea was to preposition military cargo in "floating forward depots"—initially old Victory ships operated by the Military Sea Transportation Service. The first test of this concept was held at Subic Bay in the Philippines in 1963 and declared a success. As a cheap and no doubt cost-effective substitute for adequate sealift, floating forward depots have a certain attractiveness. In the late 1970s, floating warehouses filled with heavy equipment and supplies were prepositioned in remote regions of the Indian Ocean, in anticipation of possible combat operations in the Persian Gulf. How a U.S. expeditionary force would fare if, by act of war or other happenstance, it should be separated from its heavy equipment is another matter, but one not difficult to imagine.

In Vietnam an estimated 98 percent of U.S. equipment and supplies used in fighting the war was transported by sea in a great bridge of ships stretching across the Pacific. It was America's good fortune that this bridge was never attacked outside Vietnam's internal waters. Had the war spread to sea, and had the Soviet Union's huge submarine fleet been brought into play, the navy would have had a difficult time keeping the sea lines of communication to Vietnam open.

The precipitous decline of the U.S. Merchant Marine after World War II meant that many of the ships supplying Vietnam were foreign charters or creaking relics pulled from America's reserve of leftover Liberty and Victory ships. That reserve is now mostly gone. Barring a most unlikely rebuilding of its merchant fleet, in the future America will be more dependent than ever on foreign flag vessels for support of its armed forces overseas. Certainly, finding a sufficient number of ships to supply the army in Vietnam was no easy matter.

"Counterinsurgency" was a buzzword in the armed forces of the Kennedy years. General Taylor headed a presidential "task force" that studied it. Counterinsurgency training programs at the shipboard level became checkoff items in navy administrative inspections, their preparation typically assigned to one of the more junior officers on board. Lectures were given on the evils of communism, and the importance of the navy's role in providing security for threatened societies overseas as they went forward with the essential business of "nation-building."

Ship's force landing parties were outfitted with musty equipment dredged from the bottom of long-neglected lockers. The men were arrayed in ragged ranks and drilled. When the opportunity presented itself, they were sent ashore for training under the watchful eyes of tough marines. The crackle of small-arms fire on the fantails of underway ships was heard with regularity for the first time in years. Whaleboats were launched and sent porpoising off in the open sea to investigate imaginary contacts.

Gunfire support exercises were scheduled more frequently for the relatively few gun ships still in the active fleet. The emphasis in the 1950s had been on missiles and submarines and aircraft carriers. In 1963, with all the battleships and most of the cruisers decommissioned, there were no 16-inch, and only eighteen 8-inch and eighteen 6-inch guns in the active fleet. The number of 5-inch guns, the main battery of the destroyer force, had fallen to but 463.[6] Due to low levels of procurement, gun ammunition was in short supply.

As the United States edged ever closer to direct combat participation in the Vietnam War, its navy was still the most powerful in the world. The Pacific Fleet alone numbered 434 ships, including 13 attack and antisubmarine aircraft carriers. Though material readiness for conventional war had improved under Kennedy and McNamara, little had been done to reverse the overall aging of the fleet, the shortage of navy sealift, and the decline of the merchant marine.

What was not, what perhaps could not have been, foreseen was the very unconventional nature of the war the navy would be called upon to fight in Vietnam, and the pernicious influence of a defense secretariat that insisted on involving itself in tactical areas where it had no competence and in dictating decisions, from Washington, that in past wars, wars the United States had won, were properly made by commanders in the field.

5

The Tonkin Gulf— Beyond the Point of No Return

Ah! What avails the classic bent
And what the cultured word,
Against the undoctored incident
That actually occurred?

—Rudyard Kipling

Within three weeks of the overthrow and murder of Diem and his brother, Nhu, President John F. Kennedy was himself assassinated in Dallas. Kennedy's successor, Lyndon B. Johnson, caught up almost immediately in the politics of engineering his own election, could not afford to rock the leaky boat that was Vietnam. He decided to retain, for the time being at least, senior members of the Kennedy national security team, and to follow the course they had charted in Vietnam.

Diem's overthrow, contrary to U.S. hopes and expectations, did not lead to greater political stability nor improved military performance in Vietnam. Saigon, more than ever, became a snakepit of intrigue and political maneuvering for personal power and position within the government and the army. The Viet Cong virtually ruled the countryside. Terrorist acts and attacks on government outposts multiplied.

The junta headed by Major General Duong Van Minh, which had toppled Diem, was itself overthrown on 30 January 1964 in a bloodless coup led by another major general, Nguyen Khanh. A week later, Khanh, having received a pledge of U.S. support, formed a new government with himself as premier. The popular Minh was named to the ceremonial post of "chief of state." Despite the best efforts of his American advisors, Khanh would retain power for only a little more than a year.

Viewing this turmoil from Hanoi, Ho Chi Minh decided the time was right to move to "stage three" of the insurgency, infiltrate regular North Vietnamese Army (NVA) troops into South Vietnam, and prepare for pitched battles involving large units.

Until 1964 the Viet Cong were not equipped with standardized weapons, but rather a variety of French, Russian, Chinese, Japanese, and American arms. The supply of ammunition for all of these weapons was an increasingly vexing problem. It was decided, therefore, to shift to a standard family of small arms, employing the same caliber of ammunition, and to provide more modern supporting weapons. The introduction of these, particularly the AK-47 assault rifle, required greatly increased tonnages of resupply and committed Hanoi to a sharp expansion of its infiltration effort.

The most economical and direct routes for supplying its forces in the south were sea routes, and there were many likely points of entry on the long and lightly guarded coast. Though the number of VNN ships available for coastal patrol had increased, detection probability remained low. The Junk Force was seriously undermanned, some coastal groups having less than 50 percent of authorized strength. In this period, Junk Force crews were still "paramilitary," not part of the regular navy, and paid even more poorly than VNN sailors were.

If direct sea routes were blocked by some unforeseen increase in the strength and effectiveness of offshore naval patrols, equally exploitable water routes existed on the inland river systems, which were then scarcely, if at all, patrolled. The most important of these ran from and along the border with Cambodia. Communist arms reached the rivers either by way of clandestine shipments through ostensibly neutral Cambodian ports, or overland by way of Laos and a torturous system of roads and jungle paths already being called the "Ho Chi Minh Trail." Almost incredibly, the Mekong River, running through the very heart of South Vietnam's great delta, remained an international waterway open to ship traffic proceeding to and from Cambodia well into the war. Without doubt, supplies reached Communist forces fighting in South Vietnam by way of this route also.

"I knew about it," General Westmoreland told me in an interview in January 1988, "but I couldn't do anything about it."

In January 1964, Admiral Felt sent a team of naval officers to Vietnam to see what could be done about the steadily worsening security in the Mekong Delta. Officially known as the "Vietnam Delta Infiltration Study Group," the team was headed by Rear Admiral Paul Savidge, Jr., commander Amphibious Training Command, U.S. Pacific Fleet. The next most senior officer was Captain Phillip H. Bucklew, commander of the Pacific Fleet's Naval Operations Support Group. Included on the team were representatives of the Pacific Fleet, the First Fleet, MACV, the Navy Section of the MAAG, and SEAL Team One. According to Bucklew, Felt's instructions to the group were blunt and to the point. The team was to find out "why all I get are messages of success stories and accomplishments, and meanwhile we're getting our ass kicked out there."[1]

In Saigon, Savidge became ill and Bucklew took charge. On 15 February 1964 he reported the team's findings to General Paul D. Harkins, commander U.S. Military Assistance Command Vietnam.

In general, what became known as the "Bucklew Report" acknowledged that infiltration of men and supplies from the north existed on a scale sufficient to support an expanded level of operations, and only minimal resistance to that infiltration was being made.

"Viet Cong operations, supported by minimum effort in diversion, deception or harassment cover, can feasibly infiltrate personnel and equipment by land, sea or air at times and areas of their own choice," the report stated.[2]

The team was critical of the sea patrol then in effect and recommended its augmentation by U.S. Navy forces. It pointed out, however, that a sea quarantine would be futile in the absence of a companion effort to block inland infiltration routes. It recommended the creation of a mobile patrol force along the Cambodian and Laotian borders, citing the need to equip such a force with high-speed small craft. It further recommended that the Vietnamese Navy be assigned a permanent landing force component, in order to better support inshore patrol craft operations.

Surprisingly, in a period of rapid expansion of in-country military assets, the team did not recommend the turnover of additional U.S. ships and craft. It sharply questioned the use being made of those already supplied.

"Introduction in-country of additional U.S. type amphibious or river craft is not justified. Reallocation of some items, e.g., LCVP and SSB [swimmer support boat], from units not fully utilizing the craft to others having developed requirements is indicated. Improved maintenance and repair capabilities are warranted. . . .

"Complacency and lack of aggressiveness of Republic of Vietnam armed forces evidence inadequate leadership and lack of incentives which hinder the counter-infiltration effort."[3]

The Bucklew Report recommended increased attention to psychological warfare, to the need to establish and enforce curfews and restricted zones, and to measures necessary to prevent U.S.–furnished materials from falling into the hands of the Viet Cong. It recognized that U.S. Navy forces might have to be deployed in the Mekong Delta at a later date.

A Bucklew recommendation that the VNN play a larger role in Vietnamese Joint General Staff decision making led to the appointment, on 8 April, of Captain Chung Tan Cang to the newly created post of chief of naval operations. Cang, a participant in the coup against Diem, had succeeded the murdered Ho Tan Quyen as naval deputy to the chief of staff of the armed forces. Cang was promoted to the rank of commodore and, six months later, to rear admiral. VNN influence within the JGS was not substantially enhanced, however. The Vietnamese Navy would remain subservient to the will and the whims of ARVN generals until the very end of the war, much to the despair and chagrin of U.S. Navy advisors.

General Harkins forwarded the Bucklew Report, via an approving Admiral Felt, to the U.S. Joint Chiefs of Staff who incorporated much of it in a 1964 review of the navy's role in Vietnam. Parts of the report were echoed in General Khanh's "Victory Plan," which on 22 February 1964 formally replaced Diem's strategic hamlet program as Saigon's answer to the insurgency. By then many, perhaps most, of the stockades behind which a large part of South Vietnam's rural population had been herded lay in ruins—either at the hands of the Viet Cong or the people the hamlets were meant to protect.

On 15 May 1964, against the recommendation of CINCPAC, the Military Assistance Command absorbed MAAG Vietnam. Admiral Felt had thought it important to keep operational and advisory functions separate, believing that the MACV commander could not adequately oversee both. Secretary McNamara overruled him. The Navy Section, MAAG, was redesignated the Naval Advisory Group, MACV. Its first commander was Captain William H. Hardcastle.

The worsening security situation in Vietnam was underscored early on the morning of 2 May 1964 when the MSTS aircraft ferry *Card* was mined and sunk alongside a Saigon wharf. Viet Cong sappers, avoiding detection by moving through a sewer main, were believed responsible. The *Card* was refloated by a navy salvage team and on 20 May left Saigon under tow for extensive repairs in the Philippines.

In May, U.S. Navy carrier aircraft, in concert with U.S. Air Force planes based at Tan Son Nhut, began flying "Yankee Team" reconnaissance missions over Laos. The purpose of these flights, conducted with the approval of Prince Souvanna Phouma of Laos, was to chart the flow of arms and supplies down the Ho Chi Minh Trail. Navy carriers operated in the vicinity of "Yankee Station" off the coast near Danang. (In 1966, Yankee Station would be moved to 17 degrees 30 minutes north, 108 degrees 30 minutes east to facilitate the bombing of North Vietnam. "Dixie Station" was established in 1965 at 11 degrees north, 110 degrees east as a launching point for aircraft attacking targets in South Vietnam.)

On 6 June 1964, an RF-8A from the *Kitty Hawk* (CVA 63) was shot down while on a Yankee Team mission and the pilot, Lieutenant Charles F. Klusmann, was taken prisoner by the Communist Pathet Lao. After eighty-six days of brutal captivity he escaped, along with five Thai and Laotian prisoners. Three harrowing days later, Klusmann and one surviving companion made contact with friendly

Ho Chi Minh

Meo tribesmen. The young aviator was the first, and one of only a
very few, U.S. personnel to escape from captors during the Vietnam
War.

On 20 June 1964, General William C. Westmoreland relieved
General Harkins as COMUSMACV. A tall, handsome man, looking
every inch a general, Westmoreland was fated to become a major

General William C. Westmoreland

figure in America's failed crusade in Vietnam. He had served since January as Harkins's deputy, had traveled widely in South Vietnam, knew most of the senior ARVN officers, and was well aware of the political and military morass into which he was stepping. MACV, it might be noted in passing, was not a major theater command. Throughout the war CINCPAC, in Hawaii, was COMUSMACV's immediate military superior. When the air war commenced over North Vietnam, CINCPAC had the responsibility for running it even though, as will be shown, most of the shots were called in Washington.

By mid-1964, plans were well advanced for carrying the war to the north. Admiral Felt, prior to his 1 July retirement, had prepared a list of potential targets in North Vietnam that was then reviewed and approved by Secretary McNamara. This list was to be used in conjunction with OPLAN 37, which provided for a three-phase escalation of the war, including: (1) pursuit of enemy forces across the borders of Cambodia and Laos; (2) reprisal ("tit for tat") air strikes, raids, and mining operations in North Vietnam; and (3) all-out bombing in the north.

"Those of us in Saigon who knew of OPLAN 37 saw little possibility that the President would implement it until after the November elections," Westmoreland observes in his memoirs.[4]

If the likelihood of overt action against North Vietnam seemed remote in the summer of 1964 because of politics at home, no such restraint seemed to exist for covert attacks by South Vietnamese forces assisted, quietly, by the United States. These were conducted under OPLAN 34A, drawn up jointly by COMUSMACV and CIA Chief of Far Eastern Operations William Colby (later, director of the Central Intelligence Agency). The plan was based on an earlier one, OPLAN 34, originated by CINCPAC.

Using eight U.S.–furnished fast patrol boats (PTFs), six of them Norwegian-built *Nasties* and the remaining two converted U.S. Navy torpedo boats, the Vietnamese Navy staged a series of commando-style raids against North Vietnamese installations. These were launched from Danang, and to one degree or another were coordinated with the U.S. Navy's "Desoto Patrol," a surface-ship electronic surveillance and intelligence-gathering operation of long duration directed against the Communist Asian mainland. The first of these patrols in the Tonkin Gulf was carried out in December 1962, and while they met with "serious warnings" from Communist China, they drew little response from Hanoi until the sequence of events described below.

In the early morning hours of 31 July 1964, four VNN fast patrol boats on an OPLAN 34A mission bombarded North Vietnam's Hon Me and Hon Nieu islands, hitting targets there with 20- and 40-mm cannon and 57-mm recoilless rifle fire. The boats then returned to their base at Danang.

Later that same day, the USS *Maddox* (DD 731), with Captain John J. Herrick, Commander Destroyer Division 192, entered the Tonkin Gulf on what was supposed to be a routine Desoto Patrol.

For two days, the *Maddox* cruised without incident, proceeding in a northerly direction in international waters. Herrick's orders were to stay at least eight miles off the mainland and to come no closer than four miles to the offshore islands. (North Vietnam had made no special claims to a territorial sea, and it was assumed that the old French claim of three miles was still valid.)

On the morning of 2 August, a message from North Vietnamese naval headquarters ordering its coastal forces to prepare for battle was intercepted and read by U.S. intelligence. The force immediately available to carry out these orders consisted of Soviet-built P-4 motor torpedo boats and *Swatow*-class motor gunboats. Later on 2 August, a second message was intercepted and this one ordered an attack with torpedoes against an unspecified enemy.

Not long after the second intercept, the *Maddox* made radar and visual contact with three North Vietnamese P-4s. The ship went to general quarters, increased speed to 27 knots, and altered course to the southeast, away from the rapidly closing torpedo boats. Captain Herrick sent a flash precedence message to Commander Seventh Fleet and a navy carrier task group 280 miles distant in the South China Sea. The *Maddox*, he said, was in danger of torpedo attack and he requested air support.

The carrier *Ticonderoga* (CVA 14) sent four F-8E Crusaders armed with Sidewinder missiles, Zuni rockets, and 20-mm cannon. The destroyer *Turner Joy* (DD 931), on forward picket station and the surface unit nearest the *Maddox*, was also ordered to the scene.

Shortly after 1600, the torpedo boats having closed to within five miles, the *Maddox* opened fire with her 5-inch and 3-inch guns. Her sweating gun crews had no way of knowing it, but these were the opening shots in what would become the U.S. Navy's longest war.

In this engagement, the *Maddox* fired 283 rounds. At least four torpedoes were fired at her, two of them passing within 200 yards of her starboard side. One torpedo boat was hit by a 5-inch shell and badly damaged. The *Maddox* was struck by a 14.5-mm round that lodged in the base of the ship's main battery fire-control director. That round is now on display at the Navy Museum in Washington, D.C.

When the *Ticonderoga*'s Crusaders arrived over the *Maddox*, the torpedo boats had broken off the action and were headed to port.

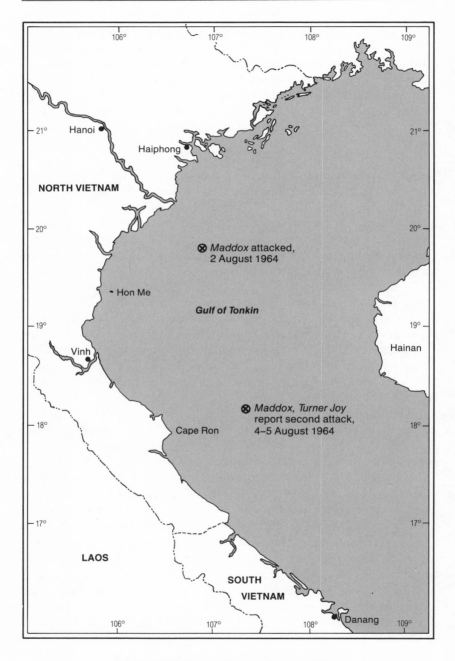

Gulf of Tonkin Incidents, August 1964

The navy aircraft, led by Commander (later Vice Admiral) James B. Stockdale, attacked the fleeing boats, leaving one of them burning and dead in the water. It later sank.

In Washington, President Johnson ruled out retaliation for the torpedo boat attack, choosing instead to issue a public warning that the United States would not tolerate further such incidents.

It is possible that the attack on the *Maddox* was ordered because the North Vietnamese believed the destroyer had engaged in the night bombardment of Hon Me and Hon Nieu, a thesis seemingly shared by William Colby. In a 9 June 1980 interview, he conceded that "the North Vietnamese could have been confused by the Desoto Patrol— whether it was part of the same 34A patrol. I mean, if one batch of boats comes up and shoots at you one night, and another boat comes up the next night, from their point of view it could be pretty easy to associate them. They don't see the one marked 'top secret' and the one marked 'secret.' "5

The Desoto Patrol was resumed on 3 August, the *Maddox* being joined by the *Turner Joy.* The ships were provided continuous daytime air cover, and Herrick was ordered to stay at least twelve miles off the coast.

What occurred next became one of the most controversial actions of the Vietnam War. It led directly, and some would say precipitously, to the first U.S. bombing of North Vietnam.

On the night of 4 August the two navy destroyers, the *Maddox* and *Turner Joy,* were steaming in formation away from the coast of North Vietnam toward the relative safety of the central Tonkin Gulf. Earlier that day, U.S. intelligence had again intercepted an order from North Vietnamese naval headquarters alerting its forces for combat. Only hours before this intercept, South Vietnamese PTFs had bombarded a radar facility near Vinh Son and fired on a security post at the mouth of the Ron River.

At approximately 2145, the *Maddox* radar picked up three high-speed surface contacts some forty-two miles to the northeast. Herrick signaled a turn to the southeast, and ordered his ships to run at best speed in the direction of the carrier task group. The radar contacts were lost and then regained. Fire-control radars on both ships reported locking on targets astern of the formation at ranges of about twelve miles.

At 2210 an F-8E (flown by Commander Stockdale) and two A-4D Skyhawks from the *Ticonderoga* arrived to provide air cover. During the night, thirteen additional aircraft were scrambled by the *Ticonderoga* and *Constellation* (CVA 64) to support the two destroyers.

The night was exceptionally dark, and a low ceiling limited visibility from the air, contributing to the confusion and uncertainty marking later accounts of the incident.

At 2234, the destroyers' radar picked up yet another target. This one approached from the east at a high rate of speed. At 2239, when the target had closed to 7,000 yards, the *Turner Joy* opened fire. The *Maddox* soon joined in.

Moments later, a sonarman on the *Maddox* heard what sounded like torpedo noises. Both ships maneuvered to parallel the torpedo's supposed track. An officer on the *Turner Joy* spotted what he believed to be a torpedo wake passing the ship's port side.

There were numerous other reports of torpedoes in the water during the course of what became a night of radical maneuvers and rapid fire at swiftly moving targets that suddenly appeared on radar scopes and just as suddenly disappeared. Sailors on the *Turner Joy* saw what they said was "definitely" a PT boat silhouetted for a brief moment in the light of a star shell. Others said they saw machine gun fire raking the water close aboard. A bright light, possibly a searchlight aimed at the sky, was seen aft of the *Turner Joy*. The light was extinguished when aircraft were sent to investigate. Believing that torpedo boats were following in their wake, both destroyers dropped depth charges.

None of the aviators circling overhead saw enemy boats, and Stockdale later would declare publicly, often, and with conviction that hostile boats in fact were not present. Two of his fellow aviators from the *Ticonderoga,* however, reported seeing what they took to be antiaircraft fire. One said he saw a wake ahead of the *Maddox,* and the other that he saw a "dark object" between the two destroyers.

Shortly before 0100 on 5 August, the last of the radar contacts vanished and the two Desoto Patrol ships resumed their run to the southeast. The next day they were ordered back into the Tonkin Gulf.

News of a second "unprovoked attack" on U.S. warships steaming in international waters sent official Washington to general quarters. President Johnson met with his senior advisors and it was agreed that retaliatory action would be taken. The Joint Chiefs proposed attacks by navy planes on North Vietnam's patrol boats, supporting bases and fuel facilities. Secretary McNamara ordered the airlift of mines to navy attack carriers. The president prepared a radio and television address to the nation.

Captain Herrick in the *Maddox,* however, was having second thoughts. In a message to Commander in Chief Pacific Fleet

(CINCPACFLT), who was then Admiral Thomas H. Moorer, Herrick said "Review of action makes many reported contacts and torpedoes fired appear [doubtful] . . . freak weather effects on radar and over-eager sonarmen may have accounted for many reports. No actual visual sightings by *Maddox*. Suggest complete evaluation before any further action taken."[6]

The stir Herrick's message caused is not difficult to imagine. It made the earlier "general quarters" in Washington look like happy hour. The director of the Joint Staff telephoned CINCPAC (Admiral Ulysses S. G. Sharp) in Hawaii. Admiral Sharp queried Admiral Moorer, Admiral Moorer the Seventh Fleet commander, Vice Admiral Roy L. Johnson. Everyone tried to interrogate, at the same time, a bleary-eyed Captain Herrick. Secretary McNamara himself tried to "get on the horn with" (talk directly to) Herrick, and was furious when navy communications could not, or would not, put him through.

Hours of frantic discussion back and forth finally produced, despite the on-scene commander's uncertainty, a consensus that an attack had occurred. At 2236 EDT on 4 August (it was then twelve hours later in the Tonkin Gulf), President Johnson went on radio and television to announce that "as I speak to you tonight" air raids were being carried out against North Vietnam's torpedo boats and their bases. (Aircraft from the *Ticonderoga* and *Constellation* in fact were not over their targets until almost two hours after the president spoke.) The president repeated a theme first expressed months before: "We still seek no wider war."

Of the estimated thirty-four PTs and *Swatows* in North Vietnam's coastal force on 5 August, naval aircraft scored hits on all but one. Seven were sunk and ten were heavily damaged. The primary shore installation targeted, the fuel storage facility at Vinh, was 90 percent destroyed. Sixty-seven aircraft participated in the raids. Two planes were shot down and two were damaged.[7]

Lieutenant (j.g.) Everett Alvarez, Jr., was shot down near Hon Gay. He survived and became the first American prisoner of war to be held in North Vietnam. He would spend the next eight and one-half years of his life in captivity. A fellow aviator from the *Constellation,* Lieutenant (j.g.) Richard C. Sather, was hit near the Lach Chao estuary. He was the first naval aviator to die in combat in Vietnam.

On 7 August 1964 the "Tonkin Gulf Resolution" was passed without a dissenting vote in the House of Representatives. In the Senate, only Ernest Greuning of Alaska and Wayne Morse of Oregon were opposed. The resolution stated that the United States was prepared "as the President determines, to take all necessary steps, including the use of armed force, to assist any member of the protocol states of the Southeast Asia Collective Defense Treaty requesting assistance in defense of its freedom."

The SEATO treaty dated to 1954, and its signatories were Australia, France, New Zealand, Pakistan, the Republic of the Philippines, the Kingdom of Thailand, Great Britain, and the United States. "Protocol" states in the treaty were "Cambodia and Laos and the free territory under the jurisdiction of the state of Vietnam."[8]

The Tonkin Gulf Resolution, considered by some to be the near equivalent of a declaration of war, gave President Johnson broad powers to employ the armed forces of the United States wherever "requested" in Indochina. Interestingly enough, the resolution had been drafted in late May, months before the incidents involving the *Maddox* and *Turner Joy*, by William P. Bundy, assistant secretary of state for East Asian and Pacific Affairs. Bundy, assistant secretary of defense for international security affairs in the Kennedy administration, was the brother of McGeorge Bundy, President Johnson's national security advisor.

The decision to attack North Vietnam would receive much critical scrutiny later when support for the war began to wane. Questions were raised concerning the sequence of events in the Tonkin Gulf on 4 and 5 August 1964. The lack of physical evidence confirming a second attack by North Vietnamese torpedo boats (no enemy rounds struck the destroyers, and no debris was found in the water), the failure of aircraft at the scene to report positive sightings, and a spate of sensational, sometimes irresponsible, published accounts of the incident fueled suspicion that the *Maddox* and *Turner Joy* had engaged not North Vietnamese torpedo boats on the night of 4–5 August, but bogus blips on a radar scope—false targets whose presence in the Tonkin Gulf was widely noted, but never adequately explained.

I myself had an encounter with the famed Tonkin Gulf "ghosts." In January 1973, just before the signing of the Paris cease-fire agreement, I was the commanding officer of the USS *Blakely* (DE 1072), then deployed in the northern Tonkin Gulf.

One night, well into the midwatch, I was called to the combat information center by an excited watch officer. Surface-search radar had picked up what appeared to be a formation of rapidly closing contacts. My weapons officer, then also on the scene, requested "weapons free," wishing to plaster the contacts with our "interim" surface-to-surface missile system.

I hesitated. The contacts were speeding across the radar scope faster than any surface contact I had ever seen. Could they be low-flying aircraft? If so, whose? Even as I watched, the contacts, sharp and well-defined one moment, vanished the next.

From conversations I later had with other ship captains, I am convinced that the *Blakely*'s experience was far from unique. The Tonkin Gulf ghosts most often were attributed to freak weather conditions or "ducting" of electromagnetic waves.

In an April 1988 taped interview, I asked Admiral Thomas H. Moorer what he remembered about the second Tonkin Gulf incident.

"I was commander of the Pacific Fleet then," he said, "and I sent Admiral Johnson, who was commander of the Seventh Fleet, down south to make a complete investigation.

"What had happened was that the North Vietnamese sent out a message that said—well, the English translation I remember very distinctly was 'Get ready to make war.' That was that afternoon [4 August] about dusk or so when we intercepted the code and broke it. Now, when the discussions of whether it [the second incident] was real or not came up—at the outset no one would say this happened or that the message was sent because we didn't want the North Vietnamese to know we were breaking their code. So that, I thought, was the key element in whether or not there was an attack.

"They were sure as hell ordered to attack. And if you're out there on a destroyer in the pitch-black dark and you get a message from the enemy or a decode ordering these groups to attack—well, you're going to start shooting. And there's nothing as uncertain as a night action at sea. No one will tell you the same thing happened. . . .

"But certainly they can't say, no one with any validity can say, that [President] Johnson or the American government lied about it as an excuse to attack Vinh. . . .

"Admiral Johnson came back with a conclusion that there was an attack, that there were enemy ships—boats—in the area and so on.

"What does the public want to happen? Do they want us to get movies of torpedoes dropping out of torpedo boats? . . . The only thing I can tell you for sure is that there was an order to attack and there were hostile ships—boats—in the area. As you know, down there, there were all kinds of false targets in the form of sampans, fishing boats—there was just a maelstrom of Chinamen.

"So what the hell difference does it make?"

Who, Admiral Moorer wanted to know, ever heard of having to have two attacks on your ships before you retaliated?[9]

Admiral Thomas H. Moorer

Who indeed? The 2 August attack on the *Maddox,* though perhaps not unprovoked, was as certain as it was deliberate, and by itself should have provided all the justification needed for an administration that, clearly not prepared to see its mission in Vietnam fail, was just as clearly steering the nation into war. When it chose to respond instead to the second incident, which could not be proven with the same degree of certainty as the first, it unwittingly played into the hands of those who later would say that it and/or senior U.S. military officers had engaged in a conspiracy to get the United States into the war.

The destroyers *Morton* (DD 948) and *Richard S. Edwards* (DD 950) were involved in a third incident in the Tonkin Gulf while conducting a Desoto Patrol on the night of 18 September 1964. Again, the targets were high-speed, rapidly maneuvering radar contacts. In a two-hour period, the ships fired 170 five-inch and 129 three-inch rounds, and supporting aircraft were scrambled from the carrier *Bon Homme Richard* (CVA 31).

In his memoirs, Admiral Horacio Rivero, vice chief of naval operations at the time of the Tonkin Gulf incidents, says he met with Secretary of Defense McNamara and Secretary of the Navy Paul Nitze in Nitze's office on the evening of 18 September (the CNO, Admiral David L. McDonald, was out of town). Rivero had gotten direct communications with the people on the scene and had developed a plot of the third incident that suggested there was no attack on the ships.

"McNamara said, 'What do you think we should do?' and I said, 'I don't think we should do anything. I'm not sure there was a target. . . . I just can't prove anything because the plot doesn't make sense the way it comes out, the movements of the enemy torpedo boats or whatever they are expected to have.' "[10]

Rivero sent experts from the Naval Research Laboratory to the Tonkin Gulf, looking for answers.

"I think a report came back," he said, "which indicated . . . there was a very high probability that there was a lot of ducting of the radar electromagnetic waves, so ghosts had appeared on the screen which could be explained scientifically, but which could have been mistaken for actual ship targets that the ships fired on."[11]

Furious over supposed "leaks" to the press and suspecting they had originated in the office of the Chief of Naval Information (CHINFO), Secretary McNamara ordered Rear Admiral (later Vice Admiral) William P. Mack and his deputy to take lie detector tests.

"I thought that was a rather poor way to do things," Mack recalls in his memoirs, "and told Mr. McNamara so, but that's all I told him because I had to be loyal to the secretary of the navy and I didn't want to tell Mr. McNamara that he was a jackass and the group working for him were jackasses, and if he couldn't do anything else but have me take a lie detector test, I would resign.

"Mr. Nitze [the secretary of the navy]—I didn't want to get him into any more trouble, so I came back and told him what had happened, and that I would go and take the lie detector test, much against my principles. He was very unhappy about this and he wanted to go and tell Mr. McNamara that he was going to resign, too.

"I said, 'No, you're too valuable. You can't do that. I'll go and do this and my deputy will go and do it.'

"We did and we passed it, and I told him what I had found out from my investigation as to how this 'leak' had occurred. It wasn't a leak at all. It was simply speculation by this reporter. The reporter told us that was what he had done. He used his common sense and speculated. . . .

"Mr. McNamara never apologized to me. . . ."[12]

On 8 April 1987, Vice Admiral James B. Stockdale spoke to the American Society of Newspaper Editors in San Francisco. Describing himself as "the only person in the world who was an eyewitness to both the actions of the real PT boats on Sunday [2 August 1964] and the 'phantom battle' on Tuesday night [4 August]," he stated his conviction that America had been deceived by its "best and brightest."

"What the hell kind of scale of values has this 20th century world lured us into?" he asked. "Those Whiz Kids and their mentors played games with the great good will of Middle America, squandered it, 'got religion,' bugged out, left a generation of their sons face down in the mud, and got away with it. They bragged about running a war without the emotional involvement of the mob, the men on the street. They decided it was best to keep the American public in the dark, and rely on their own 'creative thinking.'

"As a matter of fact, the 'game play' in the Tonkin Gulf was hailed by the American game theory elite as an artful piece of politico-military maneuvering."

On 4 November 1964, Lyndon B. Johnson was elected president of the United States in his own right, defeating Senator Barry Goldwater of Arizona in a landslide. The election was viewed by many as an endorsement of Johnson's firm, but moderate, stand on Vietnam.

Two attacks against Americans in Vietnam, one before and one after the election, went unanswered. On 1 November, Viet Cong guerrillas mortared a U.S. barracks at the Bien Hoa airfield, fifteen miles northeast of Saigon. Five U.S. servicemen were killed and many more wounded. Six B-57 bombers were destroyed and twenty other aircraft were damaged. On 24 December, a car bomb exploded in the parking lot outside the Brink Hotel, a U.S. bachelor officers quarters in downtown Saigon. Two Americans were killed and more than one hundred Americans, Australians, and Vietnamese were wounded. (In January 1989 I visited the air base at Bien Hoa. It was then largely grown up in weeds, with what looked like only a small caretaker force in charge. A few U.S.–built fighter aircraft and helicopters, abandoned by the South Vietnamese military in 1975, were for sale by a Socialist Republic clearly strapped for cash. The Brink Hotel at this time was shuttered, plans to convert it into an office building "temporarily" on hold. A brass plaque at the entrance to the Brink memorialized those who had carried out the Christmas Eve bombing.)

Though the navy had carriers on station and ready for reprisal raids, President Johnson in late 1964 was still wrestling with the question of how far and how fast to involve the United States in combat. It was clear, however, that he could not afford to delay much longer. The military and political situation in South Vietnam was chaotic. A new clique of young officers, including Air Vice Marshal Nguyen Cao Ky and General Nguyen Van Thieu, threatened the shaky rule of General Khanh. Buddhist demonstrators were again in the streets. Viet Cong attacks were becoming stronger and bolder. Yankee Team reconnaissance flights over Laos confirmed that Communist troops and supplies were pouring into South Vietnam by way of the Ho Chi Minh Trail.

As 1964 drew to a close, there were 23,000 American servicemen in Vietnam, 235 of them U.S. Navy advisors. During the course of the year, 140 Americans had been killed in action, 1,138 wounded, and 11 listed as missing in action.

Contingency plans were drawn to concentrate Americans in coastal enclaves for emergency evacuation, should President Johnson decide to abandon South Vietnam to its fate. (There was concern that U.S. advisors might have to fight their way out—not against the Viet Cong and the NVA, but against South Vietnamese forces outraged by a perceived betrayal.)

Lyndon Johnson, however, had passed the point of no return. He was determined not to be the first American president to lose a war.

6

1965—The Origins of Market Time and Game Warden

"Well, in our country," said Alice, still panting a little, "you'd generally get to someplace else—if you ran very fast for a long time, as we've been doing."

"A slow sort of country," said the Queen. "Now here, you see, it takes all the running you can do, to keep in the same place. If you want to get somewhere else, you must run at least twice as fast as that."

—Lewis Carroll, *Through the Looking Glass*

The land area of South Vietnam was divided for command and control purposes into four "corps tactical zones" (CTZ) numbered from north to south. I Corps (the "I" always pronounced "Eye") ran from the Demilitarized Zone to a latitude approximately sixty miles north of Qui Nhon. There were five provinces in I Corps, and within its boundaries were the important cities of Quang Tri, Hue, and Danang, as well as a remote village near the Laotian border that would become the scene of heroic battle by U.S. Marines in 1968—Khe Sanh. The small hamlet of My Lai, not far from the Batangan Peninsula, was also in I Corps.

II Corps's twelve provinces contained the central highlands, the Ia Drang Valley, the cities of Kontum, Pleiku, Dalat, and, along the coast, Qui Nhon, Nha Trang, Cam Ranh Bay, Phan Rang, and Phan Thiet.

III Corps consisted of eleven provinces surrounding Saigon. Within its boundaries were War Zones "Charlie" and "Delta," the "Iron Triangle," and the cities of Loc Ninh, An Loc, Tay Ninh, Long Binh, Bien Hoa, and Vung Tau. Saigon itself was in a separate command called the Capital Military District. Separate, too, was the Rung Sat Special Zone (RSSZ), the "Forest of Assassins." Through it ran Saigon's two ship channels, the Long Tau and the shallower and less important Soirap.

IV Corps embraced the vast Mekong Delta. Within its sixteen provinces lived an estimated 60 percent of South Vietnam's people. It had two great rivers, the Mekong and the Bassac, and was interlaced with countless smaller streams and canals. The Plain of Reeds, the U Minh Forest, and the Ca Mau Peninsula were in IV Corps, as were the cities of Chau Doc, Sa Dec, Vinh Long, My Tho, Can Tho, Ha Tien, Rach Gia, Bac Lieu, Ca Mau, Nam Can, and the huge U.S. base called Dong Tam ("United Hearts and Minds") that General Westmoreland ordered dredged from the Mekong mud.

The ARVN generals who commanded the corps tactical zones were responsible for both military and civil administration, all of Vietnam being under martial law. The regular army divisions reported to the corps commanders, as did the province chiefs.

Province chiefs were usually ARVN colonels or lieutenant colonels, and they commanded "Regional Force" (RF) troops whose purpose was to maintain province security. Under the province chiefs were the district chiefs (ARVN majors or captains). Their troops were "Popular Force" (PF) soldiers ordinarily employed in defending home villages. The Regional and Popular forces together were sometimes called "Ruff-Puffs" by American advisors.

Within each CTZ there was thus a dual command structure. The ARVN chain of command ran from the corps to the division, the regiment, the battalion, etc. A second chain ran from the corps commander to province, district, village, and hamlet chiefs.

Outside the corps command, there were a number of Vietnamese military organizations that reported, more or less directly, to the Joint General Staff (JGS). These included the navy (VNN), the air force (VNAF), the marines (VNMC), and the special forces (LLDB—*Luc Luong Dat Biet*).

The LLDB was patterned after the U.S. Special Forces, and its members wore the green beret. LLDB officers commanded Civilian Irregular Defense Group (CIDG) companies, recruited from montagnard tribes primarily for the purpose of manning remote outposts in the highlands athwart infiltration routes near the Laotian and Cambodian borders.

Over the JGS was the minister of defense, almost invariably a senior ARVN general. He, in theory, was answerable to the premier or the president.

The ARVN command structure, complex and riddled with graft and corruption, encouraged the rise of petty warlords who not infrequently placed the parochial interest of the hamlet, the village, the district, the province, or the corps tactical zone over the national interest. The structure also made it easy to organize plots, coups, and counter-coups against the central government.

The command structure of the Vietnamese Navy mirrored somewhat that of the Vietnamese Army, VNN coastal zone commanders having authority over naval forces that resembled, though on a much more modest scale, that of ARVN corps commanders over ground forces.

Headquarters for the Vietnamese Navy's four coastal zones were established at Danang, Nha Trang, Vung Tau, and An Thoi (on Phu Quoc Island in the Gulf of Thailand). The coastal zone commanders exercised operational control over all VNN units assigned in their respective zones. As always, however, ARVN, through the corps commanders, pulled most of the strings.

On 15 April 1964, the VNN was given responsibility for "pacifying" the Rung Sat Special Zone. This was done at the urging of American advisors who were concerned over the vulnerability of the

Saigon ship channels to mining. They were unable to persuade ARVN to devote the resources necessary to secure the capital's lifeline to the sea. Such a dreary and dangerous place was the aptly named Forest of Assassins that ARVN generals seemed genuinely pleased to turn it over to the navy.

For the VNN, the term "pacification" was defined to include maintaining territorial security, gathering military intelligence, and conducting operations to eliminate Viet Cong. On the recommendation of the Naval Advisory Group, "free fire zones" that could be bombed or strafed at any time were established in the RSSZ, and river banks were burned or chemically defoliated to lessen the danger of ambush. It was suggested that little-used canals be filled in to prevent their use by the enemy, and that a River Assault Group (RAG) be stationed permanently at Nha Be, five miles south of Saigon, to patrol the ship channels on a regular basis.

(The Rung Sat, of course, never was completely secured. All through the war, ship traffic making its way to Saigon would be subject, to one degree or another, to ambush and mining. The navy did, however, make it safer.)

Later, the VNN was given similar responsibilities for pacifying Phu Quoc Island, another less than desirable place due to its remoteness from Saigon.

In 1964, the last year prior to the start of large-scale U.S. Navy participation in anti-infiltration patrols, the VNN Coastal Force reported that it stopped and searched 211,121 civilian junks and 889,335 people—11 of whom were "confirmed" Viet Cong. The River Force, statistically much less active in the interdiction effort, said that it searched 993 civilian craft and 3,620 people. It claimed twelve confirmed Viet Cong.[1]

U.S. Navy advisors were understandably disappointed, and early in 1965 there occurred an event that brought into sharp focus problems of long standing. Because of its significance and because it illustrates some of the frustrations encountered by U.S. Navy advisors in this period, the "Vung Ro Incident" will be recounted in some detail.

At 1030 on 16 February 1965, First Lieutenant James S. Bowers, U.S. Army, flying a UH-1B ("Huey") helicopter from Qui Nhon on a medical rescue mission, sighted a camouflaged ship lying in Vung Ro Bay on South Vietnam's central coast, approximately fifty miles north of Nha Trang. Bowers promptly notified the Second Coastal Zone senior advisor, Lieutenant Commander Harvey P. Rodgers, in Nha Trang.

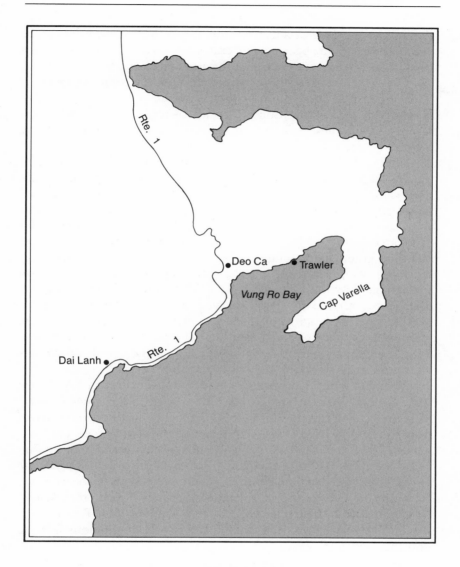

Vung Ro Incident

Rodgers reported the sighting to his counterpart, Lieutenant Commander Ho Van Ky Thoai, the Second Coastal Zone commander, and arranged for an aircraft to investigate. The ship was observed to be of the trawler type, about 80 feet in length and displacing perhaps 275 tons. South Vietnamese Air Force AD-1 Skyraiders were called in, and after a third strike the ship was awash in shallow water, resting on its port side. A fourth strike was directed at a nearby area on the beach where crates were stacked and from which small arms fire had been aimed at the attacking aircraft.

Thoai then made arrangements for an ARVN company from the 23rd Division at Tuy Hoa to be lifted into the area by a Vietnamese Navy LSM. Junks from Coastal Group 24 were also ordered to the scene, and a request was sent for LDNN divers to assist in salvaging the trawler and its cargo.

That night (16–17 February), more air strikes and illumination of the area were scheduled, but VNAF aircraft failed to appear. A U.S. observation plane reported lights and activity on the stricken ship and on the adjacent beach.

The following morning, a Vietnamese LSM, the *Tien Giang* (HQ 405), arrived at Tuy Hoa to embark the promised company of troops, but their commander refused to release them, saying the area surrounding Vung Ro Bay and the Cap Varella Peninsula was too strongly held by the Viet Cong. At 1430 on the 17th, therefore, the *Tien Giang* arrived off Vung Ro without troops. Preceded by air strikes, two attempts were made to enter the bay, but both were aborted in the face of small arms and automatic weapons fire. The *Tien Giang* anchored offshore for the night, and scheduled air services were again canceled without explanation.

The next day, 18 February, a conference was held in Nha Trang with General Westmoreland's operations officer, Brigadier General William E. DuPuy, presiding. Also attending were representatives from the ARVN 23rd Division, Vietnamese Special Forces, the Vietnamese Navy, and the U.S. Navy. An action plan was drawn up that called for a two-battalion blocking force to take position along Route 1, while one company advanced along the coast from the nearby Deo Ca outpost. A company of Vietnamese Special Forces, meanwhile, would be lifted by helicopter to Dai Lanh, south of Vung Ro, where it would be embarked on the *Tien Giang* for an amphibious landing near the sunken trawler.

As the conference progressed, the *Tien Giang* was joined outside Vung Ro by the escort *Chi Lang II* (PCE 08). Thoai ordered both ships to enter the bay where, meeting no opposition, they sprayed the area near the trawler with machine gun fire. The ships then withdrew, the *Tien Giang* proceeding to Dai Lanh to embark the company of special forces.

That night (18–19 February), the submarine chaser *Tuy Dong* (PC 04) with fifteen LDNN and the SEAL advisor, Lieutenant Franklin W. Anderson, arrived to join the growing forces at Vung Ro. In the morning, shortly after 0800, all three ships moved into Vung Ro Bay, again preceded by air strikes. The *Tien Giang* immediately began a run to the beach, but at a range of about 500 yards encountered automatic weapons fire. Engines were backed at the last moment, and the landing was aborted. A second attempt was made several hours later, moderate opposition was again encountered, and the ship backed off again. Finally, at 1100, on the third try, the troops were put ashore. Light sniper fire was taken, but by mid-afternoon the immediate area near the sunken trawler was secured. The LDNN began salvage operations.

Not far from the landing area, the special forces uncovered a large cache of about four thousand rifles and submachine guns, several thousand cases of ammunition, and large quantities of medical supplies. That night, despite heated arguments to the contrary by American advisors, and with quantities of arms and ammunition still on the beach, the *Tien Giang* embarked all troops and left the bay. The company commander reported that he couldn't hold the beachhead overnight and that with "very little arms and ammunition remaining" to be picked up, it was not worthwhile to land again.

Thoai, supported by VNN superiors, refused to order the troops back ashore. At 0215 the next morning, however, message orders from Rear Admiral Cang were received to do so immediately.

Shortly before 0600 on 20 February, therefore, troops were again landed. The special forces commander displayed great reluctance to use his men to assist in the moving of remaining cache material to the beach, and refused to order a stop to the looting of medical supplies.

That afternoon, more caches of arms and ammunition were discovered. Area clearance and mopping-up operations continued until 24 February, plagued by continued foot dragging. On the last full day of the operation, a particularly large ammunition cache was discovered and destroyed.

The total quantity of arms and supplies recovered exceeded one hundred tons, and documents removed from the trawler indicated that the ship had made twenty-two other voyages of supply to South Vietnam.

Lieutenant Commander Thoai (a former aide to President Diem) subsequently was promoted to the rank of commodore. He survived the war and escaped from Vietnam to find refuge in the United States. On 20 September 1975, in a taped interview, he related what he remembered of the Vung Ro Incident. Thoai was critical of the American advisors:

"These officers, they didn't really advise me anything, except after we landed and got more than 1,000 weapons back to the ship. The company called for help and we pulled them out. I started to fire ashore, and we hit some ammunition dump and it made the advisors happy at the meeting that night. These were officers and I don't know where they came from. But they made some commands, and they said, 'Why don't you come and land and pick up all the ammunition and bring it back?' But it was at the top of a mountain with a very high slope. I didn't think anyone would go up there and bring all the ammunition down.

"But I brought about 100 tons of ammunition to the LSM. We had made two or three trips back and forth already. But some of the dumps on top of the mountain—I just ordered naval gunfire to destroy. So I made these advisors unhappy, because they wanted to take it all back. . . .

"The only argument I had with Rodgers [his senior advisor] is that the last day of the operation he flew out with the chief of staff, Admiral Cang, from Nha Trang by helicopter. . . . They started to ask me why I did that, and why I didn't do that, and so on . . . and so I said, 'If you have room in your helicopter, how about doing me a favor by sending this advisor back home?'

". . . This was their [the trawler's] 23rd trip down south. We captured a document. And this was because at that time each coastal zone had about one or two patrol ships and some junks, and the enemy could get in any time they wanted to. . . ."[2]

The Vung Ro Incident confirmed the sea infiltration of weapons and supplies from North Vietnam. The simultaneous appearance in other coastal regions of the new 7.62 family of weapons then being introduced extensively by the Viet Cong strongly suggested that other sites were being used to receive shipments by sea. Further, the performance of Vietnamese armed forces at Vung Ro cast renewed doubt on the willingness or the ability of the Vietnamese to stop sea infiltration on their own.

On 21 February 1965, General Westmoreland asked CINCPAC and CINCPACFLT to send representatives to Saigon to plan for a joint USN/VNN offshore patrol. The conference convened in Saigon on 3 March, and in the week that followed the basic plan of the patrol was hammered out.

It was assumed that sea infiltration fell into two categories: (1) junks and fishing boats that mingled with the more than fifty thousand registered civilian craft plying the coastal waters of South Vietnam; and (2) vessels of trawler size or larger that approached the coast on a generally perpendicular course. This was, it will be recalled, the basic pattern experienced in the Indochina War.

It was the opinion of conferees that the "best tactic to interdict coastal traffic infiltration would be to assist and inspire the Vietnamese Navy to increase the quality and quantity of its searches."[3] With regard to the second category of infiltration, it was recommended that a conventional patrol be established by U.S. Navy ships and aircraft. A defensive sea area was proposed that would extend forty miles from the coast, and it was recommended that the Republic of Vietnam authorize U.S. Navy vessels to "stop, board, search and, if necessary, capture and/or destroy any hostile suspicious craft or vessel found within South Vietnam's territorial and contiguous zone waters."[4]

General Westmoreland expressed the hope that a joint operation "would inspire or shame the Vietnamese, particularly the [navy] . . . into doing a better job, since they were about the worst of the three services in Vietnam."[5]

If the navy was the worst of the three services, the army was not much better. A logistics operation does not end when supplies are deposited on the beach. ARVN units stationed in the vicinity of Vung Ro Bay had done nothing, and would do little, to root out the shore side of the enemy operation, an operation conducted under ARVN's very nose. (The 23rd Division, in Tuy Hoa, was encamped only fifteen miles away.)

The joint sea patrol was approved on 16 March, and on that very day the first U.S. Navy surface units reported for duty—the destroyers *Higbee* (DD 806) and *Black* (DD 666). Daily coastal surveillance flights by SP-2 aircraft operating from Tan Son Nhut had already begun. The code name "Market Time" was assigned on 24 March.

In his memoirs, General Westmoreland writes that prior to 1965 the Viet Cong "received an estimated 70 percent of their supplies by maritime infiltration."[6] Few senior naval officers familiar with Vietnam operations at that time would agree.

In a 1973 interview, Vice Admiral Paul P. Blackburn, Jr., who was commander Seventh Fleet when Market Time began, made these revealing, if perhaps irreverent, remarks about the army, the McNamara Defense Department, and the infiltration problem:

"I had just landed in the Philippines—I had some business to do there. Oley [Admiral U.S. Grant] Sharp said, 'You've got to get back

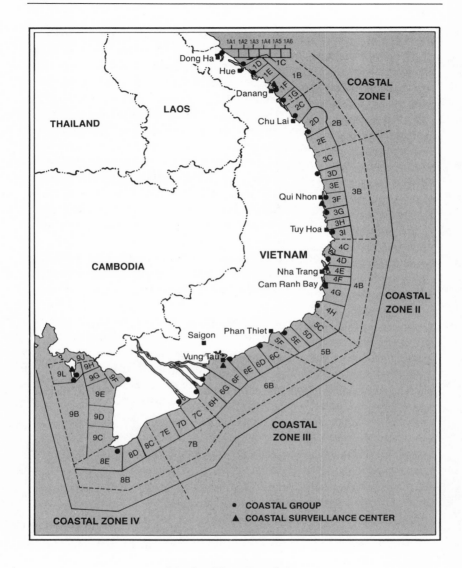

Market Time Patrol Areas

on that airplane and get back to Saigon right away.' I said, 'What's the trouble?' And he said, 'General [Harold K.] Johnson is out and raising hell about the North Vietnamese sending all their supplies to their people, to South Vietnam, by sea and we're not doing anything about it.'

"So I went in and talked with Johnson about it, and fortunately he and I had been classmates at the National War College, which helps some, but nevertheless he was taking a very stiff army attitude about it, and I knew it was horse shit. He was just trying to cover up for the failures of the U.S. Army. Nevertheless, I couldn't tell the chief of staff of the army that. . . . So anyway, he and I talked at some length and I got him somewhat calmed down. Then we started going four bells and a jingle setting this Market Time thing up.

"To give you an example, my plans officer and I were discussing the setting up of Market Time patrols, and I said, 'Jerry, you know those damned DoD guys in McNamara's outfit are nutty about mathematics and everything. If you can do it mathematically, it's perfectly all right, it's bound to be right. Now let's sit down and we'll work out a system of the area to be covered and the timing of the patrols and destroyers and airplanes, and do it so we can prove the answer by a series of formulas, that we have the optimum coverage for that area.'

"This is absolute crap, but it was the best we could do. . . . But anyway, Jerry went back and presented this line of tripe to the representatives of DoD who had come out from Washington for this. They said, 'Thank God, somebody understands the picture. That's just great!' "[7]

(Admiral Blackburn's plans officer, who helped him invent the formulas that pleased the McNamara men so, was the future Vice Admiral Jerome H. King, Jr., who, five years later, would relieve Admiral Elmo R. Zumwalt, Jr., as Commander Naval Forces Vietnam.)

Admiral Blackburn's estimate of the amount of enemy supplies reaching South Vietnam by sea as opposed to that coming by way of the Ho Chi Minh Trail was about "one-fiftieth."

"You couldn't prove these statistics at all," he continued. "We were under such heat from the army because they had been such a miserable failure at stopping the influx of supplies down through Laos and down the countryside, and so they were hollering like hell that the navy wasn't doing its part. . . ."[8]

It might be added at this time that the U.S. Navy's preferred solution to the infiltration problem was to stop the flow of war material to the south at its source. Virtually every senior navy commander in the course of this long war urged the mining or blockade of North Vietnam's ports, particularly Haiphong, through which an estimated 85 percent of NVN arms and ammunition was shipped. As will be shown, permission to do this would not be given until 1972, when for all practical purposes the U.S. part of the war in the south was over. In 1965, when closing a few North Vietnamese ports would have made a profound difference in the conduct and eventual outcome of the war, the decision was taken instead to blockade the entire *South Vietnamese* coast and to fight the interdiction battle in thousands of miles of rivers, canals, jungles, swamps, and mountain trails. The United States would do it the hard way, by stopping up the broad end of the funnel. No one seemed to realize just how broad that end of the funnel was.

Market Time operations expanded rapidly. By the first week of April 1965, twenty-eight U.S. Navy ships were assigned to patrol duty under the operational control of Commander Task Force 71. Building on planning conference recommendations of the month before, a decision was taken to deploy U.S. Navy PCFs (patrol craft fast, or "Swift" boats) and U.S. Coast Guard 82-foot cutters (WPBs) for close inshore patrolling.

The Swift boat was an adaptation of a civilian craft originally designed to carry workers and supplies to offshore oil rigs in the Gulf of Mexico. Aluminum-hulled, it was 50 feet in length, had a 13-foot, 6-inch beam, a 4-foot, 10-inch draft, and displaced 22 tons. Powered by two 475-horsepower diesel engines, it could make 25 knots in good seas. It mounted twin .50-caliber machine guns forward, and a single .50-caliber and an 81-mm mortar aft. It carried a crew of one officer, usually a lieutenant (j.g.), and five enlisted men. The first of more than one hundred Swifts would arrive in Vietnam in October 1965.

The Coast Guard's WPB originally was built for search-and-rescue work in U.S. coastal waters. It had a 17-foot, 3-inch beam, a 6-foot, 5-inch draft, and displaced 67.5 tons. The 82-foot cutter was steel-hulled, with an aluminum superstructure. Its main engine was a 600-horsepower diesel, which could drive the boat at 18 knots. The WPB mounted one .50-caliber machine gun and one 81-mm mortar forward, and four .50-caliber guns aft. It carried two officers and nine enlisted, a Coast Guard lieutenant or lieutenant (j.g.) normally commanding. The first of an eventual twenty-six WPBs arrived in July 1965.

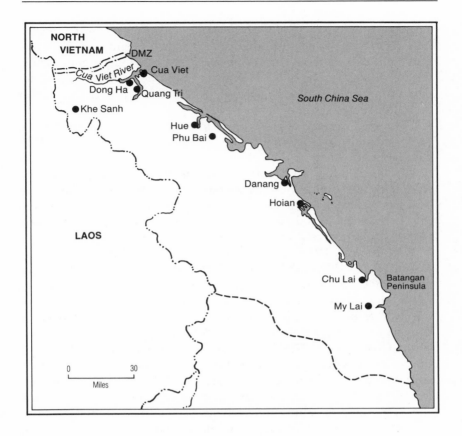

I Corps Tactical Zone

On 30 April 1965, the secretary of defense approved, in principle, the transfer of operational control of Market Time to chief, Naval Advisory Group. This marked the formal recognition of the Advisory Group's new role as an operational command, and Rear Admiral Norvell G. Ward, the first navy flag officer to be assigned to duty in Vietnam, was ordered to relieve Captain William H. Hardcastle. The change of command took place on 10 May. Hardcastle stayed on as Ward's deputy and chief of staff for another three months.

On 11 May, the government of South Vietnam granted authority for U.S. Market Time units to stop, search, and seize vessels not clearly engaged in innocent passage inside the three-mile limit of

Republic of Vietnam (RVN) territorial waters. Vessels in the twelve-mile contiguous zone suspected of infiltrating enemy supplies were also made subject to search and seizure. Beyond the contiguous zone, vessels thought to be of RVN registry could be searched, and compensation would be paid by South Vietnam if they proved to be other than RVN ships.

The first capture of infiltrators by a U.S. ship occurred in late May, when the destroyer *Buck* (DD 761) stopped a junk near the 17th parallel.

In June, a captured document confirmed initial assumptions concerning trawler infiltration. By reconstruction, the route taken by at least one enemy ship on departing Haiphong was to the north and east of Hainan Island, then due south to a point where a nearly perpendicular run could be made to the mouths of the Mekong.

On 30 July 1965, operational responsibility for Market Time passed from CINPACFLT to COMUSMACV, and operational control from CTF 71 to CTF 115, commander Coastal Surveillance Force (chief, Naval Advisory Group). When activated, TF 115 consisted of seven radar picket escort ships (DERs), two ocean mine-sweepers (MSOs), two LSTs, five SP-2H aircraft based at Tan Son Nhut, Coast Guard Division 11 at An Thoi with nine WPBs, and Coast Guard Division 12 at Danang with eight. Additional patrol aircraft were to be provided, as needed, by commander Seventh Fleet.

Market Time operations were then in their twentieth week, and almost no tangible results had been achieved to measure the effectiveness of the patrols. Though it is likely that increased U.S. Navy participation in the anti-infiltration effort caused some shift in the Communist resupply effort from the sea to inland routes, that is a proposition difficult to prove. Despite the "mathematical formulas" devised by COMSEVENTHFLT, detection probabilities at the assigned level of forces were quite low. As a result, Secretary McNamara agreed to furnish more Swift boats, bringing the approved total to fifty-four. These were to be based at Qui Nhon, Cam Ranh Bay, and Vung Tau.

In July also, the Vietnamese JGS at last agreed to integrate the Junk Force into the regular Vietnamese Navy, a move long urged by advisors and one which, it was hoped, would lead to more frequent and more thorough patrols. According to one Coastal Force advisor, not one Junk Force unit was found on active patrol during a six-week period early in the Market Time operation.[9]

CTF 115 initially carved out nine patrol areas, thirty to forty miles deep and eighty to one hundred miles long, stretching from the

17th parallel in the north along the coast to a line just north of Phu Quoc Island (the Brevie Line) separating Vietnamese from Cambodian coastal waters in the Gulf of Thailand.

Five coastal surveillance centers (Danang, Qui Nhon, Nha Trang, Vung Tau, and An Thoi) were responsible for coordinating U.S. Navy and Vietnamese Navy patrols. Though there were five coastal surveillance centers, there were only four coastal zones (matching ARVN's four corps tactical zones). Qui Nhon and Nha Trang shared responsibility in the Second Coastal Zone, whose commander was stationed in Nha Trang. A deputy coastal zone commander was assigned in Qui Nhon. Overall Market Time operations were controlled from the CTF-115 Surveillance Operations Center located at the Naval Advisory Group headquarters in Saigon.

Aerial surveillance of the sea area between Vung Tau and An Thoi was provided by SP-2H aircraft operating from Tan Son Nhut. The area north of Vung Tau to the 17th parallel was covered by Seventh Fleet P-3A patrol planes flying out of Sangley Point in the Philippines. SP-5B aircraft occasionally patrolled from temporary seadromes supported by Seventh Fleet seaplane tenders (AVs) in Cam Ranh Bay.

The primary mission of Market Time in this period was "to conduct surveillance, gunfire support, visit and search, and other operations as directed along the coast of the Republic of Vietnam in order to assist the Republic of Vietnam in detection and prevention of Communist infiltration from the sea." A secondary mission was "to improve the Vietnamese Navy's counterinsurgency capabilities and assist Vietnamese and U.S. forces to secure the coastal regions and major rivers in order to defeat the Communist insurgency in Vietnam."[10]

Late in September 1965, representatives of CNO, CINCPAC, CINCPACFLT, COMUSMACV, and CHNAVADVGRP met in Saigon to review the progress of Market Time operations to that time. At the conclusion of their meeting, recommendations were made to increase the number of offshore patrol ships from nine to fourteen, to double the patrol aircraft coverage, to increase yet again the number of Swift boats available for inshore patrolling (from fifty-four to eighty-four), and the number of WPBs from seventeen to twenty-six. A fourth LST was requested to provide radar coverage of the mouths of the Mekong Delta rivers. Three had been assigned previously to this duty.

Lastly, it was recommended that an extensive river patrol be established with 120 river patrol craft operating from LSTs anchored offshore. These patrols were to extend up the major rivers for a distance of twenty-five miles. The river patrol would not be a part of Market Time, but would be directed by the chief, Naval Advisory Group. As a result of this recommendation, Task Force 116 was formed on 18 December 1965. Given the code name "Game Warden," it was commanded, as an additional duty, by Admiral Ward.

Game Warden's mission was to assist the government of South Vietnam (GVN) in denying the enemy the use of the major rivers of the Delta and the Rung Sat Special Zone. TF-116 initially would consist of one hundred river patrol boats (PBRs), twenty LCPLs, an LSD, an LST, and eight UH-1B helicopters. The ships and patrol craft would be manned by the U.S. Navy; the U.S. Army would furnish the helicopters and, until navy pilots were trained, the crews needed to fly them. The Vietnamese Maritime Police would assign liaison personnel to the PBRs and LCPLs—essentially to act as interpreters and to assist in the inspection of watercraft for contraband.

When the river patrols began to be shot at, the maritime police refused to accompany them, and the policemen were replaced by VNN personnel. A legacy of the maritime police was an item of their uniform, a black beret, that PBR sailors adopted as their own.

The original concept of the river patrol was that the LSD and LST would anchor in the estuaries of Delta rivers and serve as support bases for the patrol boats. Each would take care of thirty PBRs. Four specially configured LSTs, capable of lifting PBRs on board and equipped with a deck for helicopter operations, were scheduled to relieve the original two support ships by September 1966.

Like the Swift boat, the PBR was adapted from a commercial design. Its fiberglass hull was 31 feet in length, and it had a 10-foot, 6-inch beam. It was powered by two 220-horsepower diesel engines that drove Jacuzzi high-speed jet pumps. The pumps pulled water through intakes in the boat's hull, discharging it through twin jet nozzles on the stern. The boat, which had neither rudders nor screws, was steered by altering the direction of the jet nozzles. The advantages of this design for shallow water operations were obvious—the PBR's draft was only 9–18 inches, and the boat was both responsive and highly maneuverable. It was capable of making 25 knots.

The PBR was equipped with twin .50-caliber machine guns forward, and .30-caliber machine guns and a grenade launcher aft. It had a crew of four enlisted men, the boat captain ordinarily being a first- or second-class petty officer. In Vietnam, PBRs patrolled most often in pairs, and the patrol officer was either a chief or first-class petty officer, though junior commissioned officers sometimes led patrols.

The worsening security situation in Vietnam prompted the evacuation of U.S. dependents in February 1965. "Tit for tat" air raids against North Vietnam were launched following enemy guerrilla attacks on U.S. advisors in Pleiku and Qui Nhon. Yankee Team reconnaissance missions over Laos were expanded to include bombing and defoliation of the Ho Chi Minh Trail.

On 21 February, General Nguyen Khanh was ousted as chairman of the ruling Armed Forces Council by a group of dissident officers who moved troops into Saigon. Replacing Khanh as chairman was General Nguyen Van Thieu, who, together with his sometime ally and sometime opponent, Air Vice Marshal Nguyen Cao Ky, would hold the slender reins of political power in Saigon until the final days. On 19 June, Ky became premier, heading the ninth government in less than two years. In 1967, by way of "democratic elections," Thieu would become president and the flamboyant Ky, vice president.

In March 1965, the first "Rolling Thunder" air strikes on North Vietnam were launched. These would continue, with occasional and, for pilots, devastating pauses, for more than three years until finally halted by President Johnson in October 1968.

On 8 March 1965, a U.S. Marine Expeditionary Brigade, 3,500 strong, landed near Danang to provide "base security." Greeted by slender Vietnamese girls bearing leis, the marines were the vanguard of a U.S. combat force that, before year's end, would number some one hundred eighty thousand. In May the brigade was redesignated the III Marine Amphibious Force (MAF).

The use of marines in I Corps, in what many (erroneously) viewed as primarily a static defense role, was controversial, particularly when the U.S. Army's Ninth Division was later deployed to the Mekong Delta as the ground component of the Mobile Riverine Force. The marines were trained for amphibious warfare; the army, presumably, was not.

Throughout the war, however, marines were used for over-the-beach operations in Vietnam (mostly in I Corps) with the Seventh Fleet Amphibious Ready Group (ARG). These operations initially were given the code name "Dagger Thrust," which was changed in February 1966 to "Batten Down" in compliance with a Washington directive ordering the use of more "moderate" code names for operations in Vietnam. The marines who made up the Special Landing

Force (SLF) were provided by both the Seventh Fleet and III MAF. ARG/SLF operations ordinarily were limited in both time (72 hours) and scope (10 miles inland). Backed by naval gunfire support, they provided a quick-reaction force designed to exploit current intelligence reports of enemy activity in coastal regions.

In July 1965, U.S. Ambassador to South Vietnam Maxwell Taylor, said to be unhappy with what he viewed as the premature decision to deploy large U.S. ground forces in Vietnam, resigned. He was replaced by Henry Cabot Lodge, back for his second tour as ambassador.

In October, Naval Support Activity Danang was established. It would grow quickly to become the navy's largest overseas shore command with detachments at Dong Ha, Cua Viet, Hue, Tan My, Phu Bai, and Chu Lai. It supported all U.S. and Free World forces in I Corps, and eventually would include security, operations, public works, repair, and supply departments, as well as a four-hundred-bed naval hospital. NSA Danang would be headed by a flag officer junior to the navy flag officer in Saigon and the commanding general, III MAF.

The year 1965 was one of explosive change and rapid growth in the U.S. commitment in Vietnam. In that year, 1,350 Americans were killed, 5,300 wounded, and 150 listed as missing or taken prisoner.

7

The Building of Naval Forces Vietnam—1966–67

Any story of the navy—even this one—should rouse the enthusiasm of the patriot because of the stirring character of the deeds that must be described; and I believe that when the reader has considered it well, he will conclude, as I do, that because of the growth of civilization and the spread of the pure doctrines of Christianity throughout the world, and the progress in the arts of making guns and armor-plate in the United States, we shall continue to pursue, for many years, our daily vocations in peace.

—John R. Spears, *The History of Our Navy* [1897]

The Naval Advisory Group's new operational responsibilities required the assignment of many additional U.S. Navy personnel. In March 1966, one year after the start of Market Time operations, there were 4,500 navy men and women "in-country," and three-fourths of them were assigned to TF-115.

On 1 April, in ceremonies on board the USS *Lowe* (DER 325) at the Saigon Naval Shipyard, Rear Admiral Ward established and assumed command of Naval Forces Vietnam (NAVFORV). He retained as additional duty the role of chief, Naval Advisory Group —in part because of the political advantage and prestige enjoyed by the Vietnamese Navy from having a U.S. flag officer as its senior advisor.

This change in the navy command structure had been under consideration for some months. Admiral Ward was a member of General Westmoreland's staff and advised him on naval matters, but he had no fully appropriate command relationship to CINCPACFLT or the type commanders with whom he was required to work most closely.

As COMNAVFORV, Admiral Ward reported to CINCPACFLT and exercised operational control, under COMUSMACV, of all U.S. Navy units assigned in Vietnam. (The marines in I Corps were designated a separate uni-service command under COMUSMACV.) On 16 April, Admiral Ward was relieved as CTF-115 by Captain Clifford L. Stewart.

The first significant payoff for Market Time occurred on the night of 9–10 May 1966, in patrol area 8 off the southern tip of the Ca Mau Peninsula. The USCGC *Point Grey* was patrolling in uncomfortable seas. The skies were overcast, and passing rain squalls limited visibility from the cutter's bridge. At approximately 2200, what appeared to be a large bonfire was observed on the beach. The *Point Grey* edged closer to the shoreline and discovered there were two fires burning near the mouth of the Rach Gia River.

At 0100 the cutter's radar picked up a contact that was tracked closing the beach on a westerly heading at a speed of 10 knots. The *Point Grey* set a course to intercept and at 0120 issued a challenge by signal light. There was no reply. The cutter then closed to within 400 yards and illuminated the contact by searchlight, identifying it as a steel-hulled vessel of the trawler type. A report of the sighting was immediately filed with the coastal surveillance center at An Thoi.

At 0200 the trawler hove to, and remained dead in the water at a position offshore from the bonfires that had been observed earlier. At

0315 the *Point Grey*, firing 81-mm illumination rounds, closed the trawler to within 100 yards and shouted instructions by hailer. Again there was no response. Three or four people were seen briefly on deck, but they soon disappeared below. The cutter's commanding officer decided to delay boarding until daylight.

At dawn, the trawler appeared to be deserted and aground, about 400 yards from shore. At 0700 the *Point Grey* cautiously approached and prepared to dispatch a boarding party. At that time she came under automatic weapons fire from the beach. Fire was returned, and the cutter withdrew to a position 1500 yards offshore to await assistance.

The USS *Brister* (DER 327) and the U.S. coastal minesweeper *Vireo* (MSC 205) were en route. CTF-115 also had ordered USCGC *Point Cypress* to the scene. The Vietnamese Navy was asked to send help.

The *Brister* arrived at 1145, but shallow water kept her well offshore. The tide, meanwhile, had moved the trawler to within 100 yards of the beach, near an area of dense mangrove swamp.

At 1315, air support became available and the *Point Grey* again attempted to put a boarding party on the trawler. At a distance of about 200 yards from shore the cutter was taken under fire, and three of her crew were wounded. She backed off.

Throughout the afternoon, surface units kept up a steady fire on the beach adjacent to the trawler to prevent any offloading of cargo. Several rounds hit the trawler, setting off fires and small secondary explosions. Late in the day the decision was taken to destroy the ship, and at 1750 shelling, bombing, and strafing began in earnest. At 2030 a violent explosion ripped the grounded vessel in two.

That night a Vietnamese LSIL, a PGM, and five junks from Coastal Group 41 arrived. The next day, 11 May, the USS *Tortuga* (LSD 26) with Harbor Clearance Unit One and a helicopter fire team on board, anchored off the coast. U.S. Navy SEALs and Vietnamese divers (LDNN) prepared to assist in salvage operations. At 1610 the commander in chief of the Vietnamese Navy steamed in on PC 10 and became on-scene commander. Air strikes were called in to suppress scattered small-arms fire that was being received from the beach.

Salvage operations ended on 13 May. Material recovered included six crew-served weapons, 15 tons of assorted ammunition, movie projectors, film, and some propaganda pamphlets.

The trawler was 110 feet long, and it had a 22-foot beam. Its machinery was of East German manufacture, much of it built in 1964. Some 120-mm mortar rounds that were recovered were made in China and dated 1965.[1]

Writing at this distance in time and space, it is difficult not to make comparisons between this trawler incident and the one more than a year earlier at Vung Ro Bay.

Economy of force was hardly a principle observed in either place (nor in the Vietnam War generally). The convergence of naval and air power off Ca Mau, the arrival of the commander in chief of the Vietnamese Navy to take personal charge—these are things that seem almost comical today. But then, this was the first fruit of what had been a long and, for many, a very boring operation. There would be other trawlers, however, and ways would be found to make the duty of those serving on Market Time patrols more interesting—and more dangerous.

The very next month, in fact, on 19 June, an SP-2H aircraft on Market Time patrol sighted and photographed a suspicious vessel in the South China Sea east of the Ca Mau Peninsula. At 0300 the next morning, the USCGC *Point League,* patrolling off the mouth of the Co Chien River, made radar contact. A visual challenge went unanswered, the cutter closed to 600 yards, and the contact was illuminated. It was a steel-hulled trawler and lying next to it was a 40-foot junk.

When illuminated, the trawler ran toward the beach, the cutter in hot pursuit. The *Point League* opened fire and received heavy automatic weapons fire in return, taking two hits, one an incendiary round, in the pilothouse. The commanding officer and the helmsman were temporarily blinded. The executive officer was knocked off his feet.

At 0350 the trawler ran hard aground. The *Point League* made three firing runs and then stood off to await help. A helicopter fire team from Can Tho was the first to arrive, followed by an SP-2H patrol plane and two U.S. Air Force F-100 fighters. The trawler was bombed and strafed, and at 0615 a large explosion ripped through it, setting off numerous fires. The USCGC *Point Slocum,* the USS *Haverfield* (DER 393), and a number of small VNN units arrived shortly thereafter.

What followed was an extraordinary bit of daring. Volunteers went aboard the burning ship and, despite the hazards of exploding ammunition, succeeded, after a struggle of more than two hours, in bringing the fires under control. Initial boarding and firefighting were conducted from VNN junks.

The after hold of the trawler suffered heavy damage from the fire and ammunition cook-off, but the forward part of the ship and the engineroom were almost intact. More than 250 tons of arms and ammunition were taken off. Some of the ammunition boxes were dated as late as May 1966, indicating the rapidity with which the material was being moved from Chinese factories to the Viet Cong in the southernmost part of South Vietnam. Most of the weapons recovered were of Chinese and Russian manufacture. A small number of North Korean rifles were found, the first North Korean arms discovered in IV Corps. The trawler was just under 100 feet in length, with a beam of 19 feet, 4 inches. Its estimated full-load draft was 6 feet, 7 inches. It was painted green with an ivory or white superstructure, and the only identification on the hull was the number 2135 painted on the bow. It was diesel-driven, and its main engine had been made in East Germany. It had accommodations for a crew of ten, one of whom, badly wounded, was captured.

Also taken with the ship were the engineer's bell book, the navigator's work book, and navigational charts. The first entry in the navigator's work book was dated 15 June and showed a position 100 nautical miles southwest of Hong Kong. The ship's track ran south to latitude 8 degrees, 35 minutes north, then due west toward Poulo Condore and the South Vietnamese coast. This again was the pattern of trawler infiltration observed in the past.

Salvage teams refloated the trawler on 21 June, and it was towed to Saigon, arriving on the 23d. The ship and selected parts of its cargo were put on display at the foot of Hai Ba Trung Street near the Vietnamese Navy Headquarters.[2]

At no time during Market Time operations were surface units attacked by enemy warplanes. On two occasions, however, they were struck by friendly aircraft and with tragic effect. The first such incident occurred in the early morning hours of 11 August 1966.

The USCGC *Point Welcome* was patrolling in area 1A1 adjacent to the DMZ when she was detected and illuminated by a forward air controller. He mistakenly identified her as an enemy infiltrator. Three U.S. Air Force planes, a B-57 and two F-4Cs, were directed to attack.

When illuminated, the cutter was under way, making about eight knots. Running and topside standing lights were immediately turned on. Colors were displayed. At the time of the initial attack, which occurred at 0340, the executive officer had the deck and the commanding officer was vainly trying to signal the aircraft with an Aldis lamp. On the first strafing run, the commanding officer was killed and the executive officer and all others on the bridge were wounded.

The senior enlisted man on board, a chief petty officer, assumed command. He ordered full speed ahead and attempted to clear the illuminated area.

The attack continued for almost an hour, the aircraft making from seven to nine passes. Signal searchlights and radio transmitters were destroyed on the first strafing runs. A fire broke out on the fantail, but it was quickly extinguished by surviving crew members.

The decision was then taken to beach the cutter and abandon ship in order to avoid further casualties. The wounded were brought topside and strapped into life jackets. The able-bodied paired off with the wounded, assisted them into the water, and began thrashing toward the shore. Their attempt to reach land was thwarted, however, when they were taken under fire from the beach.

Prior to losing communications, the *Point Welcome* had transmitted an urgent message saying that she had been illuminated, fired upon, and hit. CTG-115.1 at Danang directed the cutters *Point Caution* and *Point Orient* to the scene. Junks from Coastal Group 11 were sent to assist. At 0425 rescue operations began. The wounded were transported to Coastal Group 11 for medical evacuation by helicopter.

In addition to the commanding officer, one enlisted man from the *Point Welcome* was killed. Nine crew members, a VNN liaison officer, and a civilian newsman who had been along for the ride were wounded. The *Point Welcome* was heavily damaged topside, but was refloated and taken to Danang under her own power.[3]

A second such incident occurred almost two years later in the same general area, and under even more bizarre circumstances.

At approximately 0100 on 16 June 1968, PCF 19 reported it was under attack by unknown aircraft. From adjacent patrol areas the USCGC *Point Dume* and PCF 12 speeded to her assistance. The *Point Dume* arrived in time to observe the firing of two rockets, one of which scored a direct hit on PCF 19, which sank in less than two minutes. Two survivors, both wounded, were recovered. Five other members of the crew were lost.

On that night, and on the following night, two rocket attacks were directed against the USS *Boston* (CAG 1), and one each on the Australian cruiser HMAS *Hobart,* USS *Edson* (DD 946), USCGC *Point Dume,* and PCF 12. All were operating in patrol areas near the DMZ. Both the *Boston* and *Hobart* were hit, the latter suffering two killed and seven wounded.[4]

Many reports were circulating at this time about enemy aircraft operating in the vicinity of the DMZ. Only hours before the sinking of PCF 19, marines at Dong Ha reported that unidentified helicopters were active in their area. U.S. commanders said they had no aircraft operating there. The "contacts," if such they were, were taken under fire by marine artillery, and F-102s and F-4s scrambled from Danang.

Throughout the night of 15 June, and continuing into the early morning hours of 17 June, there were repeated sightings of unidentified aircraft, some of them by U.S. Navy surface craft on coastal patrol. There were reports of helicopter "kills," flares, rockets, and missile hits. On the night of 15 June, the USS *Boston* reported receiving hostile fire from the direction of the DMZ. Lookouts and bridge personnel said they saw unlighted jet aircraft passing overhead. Marines at Cua Viet reported a Swift boat under attack by rocket fire. Combat air patrol was launched by the USS *Enterprise* (CVAN 65).[5]

On 17 June, COMSEVENTHFLT assigned Rear Admiral S. H. Moore, CTG-70.8, to conduct an investigation. Concerning reported enemy helicopter activity, Admiral Moore concluded that "although no tangible, conclusive evidence was revealed . . . to prove the existence of enemy helicopters, there are sufficient reports that tend to substantiate at least limited enemy helicopter activity in the vicinity of the DMZ."[6]

Debris later removed from the cruisers that had been hit showed that the attacks were launched from friendly aircraft.

Throughout 1966, Market Time continued to expand. "Stable Door," a harbor defense operation under CTF-115, alone employed nearly five hundred men by the end of the year, with detachments in the ports of Danang, Cam Ranh Bay, Qui Nhon, Nha Trang, Vung Tau, and Saigon. Manned by U.S. Navy Mobile Inshore Underseas Warfare (MIUW) teams, these units provided radar and visual surveillance of anchorages, boarded and searched suspicious craft, and checked the hulls and anchor chains of visiting ships for mines.

On 23 December, a Royal Thai Navy ship, PGM 12, joined the barrier patrol in the Gulf of Thailand.

During the year, Market Time forces detected 807,946 craft, visually inspected 223,482, and boarded 181,482. Units engaged in 482 firefights, resulting in 161 Viet Cong killed and 177 captured. Friendly losses for the year were twenty-nine killed in action (sixteen U.S.) and ninety-seven wounded (forty-two U.S.).[7]

In 1967, Market Time units detected and destroyed enemy trawlers on 2 January, 14 March, and 15 July. Two were attempting to deliver shipments in the I Corps area, and the third was forced aground on the Ca Mau Peninsula.

In May 1967, the newly commissioned gunboats *Asheville* (PGM 84) and *Gallup* (PGM 85) arrived to join Market Time. These 165-foot craft, designed for speeds of 40 knots or more and armed with 3-inch and 40-mm guns, were plagued with a multitude of material problems in Vietnam and never lived up to their considerable promise.

In the same month, three Coast Guard high-endurance cutters (WHECs) reported to CTF-115 as replacements for Seventh Fleet DERs. These cutters were 311 feet long, had a beam of 41 feet, and displaced 2,800 tons. They were powered by diesel engines and could make 18 knots. They carried one 5-inch and two 40-mm guns. They had a crew of 215 officers and men.

On 20 July 1967, the Coastal Surveillance Force Operations Center moved from Saigon to newly constructed facilities at Cam Ranh Bay. In addition to providing a more centrally located command post for the operation, the move fit in well with MACV plans to reduce what had become a very large U.S. military presence in the South Vietnamese capital. Project "MOOSE" (Move out of Saigon Expeditiously) would have only limited success, as would later "Sons of MOOSE," because of rapidly escalating U.S. involvement in the war. Saigon warriors coined their own somewhat vulgar phrase for avoiding MOOSE—"Stay Here in Town Surreptitiously."

Most of the officers and men who relocated to Cam Ranh Bay no doubt were pleased by the move. The quarters, messes, and club facilities were new and better, the air much cleaner, and the beaches inviting. There were worse places to pull duty in Vietnam in the late 1960s.

In October 1967, Market Time air surveillance in the Gulf of Thailand was expanded to monitor traffic bound to and from Cambodia. By then it had become quite apparent that Communist arms destined for much of III and IV Corps were being sent via the port of Sihanoukville. From there the shipments were moved to the border in large convoys of trucks, their headlights clearly visible to American soldiers and sailors on the Vietnamese side of the border.

In November the Vietnamese Navy, urged to more fully integrate its Sea Force units into Market Time operations, assumed surveillance responsibilities in four coastal patrol areas, one in each coastal zone. The diligence with which the VNN fulfilled its Market Time duties remained suspect, however.

Overall Market Time activity in 1967 increased slightly from the year before. There were 921,121 detections, and 538,054 inspections/boardings recorded for the year.[8]

These statistics no doubt delighted the mathematicians in Secretary McNamara's office, but they produced relatively little in the way of intercepted arms and supplies, which continued to pour into South Vietnam in quantities more than adequate to keep the insurgency alive and prepare for the great battle that would mark the Lunar New Year in 1968.

The first Game Warden PBRs arrived in March 1966, and were operational a month later. Interim Game Warden bases were established at Nha Be and at Cat Lo, near Vung Tau. This placed the bases at either end of the vital Long Tau shipping channel, and the first PBR patrols were conducted in the Rung Sat. In May, as the number of available PBRs grew to forty-seven, Game Warden operations were extended into the Mekong and Bassac rivers. On 18 May, Captain Burton B. Witham, Jr., relieved Admiral Ward of his duties as CTF-116.

The mining of the Panamanian ship *Eastern Mariner* and the attempted mining of two other large merchant ships in the Nha Be anchorage on 26 May underscored the unsatisfactory state of port security there. CTF-116 assigned eight PBRs to anti-swimmer patrols at the anchorage, minesweeping boats (MSBs) were directed to make daily sweeps, and arriving ships were boarded and instructed in basic security procedures. For a time, the situation improved.

In June, the first operational test of the offshore support ship concept began when the USS *Tortuga* (LSD 26) anchored near the mouths of the Co Chien and Bassac rivers. With her were ten PBRs, a helicopter fire team, and two patrol air-cushion vehicles (PACVs).

The PACV, powered by airplane-type engines, theoretically was capable of speeds of 70 knots over water, marsh, and reasonably level ground. It was designed to climb over four-foot solid structures and could carry a dozen or more men. It was armed with 20-mm guns, 40-mm grenade launchers, and .50-caliber and M-60 machine guns. Though used with some effectiveness in later operations in the Plain of Reeds, the PACV was a maintenance man's nightmare in Vietnam and was later removed from the combat theater for further "evaluation."

Almost from the very beginning, weather was an inhibiting factor in offshore support ship operations. Monsoon winds and a long fetch over shallow waters produced frequent periods of unfavorable seas for launching and recovering small boats. On 15 July it was reported that weather was restricting PBR operations almost 50 percent of the time. Boats returning from river patrols were often unable to return to the mother ship. For PBR sailors, this made for wet and uncomfortable nights. It was obvious that changes in the support operation were needed.

In July the first successful use of PBR night ambush tactics was recorded. (Orders later would be issued to use the euphemism "waterborne guardpost" to describe the tactic of lying in wait for the enemy from concealed positions along the river banks.) Other tactics experimented with included the silent, drifting patrol—PBRs would roar into their patrol areas, cut engines, and drift with the current and tide through an assigned stretch of river hoping to catch a crossing enemy unawares.

As more PBRs arrived, the scope of river operations broadened rapidly. PBRs provided operational support to Vietnamese Navy river assault groups (RAGs). Patrols were pushed into secondary rivers, streams, and canals. By August 1966, PBRs were operating from seven "interim" bases on the rivers. In addition to those at Nha Be and Cat Lo, these were located at Vinh Long, Sa Dec, Long Xuyen, Can Tho, and My Tho.

The first LST specially configured for Game Warden, the USS *Jennings County* (LST 846), arrived on station at the mouth of the Bassac on 15 November. After three days of wallowing in foul weather, the ship was moved upriver to Can Tho. In January 1967, however, with the arrival of more favorable weather, the *Jennings County* anchored offshore once again. On the 11th of the month, during a boat-launching operation, sudden gusts of wind resulted in the loss of PBR 30 and serious damage to the ship's boat-handling equipment. The offshore basing concept was soon abandoned in favor of support bases in the rivers themselves.

Market Time (TF-115) and Game Warden (TF-116) were operations designed to interdict, in the coastal waters and river systems of South Vietnam, the flow of men and material to Communist forces fighting to overthrow the government in Saigon. The peculiar nature of these operations—that they were carried out not in enemy territory but in nominally friendly waters—led to widespread disruption of civilian life in the south. This was but one of the prices paid for Washington's refusal, until very late in the war, to mine North Vietnam's ports and interdict the enemy's lines of supply nearer their source.

The third of the U.S. Navy's major "in-country" task forces, the Riverine Assault Force (TF-117), was not created with interdiction in mind. Its express purpose was to support the U.S. Army on "search-and-destroy" operations in the Mekong Delta. The Riverine Assault Force and the 9th Infantry Division units it operated with were together called the Mobile Riverine Force (MRF). Because its ships and craft were painted olive drab, TF-117, especially after its heroics in the 1968 Tet campaign, became for many "the Great Green Fleet of the Delta."

Search and destroy was defined by COMUSMACV as "operations conducted against enemy forces and installations with the primary objectives to find, fix and destroy the enemy; to destroy or seize his equipment, foodstuffs, medical supplies and base areas; and whenever possible, destroy his political and military infrastructure. An additional objective is to keep the enemy on the move and dispersed, to prevent him from planning, assembling and executing operations on his own initiative."[9]

The Mekong Delta was and is a vast and densely populated area of rice paddies, mud flats, mangrove swamp, and forest, interlaced by thousands of miles of rivers, streams, and canals. For many years it had been dominated by the Viet Cong, and from it the enemy drew both sustenance and the manpower needed to fuel the insurgency. It is not unlikely that in the late 1960s a majority of those living in the Delta were either Viet Cong or Viet Cong "sympathizers," a term coined by American and South Vietnamese officials to describe those whose loyalty to Saigon could not be proved.

The Mobile Riverine Force thus did not have to search far to find the enemy, and in the guns of the Riverine Assault Force it had sufficient power to destroy him when he stood to fight. What the MRF lacked, what the strategy of search and destroy lacked, was the clear means to discriminate between friend and foe. As many have remarked, the innocent peasant working in the field and the Viet Cong with a grenade clutched to his breast looked remarkably alike. If it was difficult to conduct an interdiction campaign in South Vietnam without causing severe disruption to the civilian economy, it was next to impossible to engage in search-and-destroy operations in the populous delta without inflicting grave damage on those whose "hearts and minds" were the great prize in the war.

General Westmoreland credits a naval officer on his staff, Captain David F. Welch, with advancing the idea for the joint army-navy operation in the delta that grew into the Mobile Riverine Force.

"In much the same way that U.S. forces in, for example, the Seminole War and the Civil War had used waterways to facilitate military operations," Westmoreland writes, "why could we not create special units equipped to utilize the extensive waterways of the Delta to get at the Viet Cong?"[10]

In the summer and fall of 1966, therefore, the establishment of a "Mekong Delta Mobile Afloat Force" (the name would soon change) was the subject of staff discussions headed by Captain Welch in Saigon. As originally conceived, the MRF would be a highly mobile force of river assault craft and embarked troops. It would have been quite similar, in fact, to the old French *dinassault*.

As planning progressed, however, the concept expanded and evolved to provide for an afloat base capable of supporting a full army brigade, with another brigade operating from a fixed base dredged from the Mekong River mud a few miles north of the city of My Tho. U.S. Marines, traditionally the force employed in such operations, were not available, already having been committed in maximum strength to I Corps.

(General Westmoreland, sensitive to criticism over his use of the marines, told me in a 1988 interview that he had indeed considered assigning them to the MRF, but rejected the idea because marine battalions had heavy equipment unsuitable for use in the delta, and because I Corps had more miles of beach that could be used for amphibious operations.)

On 1 September 1966, the first administrative unit of the Riverine Assault Force, River Assault Flotilla One, was commissioned at the Naval Amphibious Base, Coronado, California, with Captain W. C. Wells as its commander. The first river assault craft arrived at Vung Tau on board the USS *Whitfield County* (LST 1169) on 7 January 1967, and training commenced with elements of the U.S. 9th Infantry Division. On 28 February, TF-117 was officially activated under the operational control of COMNAVFORV and the administrative control of COMPHIBPAC.

Initial operations were confined to the Rung Sat Special Zone, where increased attacks on shipping in the Long Tau channel were again being experienced. In March, the first elements of TF-117 were assigned to the U.S. Army base at Dong Tam.

Frequent delays were experienced in the delivery of river assault craft, and some boats were borrowed from the Vietnamese Navy for training and early operations. Market Time PCFs were also used as training platforms for TF-117 boat crews.

On 14 April 1967, the first Riverine Assault Force support ship, the USS *Kemper County* (LST 854), arrived at Vung Tau. Later in the month, the self-propelled barracks ship *Benewah* (APB 35) reported. With the arrival of a second APB, the USS *Colleton* (APB 36), in early May, plans were made to move the Mobile Riverine Base to Dong Tam, and on 1 June the shift was made.

The afloat mobile riverine base (MRB) initially consisted of the two APBs; two LSTs assigned on a rotating basis by COM-SEVENTHFLT; a landing craft repair ship, the USS *Askari* (ARL 30); a non-self-propelled barracks craft (APL); a repair, berthing, and messing barge (YRBM); two large harbor tugs (YTBs); and a net-laying ship, the USS *Cohoes* (AN 78). These were assigned to River Support Squadron (RIVSUPRON) Seven.

The APB was a converted LST that provided support for an army battalion and a river assault squadron of fifty boats. The 328-foot ship had berthing space for 122 officers and 1,180 enlisted men. Its armament consisted of four 4.2-inch mortars, two 40-mm quad gun mounts, two 20-mm twin gun mounts, and ten 7.62-mm machine guns. It carried a crew of 11 officers and 161 enlisted. It could make 12 knots.

The ARL was also a converted LST, with the capability of repairing and overhauling riverine assault craft. It had a crew of 12 officers and 178 enlisted. For armament it carried two 40-mm quad gun mounts. It could make a little better than 10 knots.

The 261-foot APL ("Apple") was a barge with berthing space for 39 officers and 290 enlisted. It mounted six .50-caliber machine guns.

The YRBM, a converted covered lighter, had shops and maintenance facilities for small craft, and could berth ninety-seven men. It mounted six .50-caliber machine guns and four 81-mm mortars.

River Assault Squadrons Nine and Eleven each had two command boats (CCBs), five monitors, twenty-six armored troop carriers (ATCs), one refueler, and sixteen assault support and patrol boats (ASPBs). All but the last were modifications of World War II LCM-6 landing craft. Heavily armored and displacing sixty or more tons, the LCM conversions could make little better than 6 knots on the rivers of Vietnam. Given that currents in the delta sometimes exceeded 5 knots, the low speed capability of these boats was a source of constant concern.

The CCB or "commandement" (a name borrowed from the French) was designed for use as a task group flagship and afloat command post. It was equipped with radios and a radar, and carried a crew of eleven enlisted men. A 40-mm cannon and .50-caliber machine gun were mounted in a forward turret, and one 20-mm cannon, two .50-caliber, and two M-60 machine guns were positioned aft.

The monitor, the "battleship" of the MRF, was designed primarily for fire support. Its forward turret held a 40-mm cannon and a .50-caliber machine gun. An 81-mm mortar and two M-60 machine guns were mounted amidships, and one 20-mm cannon, two .50-caliber and four M-60 machine guns were carried aft. It, too, had a crew of eleven enlisted men. A few monitors were equipped with forward flame throwers, and sailors quickly dubbed these "Zippo" boats, from the name of the popular cigarette lighter. (A Zippo boat I encountered on one of my trips in the delta had the name "Burning Sensation" painted on its hull.)

The ATC was designed to carry forty combat troops or an equivalent weight in cargo. It had a crew of seven enlisted men, and mounted two 20-mm guns, two .50-caliber and four M-60 machine guns. Some of the ATCs were equipped with a deck over the cargo well from which helicopters could "dust-off" (medically evacuate) wounded servicemen. Several carried water cannon used to destroy bank-side bunkers and spider holes. The water cannon projected a stream of high-pressure water for a distance of up to 300 meters. ATCs so equipped were called "douche" boats.

The refueler, as its name implies, was an LCM-6 conversion that carried extra diesel fuel for the squadron in bladders.

The 50-foot ASPB was the only boat designed and built from the keel up for the Riverine Assault Force (RAF). Lighter and faster than the other boats, it was meant to be the "destroyer" of the RAF. It displaced about 35 tons and could make 15 knots. It carried a crew of six enlisted men, and mounted one 20-mm gun, one 81-mm mortar, two .50-caliber machine guns, and two automatic grenade launchers. The initial ASPBs assigned to the RAF received less than critical acclaim from the sailors who served on them.

In his reminiscences, Vice Admiral Robert S. Salzer, who commanded the Riverine Assault Force during the period of its heaviest engagement with the enemy, and who later commanded Naval Forces Vietnam, tells of some of the boat's deficiencies.

"I first saw it," Salzer says, "along with a very fine staff officer who went out to Vietnam on the same plane with me. . . . We saw the ASPB at the trials at Mare Island before I left; we both looked at each other and said, 'That thing is never going to float.' The freeboard was perhaps a foot or two; it had a big open cockpit aft so they could

Vice Admiral Robert S. Salzer

mount an 81-mm mortar in there. They told me, 'We designed this; it is absolutely superb. . . . You can see it out here in the bay now, it's doing fine—look how easy it is to steer. It has a hydraulic steering system.'

"Now who the hell wants a hydraulic steering system when you are getting shot at? I looked at the engines—they were beautiful. . . . And the engine compartment was in a position where nobody could get in there to work on them."[11]

Salzer says that when the boats got into combat they began to take heavy losses. "They were always in harm's way, if you will," he says. "They were the boats we used for minesweeping because they didn't have any troops on them. . . . The ASPB was good for that. But the first thing they found out was that the armor they had put on the ASPB, which was carefully designed to preserve lightness (didn't want to make the boat so slow) and strength, had an Achilles heel. There is always one factor in armor—you make things hard and you make them light, but you make them brittle. In that narrow Can Tho River they were firing 75-mm recoilless, close range, at the boats. It would hit around the cockpit and it would smash an entire section of armor free, propelling it through the cockpit, and kill the boat captain and the coxswain—decapitate them or worse. Some of the most horrible scenes you can imagine. I have seen a lot of dead people at various times, but entering one of the cockpits after these youngsters had been mutilated was like entering a slaughterhouse, a messy slaughterhouse."[12]

Salzer also found poor welds on the boat, which caused whole sections of plate to break loose even when enemy rounds failed to penetrate it. Sighting ports in the forward gun turret fogged up in the delta environment, and gunners had to open the top of the turret, stick their heads out to find targets, and then duck down again to train the guns and fire. A wave suppressor designed to keep excessive spray off the forward guns acted like a bow plane on a submarine, driving the bow down when it bit into a wave or a wake. One boat sank during combat on the Can Tho River under just such circumstances, drowning two men. Salzer was outraged.

"I grounded the boats after that," he says, "like you ground an aircraft; and I sent out a message to CNO and BUSHIPS and CINCPACFLT and everybody else and said I was withdrawing all the ASPB boats from combat because they were a safety menace. . . . On the whole, I disliked the ASPB enormously—there was nothing right about it."[13]

Eventually, the ASPBs were refitted and returned to combat. Those already in Vietnam were upgraded at the Riverine Assault Force repair facility at Dong Tam. While they were off the line, Salzer used them for base defense, rotating crews as much as possible in the interest of equity. Though Dong Tam and the MRB were subject to frequent mortar and rocket attack, base defense was by far less hazardous duty than running the rivers.

By the middle of June 1967, TF-117 had received all of its programmed sixty-eight LCM conversions, and borrowed units were returned to the Vietnamese Navy. Fully operational, the Riverine Assault Force began a long series of operations with the 9th Infantry Division. RAF craft not only landed and extracted troops, but provided close and accurate gunfire support, medical evacuation of the wounded, and resupply of ammunition.

The Mobile Riverine Force had its own afloat artillery in the guns of the support ships, assault craft, and the barge-mounted 105 howitzers of the 9th Division. The howitzers were towed along with the base or prepositioned in advance of operations. Later, 105s were mounted successfully in the forward turrets of some monitors.

Helicopters and fixed-wing aircraft supported the MRF. From the single-spot helo deck on the USS *Benewah* alone, more than five thousand landings were recorded in the first year of MRF operations.

The ships and craft of the Riverine Assault Force were most susceptible to attack from sappers, controlled mines, and large-caliber, rocket-propelled weapons like the B-40 and RPG-7. Support ships were frequently the targets of recoilless rifle fire, even during daylight hours. Movements of the Mobile Riverine Base were routinely preceded by minesweeping, and support ships were closely escorted by RAF boats. Large-scale use of concussion grenades and tireless anti-swimmer patrols protected the MRB while at anchor.

By the end of 1967, there were 486,000 U.S. servicemen and women assigned in Vietnam—320,000 army; 78,000 marine corps; 56,000 air force; 31,000 navy; and 1,200 coast guard.

Some sixteen thousand Americans had died in the war, more than nine thousand in 1967 alone.

8

The Air War—
Clipping the Wings
of Eagles

[It was] the most asinine way to fight a war that possibly could be imagined.

—Admiral U. S. Grant Sharp

The use, or perhaps more correctly the misuse, of air power in the Vietnam War is a subject worthy of its own book. No one who flew very much over South Vietnam in the late 1960s, as I did, could escape a feeling of sadness and awe as he surveyed the cratered and ruined landscape. I recall quite vividly the words of a visiting astronaut who spoke briefly to COMNAVFORV staff in, I believe, December 1969. The astronaut had but recently circled the moon on an Apollo mission.

"Is it really made of green cheese?" someone asked, smiling.

"No," he replied. "To tell you the truth, the moon looks a lot like parts of Vietnam I've seen in the last few days." He did not smile.

South Vietnam, the country Americans were fighting to save, during the course of the war became the most heavily bombed place on earth. An estimated four million tons fell on it, almost four times as much as on North Vietnam. Add to this what was dropped on Laos and Cambodia, and the total is more than that expended in all of World War II.

The bare statistics are themselves sobering, but when one considers that the bombing of South Vietnam was not the enemy's work but our own, then one must truly wonder at the strategy and the mind-set behind it.

In truth, U.S. commanders in Vietnam were faced with an unprecedented challenge: an 800-mile open flank. Operating from bases in Laos and Cambodia, the enemy attacked at times and places of his own choosing. For political reasons ("We seek no wider war"), and out of concern for possible reaction by the Soviet Union and Communist China, President Johnson refused to authorize actions to secure the army's flank.

"The only thing that saved us," General Westmoreland told me in 1988, "was the helicopter. It was to the army in Vietnam what the horse was in our Civil War." With the helicopter, Westmoreland could quickly reinforce border outposts and keep them from being overrun by the enemy. But even with a half million troops he could not seal the border from attack.

What saved the army in Vietnam, too, in addition to the helicopter, was massive and, some would say, indiscriminate use of firepower.

"The strikes in South Vietnam were completely unrestricted," said Admiral U. S. Grant Sharp, who served as CINCPAC in 1964–68. "He [Secretary of Defense McNamara] didn't care what we struck in South Vietnam. As a matter of fact, we could strike populated enemy-controlled hamlets, towns, in South Vietnam and wipe them off the map without even asking anybody, whereas we had absolute and positive orders not to hit populated areas in North Vietnam, where the enemy was."[1]

One of the few areas of disagreement between Sharp and Westmoreland concerned air power. Westmoreland, given almost total independence in the use of forces within South Vietnam, always wanted more bombing and more close air support in the south. He wanted operational control of Seventh Fleet carriers, and he continually pleaded for more naval shore bombardment. Sharp, who kept the Seventh Fleet firmly in his own hands, wanted to concentrate on bombing the north. He believed the most effective use of air power was to strike at enemy logistics closer to their source. He wanted to close the harbor at Haiphong and cut the two railroad lines running from China. He thought that much of the bombing of jungle areas in Laos and South Vietnam was of questionable military value.

Neither Sharp nor Westmoreland was able to persuade Washington to take the steps outside the country's borders that were necessary to defeat the enemy within them. These included: (1) closing enemy ports by mining or blockade; (2) all-out, systematic bombing of North Vietnam to destroy its capacity and its will to continue the war; and (3) cutting the Ho Chi Minh Trail by either a thrust across the Laotian panhandle or an Inchon-type landing above the DMZ.

(Once, hoping to draw enemy troops north to defend their home territory, Westmoreland proposed an amphibious feint—not an actual landing, but a feint. Permission was denied, so sensitive was the Johnson administration to potential charges that it was widening the war.)

If the bombing of South Vietnam, in its severity, made little strategic sense (how many bonafide targets were there, actually, in rural South Vietnam to justify high-altitude B-52 raids?), the air campaign in North Vietnam bordered on insanity. Sharp, who was responsible for implementing it, called it a "strategy for defeat."

The bombing of the north began as a game of "tit for tat"—the *Maddox* and *Turner Joy* were attacked (maybe) in the Tonkin Gulf by North Vietnamese torpedo boats, and the boats' bases and supporting fuel facilities at Vinh were struck. U.S. military barracks were blown up at Pleiku and Qui Nhon, and in reprisal enemy barracks in North Vietnam were hit.

In February 1965, a reluctant President Johnson agreed to a sustained bombing campaign, but one that was loaded down with so many restrictions as to almost guarantee its ineffectiveness. Called "Rolling Thunder," it would continue, with periodic suspensions, until 31 October 1968 when a thoroughly disillusioned and defeated president at last ordered it stopped.

Rolling Thunder took the lives of many hundreds of brave airmen, and scores more were left to rot for years in prisoner of war camps, hostage to seemingly interminable "peace" negotiations. Aircraft worth billions of dollars were shot down. In the end, of course, the bombing, though severely damaging to North Vietnam, failed to interdict the flow of men and arms to the south, failed to destroy the war-making capacity of the north, and failed to dissuade Ho Chi Minh from his goal of unifying Vietnam under Communist rule.

On 2 March 1965 the first bombing of North Vietnam not characterized as retaliation for enemy attacks on U.S. installations occurred as some one hundred U.S. Air Force jet aircraft and sixty South Vietnamese Air Force prop-driven planes attacked an ammunition depot and a naval facility north of the DMZ. One South Vietnamese and five U.S. Air Force planes were shot down. The first Rolling Thunder strike by U.S. Navy planes was launched by the carriers *Hancock* (CVA 19) and *Ranger* (CVA 61) on 15 March 1965. Sixty-four attack aircraft struck an ammunition depot at Phu Qui, about 125 miles south of Hanoi. One Navy Skyraider from the *Ranger* was lost, along with its pilot.

On these melancholy notes did Rolling Thunder begin.

Task Force 77, operating with two to four carriers in the vicinity of Yankee Station in the Gulf of Tonkin, sent F-4 Phantoms, F-8 Crusaders, A-1 Skyraiders, A-3 Skywarriors, A-4 Skyhawks, A-5 Vigilantes, A-6 Intruders, and other first-line aircraft over North Vietnam. SH-3 Sea King and UH-2 Seasprite helicopters performed search-and-rescue work, some of it daring missions over enemy territory. Hundreds of thousands of sorties were flown. It was not a question of tools—the tools were there, the very latest of U.S. technology. Nothing was held back. It was the use that was made of air power that spelled failure.

From the very beginning, a tug of war developed between CINC-PAC and Washington over the direction of the bombing. Washington (and almost always this meant the office of the secretary of defense) specified not only the targets that could be hit, but often the time of day the attacks would take place, the number of aircraft that would participate, the bombs that could be dropped, the fusing of the bombs, and sometimes even the tactics aviators could employ in the hostile environment over North Vietnam.

Restrictions placed by Washington on Rolling Thunder caused immense problems for on-scene commanders, added enormously to the expense of the air campaign, and undoubtedly cost American lives.

Not until late April were aircraft permitted to attack in waves; the rules of engagement allowed for one strike and one strike only. This led to a concentration of aircraft over the target, and a situation made to order for enemy gunners. Restrikes could not be made the following day without JCS approval, giving the enemy ample time to repair and resupply his antiaircraft defenses.

"It's important to understand what a serious limitation these restrictions were," Admiral Sharp said. "We were not allowed to take real advantage of breaks in the weather. We were held down in the amount of force we could apply, and the restrictions were almost childish. We spent an awful lot of our time at my headquarters making up messages to go back to the JCS to get restrictions lifted."[2]

Sharp's criticism was echoed by that of Vice Admiral Paul P. Blackburn, who commanded the Seventh Fleet in the early phases of Rolling Thunder. "Like most aviators, I didn't feel that our capabilities were being used to anywhere near the extent they should have been, and also there were a lot of things that were stupid, it seemed to me, that were a waste of effort. We made proposals for strikes at this or that . . . to cut down on the North Vietnamese supply lines and things of that kind. We would have them turned down out of hand by people at the Department of Defense."[3]

Who were these people? In his reminiscences, Vice Admiral Raymond E. Peet named some of them and told how the system worked. In 1965–66, Peet, then a navy captain, served in International Security Affairs (ISA) within the Department of Defense.

"ISA was a little State Department in the Pentagon—[Adam] Yarmolinsky, myself, and a number of others," he said. "John McNaughton was very much involved. I had a very minor role. I was a staff officer working behind the scenes, trying to keep people informed. I worked with the Joint Staff and with other assistant secretaries in ISA. . . . One of the deputy assistant secretaries of defense was Mort Halperin. . . .

"There was a man on the White House staff, Francis Bator, who used to discuss State Department matters with McNaughton and Yarmolinsky. They'd pass 'non-papers' to each other. That's when I

Admiral U. S. Grant Sharp

first learned what a 'non-paper' is. That's just a piece without any letterhead or any identification of the author or the source. These papers were on most any subject—whether we should bomb this or we shouldn't bomb this, or we should take this initiative or that initiative. They were fed to the White House staff and were used to put position papers together for the president. All that type of intrigue and behind-the-scenes play went on in those days. . . .

"The CINC, Admiral Sharp at CINCPAC, and General Westmoreland would want to do certain things in Vietnam. McNamara would insist on approving their course of action. Instead of relying on the Joint Staff, McNamara would send the request to ISA and say, 'Give me your comments on it before I approve of it.' He would insist on having the initials of Adam Yarmolinsky or John McNaughton, you see, on the action papers. Working at ISA at that time was Vice Admiral Champ Blouin. . . . He had to get Yarmolinsky to approve of them. We'd go into tremendous detail sometimes. They'd want to bomb a certain section of Vietnam. We were geared to come in all hours of the day or night if they wanted something approved. We'd dig out the maps, look and see how many thatched huts were in this area, or how many people lived in that area. If there were too many civilians located in a certain area, we wouldn't give them permission to bomb. . . .

"The war was controlled in great detail. The military's hands were tied, they were definitely tied. This is the way they did it. . . . I was the military assistant to Yarmolinsky, and anything that Yarmolinsky got involved in I helped him. Yarmolinsky realized that I had a lot of experience in the Pentagon. Remember, I had been aide to the CNO, and I knew pretty much how the Pentagon worked. . . . A political appointee has a tough time making an impact. I worry about the military assistants and special assistants in the Pentagon, and I was one of them. I worry because I realize how much authority and how much power they can wield. If you get an ambitious man in there like a Bud Zumwalt or somebody else, there's no limit as to how far he can carry that authority. . . .

"It's very frightening. If I were king and could change the system in Washington, one of the things I would do would be to eliminate all of the military assistants to political appointees. I would insist that the political appointees use the organization as it is supposed to be used, get their military advice from the Joint Chiefs or the senior people in the military services as opposed to an aide. They should not rely on or turn over a lot of their responsibilities to an aide who can assume great authority without any responsibility tied to it. I think that civilians are inclined to think that the military man who is working for them is the greatest, and they're going to do everything for him to see that he gets promoted rapidly. There are many others who are equally talented and would have been able to do the same job, but they just didn't have the chance. It's wrong, in my opinion, for the political appointee to do that, just as I think it's wrong for Congress to do it. . . .

"In many ways, Yarmolinsky and McNaughton did a lot of running the war, together with some people in the State Department and with a few civilians in the White House. Oh yes, they were running the war—no question about it. . . .

"They realized we were there; they wished we weren't. They were very liberal-minded, and they were going to make sure that the war was controlled, that we didn't allow what was, in their minds, promiscuous bombing. They weren't going to let the uniformed military have too much of a head; they were going to keep them under control. This was civilian control of the military overdone. One thing led to another, and now I guess in hindsight they feel they made a horrendous mistake just being in Vietnam. McNamara felt that if we applied a little more pressure, the enemy would capitulate. It was like a slow death. Vietnam was almost like quicksand to us."[4]

In his reminiscences, Rear Admiral Kenneth L. Veth, who served on board the carrier *Yorktown* (CVS 10) in 1965, and later relieved Admiral Ward as COMNAVFORV, recalled that bombing orders typically were received between one and three o'clock in the morning, and that they included detailed instructions as to the target, the time for hitting it (usually 0700), the type of bomb and the type of fusing on the bomb. "Then all of the crews would have to get up and wrestle these bombs around on the decks of the carriers all night long. . . . Almost invariably at seven o'clock in the morning the target was clouded in, so that they couldn't bomb. Then they'd have to jettison all their bombs, come back and load again, and go back and do their actual bombing at two o'clock in the afternoon. . . . The only explanation I could get . . . was that back in Washington they wanted it to take place to coincide with a good time for press releases."[5]

Initially, Washington required South Vietnamese Air Force participation in each Rolling Thunder strike. Only two targets were authorized, and one of them had to be hit by the South Vietnamese—on the same day and at the same hour. The use of napalm was forbidden, even though it was the obvious weapon of choice against the wooden barracks pilots were first sent to attack. Because no alternative targets

Rear Admiral Kenneth L. Veth

were authorized, ordnance had to be dumped in the ocean when weather or other circumstances made it impossible to deliver the strike as scheduled.

Admiral Sharp succeeded in getting some of these early restrictions lifted, but as Rolling Thunder moved north to the vicinity of Hanoi and Haiphong, even more damaging ones came into play, and many of these were not rescinded (though they were, from time to time, modified).

Operations could not be conducted within thirty nautical miles of the Chinese border, for fear of provoking Chinese intervention in the war. Targets could not be struck within ten miles of the center of Hanoi, because of worry that foreign embassies might be hit. The port of Haiphong could not be attacked, nor any targets within five miles of the center of the city, in order to safeguard Russian, Chinese, and other "neutral" merchant ships that supplied North Vietnam with the arms and ammunition it needed to carry on the war.

When, in April 1965, North Vietnamese MiGs rose to attack U.S. planes, the airfields from which they operated were off-limits to American bombing. It was said that if the airfields were hit, the MiGs would be flown to China and operate from there. That this would require enemy fighters to fly farther and to have less time on station seems not to have mattered much to those who imposed the restrictions.

Even more incredibly, enemy surface-to-air missile (SAM) sites could not be struck until they were fully operational and had opened fire on American aircraft. There apparently was concern on Washington's part that had they been hit during assembly, Soviet personnel might have been endangered.

If the failure to strike the airfields and SAM sites early on was frustrating and infuriating, so too were rules of engagement that permitted cargo ships loaded with war material to steam right by U.S. warships and into North Vietnamese ports. Everyone knew the guns and missiles these ships were delivering would soon be used to blow American aircraft out of the skies over North Vietnam and to kill American soldiers fighting in the south.

These self-imposed limitations on Rolling Thunder were recognized and used to great advantage by North Vietnam, which put together a sophisticated and, for American aviators, deadly air defense system.

On 4 April 1965 the first U.S. planes, two Air Force F-105 Thunderchiefs, were shot down over North Vietnam by MiGs. The score was evened on 17 June, when two F-4 Phantoms from the USS *Midway* (CVA 41) shot down two MiGs over Thanh Hoa.

(Permission eventually was given to bomb enemy airfields, and the MiG threat diminished. Naval aviators alone accounted for fifty-seven of them during the course of the war. Two were shot down by navy prop-driven aircraft.)

Enemy surface-to-air missiles recorded the first kill of a U.S. aircraft, an Air Force Thunderchief, on 24 July. As a result, Washington authorized a special strike against SAM sites—those that were first positively identified in low-altitude photography. Excluded were five established sites near Hanoi and an area within seventeen miles of them, sites within thirty miles of the Chinese border, and those within ten miles of Haiphong and the Phuc Yen airfield north of Hanoi.[6] That pilots roaring to the attack in high-speed jet aircraft were expected to observe such precise limitations, circles overlapping circles and fine lines drawn on a map, seems droll. And because the SAMs were fully mobile, it of course did not take the enemy long to move them once the pictures were taken.

On 12 August, CINCPAC inaugurated operation "Iron Hand" to seek out and destroy enemy SAM sites. It, too, became an exercise in frustration as permission to hit individual sites still had to be secured from Washington. The height of irresponsibility on the part of those calling the shots undoubtedly occurred when navy aircraft were denied permission to strike a train carrying two hundred or more surface-to-air missiles near Hanoi.

In November 1965, Admiral Sharp recommended attacks on major port facilities and road, rail, and coastal lines of communication running from China. "Of course, this was a logical way to conduct this air war and it was just one of the many recommendations I made that got turned down," he said. "But you had to keep on making them in order to get the restrictions lifted, at least partially."[7]

On 25 December, a Christmas pause in the bombing began which lasted until 30 January 1966. North Vietnam used the pause to repair damage, speed the flow of supplies south, and build up its air defenses. Despite this, when Rolling Thunder resumed it was saddled with even more retrictions than were imposed before the pause. Operations were limited to armed reconnaissance flights south and west of a line from the coast at 20 degrees, 31 minutes north; to 105 degrees, 20 minutes east; then due north to latitude 21 degrees, and due west to the Laotian border. Iron Hand operations against SAM sites were also restricted to the above area. It was not until March that

CINCPAC, with all the muscle of the Joint Chiefs behind him, was able to get restrictions lifted to the point where bombing could continue at the same level that existed before the Christmas halt.

In the early months of 1966, in response to an increased MiG threat over North Vietnam, CINCPAC put forth a plan to strike, simultaneously, the airfields from which the MiGs operated. Permission was given to hit them—one at a time.

News leaks affected the bombing campaign, and once President Johnson abruptly canceled authorization to strike a number of petroleum (POL) handling facilities in North Vietnam because word that the strikes were planned had appeared in the newspapers.

"This was one of the difficulties we had continually," Admiral Sharp said. "While we were being directed to take the utmost of care to be sure that no civilian casualties were incurred . . . someone in Washington would leak the fact that we were going to make a strike, thereby making the accomplishment of the mission many, many times as hazardous for our pilots. But this never seemed to worry the administration, for some reason which has never been apparent to me."[8]

As disclosed in "The Pentagon Papers," independent studies and intelligence assessments disputed many of the military's positive reports concerning the bombing's effects throughout the air war in the north. President Johnson's men thus tended to think in terms of sending "signals" to Hanoi, hoping that each Rolling Thunder raid would trigger a favorable response and a negotiated settlement. It was thought important not to "kill the hostage"—North Vietnam's industrial assets, the preservation of which was thought to weigh heavily on Hanoi's mind. This was a gross miscalculation.

For purposes of the bombing campaign, North Vietnam was divided into six zones or "route packages," numbered generally from south to north. Route package 5 was the northwestern part of the country. Route package 6 was the northeastern part, and it was further divided into A and B zones.

In March 1966, General Westmoreland asked that he be given authority for bombing in route packages 1 and 2, on the ground that these areas were extensions of the battlefield in the south. In April, Admiral Sharp assigned Westmoreland primary responsibility for route package 1. At the same time, he gave the air force responsibility for route packages 5 and 6A, the areas closest to its bases in Thailand. The navy thus had as its primary responsibility route packages 2, 3, 4, and 6B.

"Of course," Sharp said, "the secretary of defense had to get into this act, so he sent a message to the effect that . . . operations north of route package 1 would be conducted only when they could be performed without penalty to required operations in the extended battlefield. This . . . was just another example of the complete lack of appreciation by the secretary of defense for what the air campaign against North Vietnam could do, and his preoccupation with the ground campaign in South Vietnam. We were continually justifying and re-justifying the air campaign against the North, and had to be very careful never to let him think that there was any restriction on the amount of air being supplied to South Vietnam."[9]

McNamara's concept of the air war clashed directly with Sharp's—the secretary of defense viewed it as an interdiction campaign only; the admiral, perhaps realizing better than anyone that air power alone could never cut enemy lines of supply running through Laos and Cambodia, kept insisting that North Vietnam's ports, and railroads, and bridges, and power plants, and fuel distribution systems be hammered and hammered again until the Ho Chi Minh Trail's spreading tendrils withered and died from lack of nourishment at its roots.

Over and over, CINCPAC and other senior naval commanders pleaded, almost plaintively, for permission to mine North Vietnam's ports. Early in the Rolling Thunder campaign, it appeared that Washington was about to give that approval, but after a July 1965 visit to Saigon, McNamara backed off. He sent CINCPAC a memorandum stating that mining North Vietnam's ports would be permitted only as a possible "severe reprisal should the Viet Cong or the North Vietnamese commit a particularly damaging or horrendous act such as interdiction of the Saigon River."[10]

"One is led to believe," Sharp wrote, "that his recent discussions in Saigon touched on fears that should the United States mine Haiphong, the Viet Cong might then mine the Saigon River. . . . In any event, his change of heart was most unfortunate since the offensive mining operation would have been the most useful action we could have taken at that time."[11]

Enemy mines were placed in the Saigon ship channel and in other waterways in South Vietnam throughout the war, but North Vietnam clearly lacked the capability to mount a major mining campaign. The United States had that capability, and its failure to use it in 1965 greatly influenced the eventual outcome of the war.

On 11 April 1966, B-52s for the first time struck at a target in North Vietnam, the Mugia Pass in a remote area near the Laotian border. The giant bombers already were hammering other targets in remote regions of South Vietnam. The raids in the south carried the code name "Arc Light."

Flying thousands of miles from Guam (later from nearby Thailand), the B-52s dropped their bombs from great heights and with great effect on those who happened to be on the ground below. The B-52 was, for all that, a strange weapon to employ in the interdiction campaign. It was, some thought, a little like using a battleship on Market Time station to harass over-the-horizon junks and sampans. It is likely that the psychological impact of the B-52s far outweighed the tactical and strategic ones.

On 26 October 1966, a disastrous explosion and fire broke out on the aircraft carrier *Oriskany* (CVA 34) while the ship was engaged in operations in the Tonkin Gulf. A magnesium flare, used for night illumination, apparently was mishandled by a member of the crew, touching off ammunition, fuel, and other flammable material on the ship's hangar deck. Forty-three men died, including twenty-five naval aviators. Sixteen other men were injured. Four jet aircraft and two helicopters were destroyed, and the ship suffered extensive damage.

By the end of 1966, more than thirteen thousand sorties were being flown each month over North Vietnam and Laos. Strikes occasionally were permitted on more lucrative targets—bridges, railroad classification yards, missile storage areas, POL sites, power plants, etc. Washington's on-again, off-again approach to the bombing, however, allowed the enemy to repair and quickly restore damaged facilities. Targets within restricted zones would be authorized for attack, and the authorization would just as quickly be revoked. There was no system, no rationale given for the strange twists and turns in the bombing. Sharp thought it was "incredible."[12]

On 24 December a Christmas bombing pause began, but unlike the preceding year, it ended only two days later. It was followed by another two-day pause for the New Year holiday. Presumably, someone in Washington had learned a lesson from North Vietnam's response to the extended pause the year before. If so, the lesson was soon forgotten.

In January 1967, Sharp sent yet another message to the Joint Chiefs, "asking, pleading, for proper use of air power."[13] What he wanted was permission to attack target systems—power, fuel oil, ports, transportation, military support, war-supporting industry, etc.—rather than isolated parts of these systems. He wanted to go after stockpiled war materials in areas hitherto off-limits to the bombing. Most of all, he wanted to close the port of Haiphong.

Washington, however, was considering other options—scaling down the bombing, restricting it even further, building a "McNamara Line" of electronic sensors and land mines across the DMZ and into Laos. Again, Washington's focus was on stopping the infiltration of men and supplies across the borders of South Vietnam.

"I told them on other occasions," Sharp said, "that our air attacks could never stop infiltration. Air attacks on lines of communication have never been able to stop infiltration. They can hinder it, but the primary objective of using air power should never be just to stop infiltration. What you should do is attempt to destroy the sources of the material which is being infiltrated. That is the way to use air power properly. It is the way it has been used in other wars and has been very effective. But if you allow the enemy to import material into his country without attacking it, let him stockpile in a central location in a base area, such as Hanoi, Haiphong, and then not strike it until it's dispersed into small segments coming down roads, trails, and waterways, you're doing the job in the most difficult manner."[14]

As always, however, CINCPAC's pleas fell on deaf ears. The president and the secretary of defense were throughout less than enthusiastic about the bombing of North Vietnam, convinced the war had to be won on the ground and in the south.

In April and May 1967, combat in the skies over North Vietnam intensified. There were 122 "MiG incidents" in these two months. Thirty-one MiGs and nine U.S. aircraft were shot down in air-to-air engagements. Surface-to-air missile firings increased to record highs. In April alone, 246 were reported, and these accounted for the downing of five additional U.S. aircraft.

Despite the restrictions it operated under, by the second quarter of 1967 Rolling Thunder was at last inflicting heavy damage. In May it was estimated that 85 percent of North Vietnam's electric power-generating capacity was off the line due to successful bombing of thermal power plants. The resourceful North Vietnamese, however, filled essential needs through massive use of small diesel generators. Destructive U.S. attacks on POL facilities were countered by dispersal of the fuel supply, much of it cached in 55-gallon drums.

Bridges were repaired, replaced by pontoon barges, or detoured around almost as quickly as U.S. bombers were able to knock them down. North Vietnam's ability to recover from the heavy blows dealt it by the bombing both astonished and dismayed the Johnson administration.

In June 1967, Sharp was advised that McNamara was planning a trip to Saigon and that it was likely he would seek support there for reducing or even ending the bombing of the northern regions of North Vietnam. On 28 June, a week before McNamara's scheduled visit, Sharp flew to Saigon for a meeting with General Westmoreland, General William W. Momyer, and Vice Admiral John J. Hyland. Momyer commanded the Seventh Air Force, and Hyland the Seventh Fleet. Sharp wanted to be sure that all spoke with one voice on the bombing issue.

CINCPAC emphasized that North Vietnam's air defenses were becoming less effective, that material was piling up in the ports, that heavy losses had been inflicted on rolling stock and truck inventories, and that power shortages were crippling industrial activity. He told Hyland and Momyer to be prepared to amplify the remarks he planned to make to McNamara. "Statistics will be essential," he said.

On 5 July McNamara, accompanied by General Earle G. Wheeler (chairman of the Joint Chiefs of Staff), Ambassador Ellsworth Bunker, Under Secretary of State Nicholas Katzenbach, and others gathered in Saigon for briefings on the conduct of the war, particularly the air war in the north.

Sharp gave a complete review of Rolling Thunder to that date, telling how restrictions imposed by Washington had hindered and were hindering the war effort. In a presentation replete with statistics, slides, charts, and graphs, he told a visibly annoyed secretary of defense what he did not want to hear—that halting the bombing of the vital northeast quadrant of North Vietnam would be a major military mistake.

Hanoi had concentrated its air defenses in route package 6, the admiral said. "It is this area that the enemy considers he must defend. This is his base support area for the war in South Vietnam."[15] Having beaten down North Vietnam's air defenses in the region, he said, it would be folly to stop the bombing now. MiGs were no longer rising to challenge American aircraft. Surface-to-air missiles were being used with less effectiveness; out of 3,800 combat sorties flown in route package 6 in June, only two aircraft had been lost to SAMs, he said.

New weapons were enhancing the value of the bombing campaign. These included the Walleye, an electronically guided bomb; and the Destructor Mark 36, a specially fused bomb that could be dropped on land or in shallow water and act like a magnetic mine. (The Destructor was then being used extensively in the inland waterways of North Vietnam, though of course not in its major ports.) Improved electronic countermeasures were increasing the safety of attack aircraft.

"In my judgment," Sharp said, "the trend of the war in the north has changed in our favor. This change was gradual until late April. Since that time, the rate of change has increased. Our continued presence in route package 6 is having a marked effect on the North Vietnamese. We established the momentum in late April and May when 20 JCS targets were struck in route package 6 in five weeks, compared with 22 in all of 1966. We are attempting to retain our momentum by continued presence in the northeast quadrant, but we are hampered by the prohibited and restricted areas around Hanoi and Haiphong, the primary areas where our presence would have the most powerful effect on the North Vietnamese government." Mining the ports, he added, was still the most effective action that could be taken.

"By this time, McNamara was really mad," Sharp said.[16]

General Momyer and Admiral Hyland made short, supportive presentations, and Sharp concluded the briefing with a summary of Rolling Thunder operations during the preceding eighteen months.

"During these eighteen months," he said, "we have flown about 38,000 attack sorties in the northern areas, and about 185,000 in the south, including Laos. Large numbers of vehicles, rolling stock, and water craft have been destroyed or damaged in both areas. The extent of LOC [lines of communication] disruption is partially indicated by the number of bridges and ferries destroyed, although some of the trucks, rolling stock, and water craft have been replaced and many bridges repaired. The 20,000 secondary explosions observed in Laos and the lower route packages indicate significant losses are encountered in moving his supplies through these areas. Operations in the northern areas are increasing the cost of aggression to both the North Vietnamese and the people who are supporting them. Eighty-six percent of their primary electric power capacity is destroyed; 30 to 50 percent of their war-supporting industry has been disrupted; 40 percent of the major military installations in the north and all fixed installations in the south have been destroyed or disrupted. Eighty-one MiGs have been shot down or destroyed on the ground. Operations from three of his jet bases are no longer possible. Their POL stocks are widely dispersed and their distribution has become a problem. While we have no way of measuring the amount of war material actually destroyed in the northeast sector, a reliable source in Hanoi estimates that 30 percent of the war material supplied is being destroyed en route to Hanoi by U.S. air strikes. . . .

"It is again emphasized that not until late April did Rolling Thunder begin to reach the level of intensity in the northeast quadrant considered necessary to do the job. However, since late May maximum effectiveness is not being achieved because of restrictions and the lack of authority to hit the more vital targets. These restrictions come at a time when two factors are in our favor: first, the good weather months; and second, the important and perhaps decisive changes in enemy capability to defend himself. A momentum has been established. This momentum will be lost if we do not lift restrictions and strike the more vital targets. To retrench even further and limit our attacks to south of the 20th parallel will have adverse and, I believe, disastrous effects. War-supporting industry in the north would be brought back to maximum output. Morale of our own forces would decline, while that of the enemy would be greatly enhanced. It would allow North Vietnam to operate out of a virtual sanctuary with complete freedom to move supplies to the south without damage. The losses of material they are experiencing en route to Hanoi would cease. Trucks, rolling stock, water craft, and POL would be conserved. Such limitations would also permit redistribution of a large portion of the AAA and SAM order of battle, creating a defense environment similar to that in route package 6. Armed reconnaissance and interdiction operations under such conditions would be greatly hampered.

"We are at an important point in this conflict, and an incisive air campaign including sustained attacks in the northeast quadrant against all the target systems will assure interrelated effects against the enemy's military, political, economic, and psychological posture. There is ample evidence that the enemy is hurting. I consider it essential that we continue this effective, successful air campaign. The widest latitude in planning and execution during the remaining months of good weather is requested. . . ."[17]

Sharp ended his summary by reminding McNamara that CINCPAC's recommendations were essentially the same as those of the Joint Chiefs of Staff.

McNamara's preconceived notion that the air war over North Vietnam should be scaled back had found no support whatsoever in Saigon. He did not like being told what he did not want to hear, and he was angry.

As Sharp sat down, the secretary of defense turned to General Westmoreland and complimented him on "a fine presentation."

The next day, Sharp groused to General Wheeler: "You know, I'm getting Goddamn tired of McNamara turning to Westy at the end of a presentation where I'm the senior guy present and saying, 'Westy, you made a fine presentation,' and not saying anything to me."[18]

The admiral would not have to put up with McNamara for much longer. On 29 November, McNamara tendered his resignation to become president of the World Bank. Clark M. Clifford was sworn in as the new secretary of defense on 1 March 1968.

On 29 July 1967 in the Tonkin Gulf, the carrier *Forrestal* (CVA 59) was preparing to launch a strike against North Vietnam. Her planes, fully fueled and armed, crowded the after portion of the flight deck. One of them, an F-4, inadvertently fired a Zuni rocket into an A-4 parked directly ahead of it. The resulting fire and explosion took the lives of 134 men and injured 59 others. Twenty-one aircraft were destroyed and forty-three were damaged. For a time, survival of the great ship hung in the balance. Fires raged for more than twelve hours, and only the courageous actions of the ship's crew and the assistance of other Task Force 77 units succeeded in bringing them under control.

The *Forrestal*, her participation in the Vietnam War ended, was forced to return to the United States for extensive repair and over-haul. Not since World War II had a worse disaster struck a naval ship in a combat zone.

For the remainder of 1967, the bombing of the north continued as before. For the year, approximately one hundred fifty thousand attack sorties were flown over North Vietnam and Laos. Those in the latter were conducted under the code name "Barrel Roll," an operation that actually predated Rolling Thunder.

Barrel Roll had been inaugurated in December 1964 as a series of armed reconnaissance flights along the Ho Chi Minh Trail in eastern Laos. (Armed reconnaissance meant that targets of opportunity—truck convoys, staging areas, ammunition dumps, etc.—could be taken under fire and destroyed.) These flights were authorized by Prince Souvanna Phouma of Laos and coordinated with the Royal

Lao Air Force, which provided target information to U.S. forces. In April 1965, armed reconnaissance in the southern portion of the Laotian panhandle was given the code name "Steel Tiger."

In September 1967, General Thieu was elected president, and Air Vice Marshal Ky vice president of South Vietnam. They would retain these offices until the end of the war. U.S. troop strength in Vietnam increased in 1967 to more than five-hundred thousand.

In the year, 133 U.S. Navy aircraft were shot down over North Vietnam and Laos.

9

Tet, 1968

This Springtime certainly will be more joyous than all such previous seasons, for news of victories will come from all parts of the country. North and South, our people and our soldiers will compete in the anti-American struggle. Forward we go, and total victory will be ours.

—Ho Chi Minh, New Year greetings over Radio Hanoi
(January 1968)

H o Chi Minh's radio message, thought by some to be the coded order inaugurating the great Communist Tet offensive in 1968, was more than sheer bravado. The massive buildup of U.S. forces had been matched by North Vietnam's own. Despite the bombing of infiltration routes in the north and in Laos, despite "Sea Dragon" raids by U.S. Navy surface ships north of the DMZ, despite Market Time patrols off the coasts and Game Warden operations on the rivers of South Vietnam, an estimated two hundred fifty thousand well-armed NVA soldiers, supported by at least as many Viet Cong irregulars, faced General Westmoreland's army in the south as the New Year dawned. Evidence had accumulated that an offensive was planned. But where? And when?

The U.S. command believed that Khe Sanh, a small village in northwestern Quang Tri Province, fourteen miles south of the DMZ and six miles from the Laotian border, was a likely spot. Sitting astride major infiltration routes and considered by General Westmoreland to be the western anchor of his defensive line along the DMZ, Khe Sanh had been fortified by U.S. Marines in 1967. Their mission was to defend it and to use it as a base for reconnaissance and search-and-destroy operations. Its remote location, the fact that its principal means of resupply were by air, the nature of the terrain, and North Vietnam's emplacement of artillery in the hills surrounding it evoked disturbing memories in Washington of Dien Bien Phu.

On 20 January, a marine patrol clashed with an NVA battalion northwest of the base. The next day, the village of Khe Sanh and the Special Forces camp in it were overrun. A concerned Westmoreland moved to reinforce I Corps, convinced that that was where the blow would fall.

"Although the enemy could cause trouble in other areas, it was only in the north that I saw a possibility of other than temporary enemy success," he wrote in his memoirs.[1]

As in prior years, a cease-fire had been announced for the Tet holidays—over Westmoreland's strenuous objections. The wartime ban on fireworks was lifted in Saigon, and the rattle of firecrackers, so reminiscent of the more deadly sound of firefights, filled the city's streets. Fully 50 percent of South Vietnam's soldiers and sailors left their units on furlough. More were absent without leave, and those who remained on duty stood, in general, a poor watch. Tet was, after all, the one great Vietnamese holiday of the year, a time for gift giving, for feasting, for raucous celebration. It was New Year's Eve, Christmas, Thanksgiving, and the Fourth of July all rolled into one.

The cost of the war in dollar terms to the United States was then exceeding $2 billion a month, with no real end in sight. More American servicemen (9,353) had been killed in 1967 than in all the previous years of the war combined. Protests were mounting in the streets of American cities and on the campuses of great universities. Members of President Johnson's own political party were rebelling against his leadership, and it was obvious that the war would be the major issue in the 1968 election campaign.

Against this backdrop, on 30 and 31 January the Communists launched a countrywide attack, hurling an estimated eighty-four thousand combat troops at South Vietnam's cities and towns. Thirty-six provincial capitals were struck, and Hue, Vietnam's third-largest city and its ancient imperial capital, was seized and held for twenty-six murderous days.

Saigon itself was placed under siege. Commando squads seized a government radio station, attacked the National Palace and Vietnamese Navy Headquarters. Tan Son Nhut, which housed the headquarters of both MACV and the Vietnamese Joint General Staff, was hit by a multi-battalion force that succeeded, temporarily, in breaching the compound's defensive perimeter. Most shocking of all for an America hanging on every printed word and every flaming picture from Vietnam, a fifteen-man suicide squad blasted its way into the U.S. Embassy grounds (but not, as erroneously reported by U.S. news organizations, into the chancellery itself). Five marine guards died before the intruders fell in a hail of bullets.

Rear Admiral Veth, then commanding Naval Forces Vietnam, recalled that the first he knew of the attack on Saigon was when he was awakened "in the middle of the night, and all hell broke loose in the way of gunfire, explosions and that sort of thing. . . ." He spent the night on the roof of his quarters "with rockets and flares flying all over the place."[2]

U.S. facilities in Saigon, with the notable exception of the embassy, were not targeted by the enemy. Had they been, it is likely that many Americans would have died in their sleep. Billet security in Saigon was notoriously lax, and remained so throughout the war.

Navy Captain F. F. Jewett II describes what he found when, in March 1968, he was assigned additional duty as senior occupant of the Savoy Palace BOQ in southwest Cholon:

"At the beginning, even though it had been only two months since the enemy's Tet Offensive, this billet was noticeably unprepared for defense in the event of another enemy attack; specifically:

"a. The billet had only one-third its allowance of shotguns, one of its two M-14 rifles was inoperative, its .30-caliber machine gun had no tripod and hence was not usable, and there were only four clips of M-14 ammunition on hand.

"b. There were no first aid kits.

"c. There were no 'C' rations for use in the event the billet was isolated, as it had been for five days during the Tet Offensive.

"d. The billet had only one telephone (which was always over-loaded) and no back-up radio equipment except for the security guard's walkie-talkie. . . .

"e. The billet had no established defense plan for protection in the event of enemy attack.

"f. The assigned U.S. security guard could not be depended upon because he usually was drowsy as a result of very little sleep during the daytime, 12-hour all-night guard duty every night, and very little time off.

"g. The two assigned Vietnamese guards were also unreliable as they had a tendency to disappear anytime there was enemy action in the vicinity; for example, starting with the first day of the May Offensive, there was not a Vietnamese guard to be found for a week. . . .

"The problem of less-than-alert U.S. security guards was never solved because of a shortage of MPs/SGs in the area. The problem of unreliable Vietnamese security guards similarly was never solved. . . . "[3]

As an aside, a little over a year later when I reported for duty in Saigon, the general situation reported by Captain Jewett was unchanged. I was billeted first in the Five Oceans BOQ in Cholon, and shortly thereafter in the Splendid (never was a fourth-rate hotel so magnificently misnamed!) close by the National Palace. In this period (1969–70), it was not at all uncommon for U.S. vehicles to be blown up while parked adjacent to bachelor officers quarters, in full view of Vietnamese security guards. But then, vehicles were also being blown up in the street that ran alongside NAVFORV headquarters!

During the early hours of the Tet Offensive, the world's attention was focused by the media on militarily insignificant (but politically explosive) events in Saigon. The invasion of the embassy grounds was treated as a major setback. A photograph showing the chief of the Vietnamese National Police, Nguyen Ngoc Loan, summarily executing a bound Viet Cong prisoner, dominated the front pages of newspapers all over America and helped stir up revulsion against the war. Later the horrors inflicted on Hue, where two-thirds of the city was destroyed and thousands of civilians slain, many of them murdered by the Communists, would capture prime-time news.

With the exception of one memorable comment by a U.S. Army major surveying the ruins of Ben Tre in the delta ("It became necessary to destroy the town in order to save it"), relatively little was reported of the battle elsewhere in South Vietnam, certainly not the U.S. Navy's part in it. That battle led to what was by any reckoning a stunning defeat for the Communists. Through 11 February, the enemy lost 32,000 killed and 5,800 captured. U.S. losses in that same period were 1,001 killed, while South Vietnamese and other allied forces lost 2,082.

"No one to my knowledge," General Westmoreland wrote, "foresaw that, in terms of public opinion, press and television would transform what was undeniably a catastrophic military defeat for the enemy into a presumed debacle for Americans and South Vietnamese, an attitude that still lingers in the minds of many."[4]

After Tet, the guerrilla movement in South Vietnam, the Viet Cong, never again posed a major military threat, leading some to suggest (erroneously, I think) that Hanoi had engineered the offensive with a sinister eye toward eliminating potential rivals for political power in the south once the war was ended. Henceforth, the North Vietnamese Army would play the lead role in the war to topple the government in Saigon.

Despite the utter failure of the Communists to achieve battlefield success, much less to provoke the long-hoped-for "general uprising," Tet 1968 marked the end of America's effort to win a military victory in Vietnam. The task now would be to avoid defeat.

On 10 March, the *New York Times* headlined a front-page story, "Westmoreland Requests 206,000 More Men, Stirring Debate In Administration." In fact, the story was less than accurate.

Pressed by General Earle G. Wheeler, chairman of the Joint Chiefs of Staff, to state his manpower requirements in view of changed circumstances in Vietnam, Westmoreland had replied, informally, that if a new strategy were to be followed (a strategy that included an invasion of Laos to cut the Ho Chi Minh Trail and an amphibious "hook" operation north of the DMZ), then 206,000 additional troops would be needed. Westmoreland's unsigned and strongly qualified "request," which bypassed an annoyed Admiral Sharp, was leaked in Washington, where it created a predictable firestorm. It was widely interpreted as a call for emergency reinforcement. How, critics of the war wondered out loud, did this square with Westmoreland's assessment that the enemy had been dealt a major defeat?

The dispatch of additional large forces to Vietnam in all likelihood would have required mobilization and the call-up of reserves, something the Joint Chiefs, concerned by the draining of U.S. strength in Europe and elsewhere to meet Vietnam requirements, had been urging for years. With his country in near anarchy, his standing in the polls in free fall, this was a step the president was not prepared to take.

For Lyndon Johnson, brooding in the White House, the fear of monumental failure and the apparent collapse of his policy of graduated response in Vietnam weighed heavily. On 31 March 1968, in a televised address to the nation, he announced a new policy of "peace through negotiations." He said he was "unilaterally" and "substantially" reducing the level of hostilities in Vietnam. Included in the measures he would order, much to the dismay of Admiral Sharp, was a partial suspension of the bombing of North Vietnam. All targets above 20 degrees north latitude were declared off-limits to U.S. air strikes.

Almost as a postscript to his speech, Johnson declared, "I shall not seek, and I will not accept, the nomination of my party for another term as your president."

Incredibly, with Communist forces suffering their greatest defeat of the war on the battlefield, Lyndon Johnson was throwing in the towel.

When the Tet Offensive broke like a storm over the vital Mekong Delta, the Mobile Riverine Force was, literally, stuck in the mud, engaged in an operation planned by MACV headquarters that, in Captain (later Vice Admiral) Robert S. Salzer's words, "made no sense whatsoever."[5] Salzer was then commander of the Riverine Assault Force, Task Force 117. What his heavily armored boats had been ordered to do was to stop infiltration of Communist men and supplies from Cambodia through the Plain of Reeds.

"We went up there along the skinniest canal we could," he recalled, "till we ran out of water completely, then we ploughed through the mud some and flew in some artillery because we couldn't get our barge-borne artillery up there. It was just too narrow and shallow. . . .

"Well, it was just one of those what I call 'show and tell' operations because we did not have sufficient forces—we were at the utter outer limits of the boats. The boats had gotten people out there, but

ASPBs of the Mobile Riverine Force pass under a bridge raised by U.S.
Army engineers in the Mekong Delta, 1968. (PHC Dan Dodd, USN)

The YRBM 16 takes on water from YW 126 in the Mekong Delta, 1968.

Above left: Command and control boat (CCB).

Left: Armored troop carriers (ATCs) of the Riverine Assault Force.

The USS *Colleton* (APB 36) mothers riverine assault craft in
the Mekong Delta, 1968.

No place too small to land. An army helicopter prepares to touch down on the "flight deck" of an armored troop carrier, 1968.

Mobile Base II moored near Nha Be, July 1968.

A monitor, the "battleship" of the Riverine Assault Force.

Troops of the Mobile Riverine Force await the next landing, 1968.

Stuck in the Mekong Delta mud.
Mobile Riverine Force operations,
1968. (PHC Dan Dodd, USN)

Down by the stern, but not out. Crew members of a Riverine Assault Force ASPB continue the fight in a Mekong Delta river, 1968. (PHC Dan Dodd, USN)

**Ammunition handling detail in the
Mobile Riverine Force, 1968.
(PHC Dan Dodd, USN)**

The long, green line. Riverine assault craft proceed through a Mekong Delta canal in 1968. (PHC Dan Dodd, USN)

The old and the new. Riverine assault craft share the waters of a Mekong Delta canal with a Vietnamese sampan. (PHC Dan Dodd, USN)

An armored troop carrier, equipped with a helicopter landing pad, 1968.

A brave PBR in the Bassac River, 1968.

A "flying PBR" is lifted by a U.S. Army "Skycrane" helicopter, 1969.

they could not patrol any place. . . . There was no reason what-soever to be there, except they had a nice headquarters overall plan now. 'We have assigned the Riverine Force this entire infiltration mission.' If we were going to do it properly, what we had to do was to establish by helicopter small-unit patrols farther to the north, boat patrols farther to the south and west along the canal access to ambush them all about a month later. Instead we went up there and created a nice splash of coverage, theoretically to interdict the efforts of the Viet Cong to infiltrate personnel and supplies during the Tet holiday in preparation for an offensive later in the winter.

"Nothing much happened. There was no reason for anything to happen. The Viet Cong were all the way to the east of us by this time. So much for what they thought they knew. . . .

"But about noon on the second day of Tet . . . we began to hear rumors that things weren't going quite so well in our splendid isolation. Bill Knowlton, who was a brigadier general then, flew in saying, 'My God, it's Pearl Harbor all over again.'

"The entire environment of the MACV command at this point in time, until Tet '68, was that we had the Viet Cong and the North Vietnamese right back on their heels and, you know, it was a mopping up operation. I can remember talking to Admiral Veth, Ken Veth, when we were flying up together to Cam Ranh. I was summoned mysteriously sometime around the end of the year or beginning of '68 to get the hell up to Saigon and not argue about coming this time. . . .

"I didn't like going up there. I'd go up there maybe two or three times in the year—four times. What it really was, was that all the principal commanders in country were summoned to Cam Ranh Bay to meet the president, President Johnson. General Westmoreland introduced us all and he handed out Distinguished Service Medals and told us how we had won the war. That was the entire environment. . . .

"Veth and I were talking and I said, 'I don't know who knows what, but every little old lady in tennis shoes in the delta seems to have her own personal B-40 rocket launcher.' He said, 'We aren't hearing that from the intelligence people up here.'

"I said, 'Well, that's the way it is. There are weapons coming in all over the place.'

"It was self-intoxication, self-delusion of the worst kind. . . .

"Well, we were up there to stop infiltration, if you call that being ready. We were working like hell at a useless project, completely out of the way, and then all these damned cities were being attacked. And they started screaming, all the generals in the helicopters, 'When can you get out of there?' I knew what would be waiting for me downstream under those circumstances, and I wouldn't talk to them. Finally, they screamed at Bert David [Colonel Bert David, his army counterpart in the MRF] so much that he got rattled. Obviously, we were going to get out of there when the tide came in. It was the only way we could get out of there. . . .

"That satisfied the generals in the helicopters. It also satisfied the Viet Cong downstream."[6]

Salzer and David resisted orders to move the MRF immediately to Saigon, arguing, correctly, that the northeast monsoon made it impractical to relocate the base support ships there.

"Besides," Salzer later asked, "what the hell did you want waterborne tanks for to defend Saigon? They'd probably shoot up more of the city than anything else. . . ."[7]

As it was, there was much work to do in the delta.

"It was sort of like cavalry coming to the rescue of the fort besieged by Indians, or rather with the Indians already in it," Salzer recalled.[8]

One of the first "forts" the MRF had to rescue was My Tho, a major city on the Mekong, where President Thieu had been vacationing when the Tet furies began.

"This was a great time at My Tho," said Salzer. "There I was, 10 miles away in a base camp, Dong Tam. There were three goddamned U.S. generals in there wringing their hands about what was to be done, and they couldn't find out whether My Tho was secure or not. So David and I flew in there [by helicopter, landing near the headquarters of an ARVN division commander]. . . . That son of a bitch—excuse me, I shouldn't say this—was about to bug out. All he was doing was packing his car and wailing, 'My city has gone, my city has gone.' He had let half of his troops go on Tet leave and was totally unprepared. . . . We just buoyed him up and he finally came to understand that an hour away the river cavalry was coming to the rescue.

"All of a sudden he said: 'An hour? An hour? Here are the Viet Cong. You take that side, where they are, and I will guard them against infiltration to the rest of the city.' Typical. He later became a corps commander. He had just all the right attributes to be a Vietnamese corps commander."[9]

My Tho temporarily secured, the MRF, at times joined by the brave PBRs of TF-116, rebounded from threatened city to threatened city in the delta. Major actions were fought at Vinh Long, at Can Tho, at Chau Doc. Wherever there was a fire to put out the Brown Water Navy went.

"Once Tet '68 broke out in its full force," said Salzer, "I can remember receiving only three directives over the next two months as to what to do, and two of these were canceled. The rest of the time I did what the tactical situation required and reported what we had done."[10]

Most likely, the one directive Salzer refers to that was not canceled was issued by COMUSMACV on 3 March, ordering CTF-117 to detach one river assault division for duty in I Corps. This reduced the MRF's troop lift capacity by about 25 percent.

Its heroics during the Tet Offensive, when it was the major U.S. combat unit capable of counteroffensive action in the delta, earned the Mobile Riverine Force the Presidential Unit Citation. General Westmoreland himself credited the MRF with having "saved the Delta."[11] Admiral Veth summed up his observations as follows:

"Throughout the demanding ordeal of the Tet Offensive, the Army and Navy elements operated cohesively to restore order in the besieged Delta. The marriage of the best that both the Army and the Navy have to offer has resulted in a combat force unique in the annals of military history. Its heroic performance during the 34 days of the Tet campaign was in the highest traditions of both Army and Navy service, and the more than 465 individual awards and decorations received or recommended during this period attest to the courage and valor of the individual fighting men who make up this gallant force. . . . These soldiers and sailors of the Mobile Riverine Force have served with conspicuous bravery and dedication to duty; they have proved themselves worthy of the highest collective honor that can be bestowed by the United States of America."[12]

In the first three months of 1968, General Westmoreland increased troop strength in northern I Corps by more than sixty thousand men. General Creighton W. Abrams (who would relieve Westmoreland in June) was sent north with a headquarters staff to act as deputy COMUSMACV (Forward). Logistics demands in I Corps multiplied accordingly.

The fierce battles raging in Hue and at threatened Khe Sanh made it absolutely imperative that lines of communication (LOCs) to U.S. forces engaged in these places be maintained. Two water routes, the Perfume River between Tan My and Hue, and a five-mile stretch of the Cua Viet River running from the coast just south of the DMZ to Dong Ha, were vital links in MACV's chain of supply (but not vital enough to assign sufficient ground forces to secure the river banks).

Incidents of ambush and mining of logistic craft on these rivers were not uncommon even before the outbreak of the Tet Offensive. As the level of hostilities in the north increased, however, it became obvious that greater waterway security was required.

On 20 February, General Abrams sent a message to COMNAV-FORV requesting that a naval task force provide that security. The message read, in part:

"Enemy activity on banks of inland waterways has necessitated employment of PBRs, gunships, fixed-wing aircraft, and artillery for protection of LCUs and LCMs. Overall coordination of these assets presents unusual problems. Command coordination of naval units (LCUs, LCMs, and PBRs), Army and Marine helicopter gunships and ground security elements has been lacking. Therefore it is mandatory that a task force be organized to insure full coordination of these assets in order to keep the waterways secure.

"To accomplish this, I request you provide a senior naval officer to act as Task Force Commander with a small staff . . . to coordinate overall activities. . . .

"This Task Force will direct its immediate attention to improving naval supply of forces fighting in the Battle of Hue. This same force can simultaneously coordinate operations in the Cua Viet River area."[13]

Abrams asked that the task force be operational by 1200 on 23 February, less than three days hence.

Admiral Veth almost met that deadline. On 24 February, Task Force Clearwater, with headquarters at Tan My, was established under the command of Captain Gerald W. Smith. Forces immediately at Captain Smith's disposal included ten PBRs previously sent to I Corps by CTF-116, helicopter gunships, attack aircraft, artillery, and a small number of ground security troops. This force was soon augmented by the TF-117 river division Captain Salzer had been directed to send to I Corps. Early in March, ten ATCs, three monitors, and one CCB arrived at Tan My aboard a Seventh Fleet LSD.

TF Clearwater was split into two groups—the Hue River Security Group, and the Dong Ha River Security Group. On 2 March, with Communist forces at last ousted from Hue and the banks of the

Perfume River more or less secured, Captain Smith moved his head-quarters from Tan My to a small base at the mouth of the Cua Viet River.

Operations on the Cua Viet were marked by frequent groundings (ten in two convoys in March alone), fog, enemy mines, and ambush. On 4 March the convoy to Dong Ha could not get through, due to wire and bamboo obstructions emplaced by the enemy.

On 10 March the base at Cua Viet was subjected to a heavy artillery attack, and more than one-third of the base was destroyed. Repeated shelling and frequent sapper attacks continued throughout the war. (When I visited Cua Viet, late in 1969, the men stationed there were burrowed in the sand and living little better than moles. It was one of the grimmest places to pull duty in all Vietnam.)

Gradually, the convoy of navy logistic craft was phased out on both the Perfume and Cua Viet rivers. Emphasis shifted to patrolling and minesweeping. PBRs and ATCs were used for troop insertions and gunfire support. On the Cua Viet, where mines were a particular threat due to the river's proximity to the DMZ, night patrols sought to keep the enemy from re-mining. A lack of adequate bank security made this an almost hopeless task, though there were moments of isolated success. One such occurred in the early morning hours of 2 May 1968 when a TF Clearwater boat patrol surprised approximately twenty-five uniformed NVA soldiers on the north bank.

The patrol craft opened fire with small arms and M-79 grenades, and soon found itself engaged in a sharp exchange. Suddenly, a large explosion ripped the bank, sending a ball of fire forty to fifty feet into the air. At first light, navy EOD (explosive ordnance disposal) personnel recovered one complete mine and parts of another. The mines were determined to be of Soviet manufacture, influence mines of a type previously unknown in Vietnam.[14]

In the week that followed, four more influence mines were recovered and disarmed. The small stretch of river from Cua Viet to Dong Ha was for many months a virtual testing ground for North Vietnamese minemen. Both pressure and magnetic-acoustic combination mines with delayed arming and ship count features were deployed there, mines that for all intents and purposes were unsweepable by the countermeasures devices provided Captain Smith and his successors as CTF Clearwater.

The unprecedented expenditure of men and material by the Communists in the Tet Offensive led to a desperate attempt to resupply shattered enemy forces by sea. Beginning on 28 February and ending on 1 March, Market Time patrols detected four enemy steel-hulled trawlers. Three were destroyed with their cargoes; the fourth turned back before entering South Vietnamese waters and was tracked until it neared the coast of mainland China.

CINCPAC was angered by the fourth trawler's escape. Citing a 1965 decree issued by the Saigon government, he stated that even though the trawler had not entered the contiguous zone it was in "SEASIA international waters" and acting in a manner that indicated "an intent to attack U.S./Friendly forces or installations, including the unauthorized landing of troops or material on friendly territory." As such, CINCPAC concluded, "the fourth trawler . . . was probably a hostile vessel and could have been taken under fire and destroyed had it not been for misinterpretation of the Rules of Engagement. . . ."[15] Needless to say, international lawyers would have had fun with that one.

The northernmost trawler infiltration attempt occurred off the coast of Quang Ngai Province on the afternoon of 29 February. A patrol aircraft sighted a trawler 103 miles east of Cape Batangan. It was on a westerly course at a speed of 12 knots. Early on the morning of 1 March the trawler entered South Vietnam's twelve-mile contiguous zone. The USCGC *Androscoggin* (WHEC 68), two WPBs, two PCFs, and U.S. Army helicopter gunships were waiting. The trawler ignored repeated challenges, attempted to evade, and was taken under fire. At 0214 it was driven aground. Moments later, it and its cargo blew up.

The second trawler, proceeding on a southwesterly course at 12 knots, was also detected by a Market Time patrol aircraft on 29 February, ninety-one miles east-northeast of Nha Trang. Kept under surveillance until it entered the contiguous zone, it was forced aground and destroyed by Vietnamese and U.S. patrol craft.

The third trawler, under aerial surveillance since 28 February, attempted a run for the beach some forty-three miles northeast of Ca Mau Point in the IV CTZ. Early on the morning of 1 March, this trawler was sunk in deep water by the USCGC *Winona* (WHEC 65).

These actions were the high-water mark of Market Time operations. In the aftermath of Tet, the Vietnamese Navy was given increased responsibility for the coastal patrol, and plans were made for "accelerated" turnover of all patrol craft and other in-country U.S. Navy assets to the Vietnamese.

10

Sea Lords

Nelson was once Britannia's god of war
    And still should be so, but the tide is turned;
There's no more said of Trafalgar,
    'Tis with our hero quietly inurn'd;
Because the army's grown more popular,
    At which the naval people are concerned.

—Lord Byron, *Don Juan*

On 30 September 1968, Vice Admiral Elmo R. Zumwalt, Jr., the first naval officer of three-star rank to be assigned in Vietnam, relieved Rear Admiral Kenneth L. Veth as COMNAVFORV in ceremonies at Saigon. A tall handsome man, with an extraordinarily keen intellect and more than a little flair for the dramatic, Zumwalt, only forty-seven when chosen for the command, was the navy's youngest vice admiral.

He was born in San Francisco, was valedictorian of his high school class, and graduated from the Naval Academy at Annapolis. He was commissioned an ensign in June 1942. During World War II he served in the Pacific on destroyers and participated in the Battle of Leyte Gulf.

Immediately after the war, while on a port visit in Shanghai, he met, courted, and wed a beautiful White Russian, Mouza Coutelais-du-Roche of Harbin, Manchuria—even though, as he later delighted in telling, she spoke almost no English and he no Russian.

During the Korean War, he served a tour as navigator of the battleship *Wisconsin* (BB 64). He then attended the Naval War College at Newport, was assigned for duty in the Bureau of Naval Personnel, and later returned to sea as a destroyer commanding officer. A second tour in BUPERS was followed by duty in the office of the assistant secretary of the navy.

His next sea duty was as commanding officer of the USS *Dewey* (DLG 7). His bid for command of a nuclear frigate had been vetoed by Vice Admiral Hyman G. Rickover. There later would be no love lost between the two.

As a captain, Zumwalt served tours in the Department of Defense (International Security Affairs), and as executive assistant and senior aide to the secretary of the navy. In these assignments he worked very closely with the man who became his chief sponsor and mentor, Paul Nitze. (From 29 November 1963 to 30 June 1967, Nitze was secretary of the navy, leaving that office to become deputy secretary of defense.)

In 1964 Zumwalt was selected for flag rank. A relatively brief assignment as commander Cruiser-Destroyer Flotilla Seven was followed, in 1966, by a return to Washington where he became director of CNO's Systems Analysis Group.

Admiral Thomas H. Moorer, chief of naval operations from 1 August 1967 to 30 June 1970 (when he became chairman of the Joint Chiefs of Staff), personally picked Zumwalt to relieve Veth in Vietnam—a circumstance replete with irony, in view of Zumwalt's later

Admiral Elmo R. Zumwalt, Jr.

selection to relieve Moorer as CNO, over the latter's strenuous objections.

"The Army and the Air Force had four-star officers in Vietnam," Admiral Moorer told me in 1988, "and we [the navy] had only two-stars. And of course the general attitude of the administration was that the Army was the big deal at what we called Pentagon East [MACV Headquarters at Tan Son Nhut], and the Navy was just kind of floating around outside. It was hard to get promotions.

"So knowing Nitze and Zumwalt, I decided I would—well, that was the reason Zumwalt got that job, because he was probably the only one that Nitze would agree to give [a promotion to vice admiral]. . . . But then I thought he'd move on and somebody else would fill it—in other words, we'd establish the billet as three stars. . . . The Army won't talk to you if you've got two and they've got four. I mean, they're the most rank-conscious people I ever knew in my life."[1]

It was, therefore, not so much his brilliant service record as it was his personal relationship with Paul Nitze, and Moorer's maneuvering to create another three-star billet, that landed Zumwalt in Saigon at what was a critical juncture in the war. Much to Moorer's, and the navy's, astonishment, his command of the Brown Water Navy would, less than two years later, propel this newly frocked vice admiral into four-star rank and assignment as the youngest (and most controversial) chief of naval operations in the navy's history.

He cut a dashing figure in Saigon, flying off by helicopter with a small entourage in combat greens on an almost daily basis to remote locations in the delta and elsewhere in Vietnam where the Brown Water Navy was deployed. He particularly liked to visit units that most recently had been in action, and he carried with him a pocketful of medals to pin on those he deemed deserved them, later sending their names down to the awards board at his headquarters for pro-forma confirmation.[2] Once, violating security regulations for those who held special intelligence clearances, he participated in a "night waterborne guardpost"—an ambush—on one of his boats near the Cambodian border.

The Brown Water sailor loved him, this charismatic man who seemed so down to earth and who listened—really listened!—to the sailor's fears and frustrations and complaints. And there is no doubt the admiral loved his sailors, too. His visits frequently would be followed up with shipments of better food and improvements in living conditions on the rivers. Later, he would list as one of his qualifications for CNO the fact that his Vietnam experience had led to his being "requalified in youth."[3]

The staff he assembled in Saigon, almost to a man, respected and admired him, working incredibly long hours to implement the "ZWIs" ("Zumwalt's wild ideas") that poured from his fertile brain in what seemed an unbroken stream. In particular, his chief of staff, Emmett Tidd, was a tireless individual who never seemed to sleep or miss an administrative detail. Tidd, Captain Charles "Chick" Rauch (the senior naval advisor), and other key members of Zumwalt's Saigon staff would follow him to Washington where they formed a "kitchen cabinet" within the office of the chief of naval operations. (Admiral Moorer later groused that they, and Zumwalt, did more harm to the navy than "three CNOs and twelve years" could set right.[4])

As COMNAVFORV, Zumwalt completely revamped the old way of doing things. Whereas his predecessor kept a loose rein on senior commanders, allowing them to run their part of the war pretty much as they saw fit, Zumwalt was forever prodding and looking for new initiatives. He gave the impression of being a man in a hurry, as indeed he was. He knew better than anyone what "Vietnamization" of the war really meant, and he was determined to leave the Vietnamese Navy with at least a fighting chance to ward off what many, as early as the summer of 1968, already viewed as the inevitable.

There were only seven officers and men in the Navy Section of MAAG Indochina when it was established in 1950. Eighteen years later, there were 38,386 assigned to Naval Forces Vietnam when Vice Admiral Zumwalt arrived to assume command.[5] The three principal NAVFORV task forces were then either at or about to reach their full programmed strength. In terms of personnel, the Riverine Assault Force, TF-117, was the largest of the three, with 3,717 officers and men. It operated, in addition to its base support ships, 161 riverine craft, and these included 103 ATCs, 31 ASPBs, 6 CCBs, 17 monitors, and 4 refuelers.[6] In July, the task force had been split into two groups, Alpha (TG-117.1) and Bravo (TG-117.2), and with the arrival on 1 August of the USS *Mercer* (APB 39) and USS *Nueces* (APB 40), the afloat berthing capacity of the MRF was essentially doubled. Joining the *Mercer* and *Nueces* in Task Group Bravo were the USS *Satyr* (ARL 23) and a Seventh Fleet LST. The arrival of seventeen additional riverine craft in October brought TF-117 very close to its authorized allowance of 182 boats.

Task Force 116, Game Warden, was assigned 2,032 personnel, and on 30 September 1968 it had 197 of an authorized 250 PBRs. In October the number of PBRs attached to the task force increased to 220. There were in addition seven minesweeping boats (MSBs) and thirty-one other assorted craft in TF-116.

Task Force 115, Market Time, employed 1,051 officers and men, exclusive of those attached to Seventh Fleet units temporarily assigned to the Coastal Surveillance Force. In September, eighty-one of an authorized eighty-five PCFs, and twenty-four of an allowed twenty-six WPBs were on hand. Thirty-nine smaller craft, primarily employed in support of the harbor defense operation, Stable Door, were also assigned to TF-115.

At the time of Zumwalt's arrival, all three task forces individually had achieved what most likely was the highest level of efficiency permitted by circumstances that already were mandating transfer of operational responsibilities to the Vietnamese. There had been no known attempts to infiltrate large shipments of men or arms into South Vietnam by sea since the aborted four-trawler affair in late February and early March. Market Time and Game Warden patrols in, respectively, the coastal waters and rivers of South Vietnam continued to pile up impressive statistics (if, on the whole, little in the way of intercepted enemy supplies). The Riverine Assault Force pursued search-and-destroy operations in the delta, though finding it, in the post-Tet period, increasingly difficult to attract the required number of supporting troops.

Despite the success of the naval effort as measured by the criteria then employed (e.g., detections, boardings, and inspections of water craft; naval gunfire support missions fired; kill ratios, etc.), the Communists still controlled large parts of the delta and still moved troops and war material along and across South Vietnam's rivers and streams.

The Bucklew Report in early 1964 had warned that a sea barrier to enemy infiltration would be futile in the absence of land and water patrols along the Laotian and Cambodian borders. In the fall of 1968, however, such patrols were still nonexistent. This situation, ripe for exploitation, was the subject of a meeting early in October between Zumwalt and Captain Robert S. Salzer, commander of the Riverine Assault Force.

Salzer, who had little time left on his Vietnam tour and who, despite having "saved the Delta," had been passed over for flag rank, knew he was being charmed.

"He came down to the Delta and he played on my vanity a little bit," Salzer later recalled, "because he said all the nice things like, 'I don't know anything about this business, you are leaving soon and I have to learn from you, and this is going to be the focal point of my effort.' "[7]

Salzer told Zumwalt that the idea of using the river force on search-and-destroy operations was futile and a waste of resources.

"In an oriental country against an irregular force," he said, "what our tactic had to be was to force our enemy to come to us, because he had the knowledge of the terrain, the knowledge of the people. He had many advantages and we were relatively clumsy at ferreting him out. How then, I kept postulating, do you make the enemy come to you? The answer is you must, when he is an enemy depending upon an external source of supplies, choke off the supplies. And you must have many small units (which the Army hates to do) engage in that activity; also, you must keep reaction forces poised and ready for when the enemy main force comes in and tries to tangle with these little guys.

"Where were his supplies coming from? At one time it was claimed that they were coming from the sea, but that turned out wrong. Others were claiming, and intelligence people said they had hard evidence, that they were coming into Cambodia and down the trail and then down through the Ca Mau Peninsula around certain canal networks, and our intelligence people said they had them pretty well identified. What I wanted to do was to set up multiple, integrated interdiction barriers with small river units, with troops associated with them, setting up ambush patrols along these areas. The Viet Cong were pretty well canalized for a variety of reasons as to their routes and I figured we might have a 20 percent probability at any one barrier. Therefore we had to set up a pack of barriers. We needed multiple layers of interdiction patrol, such as in 'blue water' ASW.

"We had night scopes; we could detect activity; we had now just received in the country the sensors that had been bought for the McNamara Line and were told to make whatever use we could of them; they were good for these purposes. We could set up these patrols; we could have armored boats and PBRs and react quickly with a platoon or more to any ambush that was under attack. And in addition, if we could only get some helicopter gunships in there, we could take a toll. Not one of these was going to be an impenetrable barrier just as in an ASW problem. We had to set up successive layers.

But I could not really ever get the U.S. Army interested in this. You know there is very little body count associated with it; it's not the active kind of thing they love—'search and destroy.' Yet when the enemy gets desperate he will come to you. He does have to show himself and then you get the body count. But the other weeks—the two weeks statistics might be pretty abysmal and you might never ever see him—you don't really care about killing him, but you don't want him to get his supplies."[8] Zumwalt listened carefully, nodding in agreement.

A few days later, Salzer and all other senior NAVFORV commanders were summoned to a conference in Saigon. There Salzer was handed a sign to place on the conference table before him. The sign read, "SEA LORDS," an acronym standing for "Southeast Asia, Lake, Ocean, River and Delta Strategy." Zumwalt told Salzer to run the meeting and develop a program to interdict enemy logistics in the delta. At that conference, the basic operation plan was hammered out and, at Zumwalt's direction, Salzer put the concept in message form. The next morning, a Sunday, the plan was carried to COMUSMACV (General Creighton Abrams) who gave it qualified approval. The senior advisor in IV Corps, Major General George S. Eckhardt, also would have to sign off on it, Abrams said.

Zumwalt and Salzer flew to Eckhardt's headquarters at Can Tho in the delta and got his concurrence. Salzer, as "First Sea Lord" (a title he thought was "just too damn cute"[9]), would command the operation until his relief, at the end of November, by Zumwalt's flag officer deputy, Rear Admiral W. H. House.

In a long message to Eckhardt on 20 October, the overall plan was spelled out. The broad objectives of Sea Lords were stated as: (1) the interdiction of Viet Cong infiltration routes from the Gulf of Thailand to the upper Mekong River; and (2) the pacification of vital trans-delta inland waterways. In addition, Market Time units would penetrate the rivers of the Ca Mau Peninsula "to stir up the enemy and keep him off balance."[10]

Market Time, Game Warden, and Mobile Riverine Force operations unrelated to Sea Lords would continue with as little disruption as possible. The Vietnamese Navy would relieve U.S. Navy PCFs on some additional Market Time patrol stations. These PCFs would then relieve PBRs in the lower rivers, making them available for work farther inland on the proposed barriers. Riverine assault craft already were somewhat under-employed due to the shortage of ground forces.

U.S. intelligence had estimated that 175–200 short tons of enemy supplies were entering III and IV Corps each month from Cambodia. Strategically, the best place to establish an interdiction barrier was the Rach Giang Thanh–Vinh Te Canal route between Ha Tien on the Gulf of Thailand and Chau Doc on the upper Bassac River. This route closely paralleled the Cambodian border, however, and it was decided not to risk having Sea Lords throttled in its infancy by predictable political pressures that would be brought to bear once firefights on the waterways began spilling over into Cambodian territory. (As will shortly be shown, something akin to this had already been experienced.) The plan called, therefore, for the first interdiction barrier to be emplaced some thirty miles south of the border along a canal linking Rach Gia on the coast and Long Xuyen on the Bassac. To provide for "interdiction in depth," patrols would be established at the same time along a second canal, the Cai Son (or Rach Soi), which paralleled the first about five miles farther south.

Riverine strike operations would eliminate enemy resistance and pacify the land areas on either side of the two canals. Mobile Riverine Group Bravo (TG-117.2) and Vietnamese Marines were assigned these tasks, and additional support was requested from air mobile and air cavalry troops assigned to IV Corps. COMNAVFORV would provide Swift boats, PBRs, and SEAL teams to assist in the assault phase. Upon completion of the riverine operation, a permanent PBR patrol, supported as necessary by TF-117 riverine assault craft, would be established on both canals. It was planned that eventually VNN river assault groups (RAGs) would relieve U.S. Navy units.

The Rach Gia–Long Xuyen and Cai Son canals were intersected by many smaller and shallower cross canals. Clearance was sought to mine these with small anti-personnel and anti-sampan devices.

In the initial planning document, recognition was given to what had been learned during years of river operations in Vietnam: control of river and canal banks was essential to the success and safety of waterborne interdiction patrols. It was requested that "Vietnamese ground forces conduct active day and night patrols and provide bank security on a continuing basis."[11] This request would be largely ignored by ARVN commanders and unquestionably resulted in higher casualties to the Brown Water Navy from mining and ambush than otherwise would have been incurred.

COMNAVFORV proposed to make the interdiction barriers more effective by strengthening Game Warden patrols on the upper Bassac River north from Long Xuyen and through the Vam Nao crossover to the Mekong. The IV Corps commander was asked to assign Vietnamese Navy units to augment these patrols.

To accomplish the second broad objective of Sea Lords, the pacification of vital trans-delta inland waterways, COMNAVFORV requested that Vietnamese forces provide bank security while TF-117 removed obstructions blocking navigation of the Cho Gao Canal, which joined the Vam Co Dong and My Tho rivers. PBRs would be assigned to assist in the pacification of the northeastern end of the Cho Gao, an area of known Viet Cong activity. Next, he asked that two ARVN battalions be assigned to reinforce TF-117.2 and Vietnamese Marine Corps units for strike operations along the Mang Thit-Nicolai Canal, a waterway linking the Co Chien and Bassac rivers. Once the enemy was scattered and his fortifications destroyed, it was recommended that regional force (RF) troops and VNN river assault craft establish day and night patrols to keep the waterway open.

The third trans-delta canal marked for clearing was the Bassac–Bac Lieu rice route in the lower delta. Here again, RF troops were sought for patrol operations once enemy resistance was crushed by the Mobile Riverine Force. U.S. PCFs would assist by harassing the enemy in this general area through sporadic incursions of the My Thanh River.

As an adjunct to the above, clearance of the Tan Dinh and Dung islands in the Bassac River was proposed. Swift boats, PBRs, and riverine craft would blockade the islands while ground forces swept through and destroyed enemy forces. Upon completion of the clearing operations, RF troops supported by Vietnamese Navy RAG craft would maintain a presence on the islands and keep the enemy from regaining control.

The final proposal in COMNAVFORV's 20 October message concerned Swift boat raids into the rivers of the Ca Mau Peninsula. Support requested for these included daily aerial reconnaissance, helo gunships, and a provincial reconnaissance unit (PRU) of about forty men on call for air insertion when the military situation so dictated. The proposals made to Eckhardt concluded with a promise that, assuming troop and helicopter support was provided as requested, naval forces were prepared to initiate Sea Lords "at once."[12] Needless to say, all of this added up to an ambitious undertaking.

There are several things of particular significance in the early Sea Lords proposals. First, the old idea of largely independent employment of the three major task forces had given way to the concept of a

Brown Water task fleet in which the heavy, armored craft of TF-117 played the role of battleships, and the lighter and faster PCFs and PBRs performed as cruisers and destroyers. Armored troop carriers could be likened to a whole range of amphibious landing ships. Each class of boat had its own set of characteristics, and the employment of a mix of these boats in operations where their firepower, speed, maneuverability, draft, and armor could be used to complement each other seemed to make good sense.

Second, Sea Lords called for the cooperation and mutual support of sea, air, and ground forces. If it was desirable to combine the best features of the three naval task forces, it was essential that adequate air and ground forces be committed to ensure both the initial and the long-term success of Sea Lords. A major criticism of the conduct of the war to that time had been the repeated failure to establish and maintain a friendly presence in the wake of search-and-destroy operations. Once the smoke cleared from such operations, the enemy almost always was given free rein to return and wreak vengeance on those in the civilian population who had failed to support him. (Unhappily, this was a circumstance that never really changed.)

Third, if the proposed interdiction barriers were aggressively patrolled they would, in concert with Market Time, drastically reduce Communist logistic support of the entire lower delta. This region, of paramount importance in determining the final outcome of the war, for many years had been an enemy stronghold. Sea Lords offered the last, best hope for establishing firm governmental control there.

Within a few days of the dispatch of the 20 October proposals, the IV Corps senior advisor (Maj. Gen. Eckhardt) formally approved them. Salzer and a small staff set up shop in the IV Corps Headquarters compound in Can Tho. On 25 October, CTF-115, -116, and -117 were directed to report to First Sea Lord for operations. (Salzer was double-hatted as CTF-117 until 5 November, when he was relieved of those duties by Captain J. G. Now, so essentially he was ordered to report to himself!)

Command relationships were defined by letter on 29 October. COMNAVFORV was assigned the task force designator 194. First Sea Lord became CTG-194.0, and exercised operational control over TG-194.5, Coastal Raiding and Blocking Group; TG-194.6, Riverine Raiding and Blocking Group; and TG-194.7, Riverine Strike Group. First Sea Lord was directed to designate one of the three principal task force commanders to command each specific Sea Lords operation, with CTF-115 normally expected to command incursions from seaward, CTF-116 riverine and blocking operations, and CTF-117 riverine strike operations involving ground forces.[13]

A Swift boat incursion of the Cua Lon River, two days prior to the 20 October proposals, is sometimes considered the first Sea Lords operation. The first real campaign, however, was touched off on 2 November with an attack on enemy positions along the Rach Gia to Long Xuyen Canal. Acting CTF-117, Captain J. G. Now, was the officer in tactical command. Planned participation of PBRs in the assault had to be canceled at the last moment when Vietnamese maritime police and interpreters failed to rendezvous as scheduled at Long Xuyen—another example of the exasperating "maybe tomorrow" approach to the war taken by many South Vietnamese.

The assault phase of the operation lasted five days and resulted in twenty-one enemy killed in action (KIA) at the cost of one friendly KIA and fifty wounded (WIA). Quantities of arms and ammunition were seized, and seven U.S. boats were damaged. Though the operation was deemed a success, it suffered from a lack of mobile and air cavalry support at critical moments when significant enemy contact was established. The Vietnamese IV Corps commander did not commit any of his maneuver battalions to the operation and assigned the task of securing land areas adjacent to the canal to popular force (PF) companies that proved much less aggressive than had been hoped. Furthermore, the early withdrawal of Vietnamese Marine Corps units forced a decision to limit subsequent patrol operations to the western end of the canal in Kien Giang Province. Intelligence reports indicated that that was where the principal infiltration routes ran, while in the east, in An Giang Province, the canal snaked through open and relatively pacified country.

A limited patrol operation, later called "Search Turn," was established with PBRs and selected riverine assault craft. PCFs made periodic raids into the seaward ends of the targeted canals in support of the operation.

While Search Turn was being established, riverine assault craft conducted clearing operations in the Cho Gao Canal. By 6 November, all navigational obstructions were removed from that waterway. Regional force and popular force troops provided bank security. No enemy opposition was encountered.

Cooperation from the Vietnamese IV Corps commander was difficult to come by, despite the efforts of the senior advisor, Eckhardt. On 7 November, Captain Salzer advised COMNAVFORV of the difficulties he was experiencing. ARVN division commanders, he said, were strongly oriented toward ground war concepts and as-

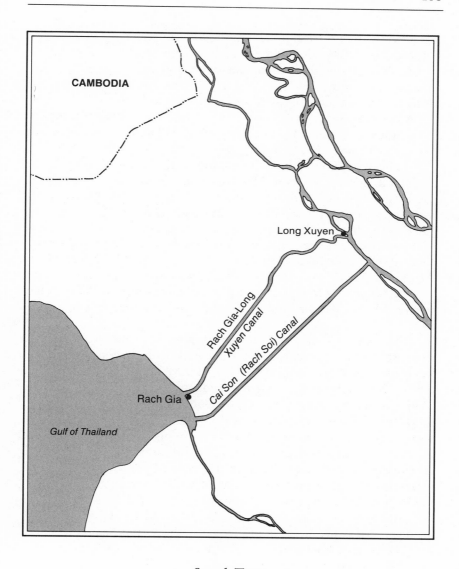

Search Turn

signed very low priority to the interdiction campaign.[14] Each division commander rigidly adhered to boundaries limiting his field of action, and as these boundaries often split rivers and canals right down the middle, the waterways themselves, and the enemy LOCs that ran along them, frequently became a strange no-man's land.

A desire to save Vietnamese "face" kept many American officers from voicing complaints, but not Salzer. He spoke his mind, and years later he was still seething.

"One operation with the Goddamn little Major General Nghi, commanding general of the 21st Division," he recalled, "is an example. I had, with a great deal of trouble, arranged a completely coordinated operation with a nice diversion plan and Nghi's troops were going to be able to storm a hill the Viet Cong had been holding at one of their primary transshipment points, right on the coast and honeycombed with caves. We had columns coming from the north and from the east and from the south, and I had an inshore fire-support ship, an LSMR, coming from seaward to supply fire support. We even had arranged U.S. close air support for Nghi and provided helicopters for him. . . .

"The night of the operation everything was put together—and with great security, incidentally. I persuaded the senior advisor that we could not allow even MACV to know about it, because they talked abut everything in Saigon. Suddenly, General Nghi, at three o'clock in the morning, after all the Goddamn boats are converging, said, 'I will not go; my troops will not go.' They were supposed to have loaded two hours before that on the boats coming up from Rach Gia. He wouldn't go because he said he did not think he had enough air support, and he was obdurate. He wanted a B-52 strike. It took two days to arrange a B-52 strike out of SAC Control all the way back to Omaha. Anyhow, it was not possible to have a B-52 strike in there with the boats as close as they would be. And laying off while we arranged it was just inviting fire from the shore. But he just wouldn't go. The corps commander said, 'Well, if he won't go, I guess that's that. We'll just have to cancel.'

". . . I think really what happened was that he got chicken; he didn't like the infantry assault even with the helicopters and the gunfire support and everything else. He was a major general then, and he was rewarded for various acts of valor like that with a third star later on."[15]

Stories like the above were legion in Vietnam.

On 11 November a naval blockade was established around islands in the Bassac River near the Can Tho crossing. Salzer originally had planned to initiate the cordon-and-search phase of this operation on 20 November when TG-117.2 riverine craft would be available to assist, but scheduling conflicts within IV Corps persuaded him to make an earlier start.

Eighteen PBRs were assigned to the blockade, and ground forces swept the two largest islands. In the operation thirteen enemy were killed and thirty captured, at a cost of two friendly KIA and eighteen WIA. Ninety "suspects" were detained. Half of the enemy losses were inflicted when ground forces were reinserted after the operation had ostensibly terminated.

On 25 November, Dung Island near the mouth of the Bassac River was blockaded by units from all three major task forces. TG-117.2, with two battalions of troops from the ARVN 9th and 21st divisions, searched the island. Only light opposition was encountered, resulting in two enemy KIA and two captured. Twenty-two suspects were again detained. Dung Island would remain "Indian country" throughout the war, and it is likely that enemy troops there simply went underground (literally) or blended into the civilian population during the sweep.

Meanwhile, a junior officer's impetuosity set in motion a series of events that led to the establishment of a third barrier patrol near the Cambodian border, despite earlier concerns raised at the Sea Lords planning conference.

On 14 October 1968, Lieutenant (j.g.) Michael Bernique took his Swift boat into Ha Tien on the Gulf of Thailand for an "R & R"—a brief respite from the boredom of Market Time patrol. While there he was told that a Viet Cong tax collector had posted himself a few miles east on the Rach Giang Thanh. Acting on his own initiative, he got under way and proceeded up the river, even though it had been declared off-limits to navy patrol craft.

Upon rounding a bend, he suddenly encountered seven armed men. At a range of less than one hundred yards he took them under fire, killing three and sending the rest scurrying for cover. A few moments later, while the crew of the Swift boat was busy collecting documents and discarded weapons, small-arms fire was taken from the river bank and promptly returned. Agent reports later indicated that two more were killed and two wounded in this exchange.

When his exploit became known, Bernique was flown to Saigon to explain his action, personally, to Zumwalt. Instead of being chastised, he was awarded the Silver Star, and for a time the Giang Thanh River was called, in the Brown Water Navy, "Bernique's Creek."

This incident, for all the political repercussions it risked, led

Zumwalt, after discussions with General Abrams, to order a test transit and patrol of the Giang Thanh and the Vinh Te Canal from Ha Tien to Chau Doc. Early on the morning of 16 November, three PCFs escorted by two Seawolves (UH-1B helicopter gunships) set out on that journey. On the way they were to "interdict VC supply lines, destroy or capture suspected VC tax collectors, board and search, gather intelligence, and conduct psyops [psychological operations]."[16] The officer in charge of the lead PCF was Bernique.

Shortly after the PCFs departed Ha Tien, they received an intelligence report from a local Vietnamese regional force commander that gave the location of two Viet Cong tax stations on the river ahead. At approximately 0840, armed men were sighted at the first supposed tax station and taken under fire. Twenty minutes later, farther up the river, another group of armed men was encountered and fired upon. The Seawolves later confirmed one enemy KIA.[17] The three PCFs then continued their transit without further incident.

Within hours of the two river actions, however, the naval intelligence liaison officer (NILO) at Ha Tien informed COMNAVFORV that the Vietnamese district chief had information that the armed men taken under fire by the Swift boats were not Viet Cong, but Cambodians—members of the paramilitary Khmer Kampuchea Krom (KKK). Ten were said to have been killed and four wounded. Furthermore, "ten South Vietnamese women of Cambodian origin" reportedly were slain in a large sampan shot up by the PCFs.[18]

The incident led to a formal protest by Cambodia to the International Control Commission for Indochina. COMNAVFORV ordered Captain (later Rear Admiral) Roy F. Hoffman, CTF-115, to make an on-scene investigation. Much conflicting testimony was taken, but in his review of the investigative report filed by Hoffman, Zumwalt concluded that "the only hypothesis consistent with what is known on the U.S. side is that any civilians killed must have been hiding in the immediate vicinity of firefight with armed men. It seems clear from all witnesses that at least some bodies were carried away from scene by persons unknown."[19]

Asked to assess the probable impact on delta operations if future boat patrols along the Cambodian border were forbidden, Zumwalt made a strong case for continuing them, arguing that to stop them would be interpreted as a "lack of resolve and a sign of weakness."[20]

"I consider that it is healthy for the Cambodians to see that we intend to prevent infiltration at the border," he said, "using waterways entirely under the jurisdiction of SVN. It would be better if geography had given us a waterway deeper in SVN, but this is the only one that allows us to bring our forces to bear in this area."[21]

General Abrams, with some reluctance, supported Zumwalt's arguments, and a barrier patrol given the name "Foul Deck" was established along the border with Cambodia. (Later, when turned over to the Vietnamese, it became the first of the VNN's many "Tran Hung Dao" operations.)

Initially, PCFs patrolled the western end of the waterway, and PBRs supported by ASPBs were given responsibility for the Vinh Te Canal. Troops to provide bank security were seldom available. On 1 December, the commander of the Vinh Te patrol operation, Captain (later Rear Admiral) Arthur W. Price, Jr. (CTF-116), informed First Sea Lord (Rear Admiral House, Captain Salzer having been detached), that falling water levels were making it impossible for PBRs to bring direct fire to bear on enemy positions behind the banks of the canal. Ground forces were now a mandatory requirement, he said, for protection of his boats. After two weeks of concerted effort he had managed to acquire the assistance of but one forty-man provincial reconnaissance unit (PRU). Vietnamese Special Forces, he said, flatly refused to embark in U.S. Navy craft, and the local district chief was "totally disinterested in the [barrier] campaign or its objectives and refuses participation."[22]

Strong pressures were applied, and by the middle of December some improvement in Vietnamese attitudes (some, but not much) was realized.

SEAL operations were conducted in support of naval patrols along the border, and these continued until 20 December. As a measure designed to lessen the danger of ambush, Zumwalt requested the defoliation of river and canal banks. This was not accomplished until late January 1969, due to objections raised by province and district chiefs. The defoliation became the subject of another formal complaint by Cambodia, which alleged that crops and vegetation on its side of the border were damaged by the spraying of chemicals.[23]

(As an aside, Admiral Zumwalt later blamed himself for ordering the use of chemical defoliants in the delta, which he believed contributed to his son's fatal cancer. The younger Zumwalt was a Swift boat officer whose Vietnam tour overlapped his father's. As already stated, however, the spraying of chemical defoliants on a massive scale predated by years Zumwalt's command of NAVFORV.)

In the latter part of December 1968, falling water depths in the Vinh Te Canal forced the removal of river assault craft from the patrol and halted minesweeping operations there. As the waters continued to drop, patrol craft operated in increasingly disadvantageous surroundings and the mine threat grew worse. On 25 January 1969, COMNAVFORV temporarily suspended the Vinh Te patrol, admitting that it was "the weakest link in our chain of barriers" and warning that failure to provide supporting ground troops had created a situation where "the enemy owns the night."[24]

A foot-dragging Vietnamese Navy was drawn into the operation. On 27 January four VNN LCVPs arrived at Chau Doc to assist in minesweeping on the Vinh Te. On 8 February two VNN PCFs and six junks began patrolling the Giang Thanh from Ha Tien. Also in February, permission was given to mine land and water areas along the Cambodian border (Operation "Silent Sentinel"). The first mines were planted in early March. In April, electronic sensors were sown along the border (Operation "Duffle Bag"). Many promises of Vietnamese troop support for the patrol at corps and province levels were made; few were kept.

Despite Zumwalt's bulldog tenacity, Foul Deck became the leakiest barrier of all. In late 1969, "patrol" of the Giang Thanh–Vinh Te waterway consisted of little more than randomly posted night ambushes. The enemy owned not just the night, but the daytime as well, moving virtually at will along and across the river and the canal.

The initial results obtained by Sea Lords were not statistically impressive. Late in December 1968, however, intelligence information was received that indicated a thirty-day backlog of supplies for the Viet Cong had piled up north of the interdiction barriers.[25] Patrols began uncovering arms caches along the banks of canals; one such contained 173 rifles and four B-40 rocket launchers.

Enemy supply levels in the delta gradually recovered, however, as alternate inland routes were exploited and increased manpower was employed in the logistics effort. The net effect of the barrier patrols seemed to be that the Communists were forced to abandon large supply convoys in favor of many smaller ones. This reduced their ability to achieve a rapid logistic buildup, while greatly increasing the manpower needed to move the supplies they did manage to infiltrate.

The reappearance of civilian water traffic on patrolled canals was a cause for celebration at NAVFORV headquarters, as was a supposed improvement in the performance of Vietnamese troops. "A renewed quality of aggressiveness appears to have been instilled in the local RF/PF troops as evidenced by their willingness to conduct ground sweeps rather than remaining close to their base camp," Zumwalt reported.[26] Characteristically, he was stretching things a bit where the Vietnamese were concerned, but overall there was cause for optimism in his early evaluation of the ambitious project he had mapped out for the Brown Water Navy.

In addition to Search Turn and Foul Deck, the Cho Gao Canal had been cleared of obstructions, and pacification of the three trans-delta waterways earmarked in the 20 October proposals awaited only the provision of necessary ground forces. The Bassac River islands had been swept and strengthened patrols established. Market Time raiders in the first month of Sea Lords had penetrated fifty-nine rivers on seventy-six separate occasions and, according to COMNAVFORV, were achieving results that far exceeded expectations.[27] These Swift boat raids into areas long controlled by the Viet Cong, though daring, were also troubling. Some, including Salzer, admitted to "squeamishness" about attacking "Viet Cong civilians."[28]

Was it really necessary to destroy the homes and the livelihood of river people in order to "save" them? There were those who did not think so, but few spoke up until long after.

11

ACTOV

I deliver to you a fleet that is master of the seas.

—Lysander of Sparta, 406 B.C.

"**B**ull shit, bull shit, bull shit! All I ever get out of the Air Force is a bunch of bull shit!

"Don't you people know what is happening? Don't you have any sense for the pressure-cooker environment that the president is in back in the United States? He has no consensus for support for this war. What support he has is dwindling. It's clear that the policy is to get us out of this war and turn it over to the Vietnamese. That policy change will be implemented by the incoming administration, but let me tell you, that's Johnson's policy right today. I've got a letter in my pocket from the president of the United States that directs me to turn this war over to the Vietnamese, and I can tell you that if anybody interferes with that, I'm going to go right around them.

"You are sitting here today and telling me that it's going to be 1976 before you can get the planes turned over to the Vietnamese? No way. Can't happen. The country won't give us that time. The incoming administration won't give us that time. Besides, I now have direct orders from the president to get this thing over with as soon as possible."[1]

The speaker was General Creighton Abrams, commander of the U.S. Military Assistance Command, Vietnam, and his outburst left others in the room in shocked silence. Vice Admiral Elmo R. Zumwalt, Jr., only a little more than a month on the job as commander Naval Forces, Vietnam, mentally raced through the briefing he had prepared concerning the navy's plan to extricate itself from the war. He thanked his lucky stars he had not been called upon to give his presentation first. During a break in the proceedings, he and Lieutenant (later Captain) Howard J. Kerr, his flag lieutenant and aide, tore up their carefully prepared timetable for turning over U.S. Navy assets to the Vietnamese, sketching in its place an "accelerated" turnover that would put the navy in the van of what became almost a race among the several services to bail out of the war.

"You must always stay in front of the power curve," Zumwalt was fond of saying, and hearing Abrams rip into the air force left little room for doubt which way the power curve was surging. When his turn came to brief Abrams, he gave a virtuoso performance. No one seemed to notice the lack of slick charts and graphs. Afterwards, Abrams put his arm around Zumwalt's shoulder and led him past more senior officers into his office for a private talk. The new vice admiral had scored big.

ACTOV, "accelerated turnover to the Vietnamese," was from that moment the number one priority for the navy in Vietnam.

By the fall of 1968, "Vietnamization" of the war (though the term itself was not coined until President-elect Richard M. Nixon used it in a speech on 31 December) had become a matter of the greatest political urgency. In October, COMUSMACV directed that a program be developed to turn over U.S. assets to the Vietnamese even while the war continued. The goal would be to make the Republic of Vietnam Armed Forces (RVNAF) as self-sufficient as possible as soon as possible. This requirement was re-emphasized later in the month when Abrams returned from a visit to the United States. The decision had been made in Washington that Vietnamization was essential to continued home support of the war. Over all hung the specter of the French defeat—"in the streets of Paris rather than on the battlefields of Indochina."

At about this same time, Secretary of Defense Clark Clifford publicly signaled the change in U.S. policy. In testimony before the Senate Armed Services Committee, he cited the need to improve the combat capabilities of South Vietnam's armed forces so that U.S. troops could be withdrawn in significant numbers. In scarcely veiled criticism of his predecessor's policy, he said that insufficient effort had been expended on giving the South Vietnamese the means to defend themselves.

Prior to his relief, Rear Admiral Veth had recommended to General Abrams and to the chief of naval operations a plan to turn over two river assault squadrons to the Vietnamese Navy by 30 June 1969. Zumwalt's ACTOV plan proposed to turn over all U.S. Navy operational responsibilities in Vietnam, and the assets to meet them, by 30 June 1970. The plan further called for the transfer of all support functions, bases, and other navy facilities in Vietnam by two years after that.

The task was formidable, and the size of the undertaking could not be measured solely in terms of the number of Vietnamese Navy personnel that would have to be recruited and trained. Significant improvement in the organization, performance, and most particularly the leadership of the VNN would also be required.

Morale within that navy was low, and unit discipline was, at best, uneven. Employment of assets already in Vietnamese hands was grossly inefficient. Maintenance ran the gamut from excellent (on guns) to unsatisfactory or nonexistent (on electronic equipment and machinery). Though many studies had demonstrated its theoretical excellence, to the end user in the field the Vietnamese supply system seemingly could not or would not work. The Saigon Naval Shipyard struggled along with barely 60 percent of its authorized work force, and skilled labor could not be attracted or held because of wage scales that were chronically and substantially below market. Training activities ashore suffered from a lack of instructors and inadequate physical facilities. Training afloat depended almost entirely on the whims of individual commanding officers, there being no system in place to ensure that standards set by higher authority were in fact met. Administrative procedures were antiquated and incredibly complex. The treatment afforded VNN dependents was, in a word, deplorable.

In the fall of 1968, the naval advisory effort in Vietnam was in its nineteenth (!) year. For all this period of time, U.S. Navy officers and senior enlisted men had been sent to live, to work, and some, eventually, to die alongside their Vietnamese counterparts. Particularly in the years after 1964, enormous sums of money and huge quantities of material and equipment were furnished the VNN. It is a fair question to ask why, after such expenditures of blood and treasure, the Vietnamese Navy, in 1968, was still so burdened with problems that should have been solved years before.

The admirals and captains our navy sent to Saigon were not stupid or deceitful men. They were, almost without exception, capable and highly motivated officers. They knew the structural changes required to make the VNN a viable organization, the improvements in command and control, training, promotion, pay, and dependents' care that should have been made before more ships and boats, more bases, and more operational responsibilities were thrown at the Vietnamese. Our lieutenant commanders and lieutenants in the field were not blind to these things either, nor to the graft and corruption that all too often had become a way of life for those they were sent to advise.

The advisory system ("show them how the job must be done, don't tell them or do it for them") was to blame, not the advisors. The system simply did not permit the kind of prompt, corrective action that circumstances clearly cried out for. The heart of the problem was political and not peculiar to the Vietnamese Navy nor to the Vietnamese armed forces as a whole. It spread its roots through virtually every sector of Vietnamese society. It was a bitter pill for a whole generation of "nation-builders" to swallow, but the brutal fact was that no Vietnamese government in Saigon ever inspired in its people the loyalty, the unhesitating support, the patriotism, and spirit of self-sacrifice essential to the creation of effective armed forces and the successful prosecution of war. The wonder is not that the advisory effort accomplished so little, but that it accomplished anything at all.

It is difficult, even now, to assess the true state of the Vietnamese Navy under American tutelage. The numbers of men in uniform, the ships and craft in the fleet, the hours spent under way, the junks inspected, the "kill ratios" and "body count" achieved—these are all quantifiable, to be sure. But these statistics were often meaningless, and sometimes deceptive. Subjective evaluations, on the other hand, were prey to a whole host of subtle psychological pressures. Sympathy and affection (or hatred and disdain) for one's counterpart, over-adherence to a "can-do" spirit in "no-can-do" situations, personal frustrations and feelings of inadequacy—these are things that exerted a powerful influence on the naval advisor's judgment. His assessment of the situation, which through most of the period under discussion was required to be stated in "end-of-tour reports" submitted to the senior naval advisor, remain, however, the best evidence of what the naval advisory effort had wrought. They are firsthand, personal, and often damning statements, which will shortly be examined here in some detail, but first it is necessary to sketch in broad outline some VNN history.

In the thirteen-year period between 1955 and 1968, the personnel strength of the Vietnamese Navy increased from 1,900 officers and men to more than 17,500. U.S.–furnished ships and craft doubled and redoubled the size of the fleet. American advisors were assigned in increasing numbers to assist and to teach—although the instruction or "advice" most often was given in English or poorly translated, halting Vietnamese. (Imagine, if you will, how well U.S. personnel would fare in basic training, much less in advanced technical schools, if their instructors spoke little English!)

As the Vietnamese Navy grew in size, if not in overall effectiveness, a deliberate program was devised, well before the start of ACTOV, to have the VNN gradually relieve the U.S. Navy of operational responsibilities. Mention has already been made of progress along this line in Market Time, but in other areas of the naval war it had happened too. VNN minesweepers shared the dangerous work of keeping the Long Tau shipping channel open to Saigon and by 1968 were doing most of the sweeping. The first minesweeper lost to enemy action was a Vietnamese minesweeping launch demolished by a mine in the Long Tau on 28 August 1966.

In May 1967, a VNN river assault group was for the first time activated outside the delta. It was assigned at Thua Thien, northeast of Hue, and its primary mission was to support the ARVN First

Division in search-and-destroy operations. In the summer of 1968, a VNN river patrol group worked alongside TF-116 units in the Rung Sat Special Zone.

The forced-draft expansion of the Vietnamese Navy was not accomplished without serious shortfalls in performance and morale. The weak and uncertain political position of the VNN was a terrible handicap for Vietnamese officers. Further, the penalties for supporting the wrong faction in a time of political turmoil were severe.

The commander in chief of the Vietnamese Navy in the last years of the Diem regime was Captain Ho Tan Quyen. As previously mentioned, when President Diem was overthrown and murdered in November 1963, Quyen, who was closely associated with the fallen president and who had been instrumental in defeating several earlier attempted coups, was himself murdered by a subordinate officer sympathetic to the incoming regime.

The successor to Quyen as commander in chief of the VNN was Captain Chung Tan Cang. He found himself the victim of a "mutiny" on 8 April 1965, when his three task force commanders and several other officers rose against him, charging him with graft in the operation of a fleet of coastal freighters that had been seized by the government at the time of the 1963 coup. Cang, who had been promoted to the rank of rear admiral in the interim, was relieved of his command as were the mutineers, pending completion of an investigation of the affair. Until the last days of the war, Cang, though still holding his rank, played no active role in the Vietnamese Navy.

(As an aside, after the war Cang and nine relatives showed up on then-retired Admiral Zumwalt's doorstep in Virginia. Although the two had never met in Vietnam, Zumwalt took Cang and his relatives into his home, fixing up living quarters for them in his basement.)

After the 1965 mutiny, the commander of the Vietnamese Marine Corps was given temporary command of the navy, and this was viewed as a tremendous loss of face for the VNN. The Naval Advisory Group reported that "there were cases of failure to carry out orders and missed commitments, but not as many as might have been predicted."[2] On 26 April, a Captain Phan, the former chief of staff to Cang, was designated acting commander of the Vietnamese Navy. The situation remained chaotic, however.

"Preoccupation with politics, both national and intra-navy, continued to erode discipline and morale in the VNN," the Naval Advisory Group reported. "The mutineers . . . all returned to their original posts in May except the River Force commander, who was replaced. At the same time, COs of two River Assault Groups, the CO of the VNN SEAL/UDT team (LDNN), and several other officers reportedly were detained by the Military Security Service and held briefly in connection with an investigation concerning an attempted coup. All were released without disciplinary action. The return of the mutineers added strength to one of the unfortunate facts of political life in RVN, namely, key leaders who fail to actively support the winner during a coup can expect to lose prestige and possibly their jobs shortly thereafter."[3]

On 8 September 1966, Lieutenant General Cao Van Vien, ARVN, took command of the Vietnamese Navy. Some viewed this as a blessing in disguise, since the VNN would at least have a voice at meetings of the Joint General Staff. This peculiar command relationship was not destined to last, however. Captain (later Rear Admiral) Tran Van Chon was named to the top VNN post on 31 October 1966, and with his appointment the senior command of the Vietnamese Navy acquired, at last, a measure of stability.

Chon had served a previous tour as commander in chief in the period 1957–59, while in the rank of commander. In 1959–60 he attended the U.S. Naval War College, and his most recent assignment prior to reassuming command of the VNN was as commanding officer of the Regional Force Boat Group, a command not, strictly speaking, a part of the navy. This assignment had afforded Chon providential relief from the necessity of choosing sides in the recent political machinations of the naval officer corps.

In the fall of 1966, U.S. Navy advisors were reporting critical shortages of trained manpower in the Vietnamese Navy's operating forces. Fewer than half of the advisors assigned to coastal groups (the Junk Force) considered their units capable of carrying out assigned missions. The sea forces were undermanned in all ranks. The shore establishment, on the other hand, was fully manned and in some cases had more personnel assigned than allowed.[4]

The U.S. Navy SEAL advisor reported, with disgust, that Vietnamese SEALs (LDNN) suspended combat operations and training on 15 October 1966 to prepare for the 1 November National Day celebration and a local all-service shooting competition.[5]

Maintenance aboard most Fleet Command ships was considered below minimum U.S. standards, and engineering practices were reported to be completely unsatisfactory. The availability of junks and river craft for operations was curtailed by a lack of repair parts and skilled workmen. At most coastal groups "a sense of responsibility for maintenance was lacking."[6]

Desertion rates soared. The number of personnel absent without leave increased from 31 in November 1966 to 451 in February 1967, in part due to the Tet holidays—a circumstance that most likely did not go unnoticed by the Viet Cong. (In February 1968, at the height of the Communist offensive, the number of AWOL Vietnamese Navy personnel would climb to 786.[7])

The Saigon Naval Shipyard was in a constant state of crisis as wage scales for skilled labor fell dangerously low. Appeals to the Vietnamese government, which set wage and employment policy, ran into a solid wall of red tape and delay. COMNAVFORV warned that failure to increase the pay of shipyard workers to a level consistent with the labor market could well destroy the long-range effectiveness of the Vietnamese Navy.[8] But it was not only shipyard pay that was failing to keep pace with Saigon's ruinous inflation. In the late 1960s a cyclo driver, a coolie pedaling a wheeled vehicle through the streets of South Vietnam's capital city, earned more than a Vietnamese Navy lieutenant was paid. Was it any wonder that corruption spread like a virus? Often, VNN sailors and junior officers had to steal, had to become corrupt, simply to keep themselves and their families alive.

These were but some of the many frustrating problems U.S. Navy advisors faced in Vietnam in the months leading up to ACTOV. It may now be instructive to consider what the advisors themselves were saying about the situation in end-of-tour reports. The format for these reports provided for description of conditions both upon the advisor's arrival and departure from Vietnam. The excerpts presented below are believed in all cases to refer to conditions as they existed in the period July–December 1968, when major decisions were taken concerning Vietnamization.

Fleet Command Advisors:

"One year ago, the lack of satisfactory trained petty officers was one of Fleet Command's biggest problems. Not only were more Class 'A' and 'B' school graduates required, but observing the performance of those graduates assigned Fleet Command clearly indicated a vast effort was required to improve the quality of instruction these sailors were receiving. Now the petty officer situation is so bleak that the Fleet Commander would be better off mooring some of his ships to a pier with a skeleton (security) crew and using the personnel he has to satisfactorily operate the remaining ships. Thousands of dollars are being wasted by a lack of familiarity with the very simplest preventive and corrective maintenance procedures. Not knowing how to do their job well has contributed to low morale aboard many Fleet Command ships. On one occasion early this year a PGM got underway from Pier 'H' for patrol in the Fourth Coastal Zone. The engines stopped in the middle of the stream in front of Fleet Command Headquarters and *the engineroom crew did not know how to restart them*! That such might happen to a local harbor craft of similar size would be extremely embarrassing, but when it happens to a ship that is expected to operate independently, be on station, on time, and provide naval gunfire in support of friendly troops . . . such lack of training becomes a tragedy. . . .

"The OASD Team which visited the shipyard and Fleet Command advisors in October and November 1968 concluded in its recommendations that no more ships be turned over until the Vietnamese Navy proves its ability to maintain the ships it already has. The response to this recommendation was a big disappointment to me and indicates the U.S. Government's willingness to continue turning over ships and boats that in a very few years might be nothing more than junk. . . .

"The VNN is growing at a bewildering pace. Decisions are being made today that affect nearly every unit. A greater sense of cooperation can be achieved if more information on the accelerated turnover program is passed down to the ships and other small units. A skipper needs to know why he is losing his good men. He needs to be convinced that it is for the good of the navy and his country. A good way to begin is to convince his advisor."[9]

"The personnel picture became more stabilized throughout the year. Poor leadership and lack of aggressiveness, motivation, and professional knowledge still plague their officer and senior petty officer ranks. Progress is being made, no miracles, just good steady progress. They have a long way to go to reach our standards, but they have enough officers with the proper attributes to lead the others out of the darkness. The key item that the Advisory Group can do is to help make sure that those with good leadership ability are promoted rapidly and placed in the right jobs. . . .

"Despite a multitude of distressing factors that still exist with shipboard maintenance, indications do exist that encourage optimism. In comparison to U.S. standards, the Vietnamese still have a long row to hoe, but when I think back on the overall maintenance condition about a year ago, and the obstacles they have faced during this time, I am utterly amazed at their progress. A year ago, we had trouble getting a man to stand a watch in the engineroom. After this was corrected, we were faced with the problem of keeping the watch-standers awake. Now we are in the third and most difficult stage, getting them to properly operate and maintain their equip-ment. . . ."[10]

"When I reported aboard, PC-06 was completing an extended overhaul with VNNSY [Vietnamese Naval Shipyard]. The com-manding officer had had four other commands, but most of the other officers were going to sea for the first time. Most of the crew were new seamen with very little experience at sea. The ship had two weeks of refresher training before going on patrol. I was told by the Fleet Commander that PC-06 was very old and had several 'thin spots' in her hull. It was policy at that time to assign the ship only to those areas where calm seas could be expected. I was told that after the first patrol the ship would be used only on the rivers and that it would be scrapped at the end of 1968. I read over the docking reports and was unable to find anything substantial to support this estimate of the ship's condition. Nevertheless, the officers and crew were well aware of the 'delicate' condition of the ship and seemed to expect it to sink at any minute. On the first day of patrol, a partially flooded storeroom was discovered. The crew immediately went to abandon ship stations and put on life jackets while the OOD [officer of the deck] headed the ship toward the beach at full speed. Fortunately, things went uphill from that point on and the ship turned out to be one of the most reliable units of Fleet Command. . . .

"Food for the crew constitutes even more of a problem now than it did a year ago. The food allowance has not changed, but food prices in most areas are much higher than they were before the Tet Offensive. The upshot is that the crew does not get enough to eat and the commanding officer must waste much more time bargaining and 'big-dealing' to get the most for his money. . . ."[11]

Coastal Group Advisors:

"Forces are used regularly and a high percentage of available units are employed, but routine patrol procedures are poor. VNN officers and senior petty officers virtually never accompany or supervise routine patrols. Officers demonstrate a reluctance to use their units in any area where danger might exist. Junior petty officers in charge of patrols do not aggressively or consistently supervise conduct of the patrol but tend to stop in a protected area, anchor, and sleep. Patrols are secured early, sometimes as much as four to six hours. Although VNN officers are aware of these situations, they make no serious attempts to really improve, but only [make] token efforts to pacify the advisors for a while.

"Planning in areas of maintenance, supply, training, and administration is poor. Officers spend much of their time on liberty, shooting birds, playing dominoes and poker, etc. They are generally unaware of the material condition of their junks and generators and make little effort to stay abreast of the situation. They don't require their senior petty officers to keep up to date on these things either. No logs or maintenance records are kept on the machinery. Regular inspections of boats, buildings, grounds, and machinery are not held. Supply problems are approached in retrospect only, and the VN officers make an effort to get spare parts through official channels only if pressured by the advisors. . . .

"Although I've seen a number of isolated incidents of good performance of VNN officers, the overall picture is dim. In establishment and enforcement of routine procedures for patrols, maintenance, training, inspections, and psywarfare, only sporadic efforts are made, usually as a result of advisor cajolery, and follow-up is generally poor to nil. Acceptance and perpetuation of the current unsat status quo is the easy way out and the path most often followed.

"Senior petty officers, emulating their superiors, do little in the supervisory field. The phrase 'retire to the chiefs' quarters' could be downgraded. First class POs and above spend most of the 'working' day playing games, and sleeping, instead of supervising, following-up, and keeping records. Because of the indifference of the officers and senior petty officers, work done by the lower rated men is usually slipshod. . . .

"The Vietnamese, although hampered by a rural, nontechnical history, are capable of performing well. . . . They are, however, in need of more effective leadership than they have. I think we must have some way to force them to accept our advice or we will be here dilly-dallying for many, many years to come."[12]

"Perhaps the general sense of frustration which seems to pervade this war is a contributing factor, but it is unquestionably true that a great many coastal groups exist only to exist. And this can only be attributed to the commanding officers of these coastal groups. They pose no threat whatsoever to the enemy and their most belligerent activity consists of defending their own base or harassing the local fishermen for a few fish each day. . . .

"But the war continues and Vietnamese officers at the highest levels who have the power to effect changes do not appear to be concerned. Incompetents are rarely relieved, and then only after tedious pleadings by the zone commanders. There is a general attitude of 'don't rock the boat,' and one senses that the war could go on like this indefinitely with the Vietnamese in command making little or no response to obviously poor situations. In the past, there has been a great fuss made down in Saigon over our isolated successes. Completely unwarranted optimism about our progress in the war has been thereby generated at the expense of any realistic assessment. The advisors out in the field, and those advisors who regularly visit the field, appear to be aware that the Junk Forces are having little real effect on the progress of the war. It is questionable how significant they could ever be, but it is certain that they could be more effective than they are now if a genuine and realistic interest were shown toward their capabilities and performance by those in the highest levels of command.

"I have been fortunate to be associated with an unusually fine command and a number of Vietnamese and Americans who are officers and gentlemen in the best sense of that term. It is not to them that my suggestions are directed, but to those who are able to affect the development and philosophy of the Junk Forces as a whole."[13]

"My personal feeling is that the advisory effort is and has been a failure. The progress made over the past few years is insignificant when compared with what could have been done if the U.S. had operational control. This feeling extends to more than Coastal Group 33 and encompasses the attitude of every advisor I have ever talked with since my arrival in country. It is time to either fight the war or get out."[14]

River Assault Group Advisors:

"'Lack of control' becomes the most frustrating fact of life for the advisor. Often he becomes more familiar with the local tactical situation than the RAG CO himself, if only because he has more occasion to ride the boats on operations. The CO does not go on all troop operations, often delegating this duty to one of his junior officers.

The advisor, however, is always present on these operations. He is most ineffective in causing bad situations to change for the better. As an observer, all he can do is relay these observations to his counterpart. His counterpart may or may not be capable of taking corrective action; his counterpart may or may not be willing to take the action necessary. For example, because of poor bank security and poor command relationships between the local ARVN commander and the RAG boat group commander making resupply runs from Can Tho to Tam Binh along the Nicolai Canal in Vinh Long Sector, the RAG boats were ambushed on nine of ten transits through a specific area in the Nicolai Canal. Although these facts were brought out in clearer terms on each successive RAGREP [river assault group report], the problem continued unabated. Apparently, ARVN advisors are in the same unfortunate position as we in the RAGs are, i.e., change cannot be initiated by them, only influenced. In desperation from messages unacted upon, I informed the RAG CO that being ambushed on the next run, I would recommend that advisors do not accompany the boats through this area until some positive corrective action was taken, and positive corrective action not occurring on the next run after that, I would actually take the advisors off the boats while putting out a RAGREP explaining why the advisors were not present on the boats. He was naturally appalled at this tactic since his men and boats would lose the use of U.S. assets which the advisors coordinated and controlled on these runs. But what else was there to be done? A clearly intolerable situation was obviously being ignored and the boats were continuously subjected to a most dangerous situation. If the firm exhortations contained in messages to all concerned in the advisory chain of command didn't get the action, it was time to rattle a few cages. Fortunately, or unfortunately, we never made another run to Tam Binh since we had been so badly devastated on the ninth and last ambush. It was determined at higher levels that Tam Binh in Vinh Long Sector should have been properly resupplied by the Vinh Long RAG coming down the opposite way through the Mang Thit, even though the Can Tho RAGs are closer. A less than Solomon-like solution!

"Perhaps the best example of the discrepancy between what the advisor is theoretically thought capable of doing and what his actual capabilities are is illustrated by the PMS boondoggle. That the Vietnamese Navy is most sorely lacking in maintenance techniques, schedules and procedures is a fact that shines forth like a beacon in the night. Therefore a plan was initiated and executed within the advisory chain of command to incorporate something akin to the very successful U.S. Planned Maintenance System [PMS]. The plan and order for incorporation into Vietnamese Navy units came down to the operational field advisors with directives ordering the inclusion of this system in the Vietnamese organization. . . .

"PMS, as it was envisaged . . . is a workable and eminently worthwhile program. The maintenance procedures and checks were basic enough and few enough to enable the Vietnamese to easily accomplish them, yet the program was good enough to insure basic reliability of engines and act as a training tool for the sailor. But the advisor cannot implement this program in a horizontal fashion by merely enthusiastically presenting it to his counterpart and encouraging its use. The initiation of the program must come from the RAG CO's own chain of command and be followed up with specific requirements by his own organization. Otherwise, any program is tenuous and temporary at best, if only because it lacks the official stamp. . . .

"That formal scheduled training is almost non-existent is again a measure of the capability and success of the advisory effort. How long has this situation existed? Through how many advisors? And yet the situation remains the same. After so many advisors and so long a period of time, the organization, system and concept [of the advisory effort] should be made the target of thorough analysis and reevaluation."[15]

"I do not feel my counterparts, or the other Vietnamese officers of their caliber and experience that I have had occasion to work with, needed advisors. They did have many uses for liaison officers and it was in this capacity that I felt I functioned. I feel that my counterparts felt that the only real value they received from the U.S. advisor was his ability to 'cumshaw' material from the American units in the area, and that if he wouldn't do this for them he didn't add very much to their organization. . . . To quote one Vietnamese officer I spoke with, 'I am a Vietnamese and speak the language, and yet it takes me about three months to get a good understanding of what is going on in a new job. How can an American, who can't even speak Vietnamese, have much understanding of my problems in only one year?' I believe that if the advisory effort is to be continued serious consideration should be given to providing the prospective advisor with sufficient language training to enable him to work with his counterpart in Vietnamese. In conjunction with this I feel that serious consideration should be given to extending the advisor's tour length. . . .

"I do not feel that my efforts contributed greatly toward making the Vietnamese at my level less dependent on the U.S. for support or more inclined to use their own channels for requirements."[16]

Coastal Surveillance Center Advisor:

"I feel that the advisory effort is only about 25 percent, or less, effective. There is too much wasted talent, effort and manpower. Most coastal group advisors and headquarters personnel could be cut by 50 percent without appreciable loss of effectiveness. . . . With our Navy sense of duty in getting the job done by any method and means, all too often we end up doing the work that should be done by the Vietnamese. This is detrimental to the advisory effort. . . . The Vietnamese must do the job themselves and have higher standards of performance. I am impressed by those Vietnamese I have met and worked with who sincerely try to do a good job and actually do perform. I am equally appalled that the majority just want to get by, have no moral sense of duty to service and country, and will not even attempt to improve their performance. . . .

"Fleet Command ships are sent out for patrols from Saigon with inoperative equipment. . . . Approximately 75 percent of the Fleet Command ships have casualties that affect their operational capability, such as radars, fathometers, gyros, generators, engines and evaporators. In most cases ship's company cannot effect repairs and the casualties remain unchanged during the entire patrol. . . .

"Commanding officers of Fleet Command ships do as they want to whether they are required to enforce regulations set by higher authority or not. For example, only one ship to my knowledge actually enforces the restricted areas and curfews set by the commanding general of I Corps. . . . It is my impression that most advice given by the advisory effort is not desired and not heeded. The overall desire to improve to the extent required just does not exist."[17]

Naval Training Center Advisor:

"Although the number of officer instructors assigned to NTC has increased from 27 to 40 (allowed 45) since my arrival, the quality of instructor input has drastically declined. . . .

"At this time, NTC does not have a training ship, any long boats or any training boat larger than an LCM to conduct underway training for midshipmen. The CO is forced to place 50–60 midshipmen on PCEs, when operations permit, for 3–4 days of training. Scheduling problems definitely exist preventing much utilization of this form of underway training, and it is extremely doubtful if the middies get much if any concrete training out of the crowded conditions prevailing. The ships are unable to feed the middies, and present instructions prohibit the CO [from acquiring] VN 'C' rations. . . ."[18]

VNN Supply Center Advisor:

"Perhaps the problem that concerns me most is maintenance, or rather, the lack of it. My counterpart frequently complains to me that parts are surveyed and reordered without a proper investigation. Being an engineering officer, I believe that the stock control officer is qualified to read between the lines of a survey and conclude that lack of maintenance caused the breakdown. The LST HQ-502 seems to have been a turning point in this problem. The HQ-502 lost a main engine during a dock trial. We requisitioned and received a new engine within 10 days. No investigation was conducted to determine why a main engine was lost in port. (If one was conducted, the results are unknown at the NSC.) The fast response on the part of the advisors to get a new engine impressed the VNN. *Dai Uy* [Lieutenant] Dat reports to Headquarters (Technical, N-4) that lack of maintenance caused a breakdown. He has been told more than once, since the 502, not to worry. 'The U.S. provided an LST main engine without a murmur—the equipment you are talking about is a lot smaller.'

"CSC Qui Nhon burned out two generators within six months. I personally saw these at NSC when they were returned. The radiators were clogged with grease and dirt. The air cleaner in one had no oil and was completely rusted out. Two new generators had already been sent and installed—nothing more was done. Recently I accompanied these generators to Pacific Architects and Engineers for repair. PA&E reported that the engines were completely destroyed. New engines were ordered from the States. . . .

"Already the PCFs at An Thoi have been issued (for immediate installation) two 12V-71 main engines. I understand the PCF grounded, continued to run its engines, and burned out everything requiring raw water with the possible exception of the Onan generator.

"These are just a few examples of the overall problem. Any supply system finds it hard to compete with this type of usage. What is being done?"[19]

Medical Service Corps Advisor:

"Sanitation by no means rates less attention than any of the other items. In training, the Hygiene and Sanitation Training Program was considered a priority item by me. However . . . waste material is strewn haphazardly at every activity that I have seen or from which I have received a report. Children, adults, rats, flies, mosquitoes, dogs, etc. can be observed rummaging through the garbage every day. One of our facilities has been reported . . . as being unsanitary and in a hepatitis epidemic area. Their water is procured from the river 10 feet below the outhouse which juts out over the river. . . .

"Potable water standards are in constant abuse or are completely ignored on the majority of VNN ships, as well as use of disinfectants and proper cleaning of food service spaces. The largest sanitation eyesore in the VNN is the deplorable sanitary condition of their food service spaces and food storage areas, which is the main reason why they are plagued with such overwhelming amounts of rodent and insect life."[20]

VNN Shipyard Advisor:

"Regular overhauls and major repairs for the Vietnamese blue-water navy are performed at the Vietnamese Naval Shipyard. This shipyard is the largest Vietnamese industrial complex in the republic. It is not typical of organizations within the Vietnamese Navy. The significant differences are related to the fact that the work force is largely civilian. Shop supervisors and overhead employees are also civilian. The top management personnel, on the other hand, are active duty naval personnel. The result of the presence of large numbers of civilian workers is that the Vietnamese Navy does not control important policy matters concerning these personnel. Pay, hiring practices, job classifications, etc., involve the Vietnamese Civil Service Commission, Ministry of Labor, and Ministry of Economics, as well as the Ministry of National Defense. The 'civilian' agencies typically do not appreciate the problems peculiar to the navy, and are unsympathetic toward requests for changes which would be of help to the shipyard.

Another important fact is that the shipyard is not new. The plant has been there for 90 years, and as the Vietnamese Naval Shipyard it has functioned since the beginning of the republic. . . .

"In November of 1968 the Vietnamese Naval Shipyard was working against a huge backlog of overhaul work accumulated during the early part of 1968. The backlog was the result of some periods of time in which the shipyard was shut down completely due to Viet Cong activity in the Saigon area. The problem was compounded by the fact that the production department of the shipyard was operating with about 50 percent of the authorized strength. . . .

"The advisory effort in the shipyard was divided into two separate efforts. The shipyard advisor was expending almost all of his efforts (as had his predecessor) in attempting to obtain a pay raise for the shipyard workers, and in alleviating the personnel shortage. The remainder of the advisory team was engaged in basic skill training in the shipyard shops. . . ."[21]

Supply Officer Advisor:

"I feel that my year in Vietnam has contributed little to the war effort. I have not found the Vietnamese receptive to our advice. All they seem to want from us is material goods.

"I have serious doubts as to the merits of the advisory program and it is my belief that it is a waste of the United States Navy's talent."[22]

I read many hundreds of end-of-tour reports in Vietnam, and later here at home while researching this work. In weighing the selections presented above, several things should be kept in mind. First, without exception they were written by U.S. Navy advisors with direct, intimate, and current knowledge of the subjects addressed. Second, most (but not all) of the advisors I have quoted felt that some improvement in the overall performance of the VNN had occurred during their watch. Third, more optimistic end-of-tour reports were written (as a general rule, the more senior the advisor, the more sanguine the report—"complainers" in the field were said to lack an understanding of the "big picture"), but the reports I have selected are, I believe, representative of the true situation as it then existed. Fourth, many advisors, perhaps a majority, expressed a view that the advisory effort in Vietnam, if not actually bankrupt, was at least in dire need of revamping to strengthen the hand of the advisor in his relationship with Vietnamese counterparts.

The situation then, in the fall of 1968, was not one for faint hearts. To carry out the politically necessary task of Vietnamizing the naval war *at the current level of operations*, the Vietnamese Navy would be required to recruit an additional ten thousand men. Minimum training requirements for the buildup were estimated to be: recruit training increased by a factor of four; advanced school capacity tripled; a fourfold increase in offshore training; English language training expanded by almost thirty times.

Better training was the answer seized upon for most, if not all, of the Vietnamese Navy's many shortcomings, and it was in this area that a major part of the effort to prepare the VNN for ACTOV would be expended. It was in the training area also, as will be shown when we return to the ACTOV story, that major cracks in the structure of the turnover program first appeared.

12

Giant Slingshot and Barrier Reef

That the tone and discipline of the service were high, is true; but it must be ascribed to moral and not to physical causes; to that aptitude in the American character for the sea, which has been so constantly manifested from the day the first pinnace sailed along the coast on the trading voyages of the seventeenth century, down to the present moment.

—J. Fenimore Cooper, *Naval History of the United States* (1839)

The "Parrot's Beak" area of Cambodia, which thrusts to within thirty miles of Saigon, had long been a base of logistic support for enemy forces operating in III and IV Corps. The rockets that periodically slammed into the heart of the South Vietnamese capital and the mines that tormented shipping in the Long Tau were carried or floated across the border and delivered into the hands of enemy units which, throughout the war, operated with virtual impunity in the very environs of the city.

The Communist logistic lines of supply ran down two rivers, the Vam Co Tay and the Vam Co Dong, which flow along either side of the Parrot's Beak to a confluence fifteen miles south of Saigon. There the rivers form the Vam Co, which continues in the same south-easterly direction to a second confluence with the Soirap (Nha Be) River, and thence to the South China Sea.

Drawn on a map, the Vam Co River and its two principal tributaries form what appeared to be, in Admiral Zumwalt's eye, a slingshot, and this is what inspired the name given to the third link in the chain of interdiction barriers in the delta. "Giant Slingshot" became the most successful, in terms of contact with the enemy and interdicted enemy supplies, of all the barriers.

On 21 November 1968, First Sea Lord (Rear Admiral House), the three principal task force commanders, and the senior naval advisor met at COMNAVFORV headquarters to make preliminary plans for the operation. The inclusion of the senior naval advisor in this operational planning conference signaled Admiral Zumwalt's determination to involve the Vietnamese Navy in all NAVFORV operations, operations that, under ACTOV, would be inherited by the Vietnamese Navy almost as soon as they were fully established and "on step."

With MACV's concurrence, Giant Slingshot was set in motion on 25 November. It was defined as an operation "separate from and concurrent with Operation Sea Lords," and its objectives were to interdict enemy infiltration from the Parrot's Beak area, establish a South Vietnamese government presence on the rivers, and enforce curfews and restricted zones.[1]

Logistic support for the operation initially was provided by the USS *Askari* (ARL 30) and YRBM 18 moored at Tan An on the Vam Co Tay, and by the USS *Harnett County* (LST 831) at Ben Luc on the Vam Co Dong. Low bridges at these two places prevented the stationing of support ships farther up the rivers. It was thought that PBRs,

TF-117 riverine craft, and Vietnamese Navy RAG boats would deploy from Ben Luc and Tan An on patrols of perhaps three to four days duration in the upper rivers, subsisting on "C" rations, sandwiches, and whatever else they could beg or borrow from small ground units in the area.

The distances involved (fifty to sixty miles as the rivers flowed), the importance of local knowledge, and the perishable nature of current intelligence information, soon made it clear that a better support system was needed, a system that would allow the deployment of units to specific patrol areas for extended periods of time. Out of this requirement grew the concept of the "advance tactical support base" (ATSB).

Built on the river banks and on 30-foot by 90-foot "ammi" pontoon barges that could be towed and moored virtually anywhere on the rivers, the Giant Slingshot ATSBs typically consisted of an acre or less of high ground and three or more barges, on which were placed berthing and messing facilities, storerooms, a magazine, a tactical operations center (TOC), a communications van, a helicopter landing pad, and a machinery room containing generators and other assorted equipment.

ATSBs were established at Tuyen Nhon and Moc Hoa on the Vam Co Tay and at Tra Cu and Hiep Hoa on the Vam Co Dong. The Hiep Hoa ATSB was soon moved to Go Dau Ha, and in July 1969 an additional ATSB was placed at Ben Keo on the Vam Co Dong, near Tay Ninh. The ATSBs were supplied by shuttle boats and helicopters operating from downriver bases.

In late July 1969, I spent some time at the Moc Hoa ATSB to observe patrol operations. My notes from this visit perhaps will give the reader a taste of what life was like for the Brown Water sailor on the Slingshot rivers.

Moc Hoa. The river is narrow and twisting, usually the color of very light coffee, but sometimes a surprising jade green. The base consists of three ammi pontoons moored perpendicular to the south bank. A fuel barge is moored parallel to the river, across the ends of the ammis. The helicopter landing pad is located on the north bank, where the ATSB originally was positioned. Boats shuttle passengers and cargo from one side to the other. There is not much real estate on the south bank, barely enough for a communications van, a new TOC now under construction, and an ammunition bunker. Over the entrance to the last is a hand-lettered sign, "Issue Hours 0900–1400; Emergencies Anytime."

Where the new TOC is going up, bare-chested Seabees drive great spikes into 3″ × 12″ fir joists supported by 12″ × 12″ posts concreted firmly into the ground. The construction is solid; it will not blow down in the wind.

One of the ammis (a so-called "turtle ammi") is given over to berthing the boat crews. It is covered by a long, wooden hut, screened at the top and sand-bagged four feet up the sides and again on the roof. Inside, the racks are stacked three-high and very closely together. Over the flapping screen door on the shore side of the hut someone has tacked another sign: "The Moc Hoa Hilton." A dog-collared monkey, chained, picks fleas at the side of the door and hisses at passing sailors.

The middle ammi houses the galley and the mess hall. The food served there compares quite favorably, I think, to that provided in Saigon's army-managed messes. At meal time several Vietnamese *co* (young women) scrub mess gear in the open air outside the mess hall and collect leftovers and tray scrapings, which they place in little covered pails. The sailors complain they also collect knives and forks, which are in chronic short supply.

At the river end of the mess hall ammi there is a six-man shower and a washstand on which are placed small, plastic basins filled from a single tap. This part of the ammi also serves as the barber shop. A young Vietnamese boy is the resident barber. Cantilevered over the river is one of the base's two heads—a two-holer. The other is on the shore-side of the third or upriver ammi.

On the river end of the third ammi is the radio shack and, pending completion of the shore-side TOC, the tactical operations center. The TOC contains a status board, a large-scale map of the operations area, some communications gear, a desk, a chair, and the inevitable "short-timers" calendar. Next to the TOC and separated from it by a curtain, is the BOQ. It has six racks stacked two-high, with a single bunk for the officer in charge. Three officers normally live here—the river division commander, the naval intelligence liaison officer (NILO), and the operations officer. The first two are lieutenants and the third is a lieutenant (j.g.). The spare racks are used for visiting firemen (like myself) and when someone's relief has reported aboard. There is a wooden table, a few folding chairs, a row of footlockers, a bookcase and a radio.

Shoreward of the BOQ is a steel tower where a continuous watch of the river is maintained. At the ready on the tower are M-60 machine guns, grenades, and flares. The remainder of the third ammi is taken up by machinery and a small workshop.

Rows of concertina surround the small shore area of the base. Outside the wire there is a dirt road leading to Moc Hoa, but the town is off-limits to the Brown Water Navy. A guard is posted at the base's single gate.

A half-dozen PBRs and a few riverine assault craft are moored outboard the ammis and the fuel barge. Additional boats patrol north and south on the Vam Co Tay. The sailors who will go out on the river tonight sleep or lounge in the stifling heat. Some work on their boats. Gunners wipe and grease machine guns with loving care. An engineman sweats over an engine on a PBR. Three or four men engage in quiet, serious conversation, their legs dangling over the swiftly flowing river. A seaman belts 40-mm grenades.

Late in the afternoon, the patrol officers for this night's operations—a chief signalman and a first-class commissaryman—meet in the TOC with the three commissioned officers. Approximate locations for waterborne guardposts (ambushes) are selected partly on the basis of intelligence reports of possible enemy movements, but mostly, I think, on educated guesses. One two-boat guardpost will be positioned where an enemy-initiated firefight took place the night before, on the theory that the Viet Cong will not believe the PBRs will choose the same spot two nights in a row. The patrol officers have authority to move the ambush site if they think it wise.

Reference points are picked out on grid charts, and instructions are given to report the actual position of the boats by "north one klick" (kilometer), "south one-half klick," etc., from a predesignated point. Procedures for requesting helicopter gunship and artillery support are rehearsed. This can be crucial if the boats encounter a superior enemy force. Safety precautions are stressed, questions are asked and answered. I do not know how much of this is for my benefit, but the impression I get is that the briefing is taken very seriously. The boats are, after all, engaged in serious business.

Next, the patrol officers brief their boat captains and crews. At about 1800, engines are started, lines are cast off, and two patrols of two boats each depart the ATSB at Moc Hoa and proceed north on the river.

The PBR I am riding carries the chief signalman patrol officer.

The boat captain is a gunner's mate second class. A third-class engine-man, a gunner's mate striker, and a seaman make up the remainder of the crew. This is, overwhelmingly, a young man's war.

There is no sampan traffic on the river, and a late afternoon peacefulness prevails. Nevertheless, flak jackets are put on, and though no order is given, machine guns are uncovered and trained at the river banks.

Speed is increased and soon the PBR's characteristic whine spreads out over the flatlands of the Plain of Reeds, calling the river people out to the banks as the boats hum past. Children shout and run after the boats from point to point. The younger ones, some half naked, wave solemnly until the boats are out of sight. Adults, mostly women, simply stare. Wash from the boats' wakes slaps the river banks and rocks sampans tied up there.

A few miles up the river from Moc Hoa, the PBRs throttle down and lie to in the middle of the stream, engines turning over just enough to keep the boats headed into the current. Two nights previously, PBRs from Moc Hoa had been fired on from a tree line several hundred yards back from the bank. The boat I am riding on fires a case of 40-mm grenades into the tree line, the chief signalman crank-ing them out on the "Honeywell" grenade launcher. The grenades are fired directly over the heads of water buffalo on the river bank. The buffalo never bat an eyelash. They have heard it all before, many times.

Farther up the river we come to a regional force outpost and nudge alongside the bank for a brief exchange of information with the U.S. Army advisor there. He is a black sergeant, and he lives in the grimmest surroundings imaginable, in a shallow bunker buried perhaps three feet underground. Our patrol officer passes him the coordinates of tonight's waterborne guardposts, and the sergeant jots them down in a notebook before waving goodbye.

The Vam Co Tay north of Moc Hoa runs deep, swift, and nar-row. Clumps of flotsam—tree limbs, brush, and logs—move with the current. Large stretches of the river banks have been cleared or defoli-ated, and when the tide is high, as it is now, one enjoys a sweeping vista over the Plain of Reeds to the Cambodian border and beyond.

At dusk a stern anchor is dropped in midstream, and the bow of our PBR is driven into the river's north bank. The gunner quickly passes a bight of line around a tree stump and makes the two ends fast to forward cleats. Another member of the crew hauls the slack out of the stern anchor line, pulling the boat perpendicular to the bank. As the current takes hold, the line stretches taut, forcing beads of water out of its nylon strands. A hundred yards or so north of us the second boat in our patrol makes a similar moor. The boats are now positioned to stay afloat on a falling tide, without starting their engines. In an emergency, they can back into the stream and clear the area quickly.

Night falls. There is no moon, but continuous artillery illumination lights the border to the north. Time drags. You find yourself straining to catch some movement, some sound, some scent of the enemy you know will kill you if he detects you first. You take your turn on the starlight scope. Viewed in its eerie green glow, everything on the bank seems to move. Bushes become animate.

Intense concentration on the "out there" ebbs with the receding tide. You gradually become aware of things closer to hand, in the boat with you. Mosquitoes. More mosquitoes than you ever dreamed existed. You try to remember to brush, not slap them away. The sound of a slap would carry a long way on a night such as this.

The longest hours are those just after midnight. From somewhere far off you catch the faint wail of Vietnamese music, probably coming from a battery-operated radio in one of the river hamlets. Miles to the south, a Cobra helicopter gunship stabs the earth with twin tongues of red tracer fire. The music stops. You wonder if these two events are related.

Shortly after four in the morning the utter silence of the night is broken when our cover boat lights off its radio transmitter. It is policy for PBRs on guardpost to keep receivers lowered to the point where transmissions are just barely audible, but PBR transmitters are equipped with a blower circuit that is as noisy as an old vacuum cleaner. The voice on the radio is muffled, but the message is sharp and electrifying: "There are people on the bank just off your port bow."

All drowsiness, all awareness of mosquitoes, all secret thoughts of home are snuffed out in an instant. All eyes search the near bank. Nostrils flare and nerves stretch tighter than the stern anchor line had stretched at ebb tide. No one seems to breathe. Moments that seem like ages crawl by, but there is nothing, nothing but a few puffs of wind curling through the nipa palm. Nothing.

An hour passes. The cover boat's transmitter whines to life again. "Guess I was mistaken. Don't see anything there now. Sorry."

The patrol officer swears beneath his breath. Slowly the tension drains away, like snow melting on a roof. Someone passes the last of the coffee.

Even endless nights end. At dawn the guardpost is broken and the two boats head south toward Moc Hoa. Children are up early and wave from the banks. Bone-tired sailors wave back. Another water-borne guardpost on operation Giant Slingshot has ended and there is nothing to report.

As originally conceived, Giant Slingshot was to last only three months. There were two planned phases in the operation. Phase one would consist of a sweep of the river banks by ground forces, with day and night boat patrols established to search and inspect all river traffic. PBRs would be assigned inspection and boarding duties, and TF-117 and VNN RAG units would provide firepower and troop lift as needed. The commander of II Field Force Vietnam (a U.S. Army command) and the Vietnamese IV Corps commander were to furnish ground and air support. Phase two of the operation would make use of a proposed Vietnamese fleet of armed, motorized sampans and supporting troops to interdict the numerous waterways that ran between the Vam Co Tay and the Vam Co Dong.

On 5 December 1968, the main units of the mobile support base arrived at Tan An. Captain (later Rear Admiral) Arthur W. Price, Jr., the Giant Slingshot commander (CTG-194.9), reported that the movement of his force was "a thing of beauty," with all units arriving within minutes of each other.[2] Patrol operations began the next day, and the initial assignment of boats was as follows: Tan An—two MSMs, two ASPBs, three ATCs, eight PBRs; Tuyen Nhon—two ASPBs, one CCB, one monitor, three ATCs, six PBRs; Tra Cu—two ASPBs, one monitor, three ATCs, six PBRs.[3] Additional units arrived within the next few days and soon nineteen patrols were being mounted daily on the two rivers. A shuttle system was put in effect whereby boats were regularly returned to Nha Be for major maintenance.

In the first week of the operation, patrol boats engaged in eight firefights, seven of them on the Vam Co Dong. These actions resulted in one enemy killed at the cost of six friendly casualties and the disabling of three boats. On 12 December, in compliance with a MACV directive to tighten defenses around Saigon, the number of boats committed to Giant Slingshot was increased to eighty-one. (Ever since the Tet Offensive, the U.S. command had been extremely sensitive to signs of increased enemy movement in the vicinity of Saigon, fearing a new all-out assault on the capital.) At the same time, COMNAVFORV issued orders to extend the Vam Co Dong patrol "as far north as feasible."[4] This was in response to intelligence reports that indicated the enemy might be responding to the new interdiction effort by engaging in an "end run" movement in the north. "Duffle Bag" sensors salvaged from the ill-fated "McNamara Line" were placed in the vicinity of suspected enemy crossing sites on the rivers.

The USS *Harnett County* (LST 821), escorted by nineteen PBRs, arrived at Ben Luc early on the morning of 12 December to act as the support ship for the Vam Co Dong operations. It became the head-quarters ship for the Giant Slingshot commander, Captain Price. The river at Ben Luc is not much wider than the *Harnett County* was long, and the surrounding country, despite its nearness to Saigon, was far from secure. It was widely rumored that the enemy had offered a $100,000 reward to anyone who succeeded in sinking a U.S. Navy ship, and at Ben Luc the *Harnett County* was particularly vulnerable. The absence of any dependable bank security force dictated that the ship return each night to a relatively safe anchorage at French Fort, some twenty miles downstream at the confluence of the two Slingshot rivers. This was the routine followed until 27 December, when the ship began overnight stays at Ben Luc.

The threat to the *Harnett County* from enemy mining and sapper attack was constant, and the ship was struck by both rocket and recoilless rifle fire. One round from a 57-mm recoilless rifle went through the ship's wardroom, hit a refrigerator in the galley, and exploded in the captain's cabin. Remarkably, no one was killed in this instance, but a number of the crew were wounded by shrapnel.[5]

On 15 December 1968 the Giant Slingshot support ships and the YRBM 18 were moved on short notice to the downriver anchorage. An Alaska Barge and Transport Company tug was commandeered to tow the YRBM. The hurried move was prompted by intelligence reports that the afloat bases and the bridges at Ben Luc and Tan An had been targeted by a Viet Cong sapper battalion. Six enemy sappers were killed only days later while attempting to mine the Highway 4 bridge at Ben Luc.

The greater distances boats were then required to travel from supporting bases to their patrol areas forced a scaling back of Giant Slingshot operations just as they were becoming most productive. By 21 December, twenty-nine firefights had been experienced on the

Slingshot rivers. In the last week of December, twenty-two more were recorded and the first seven arms caches were uncovered.

Typically, enemy arms and ammunition were sealed in fifty-five-gallon oil drums or similar containers and buried on or near the river banks. Local informants, in exchange for monetary rewards, pointed out the locations of many of the caches found.

To improve the support function and increase the density of patrols, COMNAVFORV sought and received MACV permission to construct a small shore facility for joint USN/VNN use at Ben Luc. NAVFORV and NSA Saigon base development teams went to work immediately on plans for a base just south of the Ben Luc bridge. When completed, it would permit a 50 percent increase in the number of Giant Slingshot patrols on the Vam Co Dong.

If life on the upriver ATSBs was no picnic for the sailors assigned there, neither was it pleasant for the downriver support ships. The *Harnett County*'s 10 officers and 135 enlisted men, for example, shouldered a staggering workload. As Giant Slingshot got under way, message traffic on the ship increased by more than 400 percent. Commissary issues more than doubled, and the ship's galley remained open from 0600 to 0100 daily. Piping and cooling systems were constantly fouled by river mud and silt.

Special security watches required the services of twelve men on a round-the-clock basis. Bank clearance in the vicinity of the ship's anchorage (the crew called it "Operation Chop-Chop") employed an average of fifty-five men, ten hours a day, for thirty days.

The ship's principal duties involved the repair and support of PBRs and riverine assault craft rotating from the upper rivers. Helicopter operations from the ship's flight deck became almost routine, at any hour of the day or night. And no one knew when the next enemy round would slam into the ship's tender hull, or if a suspicious clump of vegetation bobbing near the ship's bow concealed a floating mine. To ward off enemy swimmers, grenades and other small explosives were tossed over the side at random intervals. The noise of their detonation rang through the ship like the sound of large hammers beating on the hull. Through it all, the men worked and slept, nights and days following in dreary succession.

What sustained these men and their brothers scattered along the rivers? One would like to think it was the fervent belief that a tide had turned and a war was being won. Some, inspired by the Zumwalt mystique, certainly fell in that category. In my view, however, most suffered no such illusion and merely did their duty even though they knew their labors were for a failed cause. These, it seems to me, were no less courageous and self-sacrificing.

On 4 January 1969, COMNAVFORV reported that of all the operations initiated since Sea Lords began, Giant Slingshot was hurting the enemy the most.[6] Navy craft had engaged in fifty-eight firefights and uncovered thirteen arms caches as of that date. The effectiveness of boat patrols on the Slingshot rivers was enhanced by ground patrols mounted concurrently by the U.S. Army in the Plain of Reeds. Two weeks later, on 18 January, the number of arms caches found had increased to forty-four, and the weight of recovered munitions totaled approximately 43.5 tons. This was believed to be the equivalent of a full month's supply for enemy forces operating in III Corps.[7] The location of the caches correlated closely with known or suspected enemy infiltration routes.

Late in January, the first use of the sampan patrols envisaged as Phase II of Giant Slingshot occurred when U.S. sailors used sampans and metal detectors to probe shallow canals along the Vam Co Tay. Two caches were discovered in the early hours of this operation, demonstrating its usefulness. It remained difficult, however, to persuade the Vietnamese Navy to follow up this initial success.

On 1 February, Giant Slingshot statistics showed a cumulative total of 55 arms caches weighing 47.4 tons, and 103 firefights resulting in 259 enemy killed at the cost of 10 friendly KIA and 82 WIA.[8] Other positive effects of the operation were noted. Commerce had increased on the rivers, and people began to resettle long-abandoned homes. Troops in GVN outposts were observed to venture more often outside the wire of their fortified positions.

As Giant Slingshot statistics were collected and studied, patterns in enemy activity began to appear. The Communists apparently attached the greatest importance to maintaining lines of communication that ran along and across the Vam Co Dong, the most direct approach to Saigon from Cambodia. As of the middle of February, the number of firefights experienced on the Vam Co Dong was nearly three times that which had occurred on the Vam Co Tay. It seemed likely that the area between Tra Cu and Go Dau Ha contained the principal enemy through-routes, and that the northern and southern ends of the Slingshot rivers were used primarily as storage and transshipment points. As the operation progressed, a gradual falloff in the number of caches found was experienced. This was interpreted as evidence that the enemy was hiding his munitions farther away from the river banks and that naval patrols, by making it increasingly difficult for the enemy to cross the rivers, were forcing the Communists to funnel their supplies overland toward the confluence of the rivers, the "crotch" of the slingshot. If adequate numbers of troops were concentrated in this area, it seemed clear that a significant enemy LOC would be severed and Saigon's security would be enhanced. This proved to be a very large "if," however.

Naval patrols on the rivers were supported whenever possible by U.S. Army troops and air reconnaissance. A line of destructor mines was sown by the army along the border, and the navy manned a Duffle Bag sensor barrier between the border and the Vam Co Dong. The combined deterrent effect of the above was heavy, but the enemy's known investment in staging areas and infiltration routes within the Parrot's Beak, and his obvious strategic interest in maintaining established LOCs close to Saigon, made it unlikely that he would shift a major portion of his infiltration effort elsewhere. Should he do so, this would be reflected immediately in increased pressure on one or more of the other naval barriers.

In February 1969, a Vietnamese Navy river assault and interdiction division (RAID) was assigned to Giant Slingshot. The RAID's thirteen ATCs, eight ASPBs, three monitors, and one CCB almost doubled the number of armored riverine craft on the rivers and permitted the gradual relief of TF-117 units.

The busiest stretch of river during February and March was that part patrolled by River Division 532, based at Tra Cu. The river division commander was Lieutenant George Stevencavage, and prior to reporting to Slingshot he had pioneered tactics in operations along the Ham Luong and My Tho rivers, tactics which were adopted as standard operating procedures by TF-116. He personally led many PBR patrols in dangerous incursions of canals and narrow waterways, and in the early months of his command RIVDIV 532 was credited with more than fifty enemy KIA, the rallying of thirty-seven "chieu hois" (Viet Cong defectors), and the capture of large quantities of enemy weapons and supplies.

On 8 February, Stevencavage's river division was assigned to the ATSB at Tra Cu. Before standing down on 4 April, RIVDIV 532 and the river assault craft it operated with accounted for more than one hundred enemy killed. Four PBR sailors died, and almost half of the assigned navy personnel, including Stevencavage himself, were wounded. Two PBRs were lost.

A firefight early on the morning of 28 February illustrates the daring nature of Slingshot operations in this period.

Stevencavage, in command of two PBRs, had joined several river assault craft on a troop insertion and sweep operation along the northern Vam Co Dong in an area of known enemy activity. The PBRs were deployed as a blocking force downstream of the troop insertion and beached in a relatively open area to observe possible enemy movement in advance of the sweep.

Not long after the beaching, nine "moving bushes" were seen on the near bank and were soon determined to be armed enemy soldiers. The PBRs took them under fire killing six. Moments later, Stevencavage's boats were raked by automatic weapons fire from concealed enemy positions farther up the river. The PBRs backed into the stream and roared to the attack, engaging the enemy at near point-blank range.

Though wounded in the head, hand, and thigh, Stevencavage remained on deck, in command, until the last enemy guns were silenced. For this action, he was awarded the Silver Star.

In March, intelligence reports were received that indicated the enemy's intent to attack the Slingshot ATSBs. A concerted effort was made to clear the perimeters of the bases by chemically defoliating, burning, bulldozing, and manually cutting brush and nipa palm. The first "douche" boat, an ATC equipped with a high-velocity jet pump, was deployed on Slingshot operations. It proved effective in washing away mud bunkers dug into the river banks, but was only of marginal use in clearing vegetation.

Also in March, captured documents confirmed how difficult Giant Slingshot was making it for the enemy to maintain logistic lines of supply. One document taken from a dead enemy soldier stated that for nine consecutive nights naval patrols had prevented his transportation company from crossing the Vam Co Dong.[9]

The discovery of large arms caches in the vicinity of the Bo Bo Canal, which roughly split the area between the Slingshot rivers, gave added credence to COMNAVFORV's earlier speculation about the funneling effect naval patrols were having on enemy logistics. The uncovering elsewhere of old and apparently abandoned caches was thought to be evidence of the heavy losses the patrols were inflicting on enemy personnel. It seemed likely that knowledge of the location of such caches had simply died with the individuals responsible for concealing them.

The rousing success of Giant Slingshot persuaded Admiral Zumwalt to continue it indefinitely, rather than ending it after three months as originally planned. Better support facilities were ordered for Tuyen Nhon, Go Dau Ha, Tra Cu, and Moc Hoa. ATSB improvement was assigned the highest priority for naval construction in Vietnam.[10]

Tactics were developed and refined. Selected PBR sailors were given sniper training by the U.S. Army. A system was devised to provide for almost instantaneous artillery response to Duffle Bag sensor activations, leading to "confirmed" enemy kills.[11] (Needless to say, in free-fire zones anyone who wandered into the way of an artillery round or a bomb was counted as an enemy.) Cooperation and coordination with air and ground forces continually improved.

In late March, a contingency plan (Operation "Double Shift") was drawn that provided for the rapid augmentation of naval forces operating on the Vam Co Dong. The plan called for an additional seventy PBRs, twenty PCFs, six monitors, ten ASPBs, thirty ATCs, four CCBs, and two refuelers to support high-density patrols and blocking forces along the river.[12]

Double Shift was not implemented until 9 July, but an enemy document captured on 2 April indicated that the enemy thought this heavy reinforcement had occurred much earlier:

"To protect the Saigon capital, the enemy has increased its activities and set up ambushes on lines of communications, especially on the Vam Co Dong and Vam Co Tay rivers, in an attempt to cut off our communications with [Saigon]. . . . This enemy scheme resulted in heavy losses inflicted on our forces. Therefore, to frustrate the above strategy, troop movement regulations should be observed even in liberated areas. Advance ground elements should be sent to clear routes, and defenses should be set up around the position at every stop."[13]

Not all captured documents were that flattering to Giant Slingshot operations, however. A document captured by U.S. Special Forces on 16 April reported disparagingly on naval patrol activity on the Vam Co Tay near Tuyen Nhon. It said night patrols were almost nonexistent, that boats moved only at full speed and under helicopter escort, and that weapons were fired aimlessly.[14] Admiral Zumwalt directed commanders to give the captured document wide dissemination and requested that "all task units be advised that originator [COMNAVFORV] desires they reveal their presence throughout their respective AO [area of operations] daily. Impress upon Charlie that we are there to stay."[15]

In June, reports were received that Slingshot forces were being targeted by NVA and Viet Cong main force units.[16] Competition was stimulated among enemy units, and efforts were made to recruit children to place explosive devices in the way of patrols, with rewards promised for successful missions.[17] Though losses were sustained, the naval barrier patrols remained in place and were strengthened. Late in June, the newly formed VNN RAID 73 reinforced patrols on the Vam Co Tay, with eleven of its boats assigned at Moc Hoa and seven at Tuyen Nhon.

The threat of enemy attacks on Tay Ninh led to the establishment of an ATSB at Ben Keo on the upper Vam Co Dong. River Division 531 arrived there on 14 June and three days later was involved in heavy action. The commanding general of II Field Force Vietnam, Lieutenant General Julian J. Ewell, sent the following congratulatory message:

"On 17 June at 2220 hours your River Division 531 engaged enemy forces south of Tay Ninh resulting in 50 enemy KIA. Please extend my hearty congratulations and a well done to all hands who participated in this most successful action. I suspect that this contact plus their other ones made an important contribution to the defense of Tay Ninh. This fine example of coordinated action between U.S. naval forces, the Vietnamese forces, and elements of the 25th Infantry Division reflects the highest standards of professionalism and demonstrates the continued effectiveness of riverine operations."[18]

(Ewell, incidentally, was a former commander of the Ninth Infantry Division whose troops had comprised the ground elements of the Mobile Riverine Force. Captain Robert S. Salzer, the former commander of the naval part of the MRF, knew Ewell well and described him as "a good combat man with one weakness: he was mad for body count, absolutely fanatic about it."[19] Salzer recollected that once Ewell had ordered his men to dig up a grave yard. "It was ghoulish," he said, but "that was the kind of degenerate statistical spectre we had foisted upon us.")[20]

The commander of RIVDIV 531 was Lieutenant Commander Thomas K. Anderson. Early on the morning of 28 June, the ATSB at Ben Keo came under heavy rocket, rocket-propelled grenade, mortar, and automatic weapons fire. A bunkered tactical operations center had not yet been built, and Anderson directed counter-battery fire and the defensive deployment of his PBRs and assigned riverine assault craft from an exposed position on a CCB. The enemy attack was beaten off, and Anderson was awarded a Silver Star.

In July the enemy threat against Tay Ninh intensified, and on 9 July Operation Double Shift was put in motion. With little advance notice, naval units relocated as far as two hundred miles in less than twenty-four hours. This concentration of Brown Water Navy assets in the upper Vam Co Dong and the work performed there was the subject of yet another laudatory message from II Field Force Vietnam:

"On 9 July Operation Double Shift was implemented in response to the Tay Ninh situation, resulting in the addition of 40 PBRs and 58 river assault craft in that area. During the period these craft were deployed, naval forces in the Tay Ninh area were involved in 78 contacts with eight enemy KIA confirmed.

"The rapid response and professional effort displayed by naval forces reflected most creditably upon your command and played an important role in preempting the enemy plan to attack Tay Ninh City.

"A hearty well done to all hands for their highly professional and effective performance. John Paul Jones is proud of you all."[21]

After about the middle of July, contact with the enemy in the upper Vam Co Dong dropped off sharply, and it became evident that the major enemy force had withdrawn to the Cambodian sanctuary. On 23 July, therefore, Operation Double Shift stood down and naval units returned to their normal operating areas.

In the meantime, on 7 July, the Giant Slingshot base at Ben Luc had been commissioned. Built on spoil dredged from the river, it was established as a joint USN/VNN base. With the movement of most command-and-support functions ashore, the saga of the *Harnett County* at Ben Luc came to a close. She had stayed on through most of the construction period, providing support and security for the dredging operation in addition to fulfilling her other heavy duties.

At Tan An on the Vam Co Tay, Mobile Base Two had arrived to support Slingshot operations. A four-ammi complex specially constructed in the United States, it had features previously all but unknown on the rivers—an air-conditioned mess hall, spacious and comfortable berthing compartments, a ship's laundry, ample supplies of fresh water, and well-equipped repair shops. It could perform almost all repair and overhaul work on the PBRs and riverine craft it supported.

It became routine for the upriver ATSBs to rotate boats to Mobile Base Two for necessary repairs and revitalization of crews. When local security conditions permitted, sailors were given a few hours of liberty in Tan An. It was one of the few places in the delta where the Brown Water Navy could "hit the beach" and find respite, however brief, from the rigors of war.

* * *

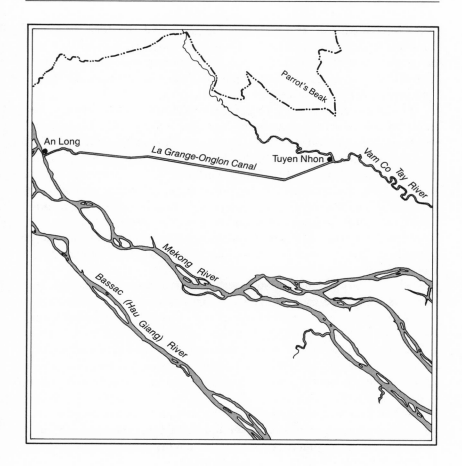

Barrier Reef

The fourth and last of the delta interdiction barriers conceived by COMNAVFORV was designed to close the gap between Giant Slingshot in the east and the two-tiered barriers in the west, Search Turn and Foul Deck. "Stop Gap" was, appropriately, the code name first chosen for this operation, but it already was assigned elsewhere and "Barrier Reef" was selected in its place.

With Barrier Reef, an unbroken chain of naval patrols was established along the Cambodian border from the Gulf of Thailand to an area northeast of the Parrot's Beak. The strategic value of closing the ring, so to speak, was obvious from the very beginning of Sea Lords, but assets were not at first available to patrol the final fifty-mile connecting link. Eventually they were provided by a further draw-down of Game Warden forces and by utilizing some units previously assigned to Giant Slingshot for patrol of the upper Vam Co Tay, a relatively quiet part of the river.

On 28 December 1968, therefore, COMNAVFORV directed that naval patrols be established on the La Grange–Ong Lon Canal, which ran from An Long on the Mekong River to Tuyen Nhon on the Vam Co Tay. The new barrier was divided into two patrol areas, Barrier Reef East and Barrier Reef West, with the intersecting Cong Hoa Canal as the dividing line. Barrier Reef East would be patrolled by boats based at Tuyen Nhon. Barrier Reef West would be the responsibility of a PBR division supported by the USS *Jennings County* (LST 846) at An Long. The senior advisor to IV Corps was asked to provide a Special Forces ready reaction platoon to support the operation.[22]

The decision to go forward with a fourth naval interdiction barrier was supported by intelligence information that indicated enemy infiltration was occurring on a large scale from the "Elephant's Ear" area in Cambodia west to the vicinity of the Cai Cai Canal. Enemy LOCs were known to cross the Barrier Reef patrol line and to continue south to Sa Dec and Vinh Long provinces. There was every good reason to believe that Barrier Reef would impede this enemy traffic.

Patrols began on 2 January 1969, and patterns observed on the earlier barriers were repeated on Barrier Reef. There was a brief period of relative inactivity while the enemy waited to see if the patrols were designed to be permanent or only transitory. This was followed by an increasing number of intelligence reports concerning planned attacks on patrol boats and, finally, the attacks themselves. The first ambush of a patrol occurred in the Barrier Reef East area on 7 January, and it included what was believed to be an attempted mining. The second week of operations was quiet, but in the third week five firefights and two mining incidents were recorded.

The employment of mines in the canal confirmed other intelligence reports, and minesweeping operations were ordered to counter the threat. MSBs were assigned for the first time on the interdiction barriers, and special chain bottom drags were designed for towing by PBRs and Boston Whalers.

An early action on Barrier Reef illustrated one of Admiral Zumwalt's favorite concepts—"synergism." Interrogation of a prisoner and analysis of combat action reports provided the following story:

In early December 1968, the Viet Cong 528th Heavy Weapons Company was organized in Cambodia and equipped with a new 12-tube 107-mm rocket launcher of Chinese manufacture. All men in the company had heavy-weapons experience, and they were led by an NVA officer. On 10 January 1969, the 528th, escorted by a Viet Cong battalion, about 250–300 strong, crossed the border into South Vietnam and, following well-established infiltration routes, approached Barrier Reef. The Communists had received intelligence reports of their own that the Ong Lon (Grand Canal) was patrolled by four PBRs, and that while two of these normally remained under way, the other two frequently took up guardpost positions. Elements of the escorting battalion moved ahead to establish their own ambush of the PBRs in order to assist in the crossing of the canal. Unfortunately for the Viet Cong, however, friendly intelligence was received giving the location of their planned ambush, and this resulted in the ambushers becoming themselves the ambushed, as a Popular Force platoon was inserted on the night of 11 January in advance of the Viet Cong.

The PF platoon, supported by six PBRs, engaged the VC ambush team, and the action led to the withdrawal of the entire enemy force to the north. Further attempts to cross the canal were made on 12 January and were again thwarted by the patrols. On 13 January, however, the Viet Cong escort battalion, now separated from the 528th Heavy Weapons Company, crossed the canal undetected. The 528th was not so fortunate, and after a firefight with the PBRs and supporting PF troops it was again forced to withdraw to the north, this time with its escorts and guides on the *other* side of the canal. On 14 January the 528th was sighted by a U.S. reconnaissance plane in a small canal just north of the Ong Lon. Delta Blackhawk gunships were called in, and in the ensuing action forty-six of the enemy were killed, sixteen prisoners were taken, and the prize 12-tube launcher and forty-five rockets captured.

COMUSMACV, perhaps cued by Admiral Zumwalt, commented:

"Though this so-called showdown on the Grand Canal was not a pre-planned exercise of integrating elements for the purpose of destroying an enemy unit or capturing a weapons system, it is an excellent example of how the sum of the results of separate agencies working together can be more effective than the sum of the results of these agencies operating independently."[23]

The enemy resorted to a variety of desperate measures designed to force the abandonment of Barrier Reef patrols. New ambush tactics were employed, and surprise attacks were launched on patrol boats from relatively open areas along the canal. Interconnecting spider holes and trenches were dug, and in areas where tall grasses grew, cleverly concealed tunnels in the grass, almost impossible to detect, were used to direct troops to and from the ambush site. One particularly clever countermeasure employed against the PBRs involved the spreading of large quantities of straw on the water in order to clog the boats' jet propulsion pumps. At times this disabled boats for ten minutes or more while pumps and strainers were cleared.[24]

With Barrier Reef, the northern ring of naval interdiction barriers in III and IV Corps was complete. In essence, the Market Time coastal patrol had been moved inland and the long-ignored recommendation of the Bucklew report concerning interdiction patrols along Vietnam's inland borders was, at least in part, addressed. (Enemy supplies continued to pour in, of course, by way of the Ho Chi Minh Trail across the largely open border with Laos.)

How effective the overall Sea Lords interdiction strategy would prove to be in the months that lay ahead would be directly proportional to the skill and courage of the Brown Water sailor manning the boats, the quantity and quality of ground and air forces mustered in his support, and to a steadily increasing degree, the ability and willingness of the Vietnamese Navy to continue the dangerous and often thankless work along the barriers as the process of Vietnamization of the naval war moved into high gear.

13

Saigon, Reductio ad Absurdum

USO Programs: *Looking for something to do this week? Stop by the Tan Son Nhut USO (next door to the Massachusetts BOQ) and catch one of the many shows highlighted there. From 1300 to 1830 hours, 24 November 1969, the Ramblers, the Jugglers, the Moon Steppers, and the High Light Show will be auditioning. Tuesday at 1300 hours a 12-piece band, the Babilone Show, will be featured, and at 1930 hours that evening, the Jewish Discussion Group will meet on the second floor balcony. Wednesday, at 1800 hours, a country & western band, the Nashville Cats, will be on board for your entertainment. On Thursday you'll be able to watch an all-Australian show, the Gold Coasters, perform while you enjoy the delicious Thanksgiving buffet dinner starting at 1130 hours and served free to all American military personnel. At 1400 hours, for the real men, a pie-eating contest! It's not only free but guaranteed to satisfy.*

Holiday Observance: *Due to requirements of military operations, the provisions of MACV Directive 630-1, setting forth 27 November 1969, Thanksgiving Day, as a legal holiday are suspended. The normal workday routine will be followed on that day. U.S. civilian personnel required to work will be compensated in accordance with applicable regulations.*

—U.S. Military Command Vietnam *Daily Bulletin,*
24 November 1969

B y the time I arrived in Vietnam in the summer of 1969, the war had assumed a surrealistic character all its own. Nowhere was this more evident than in Saigon, the headquarters of Naval Forces Vietnam and its parent, the Military Assistance Command.

In "Pentagon East," MACV staffers whose duties rarely if ever took them outside the compound, strode air-conditioned halls in heavy combat boots, jungle-green trousers neatly bloused below the knee. It was the prescribed uniform for all who worked there. At NAVFORV, on the other hand, the uniform was more optional— work khaki for officers and chiefs, undress whites or dungarees for enlisted. Combat greens could be worn anytime, of course, but ordinarily were put on only when going into the field or on the rivers.

Just as in the bigger Pentagon back home, some of the work done at MACV Headquarters—and it went on 10 hours a day, 7 days a week, 365 days a year—was of a "busy" nature and often seemed of questionable value, even to those who were producing it. Many of the plans, directives, administrative procedures, and orders that poured forth from the command were nonsensical then, and both sad and funny today.

I once went to visit a navy commander friend at Pentagon East. We had commanded MSOs in the same division a few years previously, and I knew him as a bright, ambitious "hard-charger." Shortly after reporting for duty on Admiral Zumwalt's staff, he wangled a transfer to a MACV plans job (he didn't think his NAVFORV assignment was sufficiently career-enhancing). My friend worked in a large, windowless room at MACV with, I believe, nine other officers— army, air force, and marine colonels and lieutenant colonels. Tacked on the wall over each of their desks was a large printed number on a piece of cardboard—"1," "7," "4," "8," etc.

"What do those numbers mean?" I asked.

I should have guessed. They indicated the order in which the officers in that room would "DEROS"—complete their Vietnam duty and return to the United States. DEROS was bureaucratic shorthand for "date eligible for return from overseas." Everyone who served in Vietnam kept a short-timer's calendar of one sort or another; no one believed the war possibly could end on his watch.

The plans the officers in that big room were working on, had been working on for weeks, concerned the handling of potentially large numbers of Viet Cong and NVA troops who would have to be cared for as prisoners of war when, and if, Communist forces in

South Vietnam surrendered. I could see how it might have been a bit difficult, in 1969, to tackle such an assignment with gusto.

Currency control was an objective pursued with a fanaticism that belied its essential futility in an economy as warped as Vietnam's. Initiated no doubt by bean-counting economists attached to the U.S. Mission, MACV Directive 37-6, a twenty-nine-page, single-spaced, eight-section, forty-five-subsection instruction, with three supporting annexes, set forth "the procedures and responsibilities governing certain financial transactions and the use of U.S. currency, dollar instruments, Military Payment Certificates (MPC), and foreign currencies in the Republic of Vietnam (RVN)." As stated in the directive, the policy of the command was "to conduct all financial affairs in such a manner as to reflect credit upon the U.S. Armed Forces and to avoid unfavorable publicity and international ill will resulting from financial acts in the Republic of Vietnam prejudicial to the dignity and prestige of the United States." As this policy was implemented, however, preserving "the dignity and prestige of the United States" led to such things as random strip searches of American servicemen (including officers) returning to Vietnam from R & R. The search was not for drugs—smuggling drugs into Vietnam would have been carrying coals to Newcastle—but for dollars. Dollars and dollar instruments (Treasury checks, money orders, bank drafts, travelers checks, etc.) "illegally" held or acquired in Vietnam were treated as contraband.

When I first arrived in Vietnam and stepped off the plane at Tan Son Nhut, I and all others on the flight were herded into a large, hot room in the terminal. In due course, our baggage was brought in by forklift and dumped, unceremoniously, in a huge pile in the middle of the room. As soon as we retrieved it, sweating and cursing in the sweltering heat, we were marshaled to a pay window and ordered to exchange all of our money for MPC or Vietnamese piasters. That was the very first greeting most servicemen reporting for duty in Vietnam had from MACV. No smiles, no "Nice to have you aboard to join us in the fight against Godless communism," not even any signs to direct you where to go if you were reporting to this command or that for duty. Just "Hand over all your money." It was, I suppose, a question of priorities.

On the streets of Saigon, special agents of the military police solicited dollar exchanges, practicing something that clearly smacked of entrapment.

Because the official dollar/piaster exchange rate (118 piasters to the dollar in 1969–70) was so unfavorable for Americans compared to the unofficial or market rate (400 or more to the dollar), service-men who complied with the directive and bought piasters from MACV were, in effect, paying a heavy tax to the South Vietnamese government on everything purchased on the local economy. This might have been tolerable if that government were perceived as being reasonably honest and efficient, but it clearly was not, and the invol-untary subsidies extracted from Americans in Vietnam were paid only with bitterness.

The effort to oversee and control all personal financial transac-tions led to inanities such as the detailing of field grade officers (0-4 and above) to act as "jackpot control officers" in BOQs and clubs with slot machines (and they were everywhere). The JCO was respon-sible for seeing that payoffs were in properly accounted for MPC, and that all applicable reports were filed. It would have been far better, I think, had the machines simply been removed. It certainly would have been better for those who, out of sheer boredom, became ad-dicted to playing them night after night after night.

The policy of MACV concerning marriage (Directive 608-1) was that the command would be "the final approving authority on all marriage applications processed in RVN when the proposed marriage is to a U.S. or non-U.S. citizen residing in Vietnam, or a citizen or resident of Australia." Members of the command were warned "not to enter into a marriage with a U.S. citizen outside of the fifty states and territories of the United States or with a non-U.S. citizen anywhere without first . . . receiving the written consent of COMUSMACV." The directive was written in such lawyerly language as to defy inter-pretation by the rank and file, and the administrative roadblocks it threw in the way of those seeking to marry were daunting. No fewer than sixteen forms and affidavits, including a background investiga-tion of the intended spouse, were required. Some were to be submit-ted in triplicate, the copies notarized. If the original were in Viet-namese or some other foreign language, it had to be accompanied by an "official" translation.

Applicants were ordered to undergo counseling by legal assis-tance officers and "appropriate" chaplains. It was required that they be advised specifically of "social problems concerning interracial marriage."

Nor was this all. They were told that "an individual will not be retained in Vietnam beyond his prescribed rotation because of prob-lems involving emigration or immigration of a spouse, nor will any tour of duty be extended when an approval for marriage has been requested."

Did the command have a responsibility to counsel its young men about the pitfalls of hastily contracted wartime marriages? Of course it did. In carrying out this responsibility, however, it far exceeded the bounds of common sense and human decency, and it trampled on the civil rights of Americans serving their country in Vietnam.

I was long and happily married when I went to Vietnam. I learned about the marriage directive when one of the enlisted men in our office sought permission to marry a young lady he had met while serving a tour of duty in the Philippines.

Not only love and marriage, but man's best friend fell afoul of the army in Vietnam. In the MACV *Daily Bulletin* on 14 October 1969 there appeared this rare (rare because it was short and to the point) directive:

"Effective immediately, all dogs will be removed from the MACV Compound and Trailer Park. Military police have been instructed to impound all dogs found in the area. Dogs are considered a definite health hazard and a nuisance."

One is tempted to wonder who stepped in what.

The Phu Tho motor pool in Saigon was, in a word, unforgettable. This was where NAVFORV staff vehicles were fueled and serviced. It was located some two miles west of headquarters, near a large open-air fish market. If you missed a turn, you literally could smell your way back, and that perhaps had something to do with the bad temper of the people who worked there.

After fighting your way through Saigon to reach Phu Tho's gas pumps, you encountered a stone-faced Vietnamese woman whose only duty was to turn off the pumps once thirty liters (about half a tankful) had been delivered. This rationing was not because of any shortage of gasoline in Saigon, but because the military police were said to have caught American and Vietnamese drivers selling gasoline from government vehicles. (If one is guilty, all are guilty.) Apparently, the army believed that a half-full tank was less subject to pilferage than a full one, and what did it matter that this strange policy required twice as many trips to Phu Tho through Saigon's murderous traffic?

Well, it wasn't all bad. Twice as many trips for gas meant you could make twice as many passes through Phu Tho's "automatic car wash." This consisted of one leaky garden hose and a dozen or so Vietnamese women armed with rags and buckets.

It was when you took a vehicle to the motor pool for routine service (oil change, grease job, etc.) that truly memorable things occurred. The staff section I worked with at NAVFORV (Navy History) had received, shortly after I reported aboard, a brand-new GM Scout, which was used for transport to and from the BOQs and BEQs, and for periodic trips as far away as Vung Tau on the coast and Dong Tam on the Mekong River. When the time came for its first oil change, the Scout was driven to Phu Tho and left there overnight. When we went out to pick it up the next day, the spare tire, jack, lug wrench, and horn button were missing.

I stormed into the office and confronted the sergeant in charge. "What the hell is going on here?" I demanded to know.

He broke out the book and proved to my satisfaction (and utter dismay) that a MACV directive required the removal of spare tires, jacks, and wrenches from vehicles such as ours "because they might get stolen." If we had a flat we were supposed to call Phu Tho for road service.

"From 'Ambush Alley'?" I asked.

The sergeant shrugged. "Orders is orders," he said.

Our horn button had been ripped out as part of a "maintenance" procedure ordered by the army because wiring in the steering columns of vehicles were said to "rot and short out" in Vietnam's hot and humid climate. Now, driving without a horn in Saigon traffic was almost as hazardous as driving without brakes. Eventually the horn button was replaced with a small switch mounted on the dash. It made a nice conversation piece.

Overheating of vehicles was a concern of MACV, and in the *Daily Bulletin* of 24 November 1969 there was a directive instructing drivers to "refrain from operating vehicles in high gear while in the Saigon area." (I am not making this up!)

If you lived in a BOQ in Saigon, you shared a small, spartanly furnished room with one or more fellow officers, depending upon your rank and seniority. If you were lucky, the room had a window air conditioner. As a navy commander, I was assigned a room, not air-conditioned, on the third floor of the "Splendid" BOQ. The room overlooked the street, and I could set my watch by the sudden roar of Honda motorbike traffic in the wee hours each morning when the curfew lifted.

For me, one of the great unsolved mysteries of the Vietnam War is where all these Hondas came from, and where the two, three, four, and sometimes five people riding on them were going at 4:30 in the morning. I read somewhere that an economist at the U.S. Mission dreamed up the idea of importing Hondas as a means of draining off excess piasters that were piling up in the hands of Vietnamese consumers who had not enough other things to consume. Whatever, the Honda import scheme succeeded beyond anyone's wildest imagination. By 1969, the streets of Saigon ran full of them, curb to curb, and the broad, French sidewalks of the city were given over to parking them. In some parts of town you had to walk sideways to squeeze through.

The Vietnamese police (Americans called them "white mice") spent much of their time unsnarling Honda traffic jams and investigating Honda accidents. In the evening, Vietnamese "cowboys" cruised the streets on Hondas, just as American teenagers, in my time, cruised in old Chevys.

Honda exhaust hung over the city like a pall, and killed long avenues of flowering trees that once helped make Saigon the "Paris" of East Asia.

But back to the Splendid. There were no drapes or blinds on the windows, and Vietnamese families in the apartment house across the street (we soon had a nodding acquaintance) could look directly into my room. So, presumably, could any transient Viet Cong, if they were interested.

My sometime roommate was a marine major who spent most of his time in the field, doing things he didn't like to talk about. He came "home" to Saigon about once a month, staying only long enough to dry out his boots, get blissfully drunk, and laid—not necessarily in that order. The second six months of my residence at the Splendid I "fleeted up" to an inside room that was air-conditioned. My roommate then was an army major who read the Bible a lot. He had a small refrigerator that he kept stocked with soda. He was a nice man, and I wish I could remember his name.

Each BOQ room was assigned a Vietnamese maid who did your laundry, made your bed, and kept the room reasonably clean—as clean as appallingly unsanitary conditions permitted. She scrubbed your uniforms by hand, attacking them with a brush on the shower stall floor. Starched and pressed (and always damp), the uniforms were laid out for you, along with rolled socks and folded underwear. The maid polished your shoes and boots, and made sure you always had a bottle of water for brushing your teeth. Saigon tap water was, and is, badly polluted.

You paid your maid in Vietnamese piasters or "dong," and you kept her supplied with soap, shoe polish, and bleach from the post exchange. These things and her salary were fixed in a contract negotiated by MACV with the maid's union. From time to time the union went on strike for more money. After one strike, the salary agreement was said to exceed what was then earned by an ARVN colonel, though I doubted that. It more likely was on a par with the pay of a VNN lieutenant—somewhere between dire poverty and starvation.

Strategically located BOQs had army field ration messes, and the Splendid was one of these. You could get three square meals a day there, and you paid for them individually in MPC. In the interest of decorum, and perhaps the safety of the cooks, personal weapons were checked at the desk before entering the dining room. The food was served and the tables cleared by Vietnamese waitresses who wore singularly unattractive, army-prescribed uniforms—short, black skirts, white blouses, bobby socks, and sneakers. Rats were not uncommon visitors in the dining room and elsewhere in the Splendid.

Every BOQ had a bar, open several hours over lunch (we called it "drunch") and every evening. Rolling dice for drinks (the old navy game of "horses") was a favorite pastime. The bar at the Splendid was dingy and depressing, and most of the fun-loving people adjourned to bars at the nearby "Rex" and "Brink" BOQs. These sometimes had live entertainment—rock bands mostly, and occasional Philippine strippers. Pretty sorry stuff, actually.

If you wished to escape all that, you could always find good music (recorded) and warm, quiet companionship (as much companionship as you wished or could afford) at the Embassy Hotel's roof-top bar, two blocks west of the Splendid. There you could drink under the stars in the cool night air and enjoy a truly remarkable light and sound show. Parachute flares continually illuminated the city's perimeter. Every couple of hours a "firefly" aircraft passed overhead, its strobe light blinking brilliantly. From far off, to the north and west, you could hear the rumble of bombs (B-52 "Arc Light" missions, probably) and the boom of heavy artillery.

For the price of a drink, a "Saigon tea," you could converse at your table with a beautiful, polite, nice-smelling Vietnamese girl. I don't know if this was fitting for an officer and a gentleman, but it beat the hell out of sitting next to some drunken colonel at the BOQ.

Some of my most pleasant memories of Saigon are of hours spent on that roof.

Another oasis was the International House on Nguyen Hue Street. It was a private club for diplomats, senior civilians, and military officers serving in Vietnam. It was always crowded, and there was a long waiting list for membership, but I had friends who were members and they got me in. I became a member just a few weeks before MACV abruptly ordered the club closed, supposedly because of currency control violations. The "I House" had one of the last really first-class dining rooms in the city, a piano bar, and an entertainer with a voice like an angel who sang sad songs about broken hearts and unrequited love.

Nguyen Hue (the "Street of Flowers"—so named because at Tet the city's biggest flower market is established there) was also the heart of Saigon's black market. You literally could buy anything there—cigarettes, liquor, clothing, electronic equipment, canned goods, etc.—anything, in fact, that was sold in the MACV post exchanges and commissaries, and some things that were not, including weapons and ammunition. The black market was also where they sold Vietnam campaign jackets—the ones cut out of army ponchos or jungle greens, embroidered with dragons and eagles and mottoes such as "When I die, I'm going to heaven, because I've spent my time in hell," or sometimes something simpler and from the heart, like "Fuck the Army." You saw that everywhere in Vietnam; it was to the war in Vietnam what "Kilroy was here" was to World War II.

Once, in the head at an officers club in Tan Son Nhut, I saw penciled on the wall next to a large "FTA" the following: "For God's sake, don't do it! It might multiply!"

Anytime the exchanges were sold out of something—and this could be sundries such as soap, toothpaste, envelopes, socks, etc.—you could be sure to find it on the black market, and sometimes at a better price. This is not as strange as it seems, because much of what was sold there was stolen from the army in the first place, sometimes on the docks, sometimes during transit from the docks, and sometimes from army warehouses with the connivance of dishonest exchange employees.

Could the Saigon black market have been shut down? It not only could have been, but frequently was—for a day or two at a time. The VIP hotel was next door to the Splendid, and you could tell when important people were in town by the sirens and flashing lights and jeeps with mounted machine guns that accompanied the visitors' movements to and from the hotel. You could tell, too, by the way Nguyen Hue was swept clean of its sidewalk vendors and its post exchange merchandise. Apparently, it wouldn't do to have this seen by an influential congressman or a deputy assistant secretary of defense.

In fairness, the army did everything it could, short of collaring corrupt Vietnamese officials and politicians, to restrain those who looted the post exchange and commissary systems. The military commissaries were in fact declared off limits to military personnel; they could be patronized only by authorized civilians. A complex rationing system (MACV Directive 60-7) was put in effect, limiting both the purchase and possession of items sold in the exchanges. Paragraph 6.e.(8) of the directive, for example, prohibited "the unauthorized possession of more than 10 cartons of cigarettes, 10 bottles of liquor/ wine, or 10 cases of beer/soda"—admittedly, a more than ample supply for most legitimate purposes.

I remember seeing a sign in the Cholon Post Exchange spoofing the system. It read:

No Rationing on Stateside Cameras!

(Limit—One to a Customer)

The Tu Do Street strip, a pathetic collection of bars, night clubs, brothels, "steam baths," and massage parlors catering to the GI trade, was within spitting distance of the center city BOQs and did a roaring business every night. If you had a strong stomach and were the least bit interested in social research, it was worth seeing—once. To the best of my knowledge, no serious effort was ever made to clean it up, much less shut it down. No doubt, again there were important "rice bowls" at stake.

When, for old time's sake, I revisited Tu Do Street in 1989 (the Communists had by then renamed it), it was a place of small shops and quiet, apparently legitimate hotels and rooming houses. But behind every door lurked a thousand ghosts—black-haired girls in tight-fitting mini-skirts, their haunted eyes beseeching, their slender arms beckoning.

"Hey Joe! You wanna' have a good time?"

And as I turned away, "Ah, you cheap Charlie! You number ten!"

The performance and decorum of headquarters personnel, and the mood of the city in which they lived, were indicative, I think, of a general and wide-spread decline in the quality and morale of the American expeditionary forces after Tet 1968. Washington's decision to seek "peace through negotiations" clouded an already ill-defined horizon for American servicemen in Vietnam. The failure to mobilize, to call up reserves, to modify an unjust and discriminatory college deferment system, made it very difficult to fill the ranks with qualified people. The army, and to a lesser extent the other services as well, were forced to accept large numbers of marginally qualified recruits, including several hundred thousand classified as "Category Four" who were considered barely trainable. Standards were lowered at officer candidate schools and some with questionable intellectual and moral attributes were commissioned and sent to Vietnam.

The "best" people, those tagged as "comers," no longer considered Vietnam duty a ticket that had to be punched. Some went out of their way to avoid it.

An army on the march, on the offensive, is said to be an easy army to lead. One that is standing down, that in the absence of victory is withdrawing from the field of battle, is a very difficult army to command.

"I have nothing but sympathy for the problem that Abe [General Creighton W. Abrams] had," General Westmoreland told me in 1988. "Abrams had categorical orders from [Secretary of Defense] Mel Laird and indirectly from the president to cut down, to zero out, casualties. With that type of instruction you're not going to be very aggressive, and it's going to have an adverse morale effect on the troops."[1]

All these things wounded the spirit of the army in Vietnam. No one wished to be the last man to die in a war that had been declared past winning. Hunkered down behind barbed wire, the troops grew restless and angry. An already serious drug problem spun out of control. "Fragging"—a euphemism for the outright murder of one's own officers—entered the lexicon of the soldier. Bizarre uniforms and boorish, sometimes criminal, behavior were tolerated. Racial animosities flared, pitting white against black, and both white and black against yellow.

In November 1969, the acting assistant secretary of defense for civil rights, L. Howard Bennett, made a brief visit to Vietnam. Addressing only the black/white aspect of the racial storm then tearing through MACV, he blamed it on a lack of "communications." He said there was a need for greater "sensitivity" to the problems of black servicemen, and that there was "too much concern over the threat of black group violence, a threat that does not exist." He urged senior commanders to "get out and learn firsthand" what he, presumably, had learned in a few days of walking around.[2]

Echoes of his lengthy and cliché-ridden remarks to senior officers reverberated throughout Vietnam and elsewhere for many months to come, and did little to cool the fires that were burning. Some of his language would be echoed in later "Z-Grams" issued to the fleet by a young chief of naval operations.

In truth, the problems afflicting the army in Vietnam were not unknown in the navy. Inadequately addressed, they would lead in but a few years to incidents at sea that in other times and in other navies would have been called mutinies.

Within NAVFORV, however, they were kept manageable, and for this Admiral Zumwalt deserves a lot of credit. He kept the Brown Water Navy on the move, pushing it into areas never penetrated before, prodding his staff to come up with new ideas and new initiatives. He brought his undeniable qualities of leadership, his flair, his imagination, his powers of persuasion, his bulldog tenacity, his wit, and his sense of humor to every meeting, to every crisis.

He was not always right, not always wise. When he became CNO there were those who would change that to seldom right and seldom wise, and with them I do not totally disagree. But in Vietnam, he held things together, and as long as he was there NAVFORV had a purpose, and life was bearable both on the rivers and in Saigon.

The absurdities of the war could be laughed at, the pain endured.

14

Sea Float/Solid Anchor

Now, I saw in my dream, that just as they had ended this talk they drew near to a very miry slough, that was in the midst of the plain; and they, being heedless, did both fall suddenly into the bog. The name of the slough was Despond.

—John Bunyan, *The Pilgrim's Progress*

ome 175 miles southwest of Saigon, the Nam Can district of An
Xuyen Province comprises the southernmost part of the Ca
Mau Peninsula. It is a region of ragged forests, thick mangrove
swamps, barren mud flats, and swiftly flowing rivers and canals
whose waters churn to tidal currents.

Though an accurate census had never been taken, it was sparsely
populated in comparison with the rest of the delta. Estimates of the
number of people who lived there ranged from five thousand to
thirteen thousand.

Woodcutting was the district's principal economic activity, with
fishing ranking a distant second. Roads were virtually nonexistent
and almost all travel was by water. By the 1960s, Route 12, which
once linked the towns of Nam Can and Ca Mau, had fallen into
disuse and all but disappeared in the swampy terrain. The old French
cisterns and what few wells there were had been destroyed in earlier
fighting, and the people survived on fresh water brought in by sampan from settlements in the north. The rivers, being tidal, were
brackish.

An industrious woodcutter and his family could earn what was by
Vietnamese standards a decent living from their labors in the forests
of Nam Can. The wood they cut (it was called *cay go*) was extremely
hard and dense. Young trees were cut into long, straight poles,
stripped of their bark, and used in construction. Irregular pieces were
sawed into short lengths, split, and sold to the charcoal makers. It
was hard and demanding work. Power saws and modern lumbering
techniques were foreign to the woodcutters of Nam Can.

Fishermen harvested shrimp and several varieties of small bone-
fish that they netted in cleverly designed weirs and traps strategically
positioned to make the best use of tides and currents. The catch was
dried in the sun and salted prior to shipment by sampan to markets in
the north.

At one time, charcoal preparation had been an important source
of the region's meager wealth. In the summer of 1969 a few charcoal
kilns were still recognizable in the ruins of Old Nam Can. The town,
a pathetic oasis of nominal Saigon control in a region that had been a
Communist stronghold for many years, was finally overrun during
the 1968 Tet Offensive and later abandoned by the GVN. Most of its
people were relocated to a site roughly ten miles to the north. This
was named "New Nam Can" to distinguish it from the old district
capital. Old Nam Can was declared a free-fire zone and became, in
effect, a dumping ground for bombs and other ordnance that could

not be disposed of conveniently elsewhere in the delta. Within a short time of its capture by the Viet Cong, Old Nam Can presented a scene of utmost devastation, and scarcely two stones were left standing one upon the other, save for the brick heaps of the ruined kilns.

Prior to the establishment of Market Time operations, Nam Can had been a terminus for Communist arms shipments arriving by sea. Enemy trawlers discharged their cargo in or near the mouths of major rivers, and from there the supply chain ran north and east to the upper delta and III Corps. When Market Time raised the risk of sea infiltration to unacceptable levels, the logistics flow reversed itself and Viet Cong in the lower end of the peninsula were supplied with munitions infiltrated by land from Cambodia. What could not be procured in this way was sometimes manufactured locally, utilizing explosive material salvaged from dud rounds. Given the huge amounts of ordnance expended over the years in Vietnam, these were always in plentiful supply.

Food, clothing, and other necessities were obtained by the enemy through the levying of "VC taxes" collected by way of armed sampans that took up stations on heavily traveled rivers and canals. It was estimated that several million piasters were extorted from the Nam Can each year to fuel the Communist war effort in the lower delta.

In October 1968, U.S. Navy Swift boats began regular incursions of the Bo De and Cua Lon rivers, threatening the enemy's sovereignty in an area he had come to consider his own. As stated in the initial Sea Lords proposal, the objective pursued was "to stir up the enemy and keep him off balance." When "Market Time raiders" drew fire, it was returned with a vengeance.

The people of the rivers, many of whom were at worst apolitical, but almost all of whom in the peculiar and uncompromising climate of the times were classified as Viet Cong or Viet Cong "sympathizers," suffered enormously. Their flimsy hootches ("Viet Cong structures") were shot up and destroyed, their sampans ("Viet Cong logistics craft") were chased down and sunk, and their fish traps were blown apart or pulled from the river bottoms as enemy "obstructions to navigation."

Nothing can take away from the daring and courage of Swift boat sailors who carried out these early raids in the Nam Can, but in retrospect they won no new "hearts and minds" for the government in Saigon or for the U.S. Navy. On the contrary, they only helped solidify disaffections already felt.

Bunkers, fortifications, and solidly constructed barricades were erected in and along the more important waterways to keep the American raiders out. This, of course, led to redoubled efforts on the part of the navy to pacify and control the region.

In December 1968, U.S. Navy SEALs and Vietnamese Navy LDNN were inserted on an intelligence-gathering mission (Operation "Bold Dragon IX"). Three sets of barricades were discovered and charted in the mouth of the Cua Lon River, one of which stretched completely across the river. These were similar in construction to fish weirs—tripods of *cay go* driven into the river bottom and lashed together at the top with wire. Air strikes were called in, but neither they nor the SEALs were able to clear the river of obstructions.

This led to Operation "Silver Mace" and the first open-sea transit of heavy riverine assault craft. Under the command of Captain J. G. Now, a force that included monitors, ASPBs, ATCs, and a company of Mobile Strike Force (MSF) troops left Binh Thuy late on 16 December and proceeded by way of inland waters to Rach Gia on the western coast of IV Corps. From there the riverine craft wallowed their way through choppy seas to "Square Bay" (Cua Song Bay Hap) at the mouth of the Cua Lon River. At the same time, a mobile riverine base composed of the USS *Mercer* (APB 39), the USS *Satyr* (ARL 23), and the USS *Iredell County* (LST 839) sailed from the South China Sea around the southern tip of Vietnam to an anchorage in the gulf of Thailand four and one-half miles east of Square Bay. Embarked in the *Mercer* were a thirty-man EOD/UDT team and a second company of MSF.

Rough seas delayed the start of the operation, and the riverine craft had difficulty finding the entrance to the Cua Lon, hidden in a maze of mud flats. A Junk Force pilot eventually led them in on the evening of 19 December. With the MSF providing bank security, EOD/UDT units blew up twelve structures in the river. Only sporadic contact with the enemy was experienced. Numerous bunkers were destroyed, as well as large quantities of fish, rice, and salt. One Viet Cong was killed and nine were taken prisoner.[1]

Silver Mace operations concluded on 22 December, and that evening the assault craft joined the ships of the mobile riverine base anchored offshore. The passage north to Rach Gia was completed without incident the next day.

In the early months of 1969, Market Time raiders continued their forays into the Nam Can. SEALs, EOD/UDT teams, MSF and RF/PF troops, VNN junks, helicopter gunships, and tactical strike aircraft hammered the region, turning it more and more into a battered wasteland. In April, Silver Mace II was launched with combined USN, VNN, ARVN, VNMC, and USAF units. The mission of this two-week operation was "to search and destroy all enemy units and their logistic support in the AO."[2] Contact with the enemy was established on seven occasions, resulting in twenty-one VC KIA and the capture of 380 weapons.[3] The navy suffered losses, too.

On 12 April, eight PCFs with UDT teams embarked were conducting a late afternoon sweep operation on the Duong Keo River with Vietnamese marines. At 1734, some four miles upstream from the river mouth, an enemy force perhaps two companies strong took the Swift boats under fire. Detonation of two claymore mines on the bank was followed by intense B-40, recoilless rifle, rifle grenade, and heavy machine gun fire. PCF 43 was hit almost immediately by recoilless rifle and B-40 rounds, which disabled her steering and mortally wounded the officer in charge, Lieutenant (j.g.) D. G. Droz. Raked by continuous enemy fire and ablaze, the Swift boat beached at high speed in the very center of the ambush.

Uninjured crewmen and UDT personnel hastily set up a defensive perimeter around the stricken boat, and PCFs 5 and 31 went alongside, even though they too were receiving heavy fire. Seawolves operating from an LST off the coast were overhead within five minutes. Enemy fire was at last suppressed, and all personnel were removed from PCF 43, which was deemed to be unsalvageable. A short time after the area was cleared, flames reached UDT explosives stored on the boat and it blew up.

In the engagement on the Duong Keo, three U.S. Navy personnel were killed and thirty-three wounded. The VNMC had two killed and thirteen wounded. In addition to PCF 43, four other Swift boats were damaged. Enemy losses were estimated to be eighteen KIA, though only two bodies were recovered.[4]

Operations in the Nam Can during the first half of 1969 relied heavily on offshore support ships, which, due to shallow water, had to anchor well off the coast. The disadvantages of this for small-boat operations were the same as noted earlier for the offshore support of PBRs during the first Game Warden patrols. It was obvious that from an operational standpoint the establishment of a permanent base on the Cua Lon or Bo De rivers, capable of supporting PCFs, riverine assault craft, and junks was highly desirable.

There were other reasons as well that argued for such a base. It had not been proposed that Vietnamization of the naval war would include transfer of the ships that made offshore support of operations possible, if less than desirable, for the U.S. Navy. If the GVN were to maintain a presence in the Nam Can after withdrawal of the U.S. Navy, a shore support base would be essential. A location on either the Bo De or Cua Lon was considered ideal, since this would permit egress to the South China Sea in the east and the Gulf of Thailand in the west, something of no small importance in a region swept by monsoon winds.

Further, pacification of the Nam Can would deny the enemy a strategic haven and a source of material and financial support. For those who put their faith in such things (not everyone did), a concerted and innovative psychological operation conceivably could succeed in winning back the loyalty of the people to Saigon. Armed with these arguments and promises of enthusiastic Vietnamese Navy participation, Admiral Zumwalt formally proposed that a joint USN/ VNN base be established on the site of Old Nam Can.

His recommendation was greeted with, to say the least, skepticism at IV Corps Headquarters. ARVN officers and their American advisors considered the enterprise of doubtful real worth, and said such a base could not be defended. Zumwalt replied that ground force commanders, looking at Nam Can from the north across many miles of difficult and enemy-controlled terrain, naturally had a different perspective than the navy, which viewed the region from the sea. Moreover, he said, they tended to discount the region's economic and strategic importance, and were ignoring history—specifically, the use made of the region by the Viet Cong over many years. IV Corps replied that efforts at population and resources control should focus on more accessible regions where the population was greater and the rewards more certain.

The debate ended with COMNAVFORV being denied permission to establish a shore base, and no promises were made concerning further troop support for Nam Can operations. The rivers, however, remained a navy area of operations, and what the navy did on them, by and large, was left at the navy's discretion. In typical Zumwalt fashion, IV Corps's objections were neatly sidestepped. Plans were made for a *floating* base in the rivers, detached from the shore, to demonstrate the correctness of the admiral's vision.

On 15 May 1969, CTF-115 recommended that a "mobile advance tactical support base" (MATSB) be built and moored in the middle of the Cua Lon River near Old Nam Can, adjacent to the site where Zumwalt had wished to build the shore base. Drawing upon lessons learned in Giant Slingshot, the base would be built on ammi pontoon barges to support "a concentrated psyops program called 'Market Place.' Operations will be aimed at building the GVN image in the Old Nam Can area and at the same time undermining the VC influence the civilian population has been subjected to in the past."[5]

It was proposed that the MATSB be large enough to support six PCFs, a psyops team, ten VNN interpreters, a commander's staff, a VNN LSIL (for base defense), and up to sixty VN transient civilians who would be fed and berthed while undergoing the psyops program. Five ammi pontoons were considered adequate to form the core of the complex. One of the five would be used as the "Market Place." The commander, his staff, and the PCFs would be assigned by CTF-115 from Market Time assets.

The plan, as eventually approved by COMNAVFORV, called for nine ammis, and it included a landing platform for Seawolf helicopter gunships. These would be supported by an offshore LST anchored in the Gulf of Thailand. More ammis would be added later, bringing the total to thirteen.

The MATSB was fitted out at Nha Be. The roofs of huts on the ammis were strengthened for defense against mortar attack, and the sides were heavily sandbagged to afford protection from small-arms fire. Automatic weapons and mortars were emplaced, though the primary defense of the floating base was considered to be the mobile firepower provided by PCFs, the LSIL, and the Seawolves. Much of the material to outfit the base was begged or borrowed from other commands, so rapidly was the project put in motion. When the work at Nha Be was completed, the MATSB was carried to the mouth of the Bo De River by three Seventh Fleet LSDs.

The combined USN/VNN operation, called "Sea Float" by the U.S. Navy and "Tran Hung Dao III" by the Vietnamese, was set in motion at 0200 on 25 June, when the nine ammis were floated from the well decks of the LSDs and made fast to tugs for the hazardous journey up the Bo De and into the Cua Lon. Escorted by six PCFs, the slowly moving convoy arrived in the vicinity of Old Nam Can at about 0900 that morning.

The mooring of Sea Float in tidal currents that sometimes reached six to eight knots was no small feat in itself. A six-point, fore-and-aft moor using 9,000-pound destroyer-type anchors backed up by heavy concrete clumps was used. The holding ground was surprisingly good, and the moor was accomplished without untoward incident, though ground tackle holding the ammis into the current took a dangerously heavy strain.

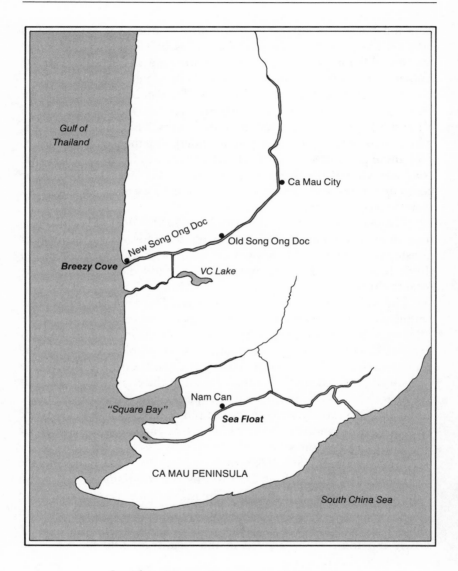

Sea Float/Breezy Cove Areas of Operations

The swift river current provided the best possible defense from swimmer/sapper attack, and on the shore an array of Duffle Bag sensors was emplaced to provide early warning of movement on the banks.

Initial reaction to Sea Float's arrival included the attempted mining and ambush of PCF patrols, and a crude form of psychological warfare. VC banners were raised along the waterways, which read "Americans and Vietnamese soldiers who come here will die," and "We kill Americans." English language leaflets were floated to the MATSB on small wooden rafts. The leaflets urged an end to the "U.S. aggressive war" and threatened to "blow the American Navy out of the water."

"Hanoi Hannah," in her daily broadcast on 15 July, took note of the new operation and predicted that Sea Float would be at the bottom of the Cua Lon by midnight on 17 July.[6] An old Vietnamese woodcutter, abducted and abused by the Viet Cong, escaped to tell VNN interrogators that his captors had boasted they would "visit" Sea Float someday soon.[7] Six weeks went by without a shot being fired at the MATSB, however.

It was Admiral Zumwalt's view that "Vietnamese Navy participation is the key to the success of this operation."[8] To underscore the importance he placed on the cooperative aspects of the venture, he insisted that a Vietnamese naval officer be assigned as second in command. No VNN officer of suitable rank (a commander or lieutenant commander) could be found to accept it as a permanent assignment, however, and VNN Headquarters soon made it a collateral duty of the IV Coastal Zone commander. He in turn detached members of his staff on temporary duty (sometimes as a form of punishment) to act for him at Sea Float/Tran Hung Dao III. This was early evidence that the Vietnamese Navy's verbal enthusiasm for the operation would not be followed by much positive action. There were exceptions, of course, but most VNN officers and sailors considered Nam Can the very end of the earth and did everything they possibly could to avoid being assigned there. Not infrequently, those forced to go were out-and-out troublemakers.

The Viet Cong warned the woodcutters and fishermen of Nam Can to stay away from Sea Float. Gradually, however, visitors came in ever increasing numbers. In addition to psyops lectures, they were given food, small gifts, and services such as outboard motor repair and axe sharpening on a grinding wheel specially acquired in Nha Trang and shipped to Sea Float by CTF-115. Simple medical treatment was also provided, and the scope of this expanded with the arrival of a VNN hospital ship (LSM-H).

On 24 July 1969, Sea Float "Annex" began operations near the intersection of the Cua Lon River and the Cai Nhap Canal, some six miles east of Sea Float. Virtually all north-south commercial water traffic passed through the Cai Nhap. Initially, the Annex was composed of two U.S. PCFs, and the Vietnamese LSIL and LSM-H. These units got under way each morning from Sea Float and returned each night. Before long, the Annex was outstripping Sea Float itself in the number of river people it attracted.

With the eviction of VC tax collectors from the waterways, and the transformation of Market Time raiders into something more akin to beat policemen, civilian traffic on the rivers increased. During the first five days of Sea Float's presence, an average of 102 sampans per day were sighted on the Cua Lon. By the middle of August the number had increased to 159 per day, and the average size of the sampans was larger as heavier cargoes, mostly wood, were moved to market.[9] By 26 August, 318 families had expressed a desire to resettle in the Sea Float AO (area of operations).[10] These statistics were compiled and distributed widely as evidence of the operation's success.

The lack of troop support for Sea Float was from the very beginning, and at the very least, worrisome. During a visit to the MATSB on 28 July, the IV Corps senior advisor said he was "fairly sure" the corps commander had issued instructions forbidding the An Xuyen province chief from employing troops in the Sea Float AO.[11] As a stopgap measure, Admiral Zumwalt approved a plan to recruit and train fifty "Kit Carson Scouts" (KCS) for defense of the MATSB. These were former Viet Cong who had rallied ("chieu hoied") to the GVN and then "volunteered" to fight against their old comrades in arms. The KCS were to be furnished building materials with which to construct shelters for themselves and their families at Old Nam Can. By the end of July, fifteen KCS and their families had arrived at Sea Float and were temporarily housed on the MATSB.

These former enemy soldiers, who would prove to be reasonably effective performers at Sea Float, were hated and distrusted by the regular Vietnamese military they came in contact with. Several were victims of savage beatings administered by VNN personnel at Sea Float.

On 2 August, a 175-man unit of the highly regarded Mobile Strike Force (MSF) was airlifted to Sea Float for a thirty-day operation. These montagnard soldiers established a base camp ashore in the vicinity of the MATSB and engaged in very successful patrols throughout the AO while providing strong bank security. A request to extend their deployment at Sea Float was denied at the JGS level. In their place, on 6 September, a newly formed company of VNN "Rangers" arrived from Nha Be aboard a VNN LSM.

The Rangers were commanded by a VNN lieutenant who had been instructed by VNN Headquarters to restrict his operations to an area within one kilometer of the river, unless "positive intelligence" indicated a lucrative target farther inland.[12] The Rangers had been assigned for a period of thirty days, which was too long for the Sea Float commander.

Neither the lieutenant nor his men spoke any English. Further, the unit had no U.S. advisor. Prior to arrival at Sea Float, the Rangers had been trained at Nha Be by a U.S. Marine captain for a period of about two months, followed by a month of restricted operations in the Rung Sat Special Zone and in an area near Ben Luc. It soon became apparent that this preparation was woefully inadequate for the kind of aggressive patrolling demanded at Sea Float.

Two U.S. Marine Corps advisors were flown in to attempt on-site training, but a quick fix of Ranger deficiencies did not appear likely. On 14 September the marine advisors accompanied the Rangers on a security patrol in the vicinity of their base camp. It turned into a fiasco.

"Shortly after passing through the perimeter wire," the marines reported, "a mud flat was crossed and the formation disintegrated as personnel put down their weapons to chase crabs. No formation was used after this point.

"Throughout the patrol all personnel, including the company commander, fired their weapons (.45's, carbines, and M-16's) at crabs, birds, and fish. . . . Such firing was completely without regard for the safety of the other personnel in the patrol and much of the firing was directed toward the Ranger base camp and Sea Float. The company commander could not be convinced by the two advisors that this firing both destroyed the security of the patrol and threatened the lives of everyone concerned.

"During the patrol the men also threw numerous grenades in the various canals in order to kill fish. . . .

"The Marine advisors contend that it is only a matter of time before someone is killed or wounded by their indiscriminate use of weapons. It is also the opinion of the advisors that the unit cannot carry out mission unless given some formal infantry training. . . ."[13]

A few days later the Sea Float commander formally asked that the Rangers be withdrawn from his AO, saying they had "balked at all training that USMC advisors have offered and company commander has informed senior advisor that when he wanted training he would ask for it. In view of the fact that the Rangers do not operate at night, their presence on the north bank detracts from rather than enhances the overall security. Should any kind of direct enemy approach be made the confusion on the banks would only compound the threat and in the event of a stand off mortar attack, our firing response would be limited by presence of VNN Rangers on opposite bank. . . ."[14]

The failure to secure adequate, committed troop support threatened the continuation of Sea Float. By then (September 1969) more than five hundred people had resettled in the area and they were considered vulnerable to VC reprisals for "collaborating" with the GVN. Without aggressive bank patrols, the narrow and forbidding Cai Nhap Canal offered the enemy almost limitless opportunities to ambush navy patrol craft. Yet the canal had to be kept open and free from VC tax collectors if the economic development of the region were to continue.

The An Xuyen province chief reluctantly agreed to furnish two Regional Force (RF) and one Provincial Reconnaissance Unit (PRU) platoons for a two-week period while COMNAVFORV searched for the troops considered necessary to provide for Sea Float security. The expiration of that two-week period without the provision of suitable relief brought into sharp focus the disagreement between the navy and the army over the long-term value of the operation. The An Xuyen senior advisor, recommending the immediate relief of the troops at Sea Float, said, "I do not agree and never did agree with Sea Float becoming involved in pacification in Old Nam Can. An Xuyen Province cannot, at this time, afford to cope with the attendant problems such as control of LOC's, government police, permanent security and organization of settlements, reconstruction, etc. . . . An Xuyen Province is being drawn into a situation it cannot afford to handle due to presence of 500–600 persons settling vicinity of Old Nam Can without permanent security and no GVN presence.

"A temporary GVN presence requires a troop commitment. A planned permanent presence requires that other resources as well as troops be made available. Procrastination simply aggravates the situation. Complete withdrawal from Old Nam Can at this time results in a disadvantageous psyop situation Province-wide. Withdrawal at a later date if the present resettlement trend continues could prove extremely embarrassing and difficult. . . ."[15]

Given this evaluation by MACV's senior representative in the province, and the less than inspiring performance of the Vietnamese Navy, why did Admiral Zumwalt continue his campaign for Sea Float? In part, I think, it was because it was not in his nature to admit to failure, and his conviction was that in the end all things he championed would turn out well. Further, by then he had made Sea Float a showcase of supposed USN/VNN progress in the essential business of Vietnamization. Almost every important visitor to Vietnam was hustled on board a helicopter for a whirlwind tour of Sea Float, conducted by the admiral himself. He was a master at this sort of thing and such was the confidence, the optimism, he exuded that almost no one came away from one of his tours lacking in enthusiasm for what he said the two navies were achieving.

He bridled at criticism, particularly of the sort that suggested the VNN was falling down on the job. When I wrote my first draft of the Sea Float story, in 1970, both he and Captain Rauch, the senior naval advisor, told me to "accent the positive" in my treatment of the Vietnamese Navy. Zumwalt told me specifically "not to be so harsh on the VNN Rangers—we think we had some marines with them who did not like Vietnamese." If the history of World War II had been written the way I seemed to want to write the history of the VNN at Sea Float, he said with a smile that was somewhere between fatherly indulgence and a razor, it would have been a story of "stolen gasoline."

To bolster his case for Sea Float with MACV, Zumwalt produced intelligence estimates that showed Sea Float costing the VC in lost revenue alone some 143 million piasters a year (nearly a tenth of what it was thought the enemy collected in all of IV Corps).[16] The Nam Can population growth was shown to be doubling the number of people in the AO every twenty-five days. By the middle of October it was estimated that more than three thousand people were living under GVN control, where before there had been none.[17] To Zumwalt, abandonment of the operation for want of a handful of troops was absurd.

More naval assets were committed. Riverine assault craft were assigned to patrol the Cai Nhap, and they were joined by VNN junks and a VNN reaction force. Maximum use was made of SEALs, EOD and UDT teams. The disgraced VNN Rangers were put through intensive retraining in preparation for reassignment to the area.

Calling upon his considerable powers of persuasion, he at last won General Abrams's consent to establish the shore base he earlier had been denied. The code name "Solid Anchor" was assigned on 24 October 1969, and described as a joint USN/VNN operation to construct a coastal group junk and PCF base at Old Nam Can.

Site clearing began immediately. A chainsaw detail went out daily from Sea Float. "Trail Dust" missions were flown to chemically defoliate large tracts of swampland. A sign was hammered into the muck: "Welcome to the Heart of Beautiful Downtown Nam Can."

In November, three Seabee teams from the Third Naval Construction Brigade were assigned to the project and began the assembly of SEASIA huts. Matting was laid to support the movement of heavy equipment. (A large bulldozer was only narrowly saved from disappearing forever into the mire.) Civilian "prospectors," escorted by Swift boats and riverine craft, were sent throughout the AO in search of sand or other suitable material to fill and build up the site. None could be found, despite NAVFORV's insistence that it would be found. Eventually, sand had to be barged, at great expense, from the offshore Poulo Condore islands. Crushed stone and gravel had to be transported even greater distances. Once a small mountain of crushed stone deposited on the southeast corner of the Solid Anchor site vanished in a matter of minutes when a thin crust of subsoil suddenly gave way. Though the Seabees and civilian contractors gave it their best effort, the land could be made to support only relatively light structures; the airstrip, when built, could handle nothing larger than small transport planes.

COMUSMACV's endorsement of Sea Float/Solid Anchor changed, almost overnight, the attitude of the An Xuyen province chief and his senior advisor. They and the Nam Can district chief visited Sea Float, and after touring the complex promised to provide a revolutionary development team, an RF platoon, two national policemen, a village committee, and possibly an armed propaganda team. The district chief even vowed to move his headquarters to Solid Anchor once the base was completed.[18]

A certain amount of peevishness surfaced, however, and the Sea Float commander reported that the province chief "stated his displeasure that so much was being done in his area of responsibility with his advice and comment not being sought except after the fact."[19]

The changes brought about by Sea Float's presence in the Nam Can were indeed impressive in the first months of the operation. Two new hamlets (not surprisingly, the Vietnamese Navy named them "Tran Hung Dao I" and "Tran Hung Dao II") were established on the north bank of the Cua Lon between Old Nam Can and the Cai Nhap. Several small shops and a restaurant opened their doors for business. New fishtraps were hammered into river and canal beds. The catch was spread on the river banks to dry, just as in other parts of the delta rice was dried along the shoulders of roads. Skilled masons appeared, seemingly out of nowhere, to begin the painstaking reconstruction of beehive charcoal kilns. In December the first baby, a girl, was born on Sea Float, much to the delight of every sailor aboard.

The number of people then living under GVN control in the AO was estimated at nine thousand.[20] This figure most likely was inflated, as many sunny statistics in Vietnam were. It was based on sampan and shelter counts and did not distinguish between permanent residents and transients. There could be no doubt, though, that the Nam Can was recovering rapidly as people who had been driven away from the Cua Lon and Bo De rivers returned to rebuild their lives. There also could be no doubt that the GVN's reach did not extend far inland from the river banks.

The new hamlets, for all their mud, hummed with activity. Sea Float sailors built schools in Tran Hung Dao I and II. The children's desks were made from ammunition boxes, as were the classroom floors. Notebooks and pencils were procured from somewhere; teachers were found and hired.

GVN flags fluttered from the tops of tall *cay go* poles in each hamlet, from crude flagstaffs on sampans, and from the fronts of most hootches and shelters. To what degree this public display reflected allegiance to Saigon, and to what degree self-preservation, was even then subject to debate. The arrival of Vietnamese officialdom sent a chill wind through the region.

On 1 December 1969, administrative responsibility for the two hamlets in Sea Float's AO was transferred to the Nam Can district chief. RF troopers and a revolutionary development team established themselves in Tran Hung Dao I. The people of the hamlet initially greeted their arrival with indifference, but after some unpleasant incidents of theft and ill-disciplined behavior on the part of the RF and RD team, the people began to move away.

The Sea Float commander complained that the RF/RD were not "professional" and that their leadership was "marginal." Many suggestions he and others had tried to give were "ignored or followed to the least extent possible." The security perimeter set up by the troops provided only for their own security, he said.[21] A month later, after closely following the performance of the revolutionary development team in a settlement whose growth and prosperity had been Sea Float's pride and joy, the most he could bring himself to say was that the "RD cadre contributions have not added significantly to the development of Tran Hung Dao I hamlet."[22]

In truth, the performance of the revolutionary development team was both uninspired and uninspiring, except when motivated by prospects of personal profit and gain, a not uncommon circumstance in many well-conceived and ill-executed development schemes in Vietnam. A case in point was the village well project in Tran Hung Dao I, an undertaking attacked with unusual energy by the RD cadre. Initially described as "a contribution to Tran Hung Dao village from a wealthy Nam Can merchant,"[23] it later turned out to be a commercial venture by a man rather openly rumored to be the district chief's brother. When pressed on such matters as the selling price of the water and distribution of the profits, the well operators became highly defensive and evasive.[24]

In early January 1970 I made my first visit to Sea Float. As was my habit, I wrote a memorandum trip report to the chief of staff when I returned to Saigon. I recounted all the positive things I had seen at Sea Float, and then discussed things I found to be not so encouraging.

"There are no new people settling in the hamlet called Tran Hung Dao," I wrote, "and I was told that many of those who live there now wish to leave. Tran Hung Dao II, on the other hand, is obviously growing, prosperous, and probably already supports more people than the older Tran Hung Dao. This phenomenon, I was told, can be traced to the arrival in Tran Hung Dao of a Revolutionary Development team and a platoon of RF. It is possible, of course, that the people are simply afraid that their presence there will attract the VC. It is also possible that the RD and RF personnel are exerting a net negative effect on the prosperity and well-being of the people.

"The only observable work being performed by the RD team in Tran Hung Dao is the well. . . . I was told that since the arrival of the RD and RF there have been incidents of terrorism, fighting, and theft. If true, there is little wonder that people would want to pull up stakes and move on.

"I noticed that the decks of at least one of the LSSLs on the river were piled high with choice wood. Perhaps there is a perfectly logical and innocent explanation, but it gives the appearance of petty extortion by the naval units dispatched there to protect the people.

"The economy of the Nam Can area appears to be on the verge of a 'take-off.' In Tran Hung Dao II charcoal kilns are in operation and others are going up. Rather large fishing and shrimping enterprises are underway. But this very prosperity poses problems for us. Fish traps are springing up all over the place, particularly in the narrow Cai Nhap. Word has been promulgated that they are not to be permitted in that waterway because they impede navigation. But the fishing is good there, and the word has not filtered down to the industrious fisherman who expends his ample time and little capital in building a trap. As time and inclination permits, our boats rip out these traps and put the fisherman out of business. No one likes to see the fruits of his labors go for naught, and there is a certain capriciousness about the enforcement of the 'no-trap' regulation when some are ripped out and others are not. A man does not know where he stands. I strongly recommend that a determination be made of what our actual navigational requirements are and that a vigorous information program be undertaken to tell the fishermen where their traps may go and where they may not go. I know that the inclination will be to say that this word was put out months ago, and that the fishermen know only too well what the rules are, but as the economy and the population of the area expand we must expect that many will not have 'gotten the word.'

"A similar information problem exists with the woodcutters. As new people arrive they find the choice claims 'staked out,' and expand their operations into areas we do not yet consider protected and freed from VC control. Here we are faced with a trade-off situation. How far do we go to encourage revival of the economy? How far can we afford to limit our operations against the VC? It is a cruel dilemma.

"From what I have observed, we have committed some of our very best people to Sea Float and in spite of living conditions which can only be described as grim, they are doing one hell of a job. . . . It is a very impressive operation."

In May I went back to Sea Float. My report to the new chief of staff, Captain W. O. McDaniel (Emmett Tidd had followed Zumwalt to Washington), included the following:

"One thing I would look for in coming months is an attempt by the enemy to re-establish sea infiltration in the Ca Mau Peninsula. . . . What might be happening now is that the enemy is hedging his bet in case his Cambodian gamble should fail. It may well be that he believes a VNN Market Time will prove ineffective in the long run and that sea supply of his forces in the Delta will once more become practicable. . . .

"An almost inescapable conclusion that I came away with is that, pragmatically, there has been no increase in VNN command and control of the operation since January. As you know, for at least six weeks there has been no VNN deputy at Sea Float and at the present time the senior VNN officer is a *trung uy* [lieutenant (j.g.)]. This reflects, I believe, an unfortunate fact of life in the Vietnamese Navy. Assignment to undesirable areas such as the Nam Can is too often successfully avoided by the more capable and more influential officers. There is a large material and strategic investment in Solid Anchor, and in my view that investment, and Vietnamization of the war in the lower Delta, are being jeopardized by less than adequate VNN personnel investment. . . ."

I doubt that I told either chief of staff what he did not already know, and certainly they had other Sea Float worries to contend with, as will shortly be shown.

In January 1970 a Mobile Strike Force company was again assigned for Nam Can operations. Stepped up patrolling and harassment of Viet Cong base camps and LOCs became the order of the day, and Sea Float morale was given a much-needed boost.

On 16 January the largest water mine ever discovered in the AO—a 750-pound dud bomb fused for command detonation—was pulled from a canal through which Swift boats frequently passed. The enemy had by no means abandoned the Nam Can. He was still there, and he was still dangerous.

Courage, individual and collective, was not an uncommon quality among the men assigned to Sea Float, and it is perhaps unfair to single out one episode to illustrate that point, but on the night of 21 January 1970 an action took place along the Cai Nuoc River that is worth recounting.

The Rach Cai Nuoc lies roughly twenty miles east of Old Nam Can, and it cuts through a region of thick mangrove swamp. On nights when there is no moon it is very dark indeed along that river. Fireflies (biological, not mechanical) wink in the heavy, drooping jungle foliage. At times they cluster in large, breeding swarms whose light, glimpsed from across the black river, seems almost otherworldly.

The night of 21 January, however, was not a moonless night. The moon was full and it rose at 1755, a great huge moon typical of the tropics. It fought back the night, etching in bold relief each twisted branch, trailing vine, and shimmering leaf along the river.

A Swift boat with embarked Vietnamese marines proceeds through a
Mekong Delta canal in April 1969.

U.S. Navy PBR, manned and ready (1969).

Swift boat "raiders" in the lower Mekong Delta, 1969.

A "Zippo" boat at rest in the Mekong Delta, 1969.

Sea Float, 1970.

Sea Float/Solid Anchor, June 1970.

The Splendid BOQ, Saigon, 1970. (Richard L. Schreadley)

Above left: Officers Club at Cam Ranh Bay, 1970.
(Richard L. Schreadley)

Left: The Annapolis Hotel, Saigon, 1970. (Richard L. Schreadley)

A PACV, the "monster" of the delta, 1969.

"White Hat Airlines," Tan Son Nhut, 1970. (Richard L. Schreadley)

Task Force 78 off the coast of North Vietnam, 1973.
(Courtesy Captain C. R. Christensen)

Boat inspection at Sea Float, July 1970.

A VNN seaman checks identification papers of a Vietnamese woman on a Mekong Delta river, 1969.

A U.S. Coast Guard WPB enters port in 1969.
(Official U.S. Coast Guard)

A U.S. Navy instructor explains the operation of a heavy machine gun
to VNN trainees, 1969.

A U.S. Navy UDT sailor makes fast a line to a barrier erected in the Bo De River, 1969.

Above right: A Swift boat speeds to patrol station off the coast of Vietnam, 1969.

Right: Twin tongues of flame dart from a "Zippo" boat in the lower Mekong Delta, 1969.

Breezy Cove before the attack, 1970.
(Courtesy Captain C. R. Christensen)

Above right: Breezy Cove after the attack, 1970.
(Courtesy Captain C. R. Christensen)

Right: The Mobile Riverine Base at anchor in
the Mekong River, 1969.

Reflections on a long flight, in a long war. (PHC Dan Dodd, USN)

An hour after moonrise, eleven men left their base camp on the north bank of the river and moved quietly in single file a distance of about fifty meters to where the Cai Nuoc intersects a small canal. Without speaking they established a rear defensive line with claymore mines and trip wires. They then dispersed to selected vantage points where they could keep silent watch. The creatures of the swamp soon resumed their private concerts. The river, almost at slack water, slapped lazily at its banks.

The patrol of ten montagnards and one U.S. sailor had taken up position on a known enemy LOC. Only the night before, this same patrol had engaged an enemy unit on this very spot, killing two and capturing two weapons. The Viet Cong were known to be creatures of habit. They would be back, if indeed they were not already there.

The men did not have long to wait. They had scarcely begun to notice the mosquitoes when the muffled sound of motorized sampans was heard approaching from the southeast. In another moment, two sampans broke into view, clearly illuminated in the moonlight. When the armed men in them reached the middle of the "kill zone" they were taken under fire. The range was not more than twenty-five meters.

At that very moment, however, the ambushers became themselves the ambushed. B-40 and automatic weapons fire poured into the patrol's position with such intensity the men could not rise up to return fire.

That the patrol was in serious danger there could be no doubt. If the survivors from the sampans were allowed to struggle ashore, the montagnards and the American soon would be caught in a deadly crossfire. Further, the claymore mines they had set out now blocked their flight or any possible reinforcement by other friendly elements in the area. In this desperate situation, something had to be done and it had to be done quickly.

The lone American in the patrol was Chief Hospitalman Donel Clifford Kinnard, a member of UDT Team 12. Firing short bursts from his M-16 rifle and hurling grenades across the narrow canal into the enemy's position, he ran the length of the patrol's right flank. One of his grenades silenced a heavy machine gun. The montagnards capitalized on Kinnard's daring by rising up to pour withering fire into the enemy.

At this moment, Kinnard received shrapnel wounds in his arms and legs from an enemy grenade. Then a body slammed into him from behind and he fell to the ground. In the darkness, he and his unknown assailant fought with bare hands. Arms flailing, the two men rolled through the underbrush and into the canal. There, as might be guessed, the American's UDT training stood him in good stead. Despite his wounds, Kinnard succeeded in wrenching a handgun from his attacker. This fight to the finish, in a shallow, jungle stream under a full tropic moon, ended as suddenly and as shatteringly as it had begun. The American dispatched his assailant with two bullets to the brain.

After a long, gasping moment, Kinnard waded ashore, dragging the body of the enemy soldier with him. The fighting on the bank was by then over and the enemy soldiers, those who had not died, were scattered and in flight. Several of the MSF troops gathered around Kinnard and tried to look after his wounds. Out on the Cai Nuoc the riddled sampans were drifting away in an ebb tide. Acting on impulse, Kinnard jumped into the river and retrieved them, along with several more enemy bodies. Only then did he permit the montagnard medic to treat his wounds.

The MSF patrol remained in position throughout the night, and nothing further marred the beauty and serenity of the moon-washed river.

At daybreak, fourteen enemy bodies were counted where they had fallen, and assorted sidearms, AK-47 rifles, B-40 rockets, and grenade launchers were collected. The sampans yielded thirty pounds of documents, which were rushed to Saigon. Papers found on the body of Kinnard's assailant identified him as an officer in the North Vietnamese Army. This was the first confirmed NVA presence in the Sea Float AO.

A picture of the dead man in uniform with rank insignia created a great deal of excitement, and later embarrassment. The Sea Float commander erroneously identified the officer, from the picture, as a "two-star general."[25] As it turned out, the NVA officer was not a general, but a lieutenant.

Kinnard, his shrapnel dug out in the field, remained with the montagnards until completion of their mission. On 16 February 1970, COMNAVFORV recommended him for the Navy Cross.

The river war in the Nam Can was brutal. The enemy, seriously shaken and his grip on the area weakening day by day, became if anything more vicious than ever. In February, MSF troops on ambush heard movement across a canal just as a sampan was approaching their position.

"The MSF took the movement in the trees under fire and heard screams from across the canal. The sampan was by this time between the two forces and the occupants of the sampan started shouting 'chieu hoi.' The MSF ceased fire and at that time came under intense fire from the VC on the east canal bank sustaining the U.S. WIA and wounding seriously one occupant of the sampan. The MSF illuminated the tree line and returned fire while the occupants of the sampan, two women and one boy, were brought to safety. . . . Later questioning of the boy revealed that the VC had forced them to go down the canal and yell 'chieu hoi.' "[26]

By the early months of 1970, there were 700 personnel assigned to Sea Float, of whom 193 were Americans. This was about the maximum number the MATSB could handle. Six PCFs, eight riverine assault craft, eleven junks, two Seawolf helicopters, one LSSL, one LSM-H, and one PGM were normally attached for operations.[27]

PCF maintenance and repair normally were accomplished at An Thoi, and Swift boats were rotated to and from Sea Float on a more or less regular basis. An APL stationed off Song Ong Doc in the Gulf of Thailand provided a repair facility for riverine assault craft. Vietnamese craft were repaired at the Saigon Naval Shipyard.

It was the Vietnamese Navy's responsibility to transport U.S. Navy–furnished supplies to Sea Float, and this task was assigned to an LSM that was to make a weekly run from Nha Be. Limited resupply on an emergency basis was possible by helicopter, but this could not provide the large quantities of food, fresh water, fuel, and ammunition needed to keep the operation going.

From the start, the VNN supply ships were "engineering casualty prone," and backups were seldom provided for canceled runs. This kept Sea Float in an almost constant state of supply crisis. Nor was this all. In January 1970, the Sea Float commander expressed his frustration and rage over what clearly had become an intolerable situation.

". . . 32,000 gallons water loaded Nha Be. LSM 402 arrived with no, repeat no, water for Sea Float. CO states he used about 90 tons to attempt to cool main engine. He further states that the water he has remaining on board, approximately 90 tons, will be used for engine cooling on his return to Saigon. . . . Due heavy seas the freeze box came apart with the entire contents lost. . . . Estimate total provisions for five days before utilizing C-Rats. . . .

"The lock on the chill box had been cut and another lock put in its place. Approximately half the contents were missing. Sea Float supply officer saw several cases of oranges in the engine room . . . large stacks of Sea Float meat below decks upon arrival of the ship. . . . On opening one crate containing miscellaneous Conex Pak boxes, it was found that all but one Conex Pak had missing items and medical supplies. Some of the remaining medical supplies were smashed. Material lost includes substantial numbers of boots, uniforms and equipment intended for KCS as well as ring sets and miscellaneous repair parts and tools intended for Sea Float.

"Originator is most appreciative of the strenuous and dedicated efforts of COMNAVSUPPACT Saigon and NAVSUPPACTDET Nha Be in supporting Sea Float/Solid Anchor and is concerned that at times these efforts are being prostituted prior to arrival Sea Float. It is therefore recommended that a regular detail of four men be assigned to ride the LSM and stand watch over the material. . . ."[28]

The senior naval advisor, Captain Rauch, discussed the resupply problem "at length" with Commodore Tran Van Chon, the VNN CNO. Chon, an amiable but thoroughly ineffective commander, was said to be "deeply disturbed over the situation," about which he claimed no foreknowledge. He promised to direct VNN Fleet Command to take "what action is necessary to preclude future recurrences of the situation reported." Sea Float was advised to let the VNN "try again" during a thirty-day evaluation period. Continuing the LSM runs was considered necessary "as a means of getting the VNN trained in the routine resupply of distant bases."[29]

Any improvement resulting from Rauch's conversation with Chon was minimal and fleeting in nature. The pilfering of supplies continued as before; the unreliability of the LSMs if anything grew worse. In early March, the Sea Float commander reported that "of the 120,000 gallons of fresh water and 69,000 gallons of diesel fuel shipped from Nha Be only 74,901 gallons of fresh water and 36,326 gallons of diesel fuel were received by originator. It should be noted that the extent of these receipts was possible only through the heavy pressure exerted by the deputy Sea Float commander and not by the decision of the LSM commander."[30]

In October, Rear Admiral Chon (he had been promoted on 1 July) was petitioned by the commander of Naval Support Activity Saigon to do what he could to improve the situation. "Nam Can's location and mission," COMNAVSUPPACT Saigon said, "do not permit the drastic reduction in operations which would result from failure to resupply."[31] Only three months later, abruptly and without warning, the Vietnamese Navy canceled its "regularly scheduled" LSM supply runs to Solid Anchor. With its ammunition, fuel, food, and water rapidly running out, the base received emergency supplies from the

Rear Admiral Tran Von Chon

USS *Park County* (LST 1077), which made a risky voyage up the Bo De and Cua Lon rivers. Airlift later would be used to keep the base going, though only at a greatly reduced level of operations.

As an interesting and somewhat humorous aside, Chon's promotion coincided with First Sea Lord and Deputy COMNAVFORV, Rear Admiral H. S. Matthews, Jr., reporting to him as deputy for the Tran Hung Dao campaigns. Matthews was given, perhaps with tongue in cheek, the additional title of "Second Tran Hung Dao."

The Sea Float/Solid Anchor AO gradually shrank to an area that extended no more than two kilometers from the banks of the Bo De and Cua Lon rivers. All the U.S. Navy had achieved through blood and sacrifice was rapidly reduced to naught. Tran Hung Dao I and II became hunting grounds for the Viet Cong. Villagers were killed or kidnapped at will. Attacks on Sea Float and Solid Anchor became bolder and more deadly.

On the night of 21 April 1970, four enemy swimmers carrying what was judged to be "enough explosives to completely destroy the MATSB" approached Sea Float.[32] At about 2050, sentries saw bubbles in the vicinity of the base and immediately threw grenades in the water. The bubbles ceased. Five hours later, however, swimmers using snorkels were detected approaching from two directions. One of the swimmers actually reached the ammunition storage ammi before being seen. Sea Float went to general quarters and saturated the surrounding water with small arms fire and concussion grenades. The swimmers, believed to be four in number, submerged. UDT personnel inspected the underwater portions of the MATSB and found nothing. Between then and the afternoon of 24 April, four bodies were spotted in the river, and three of these were recovered. They were equipped with Soviet offensive grenades, time fuses, blasting caps, nylon line, snorkel breathing tubes, etc. One of the swimmers carried a case containing 250 quarter-pound blocks of TNT interspersed with 10 pounds of plastic explosive.[33]

On 6 July, the USS *Krishna* (ARL 38) was mined while anchored in the vicinity of Sea Float. The explosion tore a twenty-foot by seventeen-foot hole in the ship's port quarter below the waterline. There were no casualties on the *Krishna*, though a VNN sailor on a PCF nested alongside was killed. Flooding on the ARL was brought under control in forty minutes, and after emergency repairs the ship departed the Sea Float AO the next afternoon.[34]

Early on the morning of 30 July, the VNN LSSL 225, moored to a buoy east of Sea Float, was mined. It took on water rapidly, capsized, and went down within minutes. Enemy swimmers had tied a mine to the ship's mooring cable, and the shifting tide had done the rest. Seventeen VNN sailors were missing and presumed lost.[35]

By 1 September 1970, construction at Solid Anchor (the Seabees called it "Challenge City") had progressed to the point where the Sea Float commander could move ashore. The navy task group designation, with the disestablishment of TF-115, was then TG-116.1. It would remain so until Solid Anchor passed finally into Vietnamese hands. Sea Float itself was broken up and towed out of the rivers.

CTG-116.1 did not sleep easy in his new surroundings. He advised COMNAVFORV the "physical Solid Anchor site is considered unsatisfactory from a defensive point of view. The frontage is long and the depth is narrow. The appendage of a helo pad and airstrip, the lack of adequate ammo and POL storage, and the neat symmetry of the quarters and warehouses all provide advantages to the attacker."[36]

His peace of mind was not enhanced by the disestablishment of the Kit Carson Scouts at Solid Anchor that same month, or by the utterly deplorable condition of the VNN units assigned to the operation. Of eleven River Interdiction Division (RID) boats at Solid Anchor on 25 September, nine were nonoperational due to material deficiencies. The other two were sunk.[37] VNN boats were ambushed thirteen times during the month of September.

This was but the beginning. On 12 December, eighteen of the assigned twenty-five riverine assault craft were in need of outside repair, and only nine were able to get under way for patrol. On 20 December, only one of ten PCFs was fully operational, a situation not improved when two relief PCFs reported with only one operational engine apiece. Theft of both personal and U.S. government property was rampant, and CTG-116.1 requested the assignment of a six-man internal security force. His request was denied.[38]

On 9 December, the VNN Explosive Ordnance Disposal (EOD) team refused to do any more work at Solid Anchor. They then packed their gear and departed for Saigon, leaving the two-man U.S. advisory team to handle all EOD assignments.[39]

As if all of the above were not enough, a cholera epidemic broke out in the nearby hamlets, resulting in four dead, thirteen medevaced, and thirty-one sick. Through it all, a resurgent enemy kept up the pressure with minings, ambushes, and mortar attacks.

Solid Anchor, which was to have been turned over to the Vietnamese Navy on 1 September 1970, became the last U.S. Navy–run operation in Vietnam. The turnover date slipped, and then slipped again.

In January 1971, the base was heavily bombarded on four occasions. Three men were killed and forty wounded. Offensive capability remained almost nil. Fewer than half of Solid Anchor's riverine assault craft and only one PCF could get under way on any given day. CTG-116.1 pleaded for replacement of the PCFs at Solid Anchor with PBRs, which he thought the Vietnamese sailors were better equipped to maintain. COMNAVFORV denied the request.[40] In February, the failure of a VNN tanker to make a scheduled POL (petroleum, oil, lubricants) supply run led to even further curtailment of Solid Anchor operations.

On 1 April 1971, the operation was at last turned over to the Vietnamese Navy. Perhaps to confuse the enemy (or future historians), the VNN redesignated it "Tran Hung Dao IV." U.S. Navy advisors, Seawolf helicopter fire teams, OV-10 "Black Pony" tactical aircraft, and logistics personnel continued to support this faltering operation in the Nam Can until they, too, were withdrawn from Vietnam. On 1 February 1973, the last Americans left Solid Anchor when the Naval Advisory Unit Nam Can was disestablished.

For the remainder of the war, the enemy kept heavy pressure on the base, though never, apparently, did he seek to overrun it. He didn't have to.

COMNAVFORV's failure to persuade or coerce the Vietnamese Navy into fulfilling its responsibilities at Sea Float/Solid Anchor illustrates, perhaps better than any other naval operation in Vietnam, the utter bankruptcy of the advisory system as U.S. participation in the war drew to a close. In such circumstances, the refusal to withdraw Americans whose lives were put at risk in an operation the VNN would not or could not support is almost inexplicable, except in terms unflattering to senior U.S. Navy officers whose careers and service reputations were most at stake. They left many brave men twisting in the wind in a godforsaken corner of Vietnam. It was not, I think, their finest hour.

15

The Naval War in the North

There are about 100 kinds of snakes in Vietnam. Ninety-nine percent are poisonous, and that last son of a bitch will swallow you.

—Chief Boatswain's Mate Wright, survival tactics instructor at the Naval Amphibious School, Little Creek, 2 July 1969

The Saigon government Thursday claimed control over 92.7 percent of the country's population, the highest level in the history of the Vietnam war.

—*Pacific Stars and Stripes*, 12 January 1970

CTOV (accelerated turnover to the Vietnamese), Sea Float, and Sea Lords captured most of COMNAVFORV's attention in the last years of the navy's operational participation in the war, but significant action continued in I Corps and in northern coastal waters. Task Force Clearwater, it will be recalled, was established in an atmosphere of crisis brought about by the battle for Hue and the threatened interdiction of vital LOCs on the Perfume and Cua Viet rivers. As the furies of Tet 1968 waned, however, the role of the operational navy in I Corps expanded to include action "to deny the waterways of northern I CTZ to the NVA/VC."[1]

In the fall of 1968 there were twenty PBRs, three PACVs, eight LCPLs, and four LCMs assigned to TF Clearwater.[2] One division of river patrol boats was based at Cua Viet and the other at Mobile Base I at Tan My.

Cua Viet, only five miles south of the Demilitarized Zone, was under the enemy's guns, and frequently subjected to artillery and rocket attack. The pressures of life at this exposed forward base were severe. The men lived in heavily bunkered huts burrowed in the sand dunes. During the long months of the northeast monsoon, the climate at Cua Viet is the country's worst, and cold, grey, and rainy days at the base followed each other in seemingly endless succession. When the rain stopped falling, the sand, fine-grained and gritty, began to blow, accumulating in drifts outside the huts, sifting through screens and under doors, finding its way into lockers and between sheets and even into the food the men ate.

In October 1968, Cua Viet was already on its third mess hall, the first two having been destroyed by NVA artillery. The enlisted men's club and the crew's shower also had been hit. Three rounds of "friendly" 8-inch had slammed into the base.

Outside the river mouth, there was a pounding surf and restless shoals. The year before, two Market Time Swift boats had gone down in heavy seas off Cua Viet, and the memory still burned in those who were required to navigate the treacherous channel. On 6 November 1967, PCF 76 had capsized, sunk, and been pounded to pieces in the surf. Remarkably, no member of the crew was lost. On 30 November, PCF 14, while attempting to rescue Vietnamese civilians whose sampans had swamped, also capsized. PCF 55, coming to her assistance, took an 85-degree roll and all of her crew except one man were washed overboard. All crewmen from both PCFs, and the Vietnamese fishermen then in the water, were returned safely to port in what surely must have been an act of Providence.[3]

A year before that, in stormy seas off the entrance to the Hue

River, the crew of PCF 77 had not been so fortunate. The Swift boat was standing by just outside the surf line to assist in the recovery of a man swept overboard from another boat. A wave, estimated to be 30 feet high, lifted her stern and flipped the Swift boat end over end. Water rushed in through a sprung pilothouse door. The officer in charge, Lieutenant (j.g.) David G. Wilbourne, pulled one man clear. Chief Petty Officer W. S. Baker, a qualified diver, was last seen entering the aft compartment of the boat where it was believed Radioman Third Class B. A. Timmons was trapped. Less than two minutes after upending, the Swift boat went down, keel up.

Chief Baker's body and that of Boatswain's Mate Third Class Harry B. Brock were later recovered. Timmons's body could not be found and he was listed as missing and presumed dead. Ironically, the man overboard from the other boat was recovered safely.[4]

The drama of men against the sea in northern I Corps was not played solely by those on Swift boats. It required both courage and skill to bring low-powered and frequently age-weakened supply ships and craft into the region's makeshift ports. "Though it reads easily today," a former commander of Naval Support Activity Danang wrote, "it was in these areas that individual officers and men became heroes in the truest sense. The lieutenant who took his LST into Chu Lai through a partially dredged, poorly marked channel in the midst of the monsoon weather knowing he had only inches or less over the sand bar, and coral all around, is a hero. . . . The same was true of the MSTS oiler captain who fought to stay moored off Chu Lai though his 32-foot-draft ship in 50-plus feet of water was bottoming out in some of the seas. At one time, 14 anchors were being searched for off Chu Lai from ships striving to keep up the supply lines in the face of terrible weather. That casualties were few is a tribute to their ability."[5]

Naval craft moored at Cua Viet, in addition to rocket and artillery attack, had to contend with enemy sappers, whose raids were thought to be launched from a refugee hamlet directly across the river. On 21 February 1969, one LCM-6 was sunk and two LCM-8s were heavily damaged in one such raid. In this action one U.S. sailor died and one enemy swimmer was killed. The dead swimmer was equipped with a Russian-designed, closed-circuit, underwater breathing apparatus, a head mask of Chinese manufacture, and adding to the international nature of his rig, Spanish swim fins. One unexploded limpet mine, with Russian markings, was discovered in the vicinity of the damaged LCM-8s.[6]

There were at least a half dozen separate U.S. Army, Navy, and

Marine Corps units based at Cua Viet, and this created special problems for CTF Clearwater, the senior officer present. Base defense was a particular concern, and divided responsibility for various sections of the perimeter wire, etc., frequently caused friction between the various services. This was the period, too, when the anti-war movement in the United States was spreading to the troops in Vietnam.

"Although there were many fine officers and enlisted personnel at Cua Viet," a former CTF Clearwater wrote, "a few left something to be desired. . . . As examples, a few officers presented an entirely unkempt appearance and didn't understand even the basic rudiments of courtesy—military or otherwise; some personnel saw fit on one occasion to cut the fresh water bladders (thus causing a water shortage for a period on the base), on another occasion to cut the fuel lines leading from the fuel farm to the waterfront, on at least three occasions to detonate tear gas grenades (thus driving everyone to gas masks), and on other occasions to detonate fragmentation grenades (thus hazarding other personnel in the camp); one enlisted man even arrived from Danang with the 'Hippy' Peace Symbol inscribed on his flak jacket and helmet.

". . . CTF Clearwater in his role as Senior Officer Present/Senior Officer Present Afloat, Cua Viet, duly rectified this situation to the extent possible and upgraded the military standards at the Cua Viet base. With regard to the grenadings and sabotage to water and fuel lines, CTF Clearwater reported these matters to XXIV Corps headquarters [the senior U.S. Army command in northern I Corps] and further discussed them at length with Naval Investigative Service officers whose efforts, combined with those of marine investigators, eventually led to the apprehension of one marine and transfer of another. One significant deficiency became apparent, however; because of the very few members of the Naval Investigative Service in-country, they normally would not investigate any incident involving a grenade unless someone were wounded in the process."[7]

One can well imagine how these circumstances affected not only tradition-bound senior naval officers at the base, but the large majority of men there who were trying to do a job to the best of their ability.

Divided authority in northern I Corps created other problems. CTF Clearwater's AO ended at the water's edge, and U.S. Marine Corps, U.S. Army, and Vietnamese Army units had responsibility for the land. Naval craft, except in self-defense when returning hostile fire, could not engage enemy forces on the river banks without first obtaining clearance from the proper AO commander. This was neces-

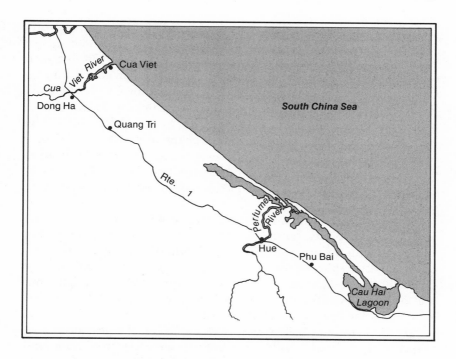

Task Force Clearwater Area of Operations

sary to protect friendly units that might be operating in the area, but it nonetheless added to the daily frustrations experienced on the rivers. "I personally watched what turned out to be enemy troops escaping in my very gun sights, while awaiting permission to fire," Commander S. A. Swartztrauber, a former CTF Clearwater, wrote.[8]

Naval craft were fired upon by enemy forces equipped with B-40 rockets, recoilless rifles, and heavy machine guns, but mines posed the principal threat, particularly in the six-mile stretch of river running from Cua Viet to Dong Ha. It should have been relatively easy for bank security forces to keep the enemy from mining this short piece of river, which ran through mostly open country, but somehow or other there were never enough troops, or enough alertness or diligence on the part of the ones there were, to stop the mining.

"We would have liked," said Swartztrauber, "to have seen the ARVN effectively engage the enemy in his area of operation between the DMZ and the Cua Viet River, notably the II ARVN Regiment's AO at the confluence of the Song Nieu Giang and the Song Thach-

Han, an area selected by the enemy to concentrate interdiction efforts against water traffic. We would occasionally get advance intelligence warning of enemy sapper plans to mine the Cua Viet. On one such occasion we were fortunate enough to obtain radar contact on an enemy patrol proceeding from the DMZ toward the Cua Viet via the II ARVN Regiment's AO. This was reported immediately, with exact coordinates, by the marines at Ocean View to the ARVN TOC. The ARVN did not send a patrol to intercept the infiltration, even after follow up reports. Nor did they investigate the reported infiltration until the following morning. From events like this, I obtained the impression that the ARVN preferred not to engage the enemy in operations at night."[9]

Many strange devices were encountered by the navy in the Cua Viet. Floating objects, regardless of their innocent appearance, had to be treated with the utmost caution. C-Ration boxes, tree limbs, cans, drums, plastic spheres and fish floats, a bright blue swim fin, and other flotsam and jetsam of no particular distinction—all might conceal or buoy a drifting mine. Recovered devices included some that were manufactured in part from scrap styrofoam, cloth, string, wicker baskets, and innertubes. The explosive charges these contained ranged from small fragmentation grenades to 750-pound bombs. Moored mines were sometimes anchored by mud-filled plastic bags on the river bottom. Some mines were free-floating. In message traffic they often were described as being of "poor and unprofessional construction,"[10] but the number of successful enemy mining incidents spoke for itself.

In the first year of TF Clearwater operations, command-detonated and floating contact mines were the kind most frequently encountered; later, sophisticated magnetic and acoustic influence mechanisms of Russian manufacture began to show up. Because of the nearness of the DMZ, the Cua Viet became the most heavily mined river in South Vietnam.

The enemy units responsible for mining the river were highly trained and well motivated. Interrogation of a prisoner captured on 17 January 1969 gave a reasonably good picture of how the operation worked. All men in the prisoner's company were Communist Party members of proven loyalty and were carefully screened to ensure they possessed required physical characteristics. They received five months of intensive training in their specialty. Organized in small teams and working at night, they transported three or more mines over the DMZ at a time, floating or dragging them in skids made from hollowed-out logs. Naval patrols on the Cua Viet were reconnoitered in advance and when it was determined safe to do so, selected team members floated the mines into position and planted them, while other members of the team established defensive positions on the river bank. The daylight hours of the next day were usually spent in concealed underground bunkers, and the return trip to the north was accomplished on the following night.[11]

On 29 January 1969, a conference was convened at Danang to review the Cua Viet mine threat and the countermeasures that could or should be taken. Rear Admiral Emmett P. Bonner, commander of the Naval Support Activity Danang, chaired the meeting. Other attendees included Commander Swartztrauber, a representative from COMNAVFORV, and the officer in charge of the Naval Support Activity Detachment, Cua Viet/Dong Ha. The conferees concluded that while the enemy had the capability to place small numbers of influence mines anywhere along the Cua Viet, he was much more likely to concentrate these mines near the mouth of the river where the targets were more lucrative. It was thought that the principal threat in the river from Cua Viet to Dong Ha would continue to come from command-detonated and small contact mines. Accordingly, it was requested that MSBs from Mine Division 112 be tasked to conduct influence sweeping in the mouth of the Cua Viet and in the turning basin opposite the base, and that armored riverine craft continue as before with chain bottom drags of the lines of communication to Dong Ha. As a form of added insurance, it was requested that four MSLs (minesweeping launches) be furnished by Seventh Fleet to conduct limited influence sweeping in the river.[12]

The recommendations seemed reasonable, if the conclusions concerning enemy intentions, in retrospect, do not. It is likely that the enemy was more intent on cutting the Cua Viet/Dong Ha LOC than in going after the LSTs and LCUs that made the ramps at Cua Viet to discharge cargo. It was certainly true that the enemy found it easier to mine the river than the river mouth. There would be little evidence of mines in the turning basin or the seaward approaches to the base, except for the occasional floating one that came down the river, and the MSBs assigned to sweep there achieved little other than perhaps adding, marginally, to the peace of mind of LST and LCU skippers coming from Danang. MSLs were not furnished, because senior commanders considered them "too valuable" to risk in the riverine environment of Vietnam.

In April 1969, an odd device was recovered in the sweep gear of one of the MSMs employed in the Cua Viet to Dong Ha chain bottom drag. In appearance, the device was a rubber bag enclosed in a wire cage attached to a metal cylinder about eight inches in length and four inches in diameter. The device apparently had been torn loose from another object to which it may have been attached by string and an electrical wire. Again, the device was described as being of "crude manufacture." Electrical connections were insulated by what appeared to be, and were, condoms. Not long after discovery of this device, others were recovered, some of which were still attached to what had been the missing half of the first mechanism—a wicker basket filled with high explosives.

Captain Frederick F. Jewett II, who had relieved as CTF Clearwater in February, was an officer knowledgeable in mine warfare. He recognized the threat posed by this device, which he judged, correctly, to be a pressure mine. Utilizing to the fullest the meager resources at his command, he ordered a resumption of influence sweeping in the river and took other steps to ensure, as far as possible, the safety of his craft. A magnetic/acoustic sweep of primitive design was conducted using a magnetized rail and clapper bars (1B/2G gear) towed by LCMs and MSMs. Concussion grenades and the chain bottom drag were the only active countermeasures available against pressure mines. When U.S. supplies of the grenades ran out, "U.K. scare charges" imported from England were used in their place and proved to be surprisingly effective. Fortunately for the U.S. Navy, the enemy pressure mine lacked countermining features that could have made it all but invulnerable to explosive sweeps.

Scare charges were thrown along the LOC each morning by a swiftly moving "skimmer" boat (a Boston Whaler) that preceded the LCM and MSM sweeps. Secondary explosions became an almost common occurrence and were observed ahead, astern, and to port and starboard of the skimmer. The heavy, steel-hulled minesweepers that followed the skimmer were themselves in grave peril from influence mines. It was openly acknowledged that the "signatures" of these craft were probably greater than the influence fields produced by the sweep gear they towed. Minesweeping on the Cua Viet was hazardous duty carried to the extreme. It took both raw courage and luck for the minesweeping effort to succeed as well as it did. As it was, four river craft (including two PBRs) were sunk or damaged by mines on the Cua Viet during the first half of 1969, resulting in eight killed and twenty-seven wounded. Enemy pressure mines were also believed to be responsible for the loss of a PBR on 16 November

1969, and the heavy damage of an LCM-6 on 7 February 1970. These two minings took the lives of four more men and wounded seven.

Additional losses undoubtedly would have been experienced were it not for passive countermeasures taken by CTF Clearwater. By local, on-site experiments using recovered influence mechanisms, "safe" speeds were established for various craft transiting the river.

The capture of an enemy swimmer on 2 January 1970, following an unsuccessful attack on the Cua Viet base, produced intelligence that magnetic mines with Soviet mechanisms were about to be deployed again in the river.[13] CTF Clearwater, then Captain James E. Edmundson, another officer skilled in mine warfare, renewed earlier urgent requests for a skimmer detachment capable of towing magnetic gear.[14] This request was turned down, too.

Mine warfare might have been the principal concern of the navy at Cua Viet in the latter part of 1969 and the beginning of 1970, but it was not the only one. On 2 September, a typhoon swept ashore, sinking an MSB and beaching several LCPLs. Roofs were blown off berthing hootches and the galley/mess hall. All power was lost, except for one small emergency generator. A security tower was toppled, and much of the perimeter wire was either down or under water. Civilian rock barges, pusher boats, causeway sections, and LCMs were scattered, and some of them were aground. Channel markers were swept away, and the entrance range was rendered inoperative. "Able to continue mission," CTF Clearwater reported, with perhaps more than a little bravado, "but with 25 percent degradation in effectiveness."[15]

Firefights on the river were not infrequent, but the enemy's presence sometimes was revealed in other ways. In exchange for small cash rewards, children turned in grenades, firearms, ammunition, and other material discovered during their play along the river banks. Sappers were discovered in the water off the Cua Viet ramps on several occasions. On 13 December 1969 they succeeded in sinking the YOG 76 with two well-placed charges while the vessel was riding to a buoy in the turning basin.

Base defense, always worrisome, became even more so with the withdrawal in November of the Third Marine Battalion and its 105-mm battery. Attempts to have ARVN relieve the marines were not successful, and ground support for the base was reduced to a single U.S. Army platoon that rotated there from field assignments. Perimeter defenses were consequently spread very thin.[16]

In January 1970, with the withdrawal of U.S. forces from northern I Corps and at least the temporary abandonment of the Cua Viet/ Dong Ha LOC, TF Clearwater's mission was again redefined. The task force was to "conduct patrol operations on the inland waterways of NICTZ to deny the enemy their use as logistic LOCs or infiltration routes, and in coordination/conjunction with GVN/ARVN/VNN forces, conduct visit, search, and psychological operations to enforce curfews, recover contraband, and extend pacification efforts." TF Clearwater was to continue mine countermeasures operations in assigned areas and "maintain the capability to reopen the Cua Viet LOC when required for resupply or reinforcement." Lastly, the tiny task force was to give combat support to "U.S. and RVN ground operations in coordination with area commanders."[17]

This was, needless to say, a pretty tall order for the navy, while the army and the marines were bailing out.

Following the new mission statement, the base at Cua Viet was reduced to the status of an advance tactical support base, and CTF Clearwater and his staff relocated south to Tan My on 14 February. Pending assumption of patrol responsibilities by the VNN, the Dong Ha River Security Group was reduced to six LCPLs, five MSMs, four LCM-6s, and four Kenner ski barges.[18]

Operations by the Hue River Security Group, meanwhile, had undergone significant change. After the brutal fighting during Tet 1968 and its immediate aftermath, there was little enemy effort to disrupt the water LOC from Tan My to Hue on the Perfume River. Though daily chain bottom drags were conducted, there was no known enemy mining activity. Occasional firefights did occur along the LOC, but the environment for patrol boat operations was vastly different from that experienced on the Cua Viet. The Perfume River was relatively broad and deep, while the Cua Viet was a nightmare of shoals. Though the Perfume, with its numerous graveyards and tree lines, offered considerably more opportunity for ambush than the barren and bleak banks of the Cua Viet, the former was largely pacified territory after the middle of 1968, and this by no means could be said of the latter.

Living conditions for the men of the Hue River Security Group were among the best offered anywhere in-country. Mobile Base I, like its counterpart in the delta, Mobile Base II, was air-conditioned, clean, and for the most part run like a taut navy ship. Compared to their brothers at Cua Viet, the men at Tan My were very fortunate indeed. (A rotation system, however, ensured that no one had to spend more than six months at Cua Viet unless he volunteered to do so.)

Operations in the south were not allowed to lag. Navy patrols gradually were extended into Cau Hai Bay and into the many tributary streams that fed it. The number of firefights in this area was comparable to the number experienced on the Cua Viet. Psychological operations were vigorously pursued, and the Mobile Base supported one of the best medical civic action programs (MEDCAPS) in the country. The "soft life" at Tan My was not an inactive life. Working hours, as they were everywhere for the navy in Vietnam, were long. (Admiral Zumwalt said at a commanders' conference once that "the greatest crime" in Vietnam was to have somebody working only one job when that job required less than twelve hours a day. If that were so, someone at the conference muttered sotto voce, then there was an awful lot of criminal activity going on within the Vietnamese Navy.)

The navy patrol air-cushion vehicle (PACV) saw its last operational employment in Vietnam with TF Clearwater. The enthusiasm generated for the PACV during the 1966 flood campaign in the Plain of Reeds had ebbed with the receding water. The craft could not climb the steep banks characteristic of delta rivers at low tide, and its great speed could not be used to full advantage in narrow, twisting waters. Furthermore, once the enemy overcame his initial fright (and became better armed), the PACV made a handsome and vulnerable target.

In the mud-flat regions of I Corps, however, the air-cushion vehicles gained a new, though brief, lease on life. In the spring of 1969 the PACVs were already six years old and increasingly difficult and expensive to maintain. In the dry season they raised immense clouds of dust that shortened engine life and further complicated maintenance procedures. Money for replacements was not budgeted. A last-ditch effort was made to keep them in-country by transferring them to III MAF, but the marines, perhaps wisely, turned them down. On 24 May 1969, the navy sent the last three "monsters" of the Plain of Reeds back to the United States. The U.S. Army continued to operate three air-cushion vehicles of its own in III Corps well into 1970, with maintenance problems similar to those experienced by the navy. These occasionally were used in support of navy operations.

The first PBRs assigned to I Corps had arrived on 18 September 1967 as part of Operation "Green Wave." The USS *Hunterdon*

County (LST 838) supported a division of ten boats, which established patrols on the poorly charted Cau Dai River, southeast of Hue, in an area effectively under enemy control. Numerous groundings plagued the operation, and the boats were fired on from heavily bunkered positions on the banks. At one time half of the assigned PBRs were out of commission due to grounding or battle damage. After three weeks, the operation ended and the PBRs were withdrawn. In December 1967, however, Mobile Base I and another division of PBRs arrived at Danang to establish a permanent river patrol boat presence in I Corps. These provided the nucleus for TF Clearwater.

Early in 1969, Market Time raiders began random incursions of the Cua Dai River, and by April these were being conducted on a regular basis. On 25 April the Swift boat operations were given the code name "Sea Tiger," which was described as "a continuing PCF operation on Song Cua Dai/Song Hoi An to interdict enemy LOC and ensure unimpeded passage for friendly water traffic."[19]

The Sea Tiger AO possessed numerous shoals, fish weirs, and other hazards to navigation. In the early weeks of the Swift boat raids, only Giant Slingshot among the other naval interdiction campaigns experienced a higher number of firefights.[20] Curfews and restricted zones were established, bunkers taken under fire and destroyed, and psychological operations were pursued. Psyops typically consisted of the playing of tapes over loudspeaker systems on the boats, tapes that extolled the virtues of the Saigon government and solicited the defection of Viet Cong by way of the government's *Chieu Hoi* ("Open Arms") program. The tapes were at best of doubtful effectiveness, and most patrol boats hated playing them—often they drew enemy fire.

Medical and dental civic action programs were much better received by the people of the rivers. I accompanied several of these in I Corps and recall vividly the lines of people, mostly women, children, and old men, waiting patiently to see a doctor, a dentist, a nurse, or as was most often the case, a navy corpsman. One old man I remember in particular. He was tall for a Vietnamese, and over a tattered pair of pants chopped off at the knees he wore a French legionnaire's dress coat. The old man was nearly blind, and he was led by a small girl whom I took to be his granddaughter. The MEDCAP corpsman looked at the old man's eyes, shook his head, and handed the girl a few aspirin. "Cataracts," he said to no one in particular, and turned to his next patient.

In spite of the strain of combat in the Sea Tiger AO, occasional black humor crept into spot reports filed by Swift boat officers. One such concerned a "probable" Viet Cong taken under fire while attempting to evade a patrol.

"During random patrol of Song Thu Bon PCF 79 sighted one male running . . . and took him under fire but failed to hit him before he reached tree line and bunker complex. PCF 79 resorted to psyops speaker but the man would not come out—not altogether surprising under the circumstances."[21]

In another incident, a two-boat patrol sighted what were thought to be enemy troops in a tree line not far from where eight children were tending several water buffalo. The PCFs beached in the immediate vicinity and called the children to the boats and managed to keep them close by with random chatter and ice cream. In the meantime, air strikes were called in on the unsuspecting people in the tree line, who did not know they had been spotted.

"Normal Sea Tiger patrol," the spot report of this incident read. "PCF 61 expended eight rounds 81-mm WP [white phosphorus]. PCF 18 expended 12 cups of ice cream. . . . GDA [ground damage assessment] not available."[22]

In May 1969, Sea Tiger units supported USMC and ARVN search-and-destroy operations on Barrier Island some twenty miles south of Danang. Swift boats, joined to seaward by U.S. Coast Guard WPBs, provided a blocking force while ground troops swept the island. The U.S. Navy and Coast Guard later assisted in the evacuation of more than seven hundred newly created refugees. When the operation ended, on 24 May, CTF-115 summarized the progress of Sea Tiger to that point.

"By the most conservative estimate, it is now safe to say:

"A. That the river complex is open to civilian traffic from Hoi An to the sea with little risk of VC taxation or retaliation.

"B. That the river between Hoi An to the sea is denied for VC use as a line of communication. If he crosses at all, he does so at great risk and in the most surreptitious manner.

"C. That the ancillary waterways—Truong Giang Thu Ban, Cua Lau, Dien Binh, Ba Ren, Phuoc Trach—have been opened for US/FWMAF/VNN use, and are largely denied to the VC.

"D. That the VC/NVA have been greatly restricted in movement, logistics, leadership, firepower, manpower, and fighting spirit by this campaign."[23]

Through 24 May, Sea Tiger PCFs destroyed or damaged 331

bunkers, 178 structures, and 142 sampans. Fifty-nine Viet Cong had been killed and nineteen had rallied ("chieu-hoied"). Swift boats had been involved in 102 firefights and six attempted minings. No U.S. sailors had been lost, but seventeen were wounded.[24]

Late in May, a new enemy ambush tactic was reported. After initiating the ambush and drawing return fire from patrol craft, the enemy would withdraw to well-prepared bunkers surrounded by heavy rings of booby traps, fully expecting reaction force troops to land and assault their positions. After suffering some losses, reaction forces adopted the simple procedure of waiting until the enemy came out. This usually occurred within twenty-four hours. Before the enemy could pass through his line of booby traps, he had to disarm them, and that is when the patience of the reaction force paid off. The only other countermeasure employed against this enemy tactic was to call in heavy air and artillery strikes, and these could not always be scheduled when needed.

In June 1969, the first Duffle Bag sensors were emplaced in the Sea Tiger AO. There was evidence that direct artillery response to sensor activations may have resulted in enemy casualties. There was no way of telling, of course, whether this tactic also resulted in the killing of innocent civilians transiting, as they often did, restricted zones.

In addition to the PCF patrols, Vietnamese Navy junks and river assault craft conducted operations in the Cua Dai and its tributaries. As elsewhere in Vietnam, VNN participation was a mixed bag of pluses and minuses. The elimination of VC tax collectors not infrequently led to the Vietnamese Navy taking their place. VNN junks were observed accepting bribes in the form of fresh fish to speed up or eliminate the inspection of fishing boats proceeding to and from the rivers. RAG boats assigned responsibility for enforcing curfews often tied up to fish weirs, and their crews went to sleep for the night.

"The U.S. recourse," Commander Swartztrauber said, "was two-fold: either register a complaint through advisory channels, or take over—or try to take over—the responsibility for the operation in question. In the former case the 'advice' usually fell on deaf ears, receiving a tactful, agreeable acknowledgment but failing to trigger a change in the *modus operandi*. In the latter case, the Vietnamese resisted strongly any proposal which would result in the U.S. taking over any section of their AO. It seemed to be politically unacceptable—a matter of losing face. . . . The lesson learned here is obvious—and an old, well recognized one—too many bosses were running the war. There was no real common superior of the allied forces in northern ICTZ."[25]

On 30 August 1969, COMNAVFORV requested that Commanding General III MAF release three PBRs from CTF Clearwater assets in order to determine the feasibility of extending the Sea Tiger AO into waters inaccessible to PCFs. On 23 September three PBRs from River Division 543 made a successful transit of the inland waterway from Danang to Hoi An. A low bridge on the Song Vinh Dien proved to be something of an obstacle, but by removing boat canopies and radomes, and ballasting the boats low in the water, they managed to squeeze through. This and later PBR probes showed that an additional forty-five kilometers of the river system, not navigable by Swift boats, could be patrolled by PBRs.

The areas penetrated by the river patrol boats were rich in evidence of enemy activity. Bunker complexes, submerged and hidden sampans, fresh trails on the river banks, and several sightings of enemy troops proved that these were waters being put to maximum use by the Viet Cong and the NVA. On 3 October, therefore, COMNAVFORV proposed that VNN RAG-32 relieve CTF Clearwater PBRs of security duties in the Hue/Perfume River area and that the PBRs join Sea Tiger operations. Eight PBRs from River Division 521 were made available early in November.

Swift boats continued to see a great deal of action. On 7 October 1969, PCFs 61 and 69 were conducting a routine patrol of the Truong Giang, the waterway that separates Barrier Island from the mainland. At about noon, sporadic small-arms fire was received from the near bank on Barrier Island, and this was returned and suppressed. Both units then proceeded north with the intention of clearing the channel.

At approximately 1245, however, both boats were suddenly taken under fire from recoilless rifle, heavy machine gun, and small-arms fire from a bunkered position on the island. The officer in charge of PCF 61, who was then at the boat's helm, was hit and mortally wounded. Moments later, running at full speed, his boat ran hard aground. At the same time the PCF officer was struck, both Swift boats took recoilless rifle rounds close aboard, causing minor damage to PCF 69 but holing the port fuel tank on PCF 61. It took on water rapidly.

Both boats tried to suppress the enemy fire, and PCF 69 maneuvered to pull PCF 61 free. It was unable to do so. At about 1310, PCF

101, helo gunships, and the medical "Dustoff" helicopter arrived on the scene. The wounded officer was medevaced at about 1330, but died shortly thereafter.

While the gunships and remaining PCFs raked the enemy position, PCF 69 sped to nearby Coastal Group 14 to pick up a pump to dewater PCF 61. It returned with the pump by 1400. PCF 61 was finally refloated, and by 1600 all units cleared the area.[26]

This action took place, mind you, not more than twenty miles south of Danang, and the island itself had been "swept" by ground forces only five months before, causing a major relocation of the civilian population. That it was still hostile territory speaks volumes about the effectiveness and lasting value of the campaign to pacify the land and the people.

Throughout the remainder of the year and into 1970, action continued to be heavy in the Sea Tiger AO. Combined operations were held with Korean and ARVN troops. Seventh Fleet amphibious ships landed U.S. Marines on Barrier Island, and an increasing number of "ralliers" was thought to reflect a weakening of enemy resolve. CTF-115 gave Sea Tiger units the following pep talk:

"Your operations in the Sea Tiger AO have resulted in 14 ralliers in a 24-hour period. This is surely striking a serious blow to the morale of the VC/NVA forces in the area. Keep the pressure on the enemy and ensure maximum psyops broadcasts capitalizing on the tendency to rally. Keep charging on the hearts and minds."[27]

A determined enemy continued to fight back, however. On the night of 25 January 1970, sappers succeeded in penetrating a forward operating base two kilometers northwest of Hoi An. They placed charges under the keels of PBRs moored there. One charge went off directly beneath PBR 91, blowing it nearly ten feet out of the water and onto the bank. A second PBR also suffered heavy damage. Two U.S. and two Vietnamese sailors were wounded and PBR 91 was declared a total loss.

Through 12 February 1970, Sea Tiger operations accounted for 473 enemy killed and 50 captured, at the cost of 28 friendly killed and 125 wounded. Patrol boats had been involved in 188 firefights and 20 mining incidents.[28]

Not an interdiction barrier in the same sense as those established in the delta along the Cambodian border, Sea Tiger was designed to destroy the enemy's hold on waterways vital to the economic life of a large civilian population. In this respect it can be considered the I Corps equivalent of Sea Float in IV Corps. By driving the enemy off these waterways, and by establishing a secure GVN presence, it was thought that the Viet Cong and the NVA would be denied important sources of material and moral support.

By early 1970, however, Vietnamization of the naval war was "progressing" rapidly, and U.S. forces already were standing down from offensive operations. On 1 July 1970, CTF Clearwater was disestablished, and responsibility for the security of the Cua Viet and Perfume rivers was turned over to the VNN. What happened thereafter was a sad and steady erosion of the GVN's defensive posture in northern I Corps. In May 1971, a "disastrous" increase in enemy activity was noted in the vicinity of Cua Viet. No fewer than seventeen mining incidents occurred that month in the river, and the sinking of a water taxi took the lives of at least thirty civilians.[29]

The Cua Viet base itself was abandoned during the NVA's 1972 "Easter offensive."

Throughout the period of U.S. participation in the war, COM-USMACV pressed the navy to provide ever larger amounts of gunfire support in northern I Corps. In 1968 alone, destroyers and cruisers on the gun line delivered almost a million rounds in support of troops ashore. This incredible bombardment depleted ammunition reserves, wore out gun barrels, strained the navy's logistics system, and tore up a tremendous amount of real estate. In all honesty, it is doubtful that it accomplished much more. What was "Indian country" remained Indian country, despite impressive numbers of "structures" and "enemy positions" blown off the map.

Because of the very few heavy cruisers in the fleet (only two could be kept in WestPac at any one time), and the insatiable demands of ground force commanders who feared a conventional attack across the DMZ by NVA armor, Secretary of Defense McNamara was persuaded to approve, on 1 August 1967, the recommissioning of the USS *New Jersey* (BB 62). The battleship was scheduled to begin operations off the coast of Vietnam in April 1968, but delays in fitting her out caused her to be five months late in reporting. She arrived off northern I Corps on 29 September.

The *New Jersey*'s primary assignment was to support III MAF by destroying hard targets in and just north of the DMZ. COM-USMACV, in coordination with COMSEVENTHFLT, was to determine when her services were needed elsewhere.

An immediate controversy arose when McNamara insisted that one of WestPac's two heavy cruisers be brought home during the period of the *New Jersey*'s deployment.

"I do not approve," he said, "more than two major naval gunfire ships (cruiser and/or battleship) in the Western Pacific, unless additional justification in terms of increased effectiveness can be provided. As you will recall, an increase in gunfire capability was not intended when the battleship activation was approved. Rather, it was to provide relief for the large caliber gunfire support ship rotation schedule and to permit the ships to begin essential overhauls. . . ."[30]

CINCPAC and CINCPACFLT wished to use the *New Jersey* and the heavy cruisers, particularly during the northeast monsoon season, to supplement the bombing campaign in North Vietnam. McNamara was unmoved, reflecting his continued disagreement with the navy concerning the bombing of North Vietnam.

In 1969, with the amount of naval gunfire support (NGFS) declining by half from the year before, the *New Jersey* was brought back to the United States and once more laid up. Had she been available earlier in the war and used to fullest advantage, the lives of many U.S. aviators and hundreds of first-line aircraft might have been saved. Many targets in North Vietnam were within easy reach of her 16-inch guns.

The ships of the Amphibious Ready Group (ARG) found most of their employment in I Corps waters. In addition to the landing of ground forces over the beach, the ARG provided safe havens for logistics craft during periods of heavy enemy activity and dangerous weather. During and after Tet 1968, its LPHs, LPDs, LSDs, and LSTs carried vitally needed supplies from Danang to offloading anchorages in northern I Corps.

Finally, the navy's only hospital ships, the USS *Repose* (AH 16) and USS *Sanctuary* (AH 17), were assigned to support operations in I Corps. At the height of the war, at least one was present in RVN waters at all times.

Originally commissioned in World War II, they were built as hospital transports to carry gravely wounded men back home. When outfitted for Vietnam duty, they were fully equipped to serve as floating surgical aid stations and recuperative treatment hospitals. A tug of war developed between COMUSMACV and COMSEVENTHFLT over the scheduled relief of these ships for periodic maintenance and rest for the staff and crews. Essentially, ground force commanders, with limited medical facilities of their own, wanted both ships on station all of the time. A request for a third hospital ship was pending when the decision was taken to withdraw U.S. forces from combat.[31]

16

A Boy Named Chou

"See, I am one of you—I am one of your children, your son, your brother, and your friend. Behold how sleek and fat I have become—and all because I am just one of you, and your friend. Behold how rich and powerful I am—and all because I am one of you—shaped in your way of life, of thinking, of accomplishment. What I am, I am because I am one of you, your humble brother and your friend. Behold," cries Enemy, "the man I am, the man I have become, the thing I have accomplished—and reflect. Will you destroy this thing? I assure you that it is the most precious thing you have. It is yourself, the projection of each of you, the triumph of your individual lives, the thing that is rooted in your blood, and native to your stock, and inherent in the tradition of America."

—Thomas Wolfe, *You Can't Go Home Again*

An Thoi is a small village on the southern tip of Phu Quoc Island in the Gulf of Thailand. The island at various times in its history has been claimed by both Vietnam and Cambodia. France, under terms of the Brevie Agreement, gave it to Vietnam. It is likely, though, that most native islanders in 1969, when I first saw it, thought of themselves first as Phu Quocese and only incidentally, if at all, as Vietnamese.

The small harbor at An Thoi was as pretty as a picture postcard. Dozens of rocky islets rose from the sea to form an offshore lee, and many of these were ringed by dazzling white beaches. The water in the harbor was unusually clear and sparkling.

Phu Quoc manufactured some of the finest *nuoc mam*, a pungent fish sauce and seasoner, to be had in all of Vietnam. In spite of the war, Phu Quoc's prized "yellow label" still found its way to the Saigon market. Great wooden vats of this delicacy bubbled away in a number of small factories near An Thoi. Alternate layers of fish and salt were tamped into the vats and when they were nearly full, water was poured in at the top. When it percolated to the bottom, it was drawn off and poured in again, and again until, in good time, the liquid, rich and darkly golden, was ready for bottling.

Phu Quoc also boasted some of the best native shipwrights in Southeast Asia. The Kien Giang junk, the mainstay of the early Junk Force, had stolen its design from the boatyard at An Thoi. Equipped with only the most primitive of hand tools, workers at the yard turned out 40- and 50-foot junks that were marvels of craftsmanship. Barefooted men stood on great wooden beams, shaping them with razor-sharp adzes, striking blows within inches of their toes, sending chips flying in small storms. Planks, similarly planed and curved, were screwed and pegged to the finished framing. The smell of the freshly worked wood mingled in a not unpleasant way with the ever-present odor of *nuoc mam* and smoke from small charcoal fires in the little town.

On the northern part of the island, pepper was grown and this, too, helped earn industrious islanders a reasonably comfortable standard of living—before "taxes." These were extorted by both the Viet Cong and equally rapacious representatives of the Saigon government. A very large and noisome prisoner-of-war camp occupied many acres in south-central Phu Quoc, not far from an ARVN security compound and a small airstrip.

The naval base at An Thoi lay to the east of and adjacent to the village. The U.S. side of the base consisted of a small collection of sea-huts, corrugated metal and raw wood, rusting and graying in the

The Boy Named Chou

salt air. The Vietnamese side was newer and the buildings a bit more substantial. It included some of the dependents' housing Admiral Zumwalt was pressing to have built wherever the VNN had a presence. Seabees were assigned to An Thoi for this purpose. The Seabees used a modified army half-ton trailer as a portable tool shed, and had fitted it out with tall plywood sides and a roof. The exterior of the trailer was decorated with truly remarkable graffiti—some of it profane, some profound, some funny, and some sad. Someone had spray-painted across the back, "War *Is* Hell—Without Sex."

Two finger piers ran out from the little base, and vessels with a draft of about eight feet or less could moor at their seaward ends. VNN junks, Swift boats, PGMs, LCUs, and other assorted craft were normally tied up there. The base had a small repair capability, though most VNN boats in need of maintenance preferred to go to Saigon, if they could make it that far. Seventh Fleet ships that occasionally anchored offshore—LSTs, ARLs, LSDs, etc.—also provided repair and supply support. Some of these had doctors and dentists on board.

On the beach in front of the base was a small boneyard of rotting Kien Giang junks. The eyes painted on either side of their bows to frighten away demons of the deep glared instead at sand and sky. The Kien Giangs had been replaced almost entirely in the Junk Force by "Yabutas"—motorized junks that were built at the Saigon Naval Shipyard. (These took their name from that of the Japanese engineer who designed them.)

An Thoi was the headquarters of the IV Coastal Zone, and theoretically its commander assigned VNN assets to Market Time patrols and to on-going "Tran Hung Dao" campaigns throughout the zone, which encompassed almost all the waters of the vast Mekong Delta. Junks and other craft from An Thoi were regularly detached to Ha Tien for patrols along the Rach Giang Thanh, and to Sea Float in the Nam Can. Because of its remote location, An Thoi was relatively secure from enemy attack during much of the war.

The senior advisor to IV Coastal Zone in late 1969 and early 1970 was James D. Beaube, a grizzled navy lieutenant commander whom I first met on a "White Hat Airlines" flight from Tan Son Nhut to An Thoi. He was traveling with a shy little girl whom he introduced as "Hao."

Beaube, like many other Americans in Vietnam, was touched by the plight of children caught up in this terrible war. He never said as much to me, but I doubt that he found his duty as an advisor very rewarding—few did—and I think he looked for other ways to justify the personal sacrifices he and others were making to serve in Vietnam. He ran across Hao, then seven years old, in a hamlet near An Thoi. The child had a harelip, a not uncommon deformity that in most Western societies is easily corrected at birth. Hao, however, was the daughter of a poor fisherman, and had never seen a doctor.

Beaube, with the help of the district chief, persuaded the little girl's father to let him take her to the Children's International Relief Hospital in Cholon. There, a Swedish doctor performed corrective surgery, leaving only a thin, white scar. When I saw Beaube and Hao on the plane, the navy officer was bringing Hao back from a postoperative checkup at the hospital.

There was a small officers club at the An Thoi base, adjoining the barracks. Above the bar was a poster, a beer advertisement, showing a long-legged, bikini-clad woman reclining on a beach. The caption on the poster read, "Next time, bring your wife." It always got a laugh from first-time visitors to the base. It was at this club that I first saw another of Beaube's charges—a little boy named Chou. Beaube had inherited him from a Junk Force advisor, Lieutenant (j.g.) Wellington Maupin Westbrook III.

Westbrook had arrived in-country on 14 October 1969, fresh from thirteen weeks of counterinsurgency and Vietnamese language instruction. He had orders to Coastal Group 15 in I Corps, but when he showed up at Naval Advisory Group Headquarters in Saigon, he was told he wasn't needed there and instead would be posted as a ship rider with Fleet Command. (Last minute changes in orders were not uncommon in Vietnam.) New orders in hand, he was walking out the door when he was hailed by a chief yeoman who asked if he really wanted duty in the Junk Force. A vacancy had suddenly "turned up" in Coastal Group 42. Westbrook said, "Sure," and five days later he was on a plane to An Thoi with orders to report as assistant advisor, Coastal Group 42.

At An Thoi he was given a briefing on local operations by the NILO (naval intelligence liaison officer) and put on a PCF for a quick passage to Ha Tien on the mainland. His junks were then engaged in interdiction patrols on "Bernique's Creek," the Rach Giang Thanh, along with assorted PCFs, PBRs, ASPBs, and some river minesweepers. He was met at Ha Tien by his boss, the coastal group advisor, who showed him around and introduced him to life on the junks. It wasn't too bad, he later said, if you were the kind of guy who "didn't mind eating rice and fish three times a day for four days in a row."[1] The junks at Ha Tien followed a routine of four days on, one day off—which most likely was not as bad as it seems. The junks rarely encountered the enemy, and the enemy even more rarely sought them out. The Viet Cong and the NVA no doubt considered the junks less than threatening to their operations and ordinarily would not waste a B-40 rocket on a junk.

In his initial month on the river, Westbrook engaged in only one firefight, and a minor one at that. At the first sign of an enemy, his instructions were to man the radio and call for air and artillery support.

After a month along the Cambodian border, Westbrook was sent to Sea Float to relieve the junk advisor posted there. Sea Float was assigned ten junks then, and their primary duty was to provide security at Sea Float Annex. Sea Float junks, when they were available, were also sent on Market Time patrols in the Gulf of Thailand and on convoy duty in the Cai Nhap Canal. Market Time assignments consisted of keeping restricted zones clear, and the boarding and search of fishing craft. While at Sea Float, the junks were sometimes sent out on ambush, but these seldom generated enemy contact, perhaps for the same reason discussed above in connection with the Cambodian border operation. In a three-month deployment at Sea Float, Westbrook's junks were fired upon (by snipers) only twice.

Once, Westbrook said, his junks participated with thirty Vietnamese Reaction Force troops in a "quite successful" sweep of a ten-kilometer by ten-kilometer piece of land within the Sea Float AO. No VC were discovered, he said, but the troops destroyed "several hundred pounds of rice and quite a few water jugs, while confiscating pigs, chickens, a VC flag and a few rifles."[2] In such ways was success often measured in this war. On another occasion, however, more substantial achievements were recorded. After the mining of a Swift boat on the Cai Nhap, troops operating with Westbrook's junks flushed two men who ran into the jungle. A search of the immediate area uncovered a blood trail, three rocket launchers, and six B-40 rockets. The next day two more launchers and four more rockets were found.

Westbrook, perhaps because of the extensive training he was given before being sent to Vietnam, adjusted well to duty as a coastal group advisor. He thought the Vietnamese officers he came in contact with were men of high caliber, intelligent, and concerned about the war. (Indeed, many were.) He developed close relationships and became fluent in the Vietnamese language. Many Vietnamese, particularly those assigned to the less than prestigious Junk Force, spoke little or no English.

In off-duty hours at Sea Float he began to visit the nearby refugee hamlets. He drank coffee and shared rice cakes with the people there, and gave small gifts to the villagers' children. They, because of the beard he wore, adopted a pet name for him—"Old Monkey." The children climbed on his back and wrestled with him on the ground.

During the observance of Tet 1970, Westbrook was invited to a round of Vietnamese parties. He recalled this with pleasure. On the afternoon before Tet, a pig was roasted and it was eaten that night. He played a game of Vietnamese "spin the bottle." A duck's head was impaled on a stick, and the stick was thrust into a large bottle of rice wine. The head was spun, and the celebrant to whom it eventually pointed was required to take a stiff drink of the wine. When midnight arrived, firecrackers were set off and pop flares were sent arching across the sky.

In contrast to what many other U.S. officers were saying both officially and in private, Westbrook said he was "most impressed" by the close cooperation he observed between the Vietnamese and Americans at Sea Float. He said that he felt "quite honored" to have been a part of it, and very happy "to live and work with the Vietnamese people—to immerse myself in another culture."[3]

Shortly after Tet, Westbrook was ordered back to Coastal Group 42, but first he caught a helicopter to Saigon to draw some field gear and, incidentally, to pull a little liberty. While there he visited a friend, a Fleet Command advisor, in Cholon. On a Cholon street, late at night, Westbrook came across a small boy dressed in a suit of tattered "tiger greens." The boy had been collared by Vietnamese military police for sleeping in an ARVN jeep. The MPs said they were going to take him to jail.

Westbrook asked if the boy had a father or a mother. He was told that he did not. (Later, Westbrook would learn that the boy's mother had been killed in Tet 1968, and that his father, a Vietnamese soldier, had placed him in an orphanage from which the boy later ran away.)

Westbrook told the MPs that if they were agreeable he would take charge of the boy and attempt to find him a home at An Thoi. The MPs seemed only too glad to oblige. Westbrook asked the boy what his name was, and the boy said it was "Chou."

The next morning, Westbrook talked himself and the boy onto a flight bound for An Thoi. He hoped to place the boy with a Vietnamese Navy family at the base, but for whatever reason Chou steadfastly refused. Perhaps he feared it was but a ploy to return him to the hated orphanage. One can well imagine the relief the prospective adoptive family must have felt. It was not easy raising one's own children on a Vietnamese naval officer's pay. Westbrook was headed back to the junks on the Rach Giang Thanh, and he was afraid that if he took the boy with him to Ha Tien, he'd wind up back on the streets. That was when he turned to Lieutenant Commander Beaube. As already suggested, Beaube was a soft touch. He took the boy in hand.

Putting him in the custody of the base's toughest hootch maid, he had him scrubbed, cleaned, and deloused. He introduced him to navy food. He had him outfitted in clean clothing, including a fresh set of tiger greens. The USS *Tutuila* (ARG 4), then fortuitously anchored offshore, was the next stop. Beaube had the boy examined in the ship's sick bay. Scabby sores on his chest were treated; iron and vitamin pills were prescribed. Arrangements were made to get him to a dentist as soon as one became available.

Back at the base, he was given a towel and soap, a place to sleep in the barracks, and a shelf to keep his few belongings on. In the weeks that followed, he was also given what mattered most—discipline, patience, and love. The entire American side of the base seemed to have adopted him.

Two weeks after his arrival at An Thoi, Chou attended his first day of schooling, in a classroom that had been built for dependent children of Vietnamese sailors at the base. He brought his first school papers "home" to the barracks in a plastic case, on the cover of which was a painted GVN flag.

Sailors taught him how to swim in the refreshing, cool waters of the beautiful harbor, and he took to it like a fish. In the evenings, under jeweled skies, he sat with the sailors on the beach to watch moving shadows on a screen, shadows cavorting in a world he had never seen—and would never see. He began to pick up a little English, beyond the few words of profanity he knew when Westbrook brought him to the island. He shined boots on the base and did other odd jobs, being careful not to intrude on the prerogatives of the hootch maids.

The changes in his life were little short of miraculous and difficult for outsiders to comprehend. The days at An Thoi were halcyon, and he no doubt wished they would go on forever. But they did not.

It would be nice if there were a happy ending to Chou's story, but there were few happy endings in Vietnam, and his was not one of them. The time fast approached when Beaube and all the other Americans at An Thoi would go home. A more permanent arrangement for the boy's upbringing had to be made. A Vietnamese priest in Ha Tien was persuaded to board him and to see to his further schooling.

Late in May 1970, I ran into Wellington Maupin Westbrook III at the airstrip in Ca Mau. I was on my way back from a visit to Sea Float. I forget where he was heading. I asked him about the boy. He told me that the day before Chou was to "muster out of the navy," so to speak, alone in one of the hootches at the Ha Tien ATSB, he apparently pulled the pin on a grenade.

There was speculation that, though only nine years old, the little boy in tiger greens had committed suicide.

17

Ready Deck

How would you have reported the shooting down of a U.S. Navy patrol boat over dry land by enemy anti-aircraft fire?

—Admiral John S. McCain, Jr., CINCPAC, during an August 1969
visit to COMNAVFORV headquarters in Saigon

Mobility and flexibility were inherent in all navy operations in Vietnam, but nowhere were these characteristics more dramatically apparent than in operations that utilized giant "Skycrane" helicopters to lift river patrol boats into the upper Saigon and Cai Cai rivers in May and June 1969.

The first such lift occurred on 3 May when six PBRs of River Division 574 were sky-hooked a distance of about sixteen miles from Go Dau Ha on the Vam Co Dong. It was thought that transit by water would have taken at least four days, but by this imaginative use of the great lifting power of the Skycranes the entire relocation was completed in three hours. Patrols were established in the new AO the same day.

The second airlift occurred on 20 June when six more patrol craft were carried from the upper Mekong River to the Rach Cai Cai. Naval operations on the Cai Cai had been under consideration for some time.[1] In the past the Viet Cong had made use of this river as a principal north-south infiltration route, and the enemy's presence in the area was still considered to be quite strong. A border surveillance and interdiction operation along the Cai Cai would add "interdiction in depth" to that portion of the border covered by Barrier Reef, in much the same way Foul Deck enhanced Search Turn in the western delta.

During the high-water season a water route was believed to be navigable by PBRs, which would permit movement to the Cai Cai from both the Mekong and the Vam Co Tay rivers. Navigational hazards associated with this route (a sudden fall in the water level might have stranded boats in transit), the usual political concerns attached to operations skirting the Cambodian border, and perhaps most of all the favorable stir created by the earlier airlifting of PBRs persuaded COMNAVFORV to "fly" them to the Cai Cai as well.

Austere berthing and messing facilities for the thirty-five navy personnel initially engaged in this operation were provided at a U.S. Special Forces camp in the village of Cai Cai. Despite severe overcrowding (the camp had been built to accommodate only fourteen men), the Special Forces element seemed genuinely pleased to have some company in this heretofore neglected corner of the war.

The Cai Cai was a narrow, winding, and nontidal river. Its banks were tree-lined and under normal water conditions were four to six feet high. In this made-to-order environment for ambush, nine firefights occurred during the first two weeks of the operation. These most likely were generated by local enemy units. Little evidence was accumulated that the river was indeed being used for significant infiltration of men and supplies; no large arms caches were found. These circumstances, and the extreme difficulty in supporting operations in such a remote place, led to the withdrawal of the boats, again by sky hook, on 21 July.

Results achieved on the upper Saigon River by the first "flying PBRs" were more promising, and Admiral Zumwalt was determined to continue and expand that operation. He proposed that a division of ten PBRs be based in proximity to the army compound at Phu Cuong on "a semi-permanent basis."[2] The army, in the person of commanding general, II Field Force Vietnam, concurred, and River Division 554 moved by water from Tuyen Nhon to Phu Cuong, arriving in its new AO on 9 June.

What COMNAVFORV believed was happening on the upper Saigon River was that, with the increasingly effective interdiction of enemy LOCs by Giant Slingshot, the enemy was engaged in an "end run" movement to the north and east of Tay Ninh, and that this was the route being used to continue the flow of men and material to vital areas surrounding Saigon. The success of the infiltration effort depended heavily upon the enemy's freedom of movement both along and across the Saigon River, particularly in the region between Dau Tieng and Phu Cuong.

An ATSB of sorts was established southeast of the bridge at Phu Cuong. Navy personnel, when they were not on their boats, lived in the mud in porta-campers and subsisted on food furnished by the army.

Through June and most of July, contact was light and sporadic. Operations were conducted with Vietnamese and U.S. Army ground units, and with VNN River Assault Group 24. While the enemy seemed to be avoiding contact, signs of his presence and activity were not hard to find. Bunkers were dug along the river banks and protected by booby traps and wire entanglements. Older bunkers in the area had faced away from the river; the new ones were turned toward it. As a rule they were well constructed. Some even had inside plumbing.[3]

In July, River Division 593, the "Iron Butterflies" of the River Patrol Force, relieved RIVDIV 554 at Phu Cuong, and shortly thereafter the pace of operations quickened. During the period 8 through 25 July, RIVDIV 593 and RAG 24 supported the U.S. First Infantry and the Fifth ARVN divisions in search-and-destroy operations along the river north from Phu Cuong. Naval forces were engaged in nine firefights that resulted in seventy-four VC/NVA killed and another eighty-one captured.[4] In early August, with the action showing no signs of slackening, COMNAVFORV reinforced the operation with a second division of PBRs.

Waterborne guardposts were particularly effective in the upper Saigon River. As in other interdiction campaigns, the enemy seemed reluctant to abandon favored, though compromised, crossing points. Several explanations were offered for this lack of "institutional memory." The most likely was the inability of the VC/NVA transportation companies to communicate with one another while on the march, and the length of time required for survivors of an ambush to report back up the line. One stretch of river northwest of Phu Cuong was called "Monzingo's Swimming Hole," and enemy units were repeatedly surprised and slaughtered there during attempted crossings.

Chief Signalman Bob Allen Monzingo was a PBR patrol officer skilled in the techniques of ambush, and it was in his honor that the "Swimming Hole" was named. The water there was relatively shallow, and the enemy ordinarily was taken under fire while wading or paddling across the river supported by rubber innertubes. Many of the enemy soldiers, it was observed, were nonswimmers.

In the deadly serious business of river war, Monzingo left little to chance. He positioned his boats on ambush with meticulous care. He had the rare gift of patience and a sixth sense that enabled him to withhold fire until the most opportune moment. This meant that at times firefights were initiated at ranges of *three feet or less*. His reasoning, grimly correct, was that at that distance it was difficult for a young and nervous sailor to miss. He had seen and perhaps at one time felt the heart-throbbing fear and split-second freeze that sometimes overcome a man when his target is another man. He half blamed that swelling of emotion for the death of a forward gunner on one of his boats, shot clean through by a B-40 rocket, and the near loss of a boat once when his "Iron Butterflies" were ambushed in the Rung Sat Special Zone.

Once Monzingo caught a whole platoon of NVA soldiers in the Swimming Hole. He had a boat hidden on either side of the river, and the first enemy soldiers were observed by starlight scope as they entered the water, made a too casual inspection of the immediate bank area, and then signaled those who followed that all was clear. Monzingo waited until the platoon was in the middle of the stream and then, illuminating the area with pop flares, he charged into the floundering troops, both boats spitting fire. The bloody melee that followed was fought at such close quarters that it became necessary to unship the M-60 machine guns and hold them over the sides of the boats to make them bear. No mercy was asked or given. It was not that kind of war. The destruction of the enemy platoon was brief, brutal, and complete.

On another occasion, on 17 August 1969, Monzingo was the patrol officer on a two-boat waterborne guardpost some four miles northwest of Phu Cuong. A heavy rain, marked by flashes of lightning and rolling thunder, masked his boats as they nosed into the river bank and took up positions near the mouth of a small canal. On this occasion, the boats were stationed on the same side of the river, about fifty feet apart. The crews donned rain gear and ponchos. Weapons were protected as much as possible from the rain, while still being kept at the ready. It was by then dusk, wet and gloomy, and night was falling fast. The men gritted their teeth and steeled themselves for a long and most likely miserable night. The rain showed no signs of abating.

The enemy troops were sighted first by Monzingo's cover boat. The voice on the radio was hoarse and barely more than a whisper.

"Chief . . . Chief, I see a *bunch* of them out there!"

Monzingo later recalled that he had to blink and look twice to make sure his eyes were not deceiving him. On the near bank, not more than forty feet from the concealed boats, a column of heavily armed men marched by in the rain, their shoulders weighted down by large packs, their faces turned away from the driving rain. The end of the column disappeared in the murky distance. Monzingo guessed there were at least fifty and perhaps twice that many in the plodding formation. It seemed incredible that the boats had not been detected by enemy scouts. For all the care that had been taken in selecting the best possible cover for the ambush, at that moment and in that proximity to such a large enemy force, his boats seemed to stand out as clearly as billboards along a stretch of barren highway.

The voice from the cover boat spoke again.

"Chief, what are we going to do?"

"Are your guns uncovered?" Monzingo asked.

"Yes."

"Well, then, open up!"

Both boats poured fire into the enemy's exposed flank. Almost simultaneously, the engines on the PBRs roared to life and the boats backed into the middle of the stream. At this time they were taken under fire from both banks, and it became apparent that the guardpost had been set right in the middle of a planned large-scale enemy crossing. The PBRs either had just beaten the enemy cover force into position or had been screened from it by the thunderstorm. One thing was certain, Monzingo recalled, and that was that his boats were in a "number ten" situation. (The Vietnamese rated things from "number one," the best, to "number ten," the worst.) Monzingo continued to pour fire into the enemy troops while calling for air and surface support. Helo gunships and Black Ponies (navy fixed-wing, tactical aircraft) were soon overhead. PBRs broke guardpost positions elsewhere on the river and sped to assist.

The firefight lasted two hours, in improving weather conditions. Most of the ammunition on Monzingo's PBRs was expended, and he rearmed from other boats in the area. Before the night was over, eight enemy dead were pulled from the river. The next day, troops sweeping the banks counted forty-one others. For his part in this action, Monzingo received his second nomination for a Silver Star.

Monzingo's battered and exhausted patrol returned to the ATSB in the small hours of the morning, and there the river division commander paid the men an unspoken compliment. Awaiting them was the last bottle of Jack Daniel's Black Label, Tennessee Sour Mash whiskey known to exist for miles around.

In this period Monzingo sported a large, red, handlebar mustache, which to some made him look more like a tenor in a barbershop quartet than a coldly proficient practitioner of the art of river warfare. His eyes, however, were steely, like those of a gunfighter in the Old West. He wore, of course, the riverboat sailor's black beret, and there was a certain cockiness in his walk and manner. He was well aware of the reputation he had earned.

"Admiral Zumwalt thinks I can do anything," he said to me once when we were discussing, among other things, the difficulty in getting VNN sailors to perform to U.S. Navy standards. (Zumwalt had handpicked Monzingo for a particularly tough ACTOV assignment, teaching the VNN how to use Kenner ski barges to patrol in shallow water.)

The successes achieved on the upper Saigon River were much talked about back at NAVFORV headquarters. One staff officer remarked that "they were really bowling them over" in the new AO, and the expression stuck. Unofficially, the operation was called "Bowling Alley," but as it turned out that code name had been assigned elsewhere. The war gobbled up even something as inconsequential as code name lists more rapidly than seemed possible. On 11

October 1969, therefore, the upper Saigon River operation was officially designated "Ready Deck." It was described as "a combined NAVFORV/VNN operation on the upper Saigon River to interdict enemy LOC."[5]

The Black Ponies that came to Monzingo's assistance were attached to Light Attack Squadron Four (VAL-4), which had arrived in-country just a few months earlier, on 19 April 1969. Flying aircraft borrowed from the army (OV-10A Broncos), VAL-4 provided the punch and staying power needed on the rivers. The radio call sign of the two-seater OV-10A was "Black Pony," and it was by this that it quickly became known by every riverboat sailor.

The twin-engine, propeller-driven Bronco carried a weapons array that included 5-inch "Zuni" and 2.75-inch rockets; a Mark 4, 20-mm gun pod; M-60 machine guns; and an SUU-11 mini-gun. The ordnance ordinarily was released with remarkable accuracy in the midst of a screaming dive. Strikes placed within twenty-five meters or less of patrol boats were not uncommon.

The normal endurance of the aircraft was three hours, but with external fuel tanks it could stay aloft for up to four and one-half hours. This proved to be adequate for most missions flown in Vietnam.

Armed reconnaissance patrols by a section of two aircraft, called a light attack fire team (LAFT), accounted for roughly 80 percent of the squadron's flight time in Vietnam. These aircraft flew a pre-planned route, checking in with each naval operations center (NOC) along the way to determine if they were needed in that particular AO. In effect, the LAFT on patrol became an airborne ready reaction force that could be diverted to any area where contact with the enemy was being experienced.

A second type of mission for VAL-4 involved continuous air cover for special operations, which included the salvage of damaged or grounded boats, the transit of newly opened or particularly dangerous waterways, or the temporary strengthening of an interdiction barrier in the face of a serious enemy threat. During operation "Double Shift" in the summer of 1969, Black Ponies provided continuous dusk-to-dawn coverage of the upper Vam Co Dong River.

The third and perhaps most important mission flown by VAL-4 was the scramble alert. The average time required to get the ready aircraft airborne was less than ten minutes. With an air speed of 180 knots, Black Ponies were ordinarily "on top" in twenty-five minutes or less anywhere navy boats were engaged in III and IV Corps.

VAL-4 arrived in-country with fourteen aircraft, and these were

Ready Deck

divided into two detachments, one assigned at Binh Thuy and the other at Vung Tau. In the first year of operations two aircraft and four aviators were lost. One aircraft and two pilots were lost in the Seven Mountains area near Cambodia. The second, with a navy pilot and a marine spotter on board, failed to come out of a dive and buried itself in a Rung Sat mud flat. A fourth pilot was killed when struck by a single round of small-arms fire during a close-support mission. The aircraft was returned safely to base by the rear-seat pilot.

Virtually all aircraft were struck by enemy fire at one time or another. On 29 October 1971, a Black Pony was shot down fifty miles southeast of Dong Tam. The pilot and an intelligence officer passenger ejected safely and were rescued by an army Dustoff helicopter.

The officers and men of VAL-4 were an elite group, though only two of the initially assigned thirty-four pilots had prior combat experience. The esprit of the squadron was most evident in a consistently high level of performance and reliability. It also was displayed in smaller ways. "Welcome to Bronco Town" signs greeted visitors at each of the VAL-4 compounds, and the squadron's symbol—a black pony with flying mane and front hoofs pawing the air—was stenciled on everything imaginable, including aircraft, vehicles, hootches, outdoor burn-out heads and, at Vung Tau, a wholly ornamental mailbox outside the command bunker.

VAL-4 was the last U.S. Navy operational unit to leave Vietnam. It departed the country on 10 April 1972.

Through November and December 1969, the level of enemy contact on the upper Saigon River remained high, though the number of enemy killed dropped off sharply. It appeared that the enemy, while not abandoning this important LOC, was breaking his logistic forces into smaller and smaller units for the purpose of diffusing the interdiction effort. Eight VNN PBRs and an entire river assault group were added to the operation, which the Vietnamese now called "Tran Hung Dao V." (Imagination in the selection of names for operations was not one of the VNN's strong suits. The profligacy of "Tran Hung Dao" operations led to a great deal of confusion, and it is doubtful if there were ever more than a handful of people in either the U.S. Navy or the VNN who could correctly, and unhesitatingly, sort them out.)

On 11 December 1969, Commander Dang Trung Hieu, the Third Riverine Area commander, was given command of the joint operation on the upper Saigon River. Ready Deck was thus the first of NAVFORV's interdiction campaigns to be placed under VNN command. It was celebrated as an early jewel in ACTOV's crown, and VNN units gradually relieved U.S.–manned boats on the operation.

The sinking of a VNN PBR in the river north of Phu Cuong on 28 December led to a prolonged and, in COMNAVFORV's eye, a successful operation.

Shortly after 2000 on the night of 31 December, VNN riverine assault craft and PBRs assigned to provide security and support to a salvage team at work on the sunken boat sighted a squad of enemy troops on the east bank of the river. The boats opened fire, and called for helo gunships and Black Ponies. The east bank was strafed and rocketed. The salvage work continued. At about 2230, the boats were taken under fire by some thirty troops on the west bank. Again, helo gunships and Black Ponies were scrambled and strikes were placed on suspected enemy positions. During the night, enemy swimmers were detected in the water on two occasions. Grenades scared them off. At 0320 in the morning, a B-40 rocket was fired at the VNN boats from the west bank. Artillery fire was called in. While this was going on, an estimated twenty enemy troops opened fire from the east bank.

The attacks were terminated at dawn. Twelve enemy dead were counted and another twenty-one were listed as "probably" killed. Salvage of the sunken PBR was completed without further incident the next day and, securely lashed between two LCMs, it arrived at Phu Cuong at 1900 on 1 January 1970.

COMNAVFORV and the senior naval advisor were nearly ecstatic. All surface units in the engagement were VNN (with USN advisors), and it was said that the operation demonstrated the Vietnamese Navy's ability to coordinate air and artillery assets.[6] What it also may have demonstrated, of course, was excessive reliance on U.S. assets that would not be available for long.

Under VNN command, Ready Deck/Tran Hung Dao V (later, "Tran Hung Dao XXVII") steadily declined in terms of operational effectiveness. Communications were difficult, logistics uncertain. Throughout 1970, contact with the enemy remained light, and in the first three months of 1971, the VNN did not inflict a single enemy casualty in the upper Saigon River. In April 1971, intelligence reports confirmed the presence of the 101st NVA Regiment and the 268th Main Force Group in the AO.[7] VNN boats, when they ventured away from their base, were attacked. Two mining incidents were recorded, the first in more than a year.

Psychologically, the VNN was not prepared to continue the operation at the level of intensity established earlier by the U.S. Navy. With relative ease, enemy LOCs were reestablished on the upper Saigon River. It was an old story, and it would be repeated elsewhere.

18

The Forest of Assassins

Any war is difficult to fight in. But the war in Vietnam was the most difficult one in which American soldiers had ever fought. Front lines were seldom clearly drawn. Enemy soldiers were often hard to identify. Our men were constantly bombarded by media reports telling them that the war was unwinnable, that our cause was unjust, and that a majority of the American people opposed it. But to their credit, our men did their duty. They honored their country. They served well the cause of freedom and justice.

—President Richard M. Nixon, *No More Vietnams*

The Rung Sat Special Zone, the "Forest of Assassins," is a four-hundred-square-mile area of dense mangrove swamp stretching from Nha Be southeast to Vung Tau and the South China Sea. It is interlaced by countless rivers and streams. Though it has little good land, at the height of the war some eighteen thousand people, many of them refugees, made their home there, living on boats or in hootches raised on stilts above the mud. Tidal ranges of six to eight feet were common; currents in major waterways often exceeded four knots. There were no roads. Travel was by sampan and small boats.

The Long Tau ship channel, Saigon's lifeline to the sea, winds for some forty-five miles through the Rung Sat, traversing four rivers—the Nga Bay, the Saigon, the Long Tau, and the Nha Be. Though broad strips on either side of the channel had been drastically defoliated, burned, and cleared, ships in transit were almost always subject to rocket, recoilless rifle, and mining attack. The inability, some would say the unwillingness, of U.S. and South Vietnamese armed forces to secure the Long Tau early on speaks volumes about the strategic conduct of the war.

The Vietnamese Navy was assigned responsibility for the RSSZ in April 1964, and at least in theory the VNN commander exercised operational control of all Vietnamese military forces within the zone. The VNN ordinarily maintained two river assault groups (RAGs), six motor launch minesweepers (MLMS's), and assorted patrol boats in its AO. The U.S. Navy conducted Game Warden operations in the ship channel. PBRs and Seawolf helicopters, operating from the base at Nha Be, responded to enemy-initiated attacks on shipping. The minesweeping boats (MSBs) of Mine Division 112 also were based at Nha Be.

SEAL operations were regularly conducted in the Rung Sat. The nature of these operations and the hazards faced by men engaged in them can be seen in the following excerpt from an end-of-tour report filed by the officer in charge of SEAL Team One, Detachment Golf, on 17 July 1968:

"Since the arrival of Detachment Golf in Vietnam, the large majority of operations conducted have been in the Rung Sat Special Zone. The missions have been dictated by first the terrain and secondly by the type of enemy encountered, and have been of a day patrol/night stream ambush nature. . . . The Rung Sat Special Zone is a jungle tidal swamp with streams flowing from 6 to 12 knots. The foliage is so thick that it is not unlikely for a patrol to be within a Viet Cong base camp and not realize it. Visibility is sometimes only 5 to

10 feet and silent movement is practically impossible. If the Viet Cong detect a patrol moving in their direction and decide that the patrol is small enough to engage, it is safe to say that a friendly patrol will take casualties in the encounter. In a firefight with a concealed enemy at a range of 5 to 10 meters the possibility of losing at least the first two members of a friendly patrol is great and was evidenced by SEAL Detachment Golf, Bravo Platoon, on 23 December 1967.

"Supporting forces are of little help in close-in firefights and, therefore, the patrol must rely on its own resources to break contact. Another example of the problems of the Rung Sat presented by its terrain is the inability to capture VC when only 30 to 50 meters away at night. Due to the noise made by a person's movement, SEAL patrols have not attempted to capture a stream or river sentry for fear of losing more than they could possibly gain. By resorting to a heavy volume of fire the only result would be one VC WIA (PROB). In each instance when a VC was spotted near a friendly ambush position, it was felt that the SEAL patrol was undetected and that hopefully the VC sentry would signal a sampan to pass.

"Another indication of the security afforded to the enemy is their use of the Rung Sat as a rest, hospital and headquarters area. Since it is not the ideal living conditions, the choice of the Rung Sat must certainly be because of the difficulty of Free World Forces in penetrating quickly and/or silently. Most large unit sweeps have been ineffective in the Rung Sat because a company or battalion is almost compelled to go single file through the jungle making it very easy for hit-and-run tactics or complete avoidance of the sweep by the VC.

"Generally the VC are located in base camps of 7 to 10 people (with exception of the T-10, where estimates of enemy strength in a single base camp run as high as 50 to 100). Because of the small VC units, movement on the streams and rivers is of an irregular and infrequent nature.

"Detachment Golf's mission was that of locating base camps and ambushing sampans at night. Locating base camps was done, but usually these camps were inactive. Ambushing sampans proved even more difficult, and successes ranged from one hit every 27 missions to the more recent one in 10 or 12. In checking through statistics it was found that the most number of 'hits' by the SEALs was obtained by using helo insertion on a 24 hour patrol/ambush. The only way to improve the one in 12 success ratio would have been through the use of agents or chieu hoi's, of which there were none. It was proposed to run a kidnap mission on a suspected VC located in one of the villages of the Rung Sat with the hope of obtaining information for later missions. Approval for this was not granted because the villages were all classified as 'friendly'."[1]

Despite the "friendly" classification of its villages and hamlets, the Rung Sat remained an enemy enclave on the very doorstep of Saigon until the end of the war. The laborious movement of large water mines, rockets, and other munitions through the area could not have been accomplished without the active support and encouragement of the people living there.

Mines were always the principal threat to ships transiting the Long Tau, or when anchored or moored to offload cargo. On 26 May 1966, the *Eastern Mariner*, of Panamanian registry and carrying a cargo of four thousand tons of bagged cement, was mined at the Nha Be anchorage, and only with difficulty was it beached on the east bank of the Nha Be River, clear of the main ship channel. Two other ships in the anchorage on that same day narrowly escaped damage. The French ship *Milos Delmar* experienced an underwater explosion while weighing anchor, and EOD personnel disarmed a third mine found attached to the anchor chain of the merchant ship *Our Lady of Peace*, which ironically, in view of the ship's name, was carrying a cargo of general-purpose, 500-pound bombs. The mine contained 130 pounds of TNT and an electrical timing device. It was attached to the ship's anchor chain with metal hooks and nylon parachute cord in such a way that it would drift under the ship with the changing tide.[2]

The first mining of a merchant ship while under way in the Long Tau channel occurred on 23 August 1966. The mining was coordinated with an ambush of Vietnamese Navy minesweepers. Two VNN minesweeping motor launches were taken under fire at 0640 while sweeping the channel south from Nha Be. One VNN sailor was killed and three were wounded. The sweep was abandoned and the two boats returned to port. At 0910, the *Baton Rouge Victory* was mined twelve miles from the channel entrance in an area left unswept. Seven crewmen were killed, and the ship was rendered dead in the water. The captain, taking advantage of the current, managed to ground his vessel clear of the channel.[3]

Prior to the mining of the *Baton Rouge Victory*, security in the Long Tau was provided by continuous daytime sweeping by USN MSBs and VNN MLMS's, and by PBR patrols. After the mining, all of these were strengthened.

On 28 August a VNN MLMS was destroyed by a mine; two crewmen were killed and five wounded, including two U.S. advisors.

The next day, on 29 August, MSB 54 was ambushed and heavily damaged. The boat made its way back to Nha Be on its own power and was soon repaired and returned to service. At 0420 on 1 November 1966, however, while engaged in a routine chain bottom drag, MSB 54 was sunk by a large, moored, command-detonated mine, four and one-half miles south of Nha Be. Two U.S. sailors were killed; four were wounded, two of them seriously.

The mine demolished the MSB from the bow to the after bulk-head of the pilothouse. A 57-mm recoilless rifle round struck the boat's port quarter almost simultaneously. Approximately four minutes later, raked by heavy automatic weapons and small-arms fire from the near bank, MSB 54 went under, bow first, in seven fathoms of water.

MSB 49, which had been operating in company with MSB 54, and two MSBs that had been sweeping 2,000 meters north on the river, sped to assist. They were joined by two VNN RAG craft and a light helicopter fire team that scrambled from Nha Be. A flare ship arrived to provide illumination, and PBRs were soon on the scene. After about ten minutes the action was broken off. MSB 49 picked up two survivors, and two more who had managed to swim ashore were rescued by one of the RAG craft.

The Long Tau channel was temporarily closed to shipping. Additional PBR patrols were established. Troops were inserted to provide bank security for salvage operations. On 3 November the broken hull of MSB 54 was pulled from the river, along with the body of one of her two missing crewmen. The body of the last missing man was never found.[4]

Thirteen well-prepared bunkers were discovered in the vicinity of the ambush site. Logs were piled in front of each to support heavy weapons. Escape trails were beaten in the heavy grass.

On 31 December 1966 a floating contact mine was sighted in the Long Tau River, the first such found in GVN waters. A navy EOD team disarmed it and it was taken to Nha Be. The mine, of Soviet manufacture, contained 500 pounds of explosive material. It was 34 and one-half inches in diameter and 52 inches in length. A 20-foot length of anchor cable was attached, and from the condition of the frayed end the mine had but recently been swept.[5]

Action in the Long Tau remained hot and heavy in the new year. In February another MSB was sunk and two were damaged. Two U.S. sailors were killed and sixteen wounded in mining incidents and ambushes during that month alone. COMNAVFORV pleaded for ground forces, and COMUSMACV responded by providing two infantry companies for a period of thirty days. Firefly missions were flown nightly, supported by a light helicopter fire team. B-52 Arc Light strikes were made on "suspected" VC headquarters in the RSSZ.

"Regardless of any mix of forces brought to bear in RSSZ," COMNAVFORV reported, "until the banks of the Long Tau are secured by troops our river forces will always take the initial blow. . . .

"Until such time when we acquire the capability to prevent a wily enemy from reaching ambush sites of his choice we will continue unfortunately to receive casualties. We are doing our best and welcome assistance."[6]

Perhaps sarcastically, and if not sarcastically then obsequiously, Admiral Ward ended his message thus:

"The close coordination, mutual support and cooperation demonstrated by COMUSMACV in solving the unique problems in this . . . area have been and continue to be most gratifying."[7]

In any event, enemy attacks on merchant ships proceeding to and from Saigon continued unabated. In 1968 there were forty-four of these, and in the first half of 1969 there were no fewer than fifty-one. Though relatively few inflicted serious damage, they demonstrated an enemy capability and a U.S./VN weakness that was difficult to toss off or hide. Further, were a large ship to be sunk in the Long Tau channel, the massive flow of supplies to Saigon would have been seriously disrupted with, as one wag at the time had it, "untold consequences for the Saigon black market."

Some of the increase in merchant ship attacks was attributed to the longer-range weapons then coming into use. These permitted the enemy to fire from relatively safe positions well back from the river banks. The RPG-7 (a rocket-propelled grenade), for example, had an effective range nearly three times that of the older RPG-2. Bank sweeps in the RSSZ in this period were also uncovering, occasionally, 107-mm and 122-mm rockets, some of which were rigged for command firing from camouflaged spider holes many meters away.

Through the middle of 1969, operations in the Rung Sat were essentially defensive in nature, and most of the forces at hand were employed in minesweeping and patrolling the river. RF/PF troops, to the extent they were available and willing, conducted random bank sweeps. On rare occasions, the highly regarded Mobile Strike Force, when it could be spared from operations elsewhere in the country (in retrospect, what other operations could have commanded higher pri-

Rear Admiral Norvell G. Ward

ority?) were assigned ad hoc search-and-destroy missions with VNN RAGs.

U.S. Navy SEALs and Vietnamese Navy LDNNs conducted intelligence-gathering and harassment operations (though, as has been shown, with indifferent results). As part of the "Phoenix" campaign, concerted efforts were made to eliminate or neutralize the Viet Cong infrastructure within the Rung Sat population. The permanent residents of RSSZ villages and hamlets were photographed and fingerprinted. Suspects "disappeared." Intensive psychological operations were carried out. Relatively little contact was made with the enemy, however.

The structure of the Viet Cong force responsible for the attacks on Long Tau shipping was well known. A sapper battalion, known as "DOAN-10," had been identified, and it was believed to consist of either nine or ten company-level elements ("DOI") of between thirty and fifty-five men. Complicating the task of engaging and destroying DOAN-10 was the fact that it was known to enjoy a relatively safe base camp area just north of the Rung Sat AO in the Nhon Trach District of Bien Hoa Province. Attacks on the Long Tau ordinarily were carried out by small groups of five or fewer men who, after expending their rockets and/or mines, simply faded back into their haven in the north. In microcosm this was the tactic enemy troops employed along the national borders with Cambodia, Laos, and North Vietnam. In this instance, however, the enemy "sanctuary" lay wholly within the territory of South Vietnam and not more than fifteen miles from the capital, Saigon. This situation, spawned by the fractured Vietnamese command structure and tolerated, almost incredibly, by senior U.S. advisors, had existed, moreover, for a number of years.

In June 1969 there were fifteen attacks on Long Tau shipping, and a concerned Admiral Zumwalt was determined to do something about it. The senior advisor in the RSSZ at this time was Commander C. J. Wages, and he proposed a temporary enlargement of the RSSZ AO to permit sweeps against DOAN-10 in its Nhon Trach base camp area. His proposal received strong backing from COMNAVFORV and from Commanding General II Field Force Vietnam. Permission was granted, grudgingly, by ARVN commanders, though they found it inconvenient to assign regular army troops to assist in the operation.

Forces eventually assembled for the operation included two battalions of Royal Thai Army Volunteers, a company from the First

Australian Task Force, some RF and National Police units, one company from the U.S. 199th Light Infantry Brigade, U.S. helicopters, VNN RAGs, U.S. SEALs, PBRs, ASPBs, and a Zippo boat. Thus, it was a truly international force that in the period 24–30 June carried out the attack against DOAN-10.

Allied sweeps through the northern Rung Sat and the Nhon Trach District accounted for fifty-one VC killed and the taking of two prisoners. Four base camps were destroyed. Three of DOAN-10's companies were forced to withdraw eastward toward Phuc Thuy Province. Allied casualties were one Thai killed, and twenty-three Thai and two U.S. wounded.

At the conclusion of the operation, COMNAVFORV sent the following congratulatory message to Commanding General II Field Force Vietnam, Commanding General Royal Thai Army Volunteer Force, and Commander First Australian Task Force:

"Perhaps the most significant single result of the recently completed joint operations in southern Nhon Trach District was its obvious effect on the enemy's previous ability to launch attacks by fire against merchant ships in the Long Tau River. During the first three weeks of June the enemy carried out his harassing actions at the much increased rate of nearly one a day. Since 22 June, however, there has not been a single such incident recorded. I am convinced that this vastly improved situation exists because of your unstinting support, close cooperation, and high degree of professionalism. I appreciate all that you have done and look forward to working with you again in the future."[8]

As was proven time and time again in Brown Water Navy operations in Vietnam, participation by trained and aggressive ground forces was the real key to success in any campaign. Without that participation, the initiative always rested with the enemy, who could choose when and where to dispute the control of a particular stretch of navigable water. In the absence of ground forces, the enemy enjoyed a further application of the strategy of sanctuary, for boats could pursue only to the maximum effective range of their weapons. Seawolves and Black Ponies, to be sure, could further that pursuit, and naval air was invaluable to the boats when they were caught up in a firefight. But a lesson that was learned in the French Indochina War and which certainly should have been relearned early in the Vietnam War is that sea power and air power are of limited effectiveness in counterinsurgency war and in the interdiction of enemy lines of communication through difficult and largely trackless terrain.

Immediately following the successful sweep of the DOAN-10 base camp area, a thirty-day campaign was initiated in the RSSZ in order to maintain the momentum that had been achieved. RF and PF units were pressured to move out from their camps and actively patrol. Known VC staging areas were hit. U.S. Navy SEALs and Vietnamese PRUs (Provincial Reconnaissance Units) collected and reacted to intelligence information. New applications of sensor devices were experimented with, including the use of airborne "people sniffers" that could detect the odor of humans on the ground. For a time the nature of operations in the Rung Sat changed from one that largely reacted to enemy initiative to a more proactive one where the emphasis was on preventing attacks on shipping.

In August 1969, two additional combined operations ("Friendship" and "Platypus") were launched against DOAN-10 in the Nhon Trach District. In September, Operation "Chuong Duong" struck at the same area. These were followed in October by the first of a series of strikes against DOAN-10 called "Wolf Pack." All of these utilized USN and VNN boats as a blocking force for ground sweeps by Australian, Thai, and VN units. Herbicides were used lavishly in southern Nhon Trach District, as were giant army "Rome plows" (armored bulldozers) to destroy the cover formerly enjoyed by the enemy sapper battalion.

The cooperation given these operations by the Nhon Trach District chief was marginal at best. A particularly aggravating situation centered on the village of Vung Gam, which was consistently identified in intelligence reports as a support base for DOAN-10. The district chief just as consistently refused to do anything about it.[9] Despite this and other equally annoying examples of official reluctance to support the navy-led campaign against the enemy sapper battalion, the results achieved exceeded almost anybody's expectations.

"I note with great pleasure," Admiral Zumwalt told his Rung Sat commander, "that the passing of January completed three consecutive calendar months during which there have been no attacks on shipping on the Long Tau. This establishes a record.

"The accomplishment of this record is tangible evidence of the continuous pressure you have maintained on the enemy through offensive operations . . . your overall professionalism and the outstanding spirit of teamwork which exists in the RSSZ. Well done."[10]

The record Zumwalt referred to in his congratulatory message was broken the very next day when DOAN-10 made its first attack on a merchant ship in the Long Tau in 117 days. The overall improvement in security operations in the Rung Sat was, nevertheless, impressive. In this period you could travel in a small boat the entire length of the Long Tau in relative safety. I myself made the trip in a Boston Whaler, and though the banks, at low water, towered over the boat, the transit and many others like it were completed without incident and without fear. Minesweeping operations, which in earlier times had been marked by ambush and death, became what they usually are—deadly boring.

"During the period 3 March 1969 to 14 February 1970," the departing commander of MSBs in the Rung Sat reported, "Mine Division 112 made over 2,000 combat sweeps covering a distance in excess of 53,000 miles in the Rung Sat Special Zone. A total of 17 wires were recovered in sweep gear, indicating the possible presence of command detonated mines."[11]

By early February 1970, the VNN operated fully half of the afloat assets assigned in the Rung Sat, and a Vietnamese officer commanded the Long Tau patrol and all but a small part of the minesweeping operation. Vietnamization was proceeding rapidly, and the U.S. Navy was getting ready to go home. Though it may have seemed so for a brief time, peace was not at hand on the Long Tau nor in the dark swamps of the Forest of Assassins. The river would never be closed to navigation, but it would never again be as secure as it then was.

On 9 November 1970, River Assault Division 153 left Nha Be, ending the U.S. Navy's patrol and assault boat operations in the Rung Sat. Later that month, Mine Division 112 went home.

19

A Swift Boat Officer's War

Now when this war is over
And all the tales are told,
Recall the Swift Boat sailor—
He wore the Blue and Gold.

—Lyrics from a drinking song, sung at the "Cat House"
(the navy officers club) at Cat Lo, in 1969–70

IEUTENANT (JUNIOR GRADE) LUTHER J. ELLINGSON ARRIVED IN-COUNTRY IN APRIL 1969 FOR DUTY AS A SWIFT BOAT OFFI-CER-IN-CHARGE. I RAN INTO ELLINGSON SEVERAL TIMES IN MY VIETNAM TRAVELS, RODE HIS BOAT ON PATROL, AND WAS IM-PRESSED BY THE QUIET, CAPABLE MANNER IN WHICH THIS YOUNG OFFICER PERFORMED HIS DUTY. ELLINGSON'S STORY MIRRORS THAT OF MANY OTHER JUNIOR NAVAL OFFICERS THRUST INTO POSITIONS OF GREAT RESPONSIBILITY AND DANGER IN THE SEA LORDS ERA.

ON 5 MARCH 1970, LIEUTENANT COMMANDER FORREST L. ED-WARDS, NAVFORV FORCE HISTORIAN, RECORDED ELLINGSON'S PER-SONAL HISTORY. WHAT FOLLOWS IS AN EDITED TRANSCRIPT OF THE EDWARDS TAPE.

I had a major portion of my swift boat training at Coronado, California, during the month of March and the first week of April 1969. My last week of training prior to departure for Vietnam was at Vallejo. We didn't have Swift boats at Vallejo, and my class was only the second one to go up there. We drove PBRs there, and the primary purpose of it was to give us a taste of riverine warfare.

I arrived in Cam Ranh Bay on 22 April. This was a one-week TAD assignment and we were given various briefings and indoctrina-tion—a little bit of the larger picture of what the situation was in Vietnam, particularly in terms of what our Swift boats were doing. I was then further assigned to Coastal Division 11 based at Danang. Danang had three coastal patrol areas at that time, and one river patrol. It also had a detachment down at Chu Lai, where there were three additional coastal patrol areas.

I started out by going on indoctrination patrols. The first one was a coastal patrol and the second one was on a river. I got a taste of riverine warfare rather quickly. On the second day of the two-day river patrol we were ambushed. We took a B-40 rocket just aft of the pilothouse, along with automatic weapons fire. It was a funny feel-ing—a bullet passed right through the spot where I had been sitting moments before. It was an interesting experience to say the least, that first firefight.

On Market Time patrols we often played policemen to fishermen who were just trying to make a living. We had many restricted zones in our patrol areas and our job was to keep these fishermen from entering them, or if they did enter them to kick them out of there, perhaps turn them in if it was their second or third offense. It often-times left a lot of room for a judgment factor, and much decision making on the part of the O-in-C. So much was left to his discretion, the grey areas were so broad and the actions you might take so varied. I'm sure they varied considerably from one O-in-C to the next, and of course this made it difficult for the fishermen, because they never knew what to expect. I tried to instill in myself a feeling of callous disregard for the people, but the letter of the law sometimes seemed quite unfair to me, and moral questions about what I was doing and what was really right gave me considerable qualms and pain.

There was a large restricted zone just south of Danang, and it had been established at a time when the coastline was in VC hands. It so happened that since then the area had been pacified by either the army or the marines—I forget which. The village that was set up there was completely under government control, and the people were almost entirely dependent on fishing as a means of livelihood. The restricted zone stretched for a long distance along the coast right in front of their village. So what were they to do? To say they couldn't fish was to say they couldn't live. Anyway, a local American officer had gotten together with the village chief, and the people of this particular village were given picture identification cards which said they could fish in the area immediately offshore of their village.

According to navy directives, however, this area was still a restricted zone. So along would come these villagers who claimed to have permission from their village chief and the U.S. officer in charge of the AO where they lived, saying they could fish there, and I as an example would come along saying they could not. What I should do in that particular instance was at first uncertain, but after going back to my boss, directives were issued saying that whenever we found any fishermen like that we were to take their identification cards and tell them that the American officer and the village chief who said they could fish there were in the wrong, and that we were in the right. What they'd have to do is talk to the village chief, who'd have to talk to the district chief, who'd have to talk to the province chief, who'd have to talk to the wheels in Saigon and persuade them to change the restricted zone. Well, needless to say, that would be a long process and as I said, fishing was their life.

I did have one rewarding experience while on a coastal patrol that I'll remember well. There were a number of coastal groups inshore of our patrol areas where we would bring detainees we'd picked up. We were frequently the coastal groups' primary means of keeping in touch with the outside world. One night a coastal group came under attack from a mountain area across from its position, and they gave us a call requesting assistance in terms of .50-caliber runs and 81-mm mortar strikes. We proceeded to do both. I don't know what the results were, but at least we put on a loud and nice-looking show. Later, at the O-club in Danang, I overheard the advisor of the coastal group relating that evening's events. He expressed great satisfaction and gave high words of praise for the Swift boat which had been his only source of outside help. It gave me a very fine feeling, a feeling of having accomplished something.

After about three months at Danang, I was transferred to our detachment at Chu Lai. This was where the living was really great. If there's any place in Vietnam that's a nice place to live, Chu Lai is the place. I lived in a hootch with one other guy, who happened to be the NILO down there. The hootch was quite large, I suppose maybe 15 by 30 feet. We had our own head and shower, and a reefer [refrigerator]. I got hold of a tape recorder and set that up. We were right next door to the O-club. It was a great place to fight the war from.

We'd patrol every other day—out for twenty-four, in for twenty-four. It was still the same policeman-type role, but there was an added factor which made the patrols seem more valuable and important. CAP [combined action platoon] units consisting of eight to ten marines were assigned as advisors in villages near Chu Lai. These marines were quite isolated, and we were their means of keeping in touch with Chu Lai and the other CAP units. We'd often get a call in the morning before returning to Chu Lai from a patrol, asking if we could stop by to pick them up and bring them in. We'd also return them to their villages if they were in Chu Lai. Their food was rather limited, and if we had extra chow we'd oftentimes give them a call and they'd come out in a little sampan and meet us, and we'd give them whatever we could spare. They'd call on us for mortar support, and they'd act as spotters for us when we put indirect fire into areas they might be concerned about. A good portion of the coastline of the patrol areas at Chu Lai was "Indian country."

I patrolled for approximately one month in Chu Lai, and from this period I have two particularly vivid experiences. These are ones I will always try to push to the back of my mind, but I'll never be able to forget them. The first is rather long and involved and I'll try to shorten it, giving only the key points.

There was a feeling that fishing restricted zones were often located where they shouldn't be, and that sometimes where they should have been, they weren't. One area where there wasn't a restricted zone was south of Chu Lai near a place called Chon Mai Point, a known VC stronghold.

Anyway, there was a CAP unit in a nearby village. Chon Mai Point was a little peninsula that stuck out in the water, and the CAP unit was always quite concerned about the place, since it was known there were VC in there. Chon Mai Point was just covered with caves and thick, heavy foliage. There was not, as I said, a restricted zone in that vicinity, and according to my book the people could fish anywhere they wanted to, anywhere around the point.

One night the CAP unit asked me to put an H&I [Harassment & Interdiction] strike into Chon Mai Point, which is about the size of a grid square, and I did so. They also put some mortar rounds into the area, and then, not too long after that, and after dark, they called me again and asked if they could get permission to fire in the water off the point. They had had reports that there were VC sampans in the area. I told them that so far as I was concerned these were innocent fishermen, and that there was no reason whatsoever that they couldn't be there. So the word I gave them was that I would not give them clearance to fire because I felt they would be hurting innocent people.

The CAP unit, though, felt otherwise, and when I refused to give them clearance they chose to go up to a higher level. They called the NOC at Chu Lai. The individual on watch there was new at the job, and here he was receiving a call from people out in the field who reported enemy activity. Not having much experience, he felt he had to rely on the people in the field, and he gave them permission to fire into my AO. After giving that clearance, he called his boss and informed him of what he'd done. His boss immediately told him "negative clearance," and directed him to call the CAP unit and tell them that they could not fire in the area off Chon Mai Point.

In the meantime, the CAP unit had told me to stand clear because a mortar platoon would be directing fire into my area. At the time I was sleeping, and I was called by my LPO [leading petty officer] on watch. We observed the first rounds fired, and they seemed to land well seaward of the point, quite close to where I knew there were large numbers of fishing craft. I immediately called the CAP unit and the mortar platoon, requesting a cease fire. At about this same time the word came down from the other end telling them they did not have permission to fire in my area.

The whole thing might have ended right there, but I decided to proceed to the area where we saw the rounds drop, to see if there were any casualties. Upon arrival, we immediately ascertained that there were.

We found one sampan half-filled with water. There were three people in it, and one guy was standing up just screaming and he was covered with blood. The sampan was just barely holding together. There was another guy in the boat with a shrapnel wound—a piece of shrapnel had ripped into his eye. He was covered with blood too, and he was curled up into a ball. The third guy in the boat was quite obviously dead. It was a terrible thing to see and something I find disagreeable to even think and talk about again.

Anyway, we got the guy who was standing and screaming, got him aboard the boat and gave him first aid. And we were able to get the second guy who was seriously wounded on board, and we administered first aid to him as best we could. I called the CAP unit and informed them of what we had found. Leaving the dead man in the nearly sinking sampan with other fishermen in the area, we proceeded to the CAP unit with the two wounded. When we got as close to the beach as we could go, we passed them to a sampan which took them ashore where there was a corpsman and where we could eventually arrange a medical evacuation.

When I left Chu Lai, an investigation was under way. Later, I was able to get additional information, sketchy though it was. Supposedly, one of the wounded men I picked up was a VC or a VC sympathizer. Needless to say, that's always the case. I talked to one of the fellows at the CAP unit who told me there were a couple of other people medevaced by the Swift boat back to Chu Lai. When I informed him that I was the Swift boat on the scene that night and that I didn't medevac anybody to Chu Lai, his comment was that well, in that case, there are a couple more missing. He went on to relate how the people who were wounded and the dead man and the missing were all from the village where he was posted, and that their CAP unit, their combined action platoon, was not then on too friendly terms with the other villagers.

The other incident I was going to relate occurred just a couple of days later. Another of the CAP units in our area called me to inquire if I had conducted any firing of any sort within the last hour or two. My response was, negative. After consulting with the other Swift boat patrolling in that rough vicinity I passed on the information that he had not conducted any firing either. The CAP unit said that, as related by one of its villagers, some type of large American boat (which to a Vietnamese villager is any boat larger than a sampan) had come along, and people standing on deck had fired shots at his sampan with a weapon of a .45-caliber nature. One of the shots had hit one of the two men in the sampan in the upper groin area and had killed him. The surviving fisherman in the boat had been able to re-create the incident quite vividly. The men standing on deck were laughing, having first fired an illumination round, a pop flare, in front of the sampan. The fisherman described how one of the men had held out the gun and fired, and how his arm went up, and how he fired again, and how his arm again went up. He said the boat was quite large, grey in color, and that all the people on deck were Americans.

I naturally sent in a spot report on the incident, relating what information I had gathered, which was nothing firsthand as I had not been in the immediate vicinity where the incident supposedly took place, nor had I been aware of any other American craft that had passed through. YFUs transit our patrol areas on occasion, as well as other large ships—LSDs, destroyers, and so forth. Their passage through our AO was nothing to be noted by us.

This incident was followed up in Danang, and it seems that a YFU was passing through when the incident was alleged to have happened, and that the YFU did have weapons of a .45-caliber nature on board. Anyway, a few days later an investigation took place and a naval officer came down from Danang. The investigating officer was the man in charge of the naval transportation unit to which the YFU belonged. I took him to the dead fisherman's village. I went ashore with him and we got statements from various people, including the other fisherman on the sampan, the American corpsman who had seen the dead man and who had checked out his wound and what he considered the type of weapon that had killed him. Statements were also taken from the village chief and the village policeman.

In my opinion, the investigating officer could not be completely impartial, even if he wanted to be. Anyway, after the fisherman finished telling us what had happened, he wanted to add to his story by talking about the damage done to his boat. He said a bullet had gone through it that had struck the propeller on his outboard motor, causing one of the blades to break off. He also said that in trying to get away, he had lost his anchor and his anchor line. His idea in relating this obviously was to get some money from the American government. We checked out his sampan and we didn't find any bullet hole in it, nor did we find any evidence of a propeller blade having been shot off. This of course tended to discredit the rest of his testimony. I think the report the investigating officer sent in was that the whole incident was concocted.

* * *

About 22 August, my Swift boat and three others were transferred from Coastal Division 11 to Coastal Division 12 at An Thoi, and on that day we headed south on the long journey down the coast and up to An Thoi. It took us about five days to make the transit. We stopped at Chu Lai, Qui Nhon, Cam Ranh Bay, and Cat Lo for fuel, repairs, and maintenance en route.

Coastal Division 12 had two detachments, one at Ha Tien near the Cambodian border, and the other at Sea Float in the delta. My first deployment out of An Thoi was to Ha Tien. What we did was to conduct night waterborne guardposts—ambushes, on the Giang Thanh River. At that time we didn't have any logistic support at Ha Tien, and every five to seven days we would have to make a trip back to An Thoi (it's about two hours each way) to get food and fuel. For a while we tied up at the foot of the hill where the MACV base is. When the single pontoon broke loose there, we began tying up at the ferry landing downtown. There were six Swift boats at Ha Tien then, and we lived aboard our boats. We were fortunate to have an Onan generator; we could cook our food and keep a reefer going. It rained quite frequently, and every time it did the guys would get out on deck and have a freshwater shower. And of course we always had the river to jump into and wash up. Whether we got ourselves any cleaner from swimming and washing in the river, I don't know.

There was a detachment of PBRs at Ha Tien, and it always perturbed us a little that they were able to take showers at the MACV base and get hot meals there.

Everyday around 1600 we'd call MACV to ask for a jeep to take us up the hill for the afternoon briefing. Other than that, we were left to ourselves. When the ferry landing on the Ha Tien side broke loose and became weakened, we shifted over and began tying up at the ferry landing on the other side of the river. Then when we wanted to go up to the briefing we'd catch the ferry to take the jeep up.

We were running night ambushes at the time, and there weren't many assets available. Consequently, we'd tie up at some spot along the river, sit for six hours or so, and then come back in. I don't think we were ever out all night. Usually we'd leave right after dark and come in at maybe four o'clock in the morning. The purpose of the operation was interdiction, but never were we able to give complete coverage to the river. For all intents and purposes, the operation was almost worthless. Not only could Charlie cross on either side of us any time he wanted to, he could wait for us to leave and then cross. And during the daytime, of course, he could go any time he wanted to because there were no patrols at all.

It had always been standard operating procedure that when Swift boats are on the rivers they operate in pairs. When we first started setting night ambushes in the Giang Thanh, we'd sometimes tie up next to each other, then maybe fifty to one hundred yards apart, or with one boat on one side of the river and the other boat one hundred yards or so downstream on the other side. Gradually, the boats were spread farther and farther apart. Directives came from the powers that be to space the boats at least one thousand yards apart. This to me was asinine and it went against all Swift boat doctrine. I raised no few words of objection to this single-unit type of operation. I was told my apprehensions were unfounded. Also, our object was to seal off the border and we had to spread the boats apart.

After forty days at Ha Tien, I returned to An Thoi for a day of maintenance and then headed south for our detachment at Sea Float. I got to Sea Float about 9 October. Operations there were considerably more diverse and not nearly so dull and boring as those at Ha Tien. We did a lot of different things—we supported SEALs, we inserted Kit Carson Scouts, we provided escort services, we made troop sweeps, we conducted psyops and night ambushes.

Sea Float at this time had been in existence for a few months. My first trip down the Cua Lon and Bo De rivers, seeing all the hootches and homes that had been razed and destroyed in our Sea Lords raids, made quite an impression on me. I personally have serious reservations about the effectiveness and value of those raids. I really think it was a sad period that we went through. But that's not my story.

We did have one particular problem at Sea Float, and it was a hindrance to our operations in the overall sense, and that was the difficulty in getting hold of troops. Without troops our ability to operate was severely limited and cramped. We could control the rivers and canals, but just inland from them we had no control. Charlie controlled the inland area, and any time Charlie wanted to hit us on the rivers he could do so. At least that's the way I felt about it, and many others felt the same. We had high hopes for a while. Some Vietnamese troops, the *Biet Hai,* arrived on the scene, but afterwards we found that they were there only to provide support and security for the construction of Solid Anchor.

One of the things we did quite frequently was to provide escort services for tugs and barges bringing material for Solid Anchor. Another task we often were called upon to perform was providing escort services for the sand-prospecting rig that was attempting to find sand somewhere in the vicinity, sand that was vitally important for the construction of Solid Anchor. We went up and down the Cua Lon, up and down canals, into some of the most hairy places you can imagine. We'd just sit around this rig while the civilians aboard looked for sand and sampled the ground. The end result of all their efforts was negative. The word I received from one person with the civilian firm in charge of this particular task was that they never expected to find any sand. The navy said they would find it, but nevertheless they didn't. The amazing thing was that all this time we spent escorting the drill rig looking for sand, we never had one incident.

One operation I and most other Swifties did not enjoy going on was a psyops mission. These were run quite frequently on different rivers and different canals in the Sea Float area. We'd just drive along, playing that loudspeaker as loud as she'd go and putting out the good word to the people on the banks. I question what good it did, what value the message that was preached over the loudspeaker really had. It did seem to rile up Charlie, because we were often hit.

On 17 October I was on one—four Swift boats headed up the Cua Lon and then the Dam Doi playing our psyops tapes. A PG had gone up with us as far as where the Bo De, the Cua Lon, and the Dam Doi come together, with the idea of providing support with her 3-inch gun. On the way back to Sea Float we overtook the PG and were a mile or so ahead of her when she was ambushed from the north bank. One B-40 hit her on the bow, putting her 3-inch out of commission. Her 40-mm was inoperative too, and all she had left were her .50-caliber guns. In essence, she was then only an overgrown Swift boat.

As soon as we got word she was hit, we turned around and headed back. About one thousand yards from the ambush, I began to receive fire from the south bank. Three B-40 rockets passed right in front of me. Thinking back on it, we were considerably closer to the south bank than we usually would have been, and the way the VC set up their aiming stakes probably caused them to fire early. Anyway, we beached and started putting in mortar fire at the two ambush positions and we were firing like crazy. Three other Swift boats scrambled from Sea Float and they began firing too, and altogether we put in a total of 256 mortar rounds. Seawolves were called in and they put in a strike with their mini-guns and .50-cal and rockets. We really saturated the area, and if nothing else we told Charlie he'd better think twice before trying to hit us again. As to the results of all our fire, I really don't know. We put a scare in somebody at least.

Night ambushes had just come into vogue at Sea Float and were proving to be rather effective. Some sampan traffic and some people were caught out at night. Some KIAs were marked up. Once Charlie caught on to what we were doing he avoided us, though, because you can hear a Swift boat from miles off and you know exactly what it is doing. After a couple of weeks, these operations, in my opinion, were rather useless. This feeling was shared by most of the Swifties, but we still conducted them because sometimes it seemed as if there wasn't enough for us to do. Anyway, we conducted them.

I remember one night ambush not so much for what happened during the ambush as for what happened to us on the way back. It was the day after Halloween. We'd gone out around midnight and broke our position about first light. We then got a message about a possible tug escort and we headed out the river to meet it. The tug we were to escort didn't show, and our four Swift boats headed back toward Sea Float. This time I was the lead boat in column. You're always trying to figure out what is the best place to be, and since I'd been hit when I was the last boat the last time, I concluded that being the lead boat was better. This time it proved to be not the case. As we were passing down the Cua Lon River I was ambushed from the south bank. Two or three B-40s and a small amount of automatic weapons fire came my way, but again none of the rounds hit my boat. My forward .60 gunner immediately took the ambush site under fire and that probably explains why we received no damage to boat or crew. We mortared the area well and called in Seawolves. A ground sweep later that morning found the spot from which the rockets were fired, and discovered three others that had not been fired.

On 14 November I completed my tour at Sea Float and returned to An Thoi for five or six days of maintenance. Around the 20th I was deployed to Ha Tien again. My stay at Ha Tien this time was again mostly uneventful. We were still conducting the same type of operations—night ambushes. There was no major contact at all, at least not by the Swift boats. The PBRs would sometimes pick up movement, which they immediately took under fire.

One night I did receive fire and that was from a PBR sitting in ambush about one thousand yards away. Tracer rounds fell all around me, on both sides of the boat.

Logistic support at Ha Tien had picked up considerably. We now had an ATSB tied up below the MACV compound area. We could get hot meals and cold showers. There was also an LST anchored off the coast where we could refuel. The LST at first had the idea that she was basically there for PBR support, as did the ATSB. Anyway, it was a lot better.

I went to Ha Tien to relieve a boat that had gotten hit in the Vinh Te Canal. The night ambushes there were a little longer. We'd head out before dark, and generally not break ambush until first light. We'd put mortar all along the Vinh Te and then take up our water-borne guardpost positions. Our operational time increased considerably; we were really turning to and working hard. During the daylight hours a few junks went out, but there was still nothing to keep Charlie from crossing.

I had something wonderful to look forward to at this time, and that was going to Hawaii on R&R to meet my girlfriend. Then on about 15 December one of the boats came in from An Thoi with mail and word that my R&R was being canceled. There just weren't enough O-in-Cs to meet all the commitments. Some had been medevaced, some were leaving country, and too many had been scheduled for R&R that month. I had asked back in November and was told there would be no problem with taking R&R as planned, but mine and two others were canceled anyway. Needless to say, it was most disappointing. I had to write my girlfriend and tell her that I wasn't coming. My feelings toward the navy at that time took a definite downward spiral. I got over it rather quickly, though.

We got mail at Ha Tien whenever a boat came up from An Thoi—this was the case at Sea Float, too. Often it seemed to take a long time to get the mail to An Thoi from Saigon. Sometimes no boats came from An Thoi for five to seven days. Mail was one thing everybody really looked forward to.

About 21 December I completed my second tour at Ha Tien. After three days of maintenance at An Thoi I headed down to Sea Float again. Boats there were still getting hit now and again. There was one good bit of news—the MSF, 179 men in all, had been sent to Sea Float. These montagnards were great troopers, and they had worked with us Swifties before.

The operations at Sea Float were as varied as ever. Once we took twenty Kit Carson Scouts and an American advisor way up the Cai Nhap Canal. We headed out about 2000 at night. The KCS objective was a VC prison camp about three klicks inland. Due to difficulty getting through VC checkpoints, however, the mission had to be aborted.

One other operation I remember well was a troop sweep along a canal. We took about thirty PF troops and inserted them on both banks. A U.S. EOD team went with one group, and a U.S. UDT went with the other. The troops swept strips along the canal banks about fifty to one hundred yards wide. I was the lead boat and the O-in-C of the operation.

I did my best to keep even with the lead troops and to keep the two groups even with each other as we proceeded down the canal. You often could not see more than ten feet or so inland, due to heavy undergrowth. Along one bank, and inland a way, the troops found booby-trapped grenades, which they dismantled. We blew up a couple of large fishtraps. After about three or four hours, and close to the time when we were supposed to head back, we heard noises up ahead. I began placing 81-mm mortar fire in front of the advancing troops.

On the north bank, some electrical leads were discovered leading from a bunker complex one hundred yards inland to the canal bottom. Some of the bunkers were brand new; the mud was still soft and you could see footprints and kneeprints in it. One of my mortar rounds had hit within ten yards of the complex, and we guessed that it had caused a hasty evacuation. A trail was followed three hundred or four hundred yards inland from the canal bank and then lost. A battery assembly was discovered that was obviously intended for use with whatever was in the canal. The electrical leads were attached to a steel support wire, and the troops pulled on it to no avail. We then connected it to my towline and I managed to yank it loose from the bottom. Because of the depth of the water and poor visibility, swimmers, going under water without gear, could not identify the object.

We next ran the towline around a tree and tried to pull the object up that way, but then the supporting wire broke. It was obvious we would somehow have to secure the towline directly to the object. We called Sea Float and a Seawolf helicopter brought SCUBA gear, which was passed to us on the fantail of my Swift boat. The EOD guys then dove down (the water was more than twenty-five feet deep) and attached the towline. We ran the line around a tree limb and managed to get the object up. Swimmers in the water had to keep pushing it out to keep it from getting hung up on tree roots. We saw that it was a 750-pound bomb that had been rigged as an electrically fired, command-detonated mine.

The divers found that it had been staked to the bottom, and that the electrical leads were well insulated. The detonator had been cemented into the nose of the bomb and it appeared to be a piece of very professional work. Needless to say, had it gone off under us, it would have given us quite a rise.

The EOD guys attached a couple of pounds of C-4 and rigged it with a two-minute time fuze. We all went roaring down the canal at full blast. We were quite a way off when it blew up, but we could still feel strong tremors from the explosion.

☆   ☆   ☆

I completed this tour at Sea Float on 24 January and went back to An Thoi and then on to Ha Tien again. Things were a little more organized there. The number of Swifts had increased from six to eight, and there were in addition two VNN Swifts. Both day and night patrols were set now, and junks were covering a portion of the river at night. We were finally getting a semblance of real coverage. We were given sensors, and this was just like having four more people on watch. I'd ordinarily plant two on one bank and two on either side of our boat on the opposite bank where I beached. You took some risk when you sent guys ashore to put them out and pick them up, but they worked well. They gave coded beeps to tell you which one had detected something—one beep for sensor one, two for sensor two, etc.

MSRs [riverine minesweepers] had been sent to Ha Tien. These were brand new craft, and their crews were quite green. Most of them had never been in a firefight before. Two MSRs had a day patrol in the upper part of the Giang Thanh River one day when I had a day patrol in the lower half. It was around 1600, and they had just put out their minesweep gear. They were sweeping down the river when they were hit by a really well-put-together ambush. One boat took about eight B-40 rocket hits, possibly a recoilless rifle round, and some machine gun fire. Both of the boats were hit, and on one of them every single man was wounded in one way or another.

As soon as I heard, I headed upriver to rendezvous with them and prepared to put some 81-mm into the ambush position. When I met them they were coming at their best speed and seemed to be running scared. I stopped them and waved them ashore at a place where a helicopter could land to medevac the wounded. One of the boats was taking on quite a bit of water, and the guys in that boat were pretty shook up—and rightly so. They talked about abandoning the boat. I sent my snipe over and found out they could make it back to Ha Tien without any problem. Two men were seriously wounded, and a third had taken a direct hit by a B-40 rocket and was dead. Seawolves arrived to put in a strike, and the two seriously wounded men were medevaced. The MSRs then continued on to Ha Tien. A VNN boat was upriver, so I escorted the one that was in the lower river up and got them together so they could resume their patrol. Then I caught up with the MSRs and escorted them the rest of the way down.

Charlie was increasing his activity. That night another MSR was fired at while in ambush—one B-40 missed, and another hit a stanchion and didn't go off. The following night two B-40s were fired at a

U.S. boat and both of them missed. The next morning a VNN boat took a B-40 right through the bow, but there were no casualties. I told my guys before we went out on patrol that we could consider our operation successful if we came back the next morning not having suffered any damage to the boat or crew.

This activity took place in just a matter of four days from 12 through 17 February. On the 18th I was relieved and headed to An Thoi to get ready for my R&R. I had a wonderful week in Hawaii and this is just a few days later when I am making this tape. I'm flying out of Saigon tomorrow morning and going back to An Thoi. Before I left, my DIVCOM told me I could have a staff job that's being established at Ha Tien. When I was up there I was the senior O-in-C and I had to take care of message traffic, scheduling, and all the administrative things as well as operate. After having been on the boats for about ten months, I had a strong desire to get off them, and now I'm going back to a staff job that will really be great. I don't have too many nostalgic feelings about getting off my old Swift boat.

In preparing this tape, I may have tended to dwell on the more unpleasant things, on the unpleasant incidents that have taken place. They're no more than anybody else experienced over here. We've seen the same things, done the same things, and I'm just one of many. It's a very strange war, and a very difficult war that's being fought over here, and if one tries to think of the bigger picture it can become very depressing and demoralizing. I'm certainly not knocking our policy and I'll certainly be the first to support our government in its efforts here, but needless to say I'm looking forward very much to heading home in another month and a half.

I RECEIVED A LETTER FROM LUTHER ELLINGSON DATED 13 MARCH 1970. HE HAD HIS STAFF JOB AT HA TIEN THEN, AND HE WAS LOOKING FORWARD TO TAKING GRADUATE SCHOOL EXAMS IN SAIGON A FEW WEEKS LATER. I NEVER SAW OR HEARD FROM HIM AGAIN.

20

Breezy Cove

South Vietnamese police used rifle butts Saturday to break up a protest march by 40 disabled war veterans toward the Presidential Palace. Some of the veterans fought back with their crutches in a brief scuffle.

Four veterans were injured. Four of the demonstrators traveled in wheel chairs. Three were amputees and one was blind.

The melee started about 200 yards from the palace in downtown Saigon after the veterans, demanding a raise in the living allowance, had marched from the National Assembly building where part of their number began a hunger strike four days earlier.

Helmeted police wearing camouflaged fatigues barred their way about a block from the palace. . . .

The living allowance of veterans now stands at $16.95 per month. There are an estimated 250,000 disabled war veterans in Vietnam.

—UPI news story, dateline Saigon, 4 April 1970

By early 1970, the social costs of the war to Vietnam were staggering. The police assault on disabled veterans reported by UPI was every bit as sickening as journalists described. For a week or so before the crackdown, the veterans and their destitute families had camped out on Saigon sidewalks, in shanty towns of sticks and cardboard and canvas. These were torn down and carted away with the demonstrators, but the problem of how to deal with a growing disaffection of the people remained.

Before the veterans, it had been saffron-robed Buddhist monks. They staged a silent, sit-down protest before the palace, and they, too, were clubbed and routed by the police. Then it was students who took up the cry against the government and its American supporters. Scores of young people, some little more than children, were arrested and jailed. Tear gas filled the streets of the capital.

Saigon newspapers attacked the government—or tried to. Despite GVN assurances that the press in Vietnam was "as free as any in the world," twenty-eight entire editions of Saigon newspapers were seized and destroyed between January and May 1970.[1] Many others were published with large blank spaces on their front pages, where censors at the last moment had pulled stories deemed inimical to the government and to the war effort.

So long as a large U.S. presence remained in Vietnam, the costs of the war, financial and moral, could be met or at least deferred. After Tet 1968, however, genuine fear began to creep into the hearts of some whose hearts before had quickened only at the prospect of diverting American largesse for their own purposes. When their U.S. protectors left, large bills were certain to be presented for payment, and not only by the Viet Cong and the NVA.

One of the objections to Operation Sea Float voiced by An Xuyen Province officials and their senior advisors in the spring of 1969 was that resources expended in the Nam Can could be put to better use farther north, particularly in Song Ong Doc District. This new awareness of a shrinking U.S. commitment was a sign of the times. After years of near profligate spending of men, money, and material, a deeply disillusioned America was preparing to disengage itself from the war, and where before there had been relatively little concern in the GVN for the principle of economy of force, now there was a general awakening to the need to conserve what America was still prepared to give.

COMNAVFORV responded to Sea Float objections by explaining that because of limiting water depths and other considerations, PBRs would be the principal asset employed in a naval operation on the Song Ong Doc. PCFs, stripped from Market Time patrols, would carry the lion's share of the operational load at Sea Float, and these were already on hand in sufficient numbers. The desirability of a Song Ong Doc patrol was acknowledged, and promises were made to establish one as soon as PBRs became available.

On 9 September 1969, therefore, First Sea Lord was instructed to prepare a plan for a joint USN/VNN operation in the Song Ong Doc AO "in support of IV CTZ pacification program. . . . [and] to provide assistance to Ca Mau District, An Xuyen Province."[2] The operation was to have a U.S. commander and a VNN deputy commander. The Americans would call it "Breezy Cove"; the VNN, "Tran Hung Dao IV" (later, "Tran Hung Dao X"). Forces assigned would include ten USN PBRs, ten VNN PBRs, and three USN riverine assault craft. These would operate from a five-ammi complex positioned fifteen kilometers downstream from Old Song Ong Doc, the district capital. LCUs would shuttle logistic support from a modified LST anchored offshore.

The Vietnamese Navy, not surprisingly, said that its participation would be delayed until late October or early November, pending the turnover of more PBRs. Admiral Zumwalt, possibly annoyed and at any rate always a man in a hurry, ordered Breezy Cove established unilaterally. It would be the last major and continuing NAVFORV operation initiated in the war.

First Sea Lord issued an operation order on 18 September. Pertinent parts read as follows:

"Situation: The Song Ong Doc is one of the principal water LOCs leading to the city of Ca Mau. As such, its freedom of use as a trade route is important to the growth and GVN control of the city of Ca Mau and An Xuyen Province. Enemy units operating along this waterway impede the flow of waterborne traffic by harassment and tax extortion operations. Transients and residents of the area are subject to intimidation and attack by fire. . . .

"Mission: Conduct patrols, night waterborne guardposts, mine countermeasures, and bank sweeps (utilizing RF/PF or 21st ARVN Div troops as available) in order to prevent tax extortion and to secure the Song Ong Doc/Song Trem Trem waterway for unmolested waterborne traffic flow. Conduct active psyop programs in coordination with Province Senior Advisor personnel and Tenth U.S. Army Psyop BN officials in order to stimulate the resettlement of the areas along the waterway and to promote the GVN image. . . ."[3]

Lieutenant Commander L. H. Thames, commander River Squadron 53, was the operation's first commander. The USS *Garrett County* (AGP 786) was anchored offshore in the Gulf of Thailand to provide support.

The ten USN PBRs, River Division 572, arrived in the AO on the afternoon of 26 September. On the same day, the first ammi pontoon barges were offloaded, in bad weather, from Seventh Fleet LSDs that had carried them from Nha Be. Two YFUs were damaged towing the ammis into the river. The seas were so choppy that Seawolf helicopters had to be securely lashed down on the *Garrett County,* giving rise to some concern over increased reaction time should a scramble be required.[4]

It is not likely that Breezy Cove took the enemy or anyone else by surprise. Several Saigon prostitutes, "firstest with the mostest," Lieutenant Commander Thames reported, were on hand to welcome the PBRs.[5]

By 29 September, the five ammis (the number later would be increased to ten) were moored in the river, approximately thirty feet from the north bank. A walkway connected the ATSB to the shore. Several 105-mm howitzers were mounted on the ammis, giving Breezy Cove, for a time, its own heavy artillery. The 105s later would be removed, and defense of the ATSB would reside primarily in its assigned boats, a Seawolf detachment, and two 60-mm and two 81-mm mortars on the ammis. A helo pad and a small barracks for Seawolf crews were located on the beach, several hundred yards distant.

With the ATSB established, PBRs began patrolling from the river mouth to Ca Mau City. The first ambush of a patrol occurred on 4 October. One of the two PBRs on the patrol received heavy damage from recoilless rifle and machine gun fire. Its crew was taken on board the second boat. One sailor was killed and twelve were wounded. Seawolves and Black Ponies were credited with killing fourteen of the enemy. The abandoned PBR was later recovered and towed out of the river for repairs.[6]

The AO, which lay to the south of the U Minh Forest, was a principal source of Viet Cong support, particularly during the rice-harvesting season. Contact with the enemy in the first three months of the operation was both frequent and sharp. The ATSB accordingly was enlarged, and additional riverine assault craft were assigned to assist in its defense. River banks were swept by local Vietnamese troops. SEALs were employed on intelligence-gathering missions.

As an operation, Breezy Cove acquired many of the characteristics of Sea Float, though on a somewhat smaller scale. In its first three weeks, 446 refugees arrived in the vicinity of the ATSB, seeking security. The village they formed there was called "New Song Ong Doc" (the navy called it "New Sod" as opposed to "Old Sod" for the established district capital, halfway up the river to Ca Mau). GVN officials wanted to move the refugees to the south bank of the river across from Breezy Cove, but could furnish no funds or material to build shelters. The navy built a school for the refugee children on the north bank, adjacent to the ATSB, and the village extended from there some five hundred yards inland and for perhaps two thousand yards upstream. This created obvious problems for the defense of the base from an enemy force attacking from the north. There was not a great deal of dry land in New Song Ong Doc village. Makeshift bridges and walkways ran from one small plot of high land to another.

By November 1969, civilian traffic was moving with relative ease on the river. A Vietnamese junk master told an American officer that for the first time in eleven years he could travel the river from Old Song Ong Doc to Ca Mau without fear of VC tax extortion.[7] Whether the junk master considered Saigon tax collectors the lesser of two evils was not asked, nor apparently was the true feeling of the refugees ascertained. Blind assumption was the rule here, as in most other regions "pacified" and placed under nominal GVN control. The truth almost certainly was that the people only wished to be left alone, and felt not much gratitude for those who, in rescuing them from the Viet Cong, had also driven them from their homes.

The arrival of VNN PBRs in November almost doubled the forces available at Breezy Cove. Two of these were soon ambushed while on patrol. Struck by recoilless rifle fire, one PBR was sunk and the other abandoned. Only light casualties were taken, and both boats were later recovered and repaired.[8]

An "unfortunate" incident of war occurred during predawn hours on 22 November. Two ASPBs on night ambush observed a small sampan entering the river from an intersecting canal. A light on the bobbing craft appeared to blink on and off, and the sampan was immediately illuminated and taken under fire. It beached, and its occupants were found to be two children, a teen-age girl, and a fifty-year-old woman. All were wounded, and the woman's left hand had been shot off. They were taken to Old Song Ong Doc for treatment and later evacuation to Can Tho.[9]

In December, barricades began to spring up on tributaries and canals leading into the river. Firefights became more frequent. Forty enemy KIA were recorded in the month, compared to sixteen in November. SEAL operations accounted for the capture of seventeen enemy soldiers.[10]

On 13 December, Duffle Bag activations only four hundred yards from the ATSB were taken under fire by mortars, resulting in two large and four small secondary explosions. The next day, PBRs received B-40 and heavy machine gun fire from a well-prepared ambush site some seven miles from the river mouth. Seawolves helped suppress the fire, and troops were inserted to end the fight. Four U.S. sailors were wounded.[11] Later in the month, a second daytime ambush of PBRs occurred.

In January and February 1970, enemy activity in the Breezy Cove AO trailed off dramatically and this, along with the continued generation of refugees living under GVN "control," was interpreted as evidence of the pacification campaign's success. On 23 February, Captain J. R. Faulk, commander River Patrol Force, told a combined USN/VNN commanders' conference in Saigon that the time had come to "reassess" the navy's mission in Song Ong Doc. The enemy had not gone away, however, and he most certainly had not been defeated. Though Breezy Cove would remain relatively quiet for six months, when full-scale fighting resumed it did so with damaging consequences.

In early September 1970, Commander Cyrus R. Christensen assumed command of Operation Breezy Cove. Christensen, a navy "mustang" (a former enlisted man who had worked his way through the ranks to commissioned officer status), was a wiry, combative, and outspoken individual who would clash frequently with U.S. and Vietnamese officers over what he viewed as unrealistic assumptions concerning the Breezy Cove AO. Highly decorated (the Legion of Merit, the Bronze Star, the Purple Heart, ten Air Medals, etc.), he had served a previous tour in Vietnam as a Junk Force advisor in 1965–66. He also spoke good Vietnamese.

Prior to assuming command of Breezy Cove, he was briefed personally by Vice Admiral Jerome H. King, Jr., then serving as COMNAVFORV. Over dinner at King's Saigon quarters, Christensen was told that Breezy Cove was "an accident waiting to happen," and that in King's opinion the ATSB was not properly defended. King warned that the current lull in activity at Breezy Cove most likely would end soon.

Only a few days after Christensen assumed command, the lull did indeed end. On 15 September, two Seawolves were shot down in the Breezy Cove AO in what came to be known as the "VC Lake Massacre." The army lost three medical evacuation (Dustoff) helicopters and two gunships in the same action.[12]

On that day, Regional Force troops were engaged on a sweep operation some six kilometers south of Song Ong Doc. In mid-afternoon the RF made contact with a large enemy force and took a number of casualties. Urgent gunship support and medical evacuation of the wounded were requested. An army helicopter, Dustoff 86, responded, but could not land in the face of heavy enemy fire. Seawolves 12 and 32 (from Ca Mau) and 62 and 65 (from Breezy Cove) were scrambled to provide cover. All were attached to Christensen's command.

At about 1700, while flying over the contact area, all four Seawolves were hit, almost simultaneously. Seawolf 62, riddled by heavy machine gun fire, went down on the shore of VC Lake. Two of its crew were killed and two wounded. Seawolf 12 also went down, the pilot crash-landing his ship in the middle of the shallow lake. Seawolf 65, damaged and barely flyable, returned to Ca Mau. Seawolf 32, which suffered many hits and was losing fuel, nevertheless remained in the area to provide cover for Dustoff 86 as it evacuated surviving crew members from the downed Seawolves. This task completed, Dustoff 86 flew the wounded to the Third Surgical Hospital in Binh Thuy. Seawolf 32 then headed down the river toward Song Ong Doc, requesting that boats be sent in case the crippled helicopter had to ditch. It did not.

At 1732, three more U.S. Navy helicopters arrived at the crash site to attempt recovery of the bodies of the two dead crewmen from Seawolf 62. These "Slicks" (unarmed Hueys) could not land because they had no air cover. An hour and a half later, an army cobra gunship arrived to suppress ground fire. It too, however, was immediately shot down, and its crew was extracted by an army Dustoff. While this was going on, a navy Slick darted in and succeeded in recovering one of the bodies from Seawolf 62. Black Ponies were by then overhead, but were denied clearance to fire into the area because of the presence of friendly troops.

Late that night, Seawolf 62 was seen to be in flames. Enemy troops, under cover of darkness, had reached the helicopter, stripped

Commander Cyrus R. Christensen

it of its usable guns and other salvageable material, and set it afire. The next morning, the body of the last crewman was found not far from the smoking ruins of the helicopter. Black Ponies destroyed the crashed Seawolf 12 in VC Lake, and an ARVN demolition team blew up what remained of Seawolf 62. The downed Cobra gunship was lifted out by an army Skycrane helicopter.

The enemy force was estimated to be five hundred to one thousand strong, armed with large-caliber automatic weapons, and well trained.[13] Its presence in Song Ong Doc District, south of the river, did not bode well for the future of Breezy Cove.

On 6 October 1970, two VNN PBRs from River Patrol Division 62 were beached within twenty-five meters of each other in a waterborne guardpost on the north bank of the Song Ong Doc, six kilometers from the river mouth. At approximately 0200 an underwater explosion ripped PBR 37 apart, sending it to the bottom. PBR 36, under fire from the near bank, backed quickly into the stream. It made an emergency radio transmission to the ATSB only moments before it too was torn by an underwater explosion, killing all aboard. Seawolves were scrambled and saturated both banks of the river with fire. Other VNN PBRs, a monitor, and a Zippo boat arrived to suppress enemy fire and search for survivors. Seaman Vincent J. Wnoroski, an advisor on one of the VNN patrol boats, jumped into the water and helped rescue four wounded sailors, one of them an American. For this action, Wnoroski was recommended for the Silver Star. The bodies of five VNN crew members from PBR 36 and an American advisor, GMG1 Edward W. Withee, were recovered the following day.

It was surmised that swimmers had attached explosives to the hulls of the two PBRs while the boats were lying in ambush. This was the first known swimmer/sapper attack in the Breezy Cove AO.[14] A VNN survivor of the attack admitted that everyone was asleep on the boats when the first explosion went off.[15]

The presence of sappers in the AO was confirmed on 11 October. On that day a VNN patrol stopped a sampan on the Song Ong Doc for inspection. The five men in the sampan could provide no identification and were taken to the ATSB for interrogation. It was soon determined that they were members of the sapper team that had carried out the successful attack on the two PBRs.

For three days prior to the attack, the men said, they had trained in the area, observing PBR tactics, performance, and the placement of night ambushes. On the day before the attack, three of the sappers hid near the intersection of a small canal and the river, where they thought it likely an ambush would be set. After midnight, they floated downstream to the PBRs with two modified 105-mm projectiles supported by innertubes. These were attached to the boats' hulls, along with detonators and timing devices. Undetected, the swimmers then cleared the area.[16]

The projectiles used were thought to be two of nearly two hundred dropped not long before by an army helicopter a few kilometers south of Ca Mau. Only eighteen of these had been recovered by friendly forces, an indication of how hazardous the very environs of the provincial capital were then considered to be.

The wealth of detailed information extracted in this instance from hardened and well-trained members of an elite enemy unit is hardly surprising. "Field interrogations" in Vietnam were often brutal and sadistic, and sometimes murderous. U.S. commanders were told to "stay out of it." Certain things were to be left in Vietnamese hands, and the treatment of prisoners was one of them. Only when prisoners were officially in U.S. custody could they expect humane, Geneva Convention treatment, and those captured by U.S. forces ordinarily were turned over to Vietnamese authorities at the earliest possible moment. This was one of the least savory aspects of the U.S. "advisory" role in the war.

Christensen, who saw the five enemy sappers both before and after they were questioned, was certain they had been tortured. It was obvious, he said, that all were brutally beaten. When he last saw them, they were laid out on deck, blindfolded, and bound hand and foot. Every one had been "bloodied," he said.[17]

On 9 October, two U.S. Navy advisors were wounded when the VNN PBRs they were riding were hit by B-40 rockets and small-arms fire on a canal five kilometers east of Old Song Ong Doc. By then, attacks on the boats up and down the river were occurring on almost a daily basis. VNN PBR crews grew increasingly reluctant to go on patrol, and waterborne guardposts were virtually abandoned. In Christensen's view, ambushes, as conducted by the VNN, were utterly useless. He established, instead, a blocking force of two PBRs and two riverine assault craft, twenty-four hours a day, at the mouth of "VC Canal," a water route running south from the Song Ong Doc approximately ten kilometers east of the ATSB. This was, he believed, the principal enemy LOC running between the U Minh Forest and the Nam Can.

Evidence of increasing enemy infiltration, and the proven presence of a large enemy force south of Song Ong Doc, led to heightened concern for the security of the ATSB. As elsewhere, the lack of adequate troop support made the base's 2,500-meter defensive perimeter extremely vulnerable. A thirty-man PF platoon was the only force assigned to defend it, and the CIA representative in Ca Mau had warned Christensen that three of their number were "known Viet Cong." He was also warned about the village chief in New Song Ong Doc. The CIA thought he might be a Viet Cong, too.[18]

Christensen and the village chief customarily ate Chinese soup together each morning in the village square, and they would talk about mutual problems. One morning, their usually friendly discussion took a different tone. The night before, one of the ATSB's Seawolves had been fired upon by automatic weapons as it overflew the village.

"We can't have this," Christensen said. "If it happens again, I'll blow this goddamned place away."

His threat was reported through Vietnamese channels to the senior naval advisor and Admiral King. Christensen was told to be more circumspect in his relationship with local Vietnamese authorities.

Two weeks later, a second Seawolf helicopter was fired upon from the village, and this time it was hit. Fortunately, it suffered only minor damage. At about three o'clock the next morning, Christensen and one of his chief petty officers went ashore and threw a hand grenade, the pin not pulled, into the village chief's house. The message apparently was received and understood. Later in the morning Christensen and the village chief ate Chinese soup together as if nothing had happened. Christensen did not mention the helicopter, and the village chief said nothing about the grenade. The Seawolves were not fired upon from the village again.[19]

The settlement of large numbers of civilians in the vicinity of the ATSB—by October there were perhaps two thousand people living in New Song Ong Doc—made it difficult to identify and isolate enemy troops believed to be hiding in the village. Christensen recommended that the base be moved to a more secure area. His concerns were scoffed at. The district chief promised to assign more troops when they became available, and to relocate the refugees when there was money to do so. COMNAVFORV asked MACV for a Mobile Strike Force company; the request was denied.

Breezy Cove, for the time being, was left to its own devices. More Duffle Bag sensors were set out (even so, there were only enough to guard the north bank), and naval gunfire support was solicited whenever and wherever available.

Christensen continued to urge that the ATSB be moved. Relocating it to Old Song Ong Doc, he argued, not only would improve the chances of defending it, but would permit more effective patrolling of the river east of the district capital. (Radio equipment on the ATSB and on the boats did not permit communications from one end of his AO to the other.) Once more his recommendation was turned down, on the ground that such a move would make it easier for the enemy to mine the mouth of the river, while making it harder for the *Garrett County* to render support. Deputy COMNAVFORV, Rear Admiral H. S. Matthews, Jr., let it be known, through his chief of staff, that he was growing tired of Christensen's "emotional messages." Breezy Cove had been established for more than a year, he said, and it had not been overrun yet.

At about this same time, Christensen was told by the senior advisor to the ARVN 21st Division that if his units were attacked on the river they were not to return fire unless clearance were obtained from the division commander.

Christensen's reply to the startled U.S. Army colonel who had brought this incredible directive is unprintable. Admiral King, while perhaps deploring Christensen's bluntness, nevertheless backed him when the issue was brought to Saigon.

The basic plan for defending the ATSB called for it to be fought much like a ship, with its men manning mortars and machine guns, and damage control parties standing by to put out fires, etc. Christensen was by this time all but certain that enemy units had his base zeroed in, and that it would be both futile and foolhardy to remain on the ammis when the shelling began. Only days before the enemy struck, he radically revised his defense plan to have his entire ship's company take to the boats and fight off an attack from preassigned positions on the river. He also took the precaution of moving 135 rounds of 105-mm from a metal "Conex" box on one of the ammis to the *Garrett County*. If a mortar round had hit that, everything would have been blown sky high.

He sent a copy of his new defense plan to seniors in the chain of command. "When I am hit," he said, "this is what I intend to do." This time, no one dared to second-guess him.

On the night of 20 October, Christensen's worst fears were realized. At 2330, the ATSB was attacked by a company-size enemy force firing mortars, rockets, and heavy machine guns from both banks of the river. Some of the mortars were fired directly over the village. As many as sixty mortar rounds fell on the ATSB within the first ten minutes of the attack. With explosions rocking the base, and gunfire erupting everywhere, the men at Breezy Cove ran to their boats. Seawolves scrambled and laid down a protective curtain of fire. The USCGC *Bering Strait* (WHEC 382), offshore in the Gulf of Thailand, began lobbing 5-inch shells at prearranged targets on the south bank. PBRs and riverine assault craft, as they cleared their berths, returned the enemy's fire. Boats began to shuttle the wounded to the *Garrett County*.

Shortly after midnight, all the men at Breezy Cove had been accounted for, except for one missing man whose body would be recovered the next day. The base was in flames and rocked by explosions as stored ammunition cooked off.

At 0010, with Black Ponies overhead, enemy fire was at last suppressed. The ATSB, almost totally destroyed, burned all night, lighting up the sky for miles around. Two PBRs were sunk by the initial mortar barrage; the remaining thirty-odd boats got under way safely. There were approximately 325 men at the base when the attack occurred and considering the ferociousness of the shelling and the extent of material damage sustained, casualties were described as "amazingly low." Two U.S. sailors were killed and twenty-six wounded by enemy fire; some twenty more suffered cuts and bruises while scrambling for the boats. Five VNN were wounded by fire and eleven injured getting into the boats. In New Song Ong Doc, seven civilians were killed and thirty-three wounded by enemy mortar rounds that fell short.

Ironically, Christensen was not present when the enemy blow fell. He had been summoned to Binh Thuy for discussions that were to lead to turning over Breezy Cove to the Vietnamese. Awakened in the BOQ there and informed that his base was under attack, he flew by helicopter to the *Garrett County*, arriving there at about 0300.

The wardroom on the support ship had been converted into an emergency battle-dressing station. Two navy corpsmen, assisted by other members of the ship's crew, rendered treatment to thirty-five U.S. Navy personnel, sixteen VNN sailors, and twenty-five VN civilians from Breezy Cove. Sixty civilians, left without shelter after the battle, were temporarily berthed on the ship.[20]

With six volunteers, Christensen sped by boat to the ATSB, arriving there at about 0400. He found every structure on the afloat portion of the base destroyed. All ten ammis were either sunk or damaged beyond repair. Remarkably, no boats other than the two PBRs were lost. The helicopter pad and its adjacent barracks were intact, as was the outpost for the Popular Forces platoon. During the attack, the PF rendered no assistance; afterwards, PF soldiers looted the Seawolf pilots' barracks, stealing everything that could be carried away.[21]

Deputy COMNAVFORV and members of his staff arrived later that same morning. "You have been defeated," Admiral Matthews told a stung and outraged Christensen. The admiral chastised him for not having raised the flag over the ruined barges. "Frankly, it didn't occur to me," said a grim-lipped Christensen.

The village chief at New Song Ong Doc later admitted that he had noticed a large influx of "strange people" prior to the attack, though he took no action to warn the base. A considerable number of B-40 rockets were fired from the village during the assault, and the accuracy of the mortar barrage made it clear that observers in the village had assisted in spotting the fall of shot. So much for "pacification."

On 26 October, COMNAVFORV gave the order to "reconstitute ATSB Song Ong Doc at original location."[22] Ammis and other parts of the now disestablished Sea Float were towed from Solid Anchor. A Seabee team arrived and began construction of barracks and a new mess hall. Given the nature of the situation, COMNAVFORV's directive was foolish and, fortunately, wiser heads soon prevailed. The order was rescinded, and in its place came plans to establish an "advance staging base" at Old Song Ong Doc. Headquarters for the operation were moved to Ca Mau City. (According to Christensen, the Vietnamese Navy refused to take command of the operation if the headquarters were not moved to the relative safety of Ca Mau.) The relocation was completed on 25 November.

In December, Ca Mau itself and the still uncompleted Breezy Cove headquarters were attacked by Viet Cong and NVA forces now clearly on the offensive throughout the western delta. There were eleven firefights on the river, even though VNN units were thought to be doing their best to avoid them.

To protect his northern perimeter in Ca Mau from attack, Christensen paid the commander of the local Provincial Reconnaissance Unit $50 a month from his own funds. His wife mailed him the $50, in U.S. greenbacks, from the United States. MACV currency controls kept him from getting the money in any other way. The PRU commander, a former Viet Cong who had "chieu-hoied" to Saigon, would have nothing to do with Vietnamese piasters or MPC.

"We were never hit from the PRU side," Christensen said. The attack at Ca Mau, when it came, was launched from the south. A B-40 rocket impacted squarely on Breezy Cove's new flagpole. If it had not, Christensen said, it probably would have wiped out the TOC, "so maybe there was something to be said about flying the flag."[23]

When Breezy Cove was finally turned over to the Vietnamese Navy on 29 December 1970, the AO was acknowledged to be one of the most hostile in IV Corps. The turnover ceremonies were held under heavy guard at Ca Mau City, with Vice Admiral Jerome H. King, Jr. (COMNAVFORV), and Rear Admiral Tran Van Chon (VNN CNO) in attendance. Commander Christensen was relieved by Lieutenant Commander Pham Thanh Nhan, and Breezy Cove became "Tran Hung Dao X." Lieutenant Commander W. D. Danheim, Christensen's executive officer and the recipient of the Navy Cross for his part in the action on 20 October, was left behind to act as Nhan's senior advisor. The operation would continue to be supported by COMNAVSUPPACT Saigon until its functions, too, were turned over to the Vietnamese.

Breezy Cove was the next to last in-country operation (Sea Float/ Solid Anchor being the last) under U.S. Navy command in Vietnam.

21

The Unraveling

We must look to the conclusion of every matter, and see how it shall end, for there are many to whom heaven has given a vision of blessedness, and yet afterwards brought them to utter ruin. . . .

—Herodotus, *The Persian Wars*

On 15 May 1970, Admiral Elmo R. Zumwalt, Jr., was relieved as commander Naval Forces Vietnam by Vice Admiral Jerome H. King, Jr. The ceremonies were held aboard the USS *Page County* (LST 1076) at the Saigon Naval Shipyard. The news of Zumwalt's selection to be the next chief of naval operations still reverberated in Vietnam, and it filled the hearts of Brown Water Navy sailors with pride and pleasure, for they knew the extent of their contribution to his astonishing rise. NAVFORV senior staff officers were ecstatic. Some would accompany him to Washington; some would achieve early flag rank and assignment to coveted commands.

In retrospect, many of us in Saigon were living in a dream world. Despite what some of us were seeing with our own eyes, we could not believe in our hearts that the tremendous investment America had made in the war was being written off and that North Vietnam would be allowed to triumph. The power and the glory of the United States were as real and virtuous as ever. And were these things not manifest in the heroic figure of Zumwalt himself?

Military airs at the change of command ceremony were played by the 25th Infantry Division band, and General Creighton W. Abrams was the principal invited speaker. Army attendees wore combat greens, in stark contrast to the navy's tropical white long. Abrams presented Zumwalt with the Distinguished Service Medal "for exceptionally meritorious service to the government of the United States in a duty of great responsibility as Commander, U.S. Naval Forces, Vietnam/Chief, Naval Advisory Group, Military Assistance Command, Vietnam from October 1968 to May 1970." The NAVFORV staff was awarded the Navy Unit Commendation.

Commodore Tran Van Chon, the Vietnamese chief of naval operations, gave a brief and almost tearful speech. No one knew better than he what a great friend and supporter of the VNN Zumwalt had been. No one had more cause to fear what the future might hold.

PBRs and riverine assault craft passed in review in the river; Seawolves and Black Ponies flew overhead in the bright blue Saigon sky. The sun beat down on those assembled on the ship, and on the larger number of official guests and spectators seated on the wharf.

When Zumwalt, tall and commanding as ever, rose to make his remarks, you could sense everyone moving forward a bit in his chair. Perhaps he would announce a new initiative for the navy in Vietnam; perhaps he would give some clue as to how he would approach his next assignment.

"Ambassador Berger, General Abrams, Commodore Chon,

Admiral King, distinguished guests, officers and men of the Free World . . ." he began.

"I want first to thank the officers and men of this wonderful ship who came in here a few days ago, with the appearance of battle and salt sea spray, and who have turned this ship into a magnificent platform for this formality. And second, to thank you distinguished guests for taking your time to participate.

"During these past 20 months I have had five sources of inspiration. My family, understanding the demands of my job, pride in a son who was willing to volunteer to come over here and join in our effort. Second, the teamsmanship of the Army, Navy, Marine Corps officers and men. Third, the tremendous association with the Vietnamese Navy, embodied personally in Commodore Chon and his wonderful family who have taken my family and me into their hearts and have helped us to understand and come to love the Vietnamese people. Next, to General Abrams—tough, demanding, compassionate, and understanding. A great military captain in war. And last, to the Brown Water Navy itself, for their sacrifices and heroism. Symbolic of this, just 11 hours ago, the president of the United States awarded the Congressional Medal of Honor to Lieutenant Commander Thomas G. Kelly, who lost an eye and stood for an ensuing five-hour period in battle in his boat.

"As I look back over these 20 months, I see a map of South Vietnam with the Navy operating along the edges. In the Cua Viet River just south of the DMZ, in the Naval Support Activity Danang—providing the sustenance to our Marine associates—in Market Time along the coast, in pacification operations in the Rung Sat Special Zone, and in the Nam Can area and in the latter part, completely along the Cambodian border in Operation Sea Lords. And I see that map changing from blue, representing the U.S. Navy, to green, representing the Vietnamese Navy, all along and throughout that area. The Marine Corps [VNMC] expanding by 50 percent and the Navy [VNN] by 120 percent.

"I welcome Admiral King, in whose selection I had the good fortune to participate, and I have to tell him that the job is only about 35 or 40 percent done. There remains in this year 29 bases to be completed to replace U.S. Navy ships, there remains 7,500 repair technicians to be trained in these bases, there remains the job of upgrading the training of these beginners to the point where they relieve our senior petty officers and junior officers and take over their own middle management.

"But I leave in the most exciting week of all. A week in which the Vietnamese Navy dramatically demonstrated its progress, in which, participating with the U.S. Navy, they opened up the Mekong River for the first 30 miles and participating without the U.S. Navy made a dramatic movement to Phnom Penh and then overnight to Kampong Cham with a three-inch gunship and armored boats. This was a tremendous feat of professionalism and navigation and during which they removed some 9,000 refugees and escorted merchant ships back down the river who had previously been denied passage.

"As I go to my next job I am following a man who was singularly well qualified and I go in with many handicaps. You in the Navy know that I have never had a numbered fleet command or never commanded an ocean. But I do think I have some advantages. First, again, I take with me my family. Second, I take with me a tremendous insight into the workings of the Army, the Air Force, and the Marine Corps. Third, I think I have a keen insight into the need for my Navy to continue to provide priority to this Vietnamization process. Next, I, as one member of the Joint Chiefs, will always understand the tremendous study, the tremendous efforts and analysis that goes into any recommendation General Abrams sends forward. And finally, despite my handicaps, in these last 20 months I have become re-qualified in youth. I have learned from these wonderful young officers and men—their aspirations, the pressures under which they operate, the inducements to be discontented, the courage with which they participate nevertheless to the fullest in the support of their country—and I pledge myself to represent them in my leadership of the U.S. Navy."[1]

At the conclusion of the ceremony, wearing the insignia of a full admiral, pinned on him by General Abrams, he stood in a reception line under a tent on the VNN's floating barge. As my turn came to bid him farewell, he leaned forward and said, "Dick, I'm not going to have to be here to see how it turns out, am I?" (He was alluding to our conversation some weeks earlier when I had made a brash statement about ACTOV's failings, Lincoln, and ten angels swearing the admiral was right if events proved him wrong.)

"No, sir," I said, "you won't."

Vice Admiral King, the new COMNAVFORV, was in an unenviable position. The charismatic officer he had relieved was credited with having "turned things around" for the U.S. Navy in Vietnam, and for putting in place daring programs to Vietnamize the naval war.

Huge cracks in these programs had opened, to be sure, but during Zumwalt's tour they were skillfully papered over. King could hardly blame the sea of troubles that would soon sweep over him on the man who had charted and sailed that sea to become chief of naval operations. Further, King was constrained in what he could do by the Zumwalt loyalists who remained on his staff. He could not easily replace them, nor could he stop them from making informal, "back channel" reports to the new CNO. Every initiative he dared undertake was certain to be second-guessed in Washington, despite disclaimers he might receive from Zumwalt himself.

Within two weeks of assuming command, King issued a five-page, single-spaced memorandum to NAVFORV staff concerning "administrative principles." In it he explained his theory of command, and what he meant by completed staff work. One section worth recounting was titled "To Tell the Truth."

"Our experience in past wars," King said, "has amply demonstrated the virtues of telling the truth. Our defeated enemies in World War II were notorious for exaggerating their victories and their enemies' losses, and minimizing their own losses and the enemies' victories. It is clear that their tendency to tell the boss only the rosy side of the story, and to embroider the facts, was a factor contributing to their downfall. The same principle is fully operative here and now. We must be wary of any tendency to mask the truth and the whole truth, by euphemisms, window-dressing, or any other device. One particular advantage of telling the truth, as regularly pointed out by one of our former CNOs, is that you then don't have to remember what you said!"[2]

It was obvious what King was driving at. Almost immediately, he had recognized a major flaw in the staff assembled by his predecessor—the tendency of those closest to the commander to shield him from unpleasant facts, to tell him only what they thought he wanted to hear. Some of this was based on legitimate concern to correct at the lowest possible level things that had gone awry, and to spare the commander from the time-devouring minutiae of his job. Some, undoubtedly, sprang from baser motives. Overpowering figures like Zumwalt (and no doubt Westmoreland before him) collected more than a few self-serving sycophants in their train. From only being told what one wants to be told, to seeing things not as they are but as they are wished to be, is a small but fatal step.

The way things were on that fine May day when King broke his flag on the *Page County* was not good—an "accident waiting to happen," in the words King himself would later use in reference to Operation Breezy Cove. Impressive statistics had been collected to prove the effectiveness of U.S. Navy operations in Vietnam—and these operations were, by and large, effective—but the U.S. Navy was going home and the Vietnamese Navy was taking over. Statistics painted an entirely different picture of the VNN, despite the compliments Zumwalt had thrown its way in his moving change of command remarks. On the barrier operations (Search Turn, Tran Hung Dao I, Giant Slingshot, Barrier Reef), for example, through 15 March 1970 the U.S. Navy had accounted for seven times as many enemy killed as the VNN, while taking three times as many casualties—this despite the "joint" nature of the operations.[3]

Applying "systems analysis" to USN/VNN operations, the indisputable fact emerged that the Vietnamese Navy had not a snowball's chance in hell of picking up the burden of operations once the U.S. Navy was gone. Reports and statistics suggesting this, however, were ignored, buried, or explained away by saying that training, the building of new bases, creation of a logistic system, dependents' welfare and "pigs and chickens" programs were sapping the energy of the VNN and draining leadership from ongoing operations against the enemy. But what did this portend for the day when Vietnamization of the naval war was complete?

Storm signals were flying well before Admiral King became the man on the spot. Some of them I had raised myself, both by bringing to Admiral Zumwalt's attention end-of-tour reports that expressed serious reservations about the way things were progressing, and by personal observations and memoranda from my trips in the field.

On 22 August 1969, I briefed Admiral Zumwalt on the impressions I had gathered while riding U.S. and Vietnamese craft in the rivers and on Market Time patrols. In this briefing and in a follow-up written report the next day, I said that up to that time I had ridden some fifteen craft based at Qui Nhon, Cat Lo, Moc Hoa, and Nha Be. Roughly half had had VNN enlisted men on board, but none that I rode had a VNN officer. Virtually all had complaints to air about unauthorized absences and tardiness among assigned VNN personnel. One U.S. officer I talked to said his division had five out of twenty-nine VNN AWOL at the time, and that another division he knew of had eleven missing. (Later I would learn that AWOL rates of 50 percent or more were not uncommon in units facing combat.)

From these and other observations I concluded in my written report that personnel and leadership resources in the VNN were "badly stretched."

I also disclosed what I had seen on board the *Ho-Tong Ham Ky-*

Hoa (PCE 09), which I boarded late one night off Vung Ro for passage to Nha Trang. The ship was then responsible for a key Market Time patrol area. The VNN commanding officer, a lieutenant commander, spoke good English and was very open and congenial. In the course of conversation with him and his officers, and from what I myself saw in a tour of the ship, I learned the following:

a. PCE 09 was operating on one shaft and had been doing so for "about eight months." The captain had no hope of restoring a damaged engine (out of commission because of a crankshaft casualty and low oil pressure) before the ship's regular overhaul, scheduled for February 1970. Ship's speed on one shaft was limited to eight knots. At that speed a constant rudder angle of about 10 degrees was required to steer a steady course.

b. The ship's radar was inoperable.

c. Flushing water, at least in the forward part of the ship, was secured, and from the smell and appearance of the heads had been for some time. If there was no flushing water, most likely there was no fire-main pressure either.

d. Fresh water was secured and the ship's evaporators were out of commission.

e. The captain said he had only 72 percent of his enlisted allowance on board, and that the wardroom consisted of himself and three officers, whereas the allowance called for seven.

f. During a brief look at the operating engineroom, I observed numerous gauges and tachometers that appeared to be broken or disconnected.

g. No radio equipment, other than hand-held "walkie-talkies," seemed to be operable.

Zumwalt expressed concern over my report, and said the PCE's material problems most certainly were correctable at the Saigon Naval Shipyard. (I knew, of course, that the shipyard already was hopelessly swamped with work.)

A few days after my meeting with the admiral, I had a call from the senior naval advisor, Captain Rauch. "Do you know," he began, "who I am?" He seemed upset that, without first consulting him, I had made a less than encouraging report to Zumwalt concerning the Vietnamese Navy. Looking back on it, perhaps he had reason to be annoyed. He, and others responsible for advising the VNN and implementing the ACTOV plan, clearly had bitten off more than could be chewed. Everybody knew it; nobody acknowledged it. The stakes had grown too large.

* * *

Zumwalt's original ACTOV plan called for the turnover of (1) nearly all the river patrol craft (PBRs); (2) all of the fast patrol craft (Swifts); (3) all of the mobile riverine assault squadrons; (4) some of the WPBs (if the Coast Guard could be persuaded to give them up; (5) some of the support craft and fleet ships engaged in Market Time; (6) eventually, all shore-based support facilities. This plan, as more and more VNN "needs" were discovered, grew like Topsy. Incredibly, it would include destroyer escorts (promised earlier during Admiral Veth's tour) and Coast Guard high-endurance cutters—ships the Vietnamese Navy clearly could not operate and maintain for long, if at all.

To cope with the lack of training facilities for so large a number of men needed to man these assets, the concept of "sequential turnover" was developed. It called for a gradual phasing in of Vietnamese personnel into all U.S. craft, bases, and operations listed in the plan. By "sequential" it was meant, for example, that a VNN sailor would be placed in the crew of a U.S. boat and trained to perform the duties of the U.S. sailor he was slated to replace. When the VNN sailor was considered ready to assume his place in the crew, his American counterpart would leave, and a second VNN sailor would report for training in the duties of the man he was to replace. Eventually, the entire crew would become Vietnamese. The U.S. boat captain would be the last to leave, and control and ownership of the boat would remain in U.S. hands as long as he remained on board.

Operational boats would be the first to complete turnover. Training programs at logistic support bases, of necessity, would be much longer and would proceed at a slower pace. U.S. Navy advisors would be the last to phase out and go home.

In the plan great reliance was placed on "on-the-job" training, and it was hoped that by living and operating with the Brown Water Navy, young Vietnamese sailors would learn much by good example. Prior to reporting to U.S. boats, VNN personnel would be given at least minimal English language training, but even so it was recognized that "show and tell" almost always would be "show and do."

Motivation to train and be trained was thought to be high. There were no spare people in the crews of U.S. boats in the rivers of Vietnam, and each man was expected to pull his share of the load. Thus, U.S. sailors, knowing that a member of their crew was going to be replaced in a relatively short period of time by a Vietnamese sailor, would ensure that the new man did in fact know how to operate, for example, the after machine gun. Vietnamese sailors, seeing that the boats and responsibility for operating them would soon be theirs, would redouble their efforts to prepare themselves.

In one respect, sequential turnover posed something of a moral dilemma, for the safety of U.S. sailors depended on how well and how fast VNN sailors were assimilated into operational crews. Later, this same dilemma would be faced in a greater order of magnitude when command of entire operations, and American lives, were placed in the hands of Vietnamese officers whose professionalism and qualities of leadership were, to say the least, often suspect.

A certain degree of flexibility was built into ACTOV. If progress in the war or political considerations at home indicated that fewer U.S. assets should be turned over, fractional Vietnamese crews could be collected from U.S. boats and brought together to man a lesser number of turnover craft. If more time for U.S. withdrawal were made available, training cycles could be lengthened.

The plan was carefully staffed and supported by reams of documents and studies. It failed, largely, because of false assumptions about the ability and the motivation of poorly supported and inadequately led VNN personnel dragooned into a war they no longer believed in.

Recommended force levels for the Vietnamese Navy constantly changed. Prior to Tet 1968, it was planned to transfer twenty ASPBs, forty PBRs, and twenty PCFs to the VNN. After Tet, the so-called "May Plan" greatly increased the numbers of craft slated for turnover, and added two destroyer escorts and two PCEs. The May Plan went through several revisions before it was replaced by Admiral Zumwalt's "accelerated" plan (ACTOV).

The admiral once told me that there were those at the time who accused him of wanting to give away the entire Brown Water Navy. "Of course," he said, "that is exactly what I wanted to do."

The ACTOV plan delivered to General Abrams on 31 October 1968 called for the turnover of 2 DEs, 8 LSTs, 1 ARL, 2 YRBMs, 8 PCEs, 22 PGMs, 100 PCFs, 250 PBRs, 354 riverine assault craft, 16 WPBs, and 104 assorted logistic and yard craft.

ACTOV would require VNN personnel ceilings of 23,391 in fiscal year 1969; 28,414 in 1970; 30,221 in 1971; and 30,805 in 1972. (These figures were later revised upwards.) That this was an extremely ambitious undertaking for a navy already suffering from severe shortages of trained officers and petty officers goes without saying.

In his forwarding recommendation, General Abrams approved the new VNN personnel ceilings, but hedged on the numbers of ships and craft to be turned over. In particular, he deferred on the decision to give the VNN the last two U.S. river assault squadrons, pending determination of possible future army participation in riverine operations in IV Corps.

In the conclusion of a long message to the CNO that reviewed the background and the reasoning behind ACTOV, Admiral Zumwalt made the following observation:

"Accelerated Turnover Plan was predicated, as directed, on providing VNN with force structure and capability to meet current threat with little or no assistance. . . . If U.S. is not to remain, and if force levels less than those recommended are decided upon, it is my view that the communists will win back uncontested control of the Mekong Delta and will be able to resume coastal infiltration. Should threat decrease during the next 19 months, we can easily adjust to force structure in existence at the time."[4]

There followed long weeks of waiting as ACTOV was held up for secretary of defense approval (the other services' turnover plans were signed off routinely). On 9 January 1969, with his eye on the imminent change of administrations in Washington, Zumwalt prodded seniors to do all they could to expedite ACTOV's approval.

"In order to get this show on the road before break in continuity of our civilian masters, recommend JCS be requested to obtain SECDEF approval ASAP," he said.[5]

It was no secret in Saigon that certain persons in the Office of the Secretary of Defense were adamantly opposed to any significant increase in the size of the Vietnamese Navy, particularly insofar as seagoing ships were concerned. Faith in the VNN's ability to maintain and operate the ships it already had was simply lacking—and for good reason.

As it turned out, ACTOV was not approved prior to the change in administrations. The plan was said to be on Deputy Secretary of Defense Paul Nitze's desk for signature the day before he left office, but for some reason he declined to sign it.

Finally, on 12 February 1969, David Packard, the new deputy secretary, approved the plan, with the exception of the destroyer escorts. Zumwalt pressed for their inclusion in ACTOV, arguing they were needed to deter Communists from a return to open-sea infiltration once the U.S. Navy's Market Time operations phased out. He found an ally in Admiral John J. Hyland, commander in chief of the Pacific Fleet.

"A matter of overall concern," CINPACFLT said, "is the effect of not meeting our previously announced intention of providing at least one DE to the VNN. Should we fail to deliver on what the VNN certainly considers a U.S. commitment to properly provide for the

VNN, the high level of espirit de corps [!] which is evident will fade. . . . Active, enthusiastic support by the VNN is essential to accomplish the ACTOV program. Any delay costs money and lives possibly far out of proportion to two DEs scheduled for inactivation soon. Additionally, we must be prepared to logically explain why we have decided that the VNN has less need for a principal combatant ship than the other U.S. supported PACOM navies. . . ."[6]

David Packard eventually succumbed to the navy's pressure and reversed himself.

"After further review," he said, "I have decided to approve the two destroyer escort ships for the Vietnamese Navy that were deferred in my decision of February 12, 1969. . . . Actual turnover of these ships to the Vietnamese Navy should depend on visible improvement in Vietnamese Navy performance and adequate capabilities to man and support them."[7]

The approval was greeted with joy in Saigon. The conditions Packard had placed on the turnover were filed away and forgotten.

To support the large expansion of the Vietnamese Navy required by ACTOV, "accelerated" training of large numbers of men would be required. For fiscal years 1969–72, staff studies showed that 19,817 recruits would have to be pushed through basic training; technical schools would have to train 10,237; advanced schools in the United States (making use of interpreters), 909. English language courses would be required by 4,275.

Training facilities and instructors to support such a large undertaking did not exist and could hardly be wished into being. The condition of the three VNN training centers as ACTOV got under way was, in a word, deplorable.

On 8 February 1969, the commanding officer of the Naval Training Center at Cam Ranh Bay, one Commander Hop, made a nervous speech before an audience that included Commodore Chon and members of the VNN general staff. In it he described with remarkable candor the situation at his command, then the largest enlisted training establishment in the VNN. The training center was an old French Army installation. In 1963 it had been turned over to the Junk Force, and two years after that it was used to house a small branch of the Naval Training Center at Nha Trang. It was then in a state of almost total disrepair.

"Formerly," Hop said, "this center was concerned with training recruits, although it had very limited means and very poor conditions. Still, it could strive to completely fulfill the recruit training mission with only the M-1 Garand rifle, a wide expanse of land, and beds to sleep in. Today the center has to train specialists for the navy. A rifle and a section of land are sufficient for training recruits, but to train specialists requires more—more support facilities, more training aids, more skilled instructors, and a well-organized supply department with sufficient authority to get what it requisitions.

"With a center that must train 1,200 students at a time, we presently have a staff of only 192 personnel consisting of 12 officers, 85 petty officers, and 95 seamen. What do you think will be the result if the center attains its target of 900 gunner's mates and boatswain's mates [students], but only 18 instructors?

"We must choose people who are skilled enough to work as instructors, people who also have a degree of education and satisfactory professionalism, because if you don't use this sort of people then the students will leave the center without sufficient knowledge, and then what will the navy do? Here I am speaking about only two specialties, gunner's mates and boatswain's mates, but there are yeomen and disbursing clerks who don't have any instructors at all! And when graduation day arrives, what will they know?

"When personnel arrive here they think it is like going to prison. It is not because the units at Cam Ranh are very hard, it is not because the water is poisoned, it is because everything is very expensive. The people at Cam Ranh are comparatively very rich, and the sailors relatively poor. The poorness of a sailor at Cam Ranh seems like a joke, because you see the people do not believe they are poor, but in truth they are really poor. Why don't they believe they are poor? Sirs, because their means are like rich people—in their homes are TVs, refrigerators, fans, etc., and these means are provided to help them by the government, and even though they have these conveniences, they still have very little pay, very little actual money, and they have to have second jobs, take in laundry, etc., in order to have enough money for their families to live.

"Now the Americans have sufficient laundry service, recreation facilities, etc. The dependent families are no longer able to make enough money to buy food. They want to sell their TVs, refrigerators, etc., in order to buy food. Yet they are not allowed to go into the village to sell things. To compare the money a sailor is paid with the price of goods in Cam Ranh, a sailor can live only 15 days out of a month.

"Perhaps you aren't able to think like this, or find it difficult to believe, but it is true. There are many sailors and petty officers who at lunch time only have bread and sugar to eat and a glass of water to drink, because it costs at least 100 piasters to eat lunch. Therefore, they are often hungry. If they eat at the staff mess and go to buy duck eggs at the Cam Ranh market, they must pay 40 piasters for two. If they go to the market at Nha Trang they lose a whole day because they have to take the bus before 0800 and there is nothing to come back on until one or two in the afternoon.

"Here is a difficult situation: A company grade officer with a wife and seven children presently is serving at the center with a salary of 15,000 piasters. His family lives in a rented house in Saigon, where his children go to school. He just arrived in this area two months ago and already has requested permission to be transferred for the reason that he can't make enough money to live. This officer neither smokes nor drinks, eats just two meals a day, but still doesn't have enough to live on.

"Personnel at the training center, especially instructors, have poor morale because they are worrying about their families and getting enough for them to eat, more than they worry about the training mission."

Commander Hop's litany of woe continued. Training aids were either obsolete, broken, or nonexistent. Recruits at the firing range were allotted only one round per man. There were no small boats to train on, even line for splicing and knotting was in short supply. A navigation class of more than one hundred students had only one small magnetic compass and two parallel rulers to train with. To berth a large influx of new students, the center was given six hundred bed springs, but only one hundred mattresses. He ended his speech almost apologetically:

"Commodore Chon, Gentlemen—I am honored to speak to you, because the future of the navy depends upon your special attention and help. All of the staff personnel are striving to their utmost to successfully remove each new obstacle, to improve morale daily so that the inside of the center will be like the outside [large new construction projects were then under way]. I am very honored to thank you and say goodbye."[8]

The conditions noted by Commander Hop were not unique to the Naval Training Center at Cam Ranh nor to the VNN training establishment as a whole. No adequate infrastructure existed in the Vietnamese Navy to support the operational forces being transferred under ACTOV. None could be created in the time that remained.

An internal NAVFORV staff memorandum recorded the initial

response to Commander Hop's speech: "Commodore Chon told various staff people to assist CDR Hop. To date, there has been no action, only promises."[9]

Later, when I ran across a copy of the speech, Captain Rauch advised me not to make too much of it. "Hop is a cry-baby," he said.

Cry-baby he may have been, but in March 1969 there were one thousand students berthed and messed at Cam Ranh in spaces designed for six hundred. Conditions were so crowded that classrooms were used for extra berthing. The instructor situation continued to be critical. There were only seven instructors for 446 boatswain's mates, six for 385 gunner's mates, two for 87 yeomen, and four for 87 disbursing clerk students. There were no instructors for the storekeeper and commissaryman ratings. Further, the U.S. Navy advisor at the training center reported that not more than 50 percent of the instructors assigned were qualified to teach.[10]

In April, a Bureau of Naval Personnel Mobile Training Team visited NTC Cam Ranh and reported the following:

"Very little training is being accomplished in the Naval Training Center Cam Ranh Bay. Less than 50 percent of students are in class during the scheduled school day. Students are used for numerous support and logistic duties which have recently included the filling of 200,000 sand bags. Further, the scheduled school day which is supposed to run from 0800 to 1200 and 1400 to 1700, actually in practice was 0830 to 1130 and 1430 to 1630; this is only five hours, less breaks between periods. . . .

"From an instructional quality control viewpoint the situation is deplorable and inexcusable. Class sizes ranged from 127 to 153 in a single room that was about 64 feet long and 18 feet wide. . . .

"Shortages of instructors is not the only reason for the extremely large classes. It is due to lack of concern for learning that was apparent throughout the school. . . .

"Tables should be provided for trainees to have something to place their note pads on (other than their knees). They presently use straight-back chairs, crowded together like sardines in a can."[11]

Mobile Training Team reports were pessimistic concerning the chances of achieving the training quotas adopted for the VNN in 1969. Team members pointed repeatedly to a lack of qualified instructors. During a visit to the ARVN Recruit Training Center at Lam Son, where VNN recruits received their first five weeks of military instruction, observers were appalled by what they found.

"Living conditions are severe. Men sleep in companies of 200 crowded into a building where they have neither mattresses nor mats. They simply lie on a concrete floor in their clothing. Rations are delivered to their quarters or to a field site, where they eat squatting in an inch of dust while passing trucks stir up a heavy cloud. . . .

"The water which they drink is contaminated and insufficient in quantity. The only opportunity they have to bathe is a trip to the river once a week. Many men were in barracks with dysentery on the occasion of the team's visit. Others were in the dispensary with malaria."[12]

And this was the raw material with which a redoubled Vietnamese Navy was to be built?

In January 1969, a joint USN/VNN Boat School was opened in Saigon to prepare VNN trainees for assignment to operational PCFs and PBRs. In addition to boat orientation, emphasis was placed on "accelerated" (that word again) English language training. The first class of 270 graduated on 17 March and 100 were selected for advanced English language training and schools in the United States. Even in Saigon, absenteeism and discipline were vexing problems, but Boat School training in general was considered a rousing success—compared to what was happening elsewhere. By 30 June 1969, 912 VNN sailors had attended; by 1 March 1970 the figure had increased to 2,127.[13]

Concerted efforts were made to improve the quality of English language instruction. (How odd it now seems that early in the advisory game someone decided it was easier to give often poorly educated Vietnamese crash courses in English, in a wartime environment, than it would be to teach a sufficient number of American advisors Vietnamese—at home, in the United States. Some advisors, of course, did receive adequate instruction in the Vietnamese language prior to their assignment as advisors. They remained an exception to prove the rule.)

As an interesting aside, in 1970 official English language examinations were sold on the streets of Saigon to Vietnamese who had to pass them to qualify for training in the United States. These included prospective aviation cadets.

U.S. Navy enlisted men with college degrees were selected by the Bureau of Naval Personnel for English language instructor duty in Vietnam. Language laboratories were established at VNN training centers, and the latest techniques and technologies were employed.

The entire Vietnamese Navy was screened for English language comprehension. The results were discouraging to those who considered a knowledge of English vital to successful prosecution of the war after the Americans were gone.

A particularly difficult problem concerned the translation of technical publications and manuals. There seemed to be no Vietnamese words for many technical terms, and suitable English/Vietnamese technical dictionaries could not be found in Saigon. COMNAVFORV even looked to Hanoi for a possible solution to this problem. A message asking help from Washington included the following:

"Have recently learned of very comprehensive English-Vietnamese technical dictionaries originating in DRV [Democratic Republic of Vietnam] which may be available in Paris and would be of considerable value."[14]

And how long had the U.S. Navy been advising the Vietnamese? Almost nineteen years! How could something so elementary as a technical dictionary not have been acquired and in use long before this? Why were there not Vietnamese translations of necessary manuals and publications?

A few U.S. petty officers with instructional ability and a good knowledge of the Vietnamese language were found and assigned to the staffs of VNN advanced schools. Training aids, devices, books, equipment, and materials to relieve desperate shortages at the VNN training centers were sought and solicited from every possible source. The senior advisor at the Vietnamese Naval Academy in Nha Trang on his own initiative procured $1,600 worth of technical books from the U.S. Naval Institute. They were, of course, written in English.

Orientation and indoctrination cruises for VNN personnel were conducted on Seventh Fleet ships. VNN trainees were sent to Guam for special instruction. The naval support activities at Danang and Saigon phased raw and unskilled VNN sailors into their highly geared operations (sowing the seeds of future logistic nightmares). The Naval Communications Station at Cam Ranh Bay established and conducted a comprehensive training program for VNN communications personnel, utilizing its own facilities and its own personnel as instructors. Many extra hours were piled on top of what were already staggering work weeks.

Statistics, painstakingly recorded, measured the training effort expended. Recruit output: 13,994; advanced (in-country) schools: 10,076; advanced (off-shore): 228; English language (Boat School): 2,127; etc., etc.[15] These were not unlike the statistics President Diem had once cranked out to prove the success of his strategic hamlet program. What they did not and could not show was what was happening to the overall quality of the Vietnamese Navy.

On 1 October 1969 the personnel strength of the VNN reached 28,400 officers and men.[16] Eight months later, the number would be more than ten thousand greater. In terms of sheer numbers, the VNN was growing a little ahead of schedule, but in numbers of officers and petty officers the situation was critical. Further, the quality of recruits then being accepted by the VNN was in decline.

The VNN had always been a favored service for young Vietnamese seeking to escape from the draft. As late as April 1968, COMNAVFORV could state:

"Because of the outstanding performance of the Vietnamese Navy in general and during the Tet Offensive in particular, its prestige is growing steadily. It is presently receiving 4,000 applicants for enlistment per month and is taking only the cream of the crop. Recently it inducted 350 high quality men holding baccalaureate degrees (two years VN college level). This growing quality level will ensure sufficient qualified technicians to maintain more sophisticated ships in the future."[17]

A year later, however, the well was drying up. In April 1969, the number of volunteers declined to 1,100, from which 1,000 had to be drawn. The VNN was hard-pressed to maintain its minimum educational standards—eight years of schooling.

When Admiral Zumwalt was relieved, the Vietnamese Navy had achieved a force level of 37,473 men, well on its way to meeting the ceiling established for it. Ominously, the number of VNN petty officers, despite very low standards for advancement, was only 4,604. This represented an actual decline from May 1969 when the record shows there were 4,785.[18] (Battle casualties and, more importantly, desertions accounted for the decline.) The ACTOV plan called for a petty officer strength of 13,800. There seemed to be no realistic chance this figure could be reached.

On 23 June 1970, Secretary of the Navy John H. Chafee, the man most often credited with overriding Admiral Thomas H. Moorer's objections to Zumwalt's relieving Moorer as CNO, participated in ceremonies at the Saigon Naval Shipyard as 273 riverine assault craft were transferred to the Vietnamese Navy.

"The Vietnamese Navy takes over today the major combat role in its own waters," the secretary said. "And with the turnover next December of the final 123 combat boats, the U.S. Navy will relinquish all surface combatant responsibilities in the country." The Navy's Vietnamization program, he added, "was on or ahead of schedule."[19]

On or ahead of schedule for what? one might have asked.

Planning for the turnover of logistic responsibilities to the Vietnamese Navy (ACTOVLOG) began in November 1968 and was essentially completed in July 1969. Much more than just a training/turnover program was required, for the plan had to address itself to certain fundamental and long-term problems in the existing system of VNN logistics. The first important decision in the development of ACTOVLOG hinged on whether the Vietnamese Navy could support the expanded force being programmed for it by simply enlarging its existing organization.

"There was general agreement," a NAVFORV logistics officer wrote, "including most of the logistics advisors, that to make the VNN logistics system at the time larger would only be making it worse. The VNN system would have to be reorganized in order to effectively absorb the USN logistic assets that would be required to support the increased force levels. It would be necessary to not only turn over our logistic assets, but the systems that made the assets effective as well. . . ."[20]

The new VNN logistics system was to follow the pattern of existing in-country U.S. Navy systems, especially those of Naval Support Activity, Saigon. It was evident that the VNN could not afford to operate afloat logistic assets, for the costs in manpower and maintenance would be too high. VNN bases were, in general, in a state of extreme disrepair, and USN bases that were considered potential turnover assets were characterized by temporary construction. Considerable rebuilding would be required prior to turnover if the VNN were to be spared heavy maintenance costs in the future.

It was assumed that the VNN would operate its expanded forces in much the same way the U.S. Navy, under Zumwalt, had employed its forces, and ACTOVLOG planning proceeded under that assumption. An additional requirement was to retain sufficient logistic capability in-country to support U.S. Navy forces until their deployment home.

In essence, ACTOVLOG called for a base-by-base turnover of the USN bases that comprised NAVSUPPACT Saigon, plus some elements of NAVSUPPACT Danang, including headquarters and systems control elements. In the event that NAVSUPPACT Danang phased out prior to the Vietnamese Navy's assumption of full logistic responsibility, NAVSUPPACT Saigon temporarily was to assume responsibilities in I Corps.

A civilian consulting firm, the Parsons Company, was given a contract to prepare a master plan for the VNN shore establishment, including individual operational and support bases. A "freeze point" was established in February 1969, and the number and location of naval bases (and floating support assets) then in use were used to shape the structure of the future VNN logistics command. The Parsons plan, when delivered, was thought to include too many bases, and NAVFORV eliminated some and consolidated others. Even so, the logistic system the VNN would be required to operate was more extensive and more sophisticated than that overseen by NAVSUPPACT Saigon.[21]

An ACTOVLOG Committee, which included representatives from NAVFORV, the VNN, NAVSUPPACT Saigon, and SERVPAC (Service Force, Pacific), worked out the details of systems development.

As it eventually took shape, ACTOVLOG consisted of three principal parts: (1) personnel requirements/acquisition/training; (2) equipment acquisition, both technical and collateral; (3) base construction/modification.

The base turnover schedule called for the entire program to be completed by the end of fiscal year 1972 (1 July 1972). A key feature of the plan was the "model turnover" section that allowed bases to be developed and turned over as fast as personnel, equipment, and buildings were assembled and completed.

Several major problems that defied early solution were identified. A strong cadre of top and middle management personnel, deemed essential for the successful operation of a new VNN Logistic Command, did not exist. Logisticians were held in low esteem, and the VNN had no supply corps and no civil engineer corps. The number of officers detailed to logistic duties was dismayingly small. Finally, the resources (personnel and plant) from which the new command was to be built were then controlled by operational commanders who most likely would resist giving them up.

It was hoped that by maximum exposure to USN counterparts in NAVSUPPACT Saigon, VNN officers who eventually would staff the Logistic Command would overcome the above handicaps. Months went by, however, before the VNN decided who these officers would be. There was no sense of crisis in the VNN, nor would there ever be until the very end.

Despite all, on 3 August 1969, ACTOVLOG was signed and

jointly promulgated by Admiral Zumwalt and Commodore Chon. Painstakingly conceived, it was doomed from the start for the very reasons its planners had identified months before.

The program to turn over U.S. Coast Guard assets in Vietnam was called "SCATTOR" (Small Craft Assets, Training and Turnover of Resources). It was developed by Captain R. W. Niesz, USCG, the commander of Coast Guard Activities Vietnam in 1968–69. Niesz had recently completed a tour on the staff of the Naval War College, was a training specialist, and a student of oriental culture. His task was to transfer sixteen (the number was later increased to twenty-six) 82-foot patrol boats (WPBs) to the VNN. No one could have been better suited to the job.

Niesz adopted the navy's system of "sequential" relief to Vietnamize WPB crews, but with an important twist. Prospective VNN commanding officers were assigned to the turnover craft first, thus allowing them to gain an understanding of operations and equipment before their juniors reported on board. The advantage of SCATTOR was that seniors, by virtue of earlier exposure to the many nuances of life on board an operational craft, were better equipped to instruct and correct their juniors when they reported on board—in other words, to exercise leadership. In addition to contributing to a better command relationship on board, the system made it easier to discipline VNN sailors and seemed to improve their morale.

"The success of the training and turnover program," Niesz wrote, "is dependent almost entirely on the quality of the personnel involved. Language, culture, and attitude differences place a stress on the program which has never before been encountered by either Coast Guard or Vietnamese personnel, and therefore special attention must be given to the selection of personnel participating in the program."[22]

When the VNN prospective commanding officer reported on board, the Coast Guard executive officer left. The Coast Guard commanding officer determined how long the training continued, basing his decision on how quickly the Vietnamese took up their new assignments. In the final stages of the program, the entire crew of the WPB, with the exception of the commanding officer, was composed of VNN personnel. USCG crew members relieved of their duties afloat were assigned ashore as instructors and staff assistants.

When the VNN crew successfully completed all its programmed training and at least one satisfactory patrol, an operational readiness inspection was conducted by a joint USN/USCG/VNN team. Upon successful completion of the ORI, a formal transfer ceremony was held.

A companion program to SCATTOR was called "VECTOR" (Vietnamese Engineering Capabilities, Training of Ratings). VECTOR provided for the phasing in of VNN engineering and repair personnel at Coast Guard repair activities in Danang and Cat Lo. Vietnamese sailors were assigned to repair and maintenance duties and worked side by side with Coast Guard counterparts until they could perform all required maintenance and minor repairs on the WPBs. The plan called for at least eight months of training to achieve minimum levels of Vietnamese competence. All engineering personnel slated for assignment to SCATTOR boats first went through the VECTOR program. The assumption was that maintenance and repair skills could be acquired much faster ashore than afloat on an often wildly tossing patrol craft.

SCATTOR officially was launched on 3 February 1969 when two VNN lieutenants reported for duty as prospective commanding officers of the Cat Lo–based *Point Garnet* and *Point League*. The principal concern in the early weeks of the program centered on disciplinary control of the trainees. Vietnamese personnel, including officers, were prone to reporting to work late, leaving early, missing movement, and disappearing for extended periods of time over Vietnamese holidays, of which there were many.

Despite these problems, by mid-April 1969 the first two turnover WPBs were sailing on regular Market Time patrols with all-Vietnamese crews, with the exception of the Coast Guard commanding officers. On 16 May, having successfully completed operational readiness inspections, the *Point Garnet* and *Point League* were transferred to the Vietnamese Navy in ceremonies at Saigon. The severe shortage of VNN petty officers delayed turnover of a third craft until September, but by April 1970 the initial sixteen WPBs scheduled for turnover were in Vietnamese hands.

In general, the performance of VNN WPBs after turnover was satisfactory. Absenteeism, particularly during monsoon periods of rough seas, continued to be a matter of serious concern, though not to the degree it was in craft turned over under ACTOV. Overall, SCATTOR ranked as one of the more successful Vietnamization programs.

The Coast Guard system of having senior members of turnover crews report first was not adopted by the U.S. Navy. It was thought that such a system, due to the lack of officers and petty officers in the

VNN, would have delayed turnover. VNN petty officer promotions during this period were based almost entirely on time spent in grade or graduation from certain training courses—which, of course, nobody failed. It was hoped that large numbers of nonrated men would "fleet up" and assume duties on boats which, when operated by the U.S. Navy, had required petty officer skills and maturity.

Admiral Zumwalt acknowledged the seriousness of the officer and petty officer situation. In January 1970, he sent a long message to navy advisors and others concerned with implementing ACTOV.

"Although the VNN was able to double in size in one year," he said, "it could not produce qualified officers and petty officers at a proportional rate. We have pushed for a promotion reform [essentially, an easing of already dreadfully lax promotion requirements], and may have a breakthrough in the next few months. We have already begun a program to train 750 VNN officer candidates at our OCS [Officer Candidate School] in Newport, R.I. The first VNN class will commence in early March. The VNN will also utilize the ARVN OCS to turn out about 1,000 officers during 1970. The petty officer situation is even more critical, and even if we double the output of Petty Officer School, the VNN will not reach 90 percent of its PO needs until FY 74. We are examining every option to bring this problem within limits well before that time.

"One program to shore up the VNN in this critical area involves leaving sufficient USN personnel in-country to provide middle-management expertise until the VNN is up to speed. As a start, we are co-manning all repair and support bases upon commissioning. As the VNN sailors gain the necessary expertise, we phase down the USN personnel to a minimum number of advisors. At the Headquarters, we have already filled some VNN billets with USN junior officers. . . .

"Progress to date has exceeded my fondest expectations, but we must accelerate still faster to stay ahead of the power curve. Go team go!"[23]

Incredibly, ACTOV had been followed, in November 1969, by ACTOV-X, which called for the turnover of even more assets to a foundering Vietnamese Navy. The rationale used to support ACTOV-X was that (a) the threat of infiltration into the delta had increased; (b) the number of USN and VNN craft in-country had increased to meet that threat since the original ACTOV levels were established; (c) interdiction operations required more than the assets then available;

and (d) because of changing circumstances, VNN force levels should actually be greater than the combined USN and VNN forces then in-country.

In addition to VNN acquisitions from U.S. Navy "residual" forces (Brown Water Navy assets earlier earmarked to support contingency planning elsewhere), ACTOV-X proposed that one hundred "Vipers," 20-knot river patrol boats having ferrocement hulls, be built in-country at an approximate cost of $13,000 each. These boats were to be part of a larger ferrocement construction program that would include PCF-type hulls and replacements for the VNN's wooden junks. The Viper was needed, it was said, to compensate for probable reductions in U.S. tactical air support, and to counter a high infiltration threat along the Cambodian border. The first experimental Viper was launched on 20 December 1969 at the Saigon Naval Shipyard. Critics contended that ferrocement construction produced a hull that was too heavy for a craft designed to "plane" at high speeds. Nevertheless, the U.S. Navy backed the project to the very end.

ACTOV-X provided for the turnover of an additional 333 craft and an increase of 7,372 VNN personnel. Significantly, it also called for 750 more U.S. Navy "advisors" to fill the VNN's middle-management gap. Tentative turnover schedules were such that virtually all ACTOV-X assets would be transferred by the end of calendar year 1970.[24] ACTOV-X was formally approved in March 1970, and a new VNN personnel ceiling of 37,645 was established (39,611 had been requested). COMNAVFORV protested this scaling back of personnel, and the figure of 39,611 was restored. It was reached in June 1970.

So fast was the Vietnamese Navy growing in this period that more VNN officers were "in the pipeline" than were actually assigned to duty. The shortage of trained officers and petty officers created by this madcap expansion was to be bridged by 4,100 U.S. Navy advisors. An air of unreality pervaded everything having to do with the turnover. People believed that Zumwalt could work miracles. Perhaps he believed it too.

As U.S. assets passed rapidly into Vietnamese hands, "AC-TOVOPS" was implemented to provide for the transfer of command of each ongoing operation. When a combined command was activated, COMNAVFORV designated a USN officer as the commander or deputy commander. CNO VNN at the same time designated a VNN officer to serve as the commander or deputy commander, as appropriate. (It has already been discussed how this worked in practice at Sea Float/Solid Anchor.) Staffs were to be manned jointly, and combined combat operations centers were established. Joint operations orders were written. Communications facilities were turned over in accordance with an "ACTOVCOM" plan.

By the middle of March 1970, VNN officers commanded operations in the Rung Sat Special Zone, Tran Hung Dao I (the northernmost barrier operation along the Cambodian border), and Tran Hung Dao V/Ready Deck. All U.S. Navy operations were to be turned over by 1 November 1970, though, as has been shown, this schedule slipped in the case of "hot spots" such as Breezy Cove and Solid Anchor. On 1 June 1970, Deputy COMNAVFORV/First Sea Lord assumed additional duty as deputy for operations to the VNN CNO, Commodore Chon. The assignment of a U.S. Navy rear admiral as Chon's deputy was one of the arguments advanced to secure Chon's promotion, on 1 July, to rear admiral.

And how did senior Vietnamese naval officers react to this bewildering display of U.S. "generosity," to ACTOV and to ACTOV-X? How much input did they have in the actual planning of their forces?

"They brought over a big chart which covered a whole wall, with arrows to depict the PBR program," VNN Captain Bui Huu Thu, a former chief of naval training, said in a 1975 interview. "It was not a mysterious thing, but the VNN officers were very much against it, except me—against the whole program. . . . The personnel chief couldn't believe it. He said it was like building castles in the sand. That was his expression. It made CNO mad, because he had discussed the program with Admiral Zumwalt, and they had agreed to it."[25]

The then deputy chief of staff for political warfare, Captain (later Commodore) Hoang Co Minh recalled that he was working in his office one day early in 1970 when he received a telephone call from the CNO's secretary telling him to come to a meeting with all the other deputies concerning something called "ACTOV-X."

"The chief of staff," Minh said, "presided over the meeting. He said, 'This is ACTOV-X which we have just received from the U.S. Navy. And we must make our reply in 24 hours.' Everybody asked, 'How can I do it in 24 hours?' and he answered that that was what the U.S. Navy wanted. So I said I could not do it. He said that CNO wanted it too. I said that even if CNO wanted it I could not do it, because it would take me about a week to only read it. It was all in English. They gave it to us for comment, but they never waited for our reply. They just went ahead with it. The whole ACTOV plan was done by the U.S. Navy. There was never enough time to even discuss it. . . . The U.S. Navy assumed that the Vietnamese Navy officers could speak very good English and could read English well. . . .

"Before the ACTOV program our navy numbered about 10,000. In two years it increased to 40,000. We increased our navy four times in two years. . . . We didn't have enough time to train the people. . . . Admiral Zumwalt's idea was to use on-the-job training. We would recruit the civilians, send them to school in Saigon for one month to learn English, because most of them could not speak English, and then send them to U.S. Navy units where they would learn on the spot. . . . After about four or five months they would be qualified to be the engineer, the gunnery officer, etc. But what really happened was that the Vietnamese were sent to the ship, and first of all they didn't like it. It was not that they didn't like Americans, but it was that they were lonesome. Second, the crews of the U.S. ships were not instructors. They had their own mission to do. They had to fight. They had no time to train the people. So the result was that the only thing the Vietnamese learned was how to cook, how to clean the boat, things like that. . . . We had about 40,000 people in the Vietnamese Navy, but I think more than half of them were not ready for the job. In many, many cases I had a chief engineman, but he had no knowledge of the engine. We called him an engineman and let him work on the engine, but the engine would not work. . . . So you can figure it out. We trained about 13,000 people to be qualified seamen in a year and a half. You can't do it. That was called Vietnamization. . . .

"Many people said that the Vietnamese Navy was very smart, very sharp because it finished Vietnamization very fast while the other services, the army and the air force, they did not finish so fast. I think Admiral Zumwalt was very proud of that. . . . I think he was a very good admiral for the U.S. Navy. I talked to many people and they said he was smart. If I were in his position I would have done the same thing. The Vietnamese Navy played a big part in his becoming the U.S. Navy CNO. He stepped on us to come up."[26]

(According to a 4 December 1987 story in the *Washington Post*, Commodore Minh, leader of the "National Front for the Liberation of Vietnam," was killed in southern Laos while leading a band of two hundred armed insurgents from Thailand to Vietnam.)

22

The Navy's Helping Hand

The fact that storms always blow over is of little help to drowned sailors.

—Sloan Wilson, *All the Best People*

For all the troublesome moral questions raised by Admiral Zumwalt's "damn the torpedoes" approach to Vietnamization of the war, no one could doubt his compassion for the Vietnamese sailor or the depth of his commitment to improve the sailor's lot. Indeed, much of the impetus for Zumwalt's later effort to "reform" the U.S. Navy unquestionably was gained in Vietnam from his personal observation of VNN living standards and conditions of service. He knew that the sailor's morale was crucial to the success of the VNN, and with characteristic vigor he set out to improve it.

VNN pay lagged far behind the rapidly inflating Vietnamese economy. Allowances for dependents were entirely inadequate (it was estimated that one-half of VNN enlisted men and two-thirds of VNN officers were married and had families). A NAVFORV staff study in 1969 indicated that rents (in Saigon) had increased an average 400 percent during a period when service pay and allowances had gone up only 30 percent. Navy housing, where it existed, was a disgrace.

In these circumstances, was it rational to believe that the Vietnamese sailor or junior officer would give his all for the government—a government that had condemned his wife and children to a life of squalor? Was it surprising that duty frequently became a thing to be endured rather than performed with honor? That patriotism gave way to cynicism as the glaring inequities, graft, and corruption that characterized Vietnamese wartime society were thrust in his face? The effort to improve the living standards, dignity, and morale of the VNN sailor was critical to the future of ACTOV.

COMNAVFORV decided that "payment in kind," not a pay raise, was the best way to address the problem. (An odd decision, actually, given one of the broad objectives of the war—saving Vietnam from an imposed socialist system.) Despite heroic and possibly illegal measures, the battle to improve VNN living standards, like ACTOV itself, would fall far short of the goals established for it.

The GVN's program for armed forces housing was administered by ARVN, and as might be imagined, available materials and funds seldom reached the VNN at its customary spot at the far end of the trough. Even the cornucopia of USAID failed the sailor, for the resources it disbursed for housing construction were channeled through province chiefs, who rarely expressed any interest in the plight of navy families. The truth was that there were only two practical ways for the VNN to acquire GVN materials for housing—by stealing them from authorized projects, or by imposing a transportation "fee" in kind when navy boats moved construction materials on the rivers for other, nonmilitary agencies.

As ACTOV progressed and the day approached when large numbers of navy personnel would take up duties at remote bases turned over by the Americans, the provision of adequate housing seemed to be an imperative.

At Midway Island on 8 June 1969, President Nixon was briefed on GVN requests for increased force levels and improved standards of living for Vietnamese servicemen and their dependents. These requests entailed, of course, U.S. funding. Among the proposals made to the president were: pay increases, free food issues, free transfer of U.S. disposable property, increased housing allowances, and various other measures designed to improve the morale and effectiveness of Vietnam's armed forces. The cost was estimated to be in excess of $1 billion for fiscal year 1970 alone.

The plan did not have the backing of the U.S. Mission in Saigon, which advised that "U.S. financial support of the magnitude involved would not only be highly inflationary, but also would tend to perpetuate and extend the dependence of the GVN on imports. Furthermore, the Mission considers that the specific elements in the financial proposals are either not warranted at this time or are insufficiently justified to merit approval."[1]

Even COMUSMACV disapproved. Concerning specifically the proposed increase in housing allowances, General Abrams said, tersely: "Not recommended. Is internal GVN problem; MACV should not address increase of standard of living for one segment of GVN population."[2]

"Economists" and "nation-builders" in the U.S. Mission, who had done, it must be stated, such a miserable job of managing the Vietnamese economy and preserving the fabric of Vietnamese society in the war until that time, apparently had carried the day.

It was true that prospects for effective GVN implementation of expensive new programs, given the record, were not good. Nor could the inflationary aspects of GVN proposals be discounted. The fact remained, however, that something had to be done if Vietnamization of the war were to have even the remotest chance of success.

There remained three programs through which possible funding for VNN dependents' shelter might be obtained:

(1) The joint US/GVN funded construction program. This was administered by the Vietnamese JGS, and the likelihood of any significant help from this source was considered remote.

(2) The Self Help program. This was a combined USN/VNN program that provided Vietnamese Navy personnel with technical assistance and construction materials declared excess.

President Nguyen Van Thieu

(3) The MILCON (military construction) program. This was a U.S. program that, if funded, could provide for construction of shelters by local contractors. Through it, materials could be furnished to the Self Help program. Admiral Zumwalt asked that $900,000 in MILCON funds be earmarked for dependents' housing, and this amount eventually was approved. He also urged subordinate com-

President Richard M. Nixon

manders to make use of local assets and to obtain excess materials and equipment wherever and whenever available to support the Self Help program. The minimum requirement established was that pilot programs be under way and materials stockpiled prior to the arrival of the first dependents at ACTOVLOG bases.

Plans were drawn for standard, 400-square-foot, concrete block shelters, some of which would feature ferrocement dome roofs (ferrocement was then much in vogue in NAVFORV). The following guidance was given local commanders for nonstandard housing:

"Internal area should be approximately 480 square feet, preferably masonry with metal/asbestos roofing; well ventilated; external central toilets with septic tank or tie into existing drains; central water sources; should have concrete pad immediately outside entrances. Minimum lighting circuits to be included; concrete flooring except wood in existing buildings. . . . Unit material cost should not exceed $400. However, maximum effort to obtain no-cost materials must be pursued. Highly desirable to conform to local design and tradition."[3]

A "dependent shelter project team" was established to coordinate the allocation of materials and to provide technical assistance. Seabees were assigned to supervise construction. All in-country commands were screened for excess materials, and a block plant was built at Cam Ranh Bay. A personal appeal went out from Zumwalt to the Navy League for donations of construction materials that could be transported to Vietnam on deploying U.S. Navy ships. The Ships Systems Command was asked to provide bunks and mattresses that might be available from navy ships being decommissioned.

"The construction of an adequate number of VNN dependent shelters," Zumwalt told his officers, "is of great importance to the success of the ACTOV program in view of the remote location of some VNN operating bases and the wide disparity between VNN service pay and the local cost of living. We cannot expect high morale, attention to duty, and retention of the trained cadre if the VNN serviceman is unable to provide suitable shelter for his wife and children. The construction of adequate numbers of VNN dependent shelters is critical to the success of our advisory effort in Vietnam and requires your best efforts. I am personally interested in hearing of ways in which local commands have made substantive, innovative contributions to any phase of this program. Move out."[4]

NAVFORV staff studies concluded that 14,000 new housing units would be required by the VNN. It appeared that appropriated funds would finance 10,500 of these. The shortfall would have to be made up elsewhere, and Zumwalt persuaded a group of U.S. executives doing business in Saigon to form a foundation to solicit and receive donations for the VNN shelter project and related welfare programs. "Operation Helping Hand Foundation" was incorporated in Wilmington, Delaware, on 31 March 1970. It was hoped that it would raise at least $3 million. The force chaplain was assigned the duty of receiving cash donations from the Brown Water Navy.

When he became chief of naval operations, Zumwalt used the forum of the U.S. Naval Institute to seek support for the foundation. In an undated letter distributed in 1971 to members of the Institute, he said that "although our training and turnover program is progressing on schedule and the Vietnamese sailor has proved himself to be a capable and courageous fighter, this rapid expansion has caused critical internal economic problems which are as much a threat to their cause as the enemy himself. Unless these problems are overcome, it is uncertain whether or not the Vietnamese Navy will be able to continue to function as a viable and professional fighting force once massive U.S. support is withdrawn." He asked Institute members to contribute "$15 or $25" each to support his goals. As CNO, he also promoted "Buddy Base" and "Sister Ship" programs to funnel needed materials and cash donations to the VNN. Wish lists were provided by Vietnamese bases and ships, and their U.S. "buddies" and "sisters" helped find and ship desired goods.

When NAVFORV bases were turned over to the VNN, U.S. officers, caught up in the Christmas spirit Zumwalt inspired, winked at the unauthorized provision of U.S. Navy rations to Vietnamese personnel.

As Vietnamese sailors replaced American sailors on the rivers, and as other manpower became available from the gradual phasing out of navy responsibilities in I Corps, Naval Construction Assistance Teams (NAVCATs) were formed. Young and sometimes bewildered U.S. Navy sailors, under Seabee supervision, became laborers, hod carriers, masons, and carpenters in the shelter project. Dozens of austere "Levittowns" sprang up at remote base sites throughout the country. At the end of March 1970, construction was under way at sixteen sites. Some 635 units were completed, and 537 were under construction.[5] Progress was slowed by less than hoped for participation by the Vietnamese Navy.

By September 1970, the number of shelters programmed had grown to twenty-two thousand ("needs" always grew in Vietnam), though available funds and personnel were sufficient to construct only about five thousand.[6] As the withdrawal of U.S. Navy personnel progressed, the burden of dependent shelter construction fell increasingly on a dwindling number of VNN shoulders. In December 1970,

110 VNN sailors were assigned to the project; by April 1971, there were only 34.[7] Construction of dependents' housing was stopped almost in its tracks.

To American advisors, the lack of VNN interest in the shelter program seemed incredible. There was, however, a quite logical explanation: many Vietnamese sailors could not afford, and did not want, to have their families at the bases being turned over. The construction of dependents' housing was another half-cocked, though well-intentioned, program undertaken without any real consultation with the Vietnamese Navy (except, of course, for Commodore Chon, who could always be counted upon to agree with anything proposed by Zumwalt).

Commodore Minh described the situation at Dong Tam, and it could be repeated to one degree or another at many other VNN bases:

"I remember at Dong Tam they built about 400 houses, and one time we received orders that on three or four days notice we had to fill every house to please Admiral Zumwalt. I said, 'No, I cannot move people in so fast.' They didn't want to live there. I talked with Admiral Chon when I became the Amphibious Force commander and was stationed at Dong Tam. I told him that two years earlier when I was deputy chief of staff for political warfare I had told him the same thing—don't build the houses at Dong Tam because nobody will live in them.

"He didn't agree. Now he was telling me to move people in. How could I? The site we chose was wrong, besides the design of the house and the size. How many rooms? Where is the kitchen? The style of the house itself. I didn't want to have dependent housing on the base because it influenced the security of the base. . . . People couldn't bring their families along to the base because they might die.

"One time Admiral Chon asked me why the families of my people didn't want to move into our dependent housing, into a free house with free water, free electricity. If they lived on the outside they paid about 1,000 piasters a month for rent. So I explained to him that if they moved to the base they could have a free house, free everything, but that would be all they had. If they paid 1,000 piasters to rent a house downtown [in My Tho], then they could do other jobs. They could sell something. They could go to market very easily. The students could go to school easily. That was the reason they lived outside.

"At Dong Tam, if they had to go someplace, they had to use a boat and they didn't have a boat. No school. No market. They couldn't do anything to make money.

"Our men were very poor. If a man served with our unit, then his wife had to have another job. . . . I tried to explain that, but nobody understood.

"In 1971 or 1972, I remember Admiral Zumwalt [was to] visit me, and I received orders from Admiral Chon who said, 'I do not want to see empty dependent housing because Admiral Zumwalt will be visiting us. So I want you to move all the dependent families to fill them.'

"I said, 'No, I cannot.' So Admiral Chon said that Admiral Zumwalt would not visit my base. So he did not come down, because if he had seen all the empty dependent housing, he would have been upset. . . .

"They built houses that were too small. Every man was provided with one house. I remember they were 2.5 meters wide and about 10 meters long. When people moved in we found that we had to provide them with two or three houses, not just one. We had to knock down the walls between them and then we had to repair it. The cost of repairing it was almost as much as building a new house. . . .

"[The house] had a kitchen and it had a toilet, and the toilet was terrible. They built every house with a toilet, but we didn't have running water like you do in America. Every house had a 55-gallon drum cut in half in which they could go to the toilet, and then take it out and throw it away every day. . . .

"I think about 30 to 40 percent of the houses were occupied. . . . I respected Admiral Zumwalt very much. He wanted to help us, but he did not do it the right way."[8]

Dong Tam, the former U.S. 9th Infantry Division base, was and always had been "mortar city." The Viet Cong and the NVA attacked it almost at will even during periods when the delta as a whole seemed to be relatively well "pacified."

Commodore Ho Van Ky Thoai, commenting on the dependent housing situation at other VNN bases, said the U.S. Navy didn't think about "what happens when you see your kid die in front of you, or your wife is dying right there and your kids are running around. Do you think that you would have the courage to abandon them and go to the bunker to fight back? Let them just take care of themselves?"[9]

There were three other parts to COMNAVFORV's original proposals for VNN welfare: resettlement of the Rung Sat Special Zone; construction of a rehabilitation center for disabled VNN veterans and their dependents; and an animal husbandry program.

The first of these called for the building of twelve "key hamlets" in the RSSZ, an area, it will be remembered, that was the operational responsibility of the VNN. Pacification of the Rung Sat was always high on COMNAVFORV's priority list, and it was thought that moving VNN dependents there would have a favorable effect.

The Vietnamese Navy Rehabilitation Center was a proposed five-hundred-family hamlet adjoining the VNN base at Cat Lai, in Gia Dinh Province, some seven miles from Saigon. Disabled veterans were to receive training in carpentry, auto mechanics, electricity, refrigeration, welding, plumbing, and typing.

Animal husbandry, the navy's "pigs and chickens" program, was designed to teach VNN sailors and their families how to raise farm animals "vital for a nourishing and balanced diet."

"The steadily rising cost of living for the VNN sailor and his family," said COMNAVFORV, "requires that we explore all possible methods of improving his standard of living. One method is self-reproducing meat sources such as pigs or chickens. . . .

"Qualified officer or enlisted volunteers to monitor implementation of subject programs with VNN [are] desired. Particularly desired are personnel with degrees in agriculture/animal husbandry or highly knowledgeable in these fields."[10]

Volunteers (they were called "pigs and chickens advisors") were not slow in answering the call. In the months that followed, the navy communications system handled a number of messages that, viewed out of context, seemed surprising, to say the least:

"Pig farm officially commissioned and in operation today," said CTF-115. "Originator cannot say enough regarding the enthusiasm, spirit, initiative, ingenuity, resourcefulness, and professionalism shown by the officers and men of CBMU-302 and those of NAVSUPPFAC CRB associated with this most worthy program."[11]

"Complete brooder and finishing houses have been constructed by VNN at CG Three Four and CG Three Six. CG Three Five will be completed in ten days. CG Three Three will be completed in three weeks. Request supply by quickest means two zero zero chicks with feed and medicine each for CG Three Four and CG Three Six. Chicks, feed and medicine for CG Three Five and CG Three Three will be requested in near future.

"High level of enthusiasm for project exists at all levels of U.S. and VNN command. Request fast action on supply of chicks, feed and medicine to maintain momentum."[12]

"Livestock projects . . . progressing well. Negligible loss of birds at Ben Luc and new permanent hog shelter constructed My Tho indicate active involvement and interest of VNN.

"Commencing new poultry project with CTF-212 staff Binh Thuy. Eight families of VNN dependents to receive 50 birds each. Written agreement between CTF-212 and participating families will ensure understanding of project purpose. Your staff to arrange delivery of 200 birds to Binh Thuy 15 or 16 February. Will advise further as project progresses."[13]

"The generous donations made toward this headquarter's Protein Project are sincerely appreciated. . . .

"These donations enabled us to purchase a prize thoroughbred Duroc Jersey boar and four female companions. The total population of the Protein Project is now ten fine quality swine. The potential of Lord Wingfoot and his female companions will be about 160 pigs a year and will prove to be a model for all in-country projects of its kind."[14]

Pigs and chickens statistics were recorded as zealously as were those for enemy KIAs and "chieu-hoi's." In March 1970 there were twenty-one projects under way, with 36 pigs, 3,300 chickens, 50 ducks, and 14 rabbits.[15] In May the numbers of animals had increased to 116 pigs, 9,180 chickens, 186 ducks, 102 rabbits, and four goats.[16] Thus was progress measured in the war against godless communism.

Enthusiasm for these pigs and chickens programs ran high. Once, a fellow member of NAVFORV staff asked me, dead pan, if I could help him find the words to "float a Silver Star" for one base commander who had put together a program that particularly impressed the admiral. Such was the climate of the times, I could not be sure he was joking.

Even something so seemingly innocent and well intentioned as "pigs and chickens" came a cropper in Vietnam. At the end of 1973, Commodore Thoai was appointed chairman of a VNN committee to study the program which, with the Americans gone, had fallen on hard times.

"For the pigs it was good," said Thoai, "but for the chickens it didn't work well, because you paid as much for the food for the chickens as you got back in profit. So it was not worth it. It was still continued because when the U.S. Navy left, they left us a lot of food—a warehouse of food for pigs and chickens. And so we fed them for free. And we still made a good profit.

"But if you look at the balance, it was not worth it for the chickens. Because, with the chickens from the States, you had to feed them good, special food. Not the Vietnamese chickens—we just sent them out and they could eat anything, even barbed wire. With the pigs, yes. We sold them very cheap to the seamen. But even that didn't help them much, because it still cost something and their salaries became nothing.

"A family had to eat a 50-kilo bag of rice, 100 kilos of rice. The pay was just enough to pay for the rice, not even the fish sauce. So how can you live? . . . You had to change the whole structure and do like the VC in the North. They kept the family away from the men and sent them very far away. He [the enemy] doesn't have any news about his family. You say, 'OK, the women will take care of the family, don't worry. Go ahead and fight the war.' "[17]

Where are they now, one wonders, the strutting Chanticleers imported from half a world away, the snuffling descendants of proud Lord Wingfoot and his "female companions"?

Buried long ago, I suppose, with other relics of the War of Good Intentions.

23

End Game

Never before have our young men been sent into war under such conditions as prevailed in Vietnam and, I regret to say, in their own country. They fought in an unfavorable jungle environment where more often than not they were unable to distinguish friend from foe. They fought under the most severe restraints ever imposed on the members of any armed force. They fought an enemy whose homeland was a land sanctuary. They operated aircraft in the heaviest anti-aircraft and missile environment ever confronted by any airmen. And they did all this while many of their own countrymen were making accusations in writings, speeches, and demonstrations that what they were doing was immoral. And in spite of all this, they carried out their duty with dedication and true professionalism—equal to, if not surpassing, the performance of American fighting men at any time, in any war.

—Admiral Thomas H. Moorer, speech given at Pittston, Pa.,
on 17 March 1973

As the U.S. Navy turned over its operational responsibilities in Vietnam to the VNN, control of the coastal waters and rivers of Vietnam began to pass once more into the hands of the Viet Cong and the NVA. What the Brown Water Navy's heroics had won was allowed to slip through the fingers of a Vietnamese Navy that remained, to the very end, singularly uninspired and ill-equipped to pursue the war to a successful conclusion.

It was not that there were no brave and capable officers and men in the Vietnamese Navy (there were many), it was just that these were overwhelmed by the impossible circumstances thrust upon them by ACTOV and the rapid recruiting of tens of thousands of men from a manpower pool that already had been drained to unacceptably low levels.

VNN operations, more than ever, became exercises in going through the motions. Ships and boats were sometimes towed on "patrol"—to anchorages where their crews could fish or sleep the hours away. U.S. helicopters and Black Ponies logged precious time checking up on the actual location and performance of VNN units, hours that should have been spent hunting down an implacable enemy. U.S. ship riders, the relatively few who remained, had less power than ever to influence Vietnamese commanding officers.

Unauthorized absences, drunkenness on duty, cowardly behavior in action—these were the hallmarks of the VNN in the war's final stages. When U.S. advisors remonstrated, their complaints, which earlier might have led to sullen and pouting behavior on the part of VNN officers, now not infrequently led to shouting matches. Friction between USN and VNN sailors escalated to fistfights and occasional shootings. The situation at many bases turned ugly.

No matter how bad things got, however, nothing was allowed to interfere with the transfer of more and more U.S. ships, boats, and bases to the Vietnamese Navy. ACTOV had acquired an imperative of its own; it would not be stopped, regardless of the consequences to the VNN or to the eventual outcome of the war.

All of the Brown Water Navy's riverine and patrol craft were in Vietnamese hands by the end of 1970, and the emphasis then shifted to transferring larger units—DEs and WHECs—to "augment the VNN's offshore patrol capability." Two U.S. Coast Guard high-endurance cutters, the *Yakutat* (WHEC 380) and *Bering Strait* (WHEC 382) were turned over on 1 January 1971. On 13 February, Vice Admiral King and Rear Admiral Chon traveled to Hawaii for ceremonies in which the USS *Camp* (DER 251) was given to the VNN.[1] The ship was renamed (what else?) *Tran Hung Dao* (HQ 1). By year's end, a second DER, the USS *Forester* (DER 334), and two more WHECs would join the VNN's "Blue Water" fleet.

"What we had before was just small craft, nothing that could be called a major ship, until we received the DER and . . . the WHEC," recalled Captain Bui Huu Thu. "We were all happy now that we had more men, more ships, and more bases, and more positions and more billets. And people kept going up in rank, and there were more captains, and more commodores, and more admirals. And everyone was very happy. . . ."[2]

At the beginning of ACTOV there were only two VNN flag officers, Commodore Chon and Rear Admiral Cang. (Cang was not then assigned to duty in the VNN.) In 1972, five new flag officers were named; in 1974, four more were promoted. It was only fitting, the argument went, for a navy that was then, in terms of personnel, the ninth largest in the world and, in numbers of ships and craft, the fourteenth largest.

Despite all the hoopla that accompanied ACTOV, despite the huge sums of U.S. money spent, the operational effectiveness of the Vietnamese Navy continued its dizzying, downward spiral in the months following King's relief of Zumwalt as COMNAVFORV. The more assets the VNN was given, the less able it became to man and maintain interdiction patrols in coastal waters and in the rivers of the delta. The sad stories that unfolded at Solid Anchor and Breezy Cove were but harbingers of worse things to come.

The Vietnamese logistics system, despite the painstaking efforts of ACTOVLOG planners, was in shambles. Department of Defense auditors were threatening to blow the whistle on long-standing practices that in other places and in other times might have led to the court-martial of senior U.S. officers.

Not long after the *Camp* turnover in Hawaii, King's health began to fail. He flew to quarters at Clark Field in the Philippines, suffering from what was said to be a bad back. Admiral Zumwalt, clearly worried by the situation unfolding in Vietnam, and not wanting to have King relieved by any of the flag officers in-country, turned to Robert S. Salzer, then on limited duty recovering from a heart attack.

Salzer, it will be remembered, had commanded the Riverine Assault Force in 1967–68 and conducted the initial Sea Lords operations for Zumwalt. He was a no-nonsense, tough-minded officer not to speak his mind. Since leaving Vietnam, he had made rear admiral, after having failed selection the first time around. No doubt he felt some obligation to Zumwalt for his promotion.

Given a green light by doctors to return to full duty, Salzer agreed to go back to Vietnam. He was briefed in Washington by Zumwalt and members of the CNO's staff, who told him it was urgent that he report to Saigon as soon as possible. On the way over, however, he stopped in Hawaii for further briefings by CINCPAC (Admiral John S. McCain, Jr.) and CINCPACFLT (Admiral Bernard A. Clarey).

"At Pearl Harbor they really didn't know what the problem was," Salzer said. "They knew there were a lot of problems. They had had some kind of an audit report—which had been looking into the logistics. The report declared that it was sort of a fetid mess."[3] Salzer asked for, and got, Clarey's promise to send a team of experts to conduct a thorough inspection of the logistics situation.

After scanning through reports detailing the operational effectiveness of the Vietnamese Navy ("I was not at all satisfied with my initial perceptions"), he asked that Zumwalt arrange to have Rear Admiral Arthur W. Price, Jr., posted as his operational deputy. Price, who had commanded TF-116 during Salzer's previous Vietnam tour, arrived in Saigon a few weeks after Salzer.

The NAVFORV change of command was unusual in that King did not return to Saigon to participate in formal ceremonies. Salzer relieved him during a brief stopover at Clark Field on 5 April 1971. In a message to NAVFORV, King said he was "deeply gratified at the performance of U.S. Navymen in Vietnam. In the final tally, progress has meaning only in terms of how well we have assisted the Vietnamese Navy toward the ability to continue, on their own, to fight against the enemy. In these terms I believe we can view the past with quiet pride."[4]

Evidence to belie King's mildly encouraging assessment of the VNN would soon appear. On 12 April, an enemy trawler loaded with munitions, only the second detected in South Vietnam's coastal waters in at least three years, was sunk off the mouth of the Cua Ganh Hao River by U.S. Navy and Coast Guard units. Vietnamese craft vectored to the scene "disappeared" en route.[5] Within a few days of the sinking of this trawler, the grounded hulk of a second was discovered in the mouth of another delta river where it obviously had beached to offload cargo. Whatever the official U.S. Navy assessment of VNN performance in Market Time operations might be, North

Vietnam apparently had decided that sea infiltration of supplies to its forces in IV Corps was once more a viable option.

"In the meantime," Salzer said, "I spent my nights getting one briefing after another on logistics. There was a strong feeling on both the advisory and on the support side of my staff that our little brown brothers had been doing very well, but we had given them more than they could take at one time. Thus we have to let them sort it out and encourage them on how they were doing. These problems would then all straighten out. Granted, they couldn't find out what they had in stock—just get them some new spare parts, so we can be sure they have stocks.

"When I questioned them what they had done about getting an accounting on this kind of thing, they said, 'Well, you know we turn this over to the Vietnamese, or we are turning this over, and we just can't step in there and show distrust. We have to help the Vietnamese; that's why we are here.'

"I would ask, 'Why didn't you do this or that?' The answer would be, 'Well, that would have been disruptive to my relationship with my counterpart.'

"I made a decision that I would do one of those things that one should never do and that is walk on board and tell your boss, 'Everything is a goddamned mess.' I had some tickets with General Abrams . . . so I went in and said, 'I am very familiar with the one-year-tour syndrome where everybody who comes out here says, "The guy I relieved just didn't get anything done,"' and I said, 'I don't know who didn't get anything done; maybe this goes back to my last tour here, but we have a fetid mess in logistics. Also, whatever you have been told about the anti-infiltration effort in Vietnamese hands is wrong unless it was described as totally ineffective and completely dependent upon the American P-3s and the American ships we still have.'

"Abrams chewed on his cigar and said, 'What are you going to do about it?'"[6]

Salzer may not have been the kind of man to blame things on his predecessors, but he was not about to take the rap for them, either. He asked for and got inspection teams from outside NAVFORV whose job it was to determine the true state of affairs in the Vietnamese Navy. The conclusions that were drawn were brutal and frank: Both the coastal force and the river force were in a state of "operational ineffectiveness."

Hoping to jack up Vietnamese commanders, Salzer began a series of unscheduled inspection visits to VNN bases, often giving only twenty minutes advance notice of his arrival.

"It was obvious," he said, "that most of the advisors were demoralized. I asked some of them why they were riding the boats with the Vietnamese and still not reporting that these boats were not going out on patrol. They said, 'If we said that I'm afraid they would throw me overboard some dark night. . . .' The whole thing was pretty bad.

"I got the report from this logistics team I had about that time. I was getting calls from Washington from members of the mini-staff [Zumwalt's "kitchen-cabinet"] . . . as to what is going on. They were pretty nervous and you could hear the exclamations of horror."[7]

He moved quickly to stop the "back-channel" reports to CNO that were being made behind his back by those he called the "Kitchen-Cabinet East"—former members of Zumwalt's Saigon staff who had stayed on. This was the sort of thing that had troubled King. Salzer ordered a full stop to the practice of sending wire-notes, informal messages of a personal nature, through NAVFORV's communications system, and he shifted Zumwalt loyalists from positions of acquired power. He knew full well that he was stirring up a hornet's nest both in Saigon and in Washington. These actions, and a twenty-page message summarizing the findings of his special logistics inspection team, brought Zumwalt hurrying to Vietnam on his first visit since becoming CNO.

"I flew over to Clark Field to meet him," said Salzer, "and briefed him on the plane about the Vietnamese and why I was having sort of a crunch point with Admiral Chon at that time. It had started under Bud [Zumwalt]. When we started jointly manning bases, we gave those Vietnamese who came on board American rations. Well, that was sensible, but illegal, and there was just no way around it. Then we started forming Vietnamese units and they were saying, 'Our food is so poor, the people aren't well enough nourished to go out and fight.' They worked out a deal where we would provide American rations to complete units. Then we built the bases we were going to turn over to them—shore bases, that was what it was, all shore bases—and we fed American rations to all the Vietnamese there. There was no legal cover for this whatsoever, and the money simply wasn't there. It wasn't provided for in the next year's budget, and I had to cut it off.

"One of the things that really hurts relations with people is when you take away their food—when you take them from steak and eggs and put them on rice and fish. The 'do-gooders' on my staff were prophesying mutiny and all this kind of thing. We explained it to the Vietnamese as best we could. Everybody accepted it except Chon.

"I wouldn't get him any new spare parts until we inventoried these old spare parts and straightened them out. He felt that I was just unsympathetic since I wouldn't get him any new engines until he started doing preventive maintenance on the engines he had and made his people work harder.

"I told Bud this, and he asked, 'What is Chon going to be asking me for?' I said, 'Admiral Chon wants you to kiss him and make it well.' That really made him mad as hell, but he took it.

"Chon and I had a confrontation in his [Zumwalt's] presence and he told me, 'You've got to be easier on Chon; he can't take this kind of pressure.' I said, 'If we don't give him that kind of pressure what will happen to his navy when we leave here sometime in the next two years? Are we going to leave Admiral Chon, as he is now, face to face with General Giap? He'll be chewed up alive.'

"Bud went around, and he couldn't believe his eyes. How could it have deteriorated so much?"[8]

At An Thoi Zumwalt was greeted by a big sign that read: "Z-Houses, Pigs, Fishes, Chickens—A Better Life for the Vietnamese Navy." At all of his stops he reminded U.S. sailors that many of their shipmates had served and died in Vietnam to help the Vietnamese people. He told them that they were now witnessing the successful results of those sacrifices as the Vietnamese Navy became more able to defend itself, and more Americans left Vietnam.[9]

Complicating things for Salzer during and after Zumwalt's four-day visit was what he referred to as "the goddamn drug scene."

"The Navy at that time had no drug amnesty program. I didn't really feel that it should, but the problem that was bothering me was how else to purge those bad guys, get them out of the way, discharge them or do something. They were useless. If I got rid of them, I would have a clean force and then we could guard against further infection by being better leaders. . . . Chick Rauch, who was by then a rear admiral, the former 'chief of staff of the kitchen-cabinet,' became officer-in-charge of drugs and stuff like that, and he came out. He was arguing that we ought to have amnesty. I would say I'd like amnesty for 30 days on a one-time basis; anybody who doesn't come forward in 30 days can hold his peace. After that we are really going to put the bricks to those boys.

"During Bud's first visit out there when he was addressing the sailors in one of the bases, he asked them for questions, which he always did. . . . Somebody asked him about amnesty—'the army has amnesty and the air force has amnesty and we don't.' Bud explained the navy's position, but somebody started begging for amnesty. Bud said, 'We'll consider this urgently.' The sailor answered, 'Urgently isn't fast enough; we need amnesty now.' And Bud made one of his famous spot decisions. He said, 'All right, we will have a trial period for amnesty in Vietnam. How long it will go on I don't know, but Admiral Salzer will have the regulations and the rehabilitation program in effect within 24 hours.' "[10]

Zumwalt's decision on amnesty for drug offenders was announced at a press conference on 30 May at Tan Son Nhut, just prior to his departure for Washington.

APLs 21 and 30 moored at Nha Be became NAVFORV's rehabilitation center. A chaplain, and a navy doctor who, Salzer said, had been "shipped out to Vietnam as punishment duty by some stupid guy in BUPERS because he was a conscientious objector," were assigned to run the center.

"The whole drug scene was the part of the tour that I disliked the most," said Salzer. Rauch told him, "We are not going to let this amnesty expire at the end of 30 days; it will be a continuing program. It is the beginning of the Navy Amnesty Program—but we won't be able to open our stateside rehabilitation centers for three months. Thus, you will have to keep them out there."

"I then forced the issue," said Salzer, "on one point—that nobody who was detected using heroin, unless I exempted them, would be permitted to serve in-country. They must get out of our brotherhood; that was my compromise. . . . To give a man pride in his job, you cannot pair him up with dope addicts."[11]

By 1 July 1971, some one hundred U.S. sailors had turned themselves in for treatment at the drug rehabilitation center. By way of comparison, the army at that time was treating 460 of its men; the air force 350.[12] The navy's center at Nha Be would remain open until 1 March 1972.

(I personally never encountered the use of hard drugs during my time in-country—alcohol abuse was much more common and perhaps even more debilitating. However, as Vietnamization of the war progressed and U.S. units assumed essentially defensive postures, the use of drugs undoubtedly increased.)

Statistics painted a vastly different picture of the navy's drug problem from that which was popularly thought to exist. For example, a routine urine test of all servicemen being reassigned from Vietnam was instituted on 1 June 1971 to detect heroin users. As of 22

September, 97,296 armed forces personnel were screened; 3,580 or 3.7 percent tested positive. Of 7,327 navy personnel screened, only 25 or 0.3 percent were confirmed positive.[13]

One, of course, was too many, but the problem within the Brown Water Navy was nowhere near as severe as had been supposed.

When Salzer took command of NAVFORV, the number of U.S. Navy personnel in-country was 12,166, less than a third of the peak strength of 39,265 achieved in October 1968. By the time he was relieved, on 30 June 1972, there were only 2,340. NAVFORV was a rapidly dwindling force throughout his command tour, and with relatively few people he had to address a myriad of inherited problems.

To help straighten out VNN logistics, Salzer persuaded Zumwalt to recall Rear Admiral Wallace R. Dowd, who had recently retired as chief of the Bureau of Supplies and Accounts. Dowd was assigned to Salzer's staff and "double-hatted" to the Vietnamese Navy as vice chief of naval operations for supply. As many as one hundred other supply specialists were assigned to NAVFORV for periods of thirty days (to stay within imposed personnel ceilings). In the first sixty days of a complete supply overhaul of the Vietnamese Navy, four container-ship loads of spare parts not needed by the VNN were returned to the United States.[14]

In actuality, what Salzer did was to reverse the ACTOV process in the supply arena by assigning U.S. personnel to do the work VNN officers and men should have been doing all along. He did the same insofar as maintenance was concerned, using advisory personnel to perform preventive and corrective maintenance on VNN ships and boats.

"The idea," he said, "was that we would get it straightened out . . . then we would gradually phase the Vietnamese back into the thing, on the theory that, having bitched it up once, they would have learned enough so that they wouldn't do it again."[15]

An ambitious program to overhaul all river craft in the delta within six months was kicked off in the last week of June 1971. It soon became apparent, however, that such a schedule could not be met. Slippage was blamed on inadequate participation by boat crews, improper supervision of repair work, and high rates of absenteeism at repair facilities.

"The difficulty appeared to be discouraged and unmotivated sailors, inadequately supervised and controlled," said the senior advisor at Logistics Support Base, Dong Tam. The Vietnamese Navy commander of the Dong Tam facility suggested that concertina wire be strung around the repair shops to prevent his men from slipping away.[16]

During Salzer's tour, the Vietnamese Navy leveled off at a numerical strength of more than 42,000 men, and 1,600 ships and craft. To make the best use of remaining U.S. Navy advisors, Mobile Operational Advisory Teams (MOATs) were established, using advisors pulled from individual VNN units. A MOAT was assigned to each "Tran Hung Dao" operation until the last advisors went home.

"The most pressing operational problem I found when I returned in-country was no longer on the rivers," Salzer said, "though God knows, if the Viet Cong had not become so disorganized they'd have had a field day there the way the Vietnamese let their river boats deteriorate. Rather, the problem was in the Market Time operation offshore. . . . Infiltration was the first threat that we participated in back in '65 and it became a very pressing consideration in 1971 and '72. . . . First of all, it was unmistakably clear that the North Vietnamese were trying major infiltration by 150- to 200-ton trawlers, loaded with ammunition."[17]

Salzer found that the inshore Market Time patrol, then 100 percent in Vietnamese hands, was almost useless, and that "the material condition of these boats [Swift boats and WPBs] was just indescribable." He also concluded that the entire concept of the inshore patrol—what the U.S. Navy had based its patrols on for years—was questionable. "Having 45 equal patrol areas, or 50 equal patrol areas all the way along the coast, really didn't make a hell of a lot of sense," he said. "Many of these areas were relatively secure; in other areas the terrain was such that it was just unsuitable for infiltration."[18] He persuaded the VNN to form task units of three or four boats (the Vietnamese called them "clouds") to operate in high-risk areas off the coast—areas the enemy had used in the past to infiltrate supplies, and areas that seemed to invite such activity in the future.

To compensate for the imminent departure of U.S. Navy patrol aircraft and ships on the outer detection barriers, he pushed through the construction of radar sites, some of them in remote regions along the coast, and some on offshore islands. This program, which had been started during Zumwalt's tour as COMNAVFORV, was called "ACTOVRAD."

At the suggestion of Rear Admiral Price, the San Francisco lightship (WLV 523), which the Coast Guard had declared excess property, was towed to Vietnam, transferred to the VNN and rechristened the *Ba Dong*. It was used as a platform for a movable, floating radar station. Moored in the South China Sea between Vung Tau and Con Son Island, it provided radar coverage of the northern Mekong Delta.

Not long after the former lightship had been towed to station, Price happened to be in Vung Tau and saw the ship alongside the pier.

"What the hell is it doing in here?" he asked.

He was told that the ship's reefer had broken down, and the captain had come in for fresh supplies.

"Why didn't they send a boat in?" he asked, getting angrier by the moment. Not getting a satisfactory answer, the usually mild-mannered Price exploded. "That ship will remain on station until hell freezes over," he said. "If it needs anything, take it out to it!"[19]

For a while, at least, the old San Francisco lightship, minus its light, remained anchored in the South China Sea, a strange bit of Americana in an even stranger war.

On the rivers, Salzer and Price found VNN bases and craft to be in "an advanced state of deterioration—shocking, with [again] boats being towed out on patrol. . . . The corps commander and the province chiefs were successfully trying to exert control over the navy river operations, as had been a tradition of the Vietnamese regional military authorities. They [the ARVN commanders] had no idea what they were doing and would use them for unsuitable purposes."[20]

A major part of VNN River Force assets that were still usable had been committed, after the 29 April 1970 joint U.S./VN invasion of Cambodia, to the convoy of supplies to a crumbling regime in Phnom Penh. Between 10 May and 19 August 1970, the VNN also had assisted in the repatriation of some eighty-two thousand refugees—Vietnamese who had fled across the border into Cambodia to escape the horrors of war in Vietnam, and who were then fleeing back across that border because of even worse horrors in Cambodia.

Admiral Chon argued against the use of his navy to ferry Cambodian supplies, saying this was a U.S. responsibility, but the convoys continued to run until almost the very end of the fighting. Phnom Penh fell to the Communist Khmer Rouge on 16 April 1975, two weeks before Saigon itself fell.

An interesting aside to VNN convoy operations in Cambodia concerns the dispatch of Commander Cyrus R. Christensen to Phnom Penh in late February 1975. Christensen, the former commander at Breezy Cove, was then serving with the Mine Force in Charleston, S.C. He was sent on short notice to see what could be done about mines in the Mekong River south of Neak Long. (Since Congress had forbidden the posting of additional U.S. military personnel in Cambodia, he was told to wear civilian clothing.)

Christensen determined that the mines were command-detonated by entrenched enemy forces on the river banks. An unsuccessful attempt was made to clear the banks, and Christensen's organization and training of a small Cambodian Navy mine-countermeasures element was aborted. When he left Phnom Penh, rockets already were falling on the airport, and the Communists had begun their final assault on the city.[21]

In January 1972, the Nixon administration decided to speed up the withdrawal of Americans from Vietnam or, in Salzer's words, "to get the hell out of there fast." This came just at the time he felt he was making real progress or at least "comforting ourselves with the illusion that we were getting order out of chaos."[22] It seemed obvious the White House wanted everyone home before the November elections.

On 6 March 1972, the last navy Seawolf left Vietnam. HAL-3, the Seawolf squadron, was formally disestablished ten days later. On 10 April, the Black Ponies of VAL-4 stood down and left the country. Henceforth, the Vietnamese Navy would have to rely on ARVN and the VNAF for air support in the rivers.

More shiploads of supplies and equipment arrived to overload the Vietnamese logistics system, and now there simply were not enough Americans left to manage the situation. Many more millions of dollars went swirling down the Vietnamese drain in a final orgy of "accelerated" turnover. To many, the whole thing bordered on insanity.

In the midst of the Nixon administration's near-frantic effort to get the last Americans out, Hanoi launched the "Easter Offensive" of 1972. Commencing on 30 March, twelve NVA divisions and an estimated five hundred tanks rolled across the DMZ, sending ARVN and VNMC defenders reeling back in near panic. The "conventional" war American generals had prepared for in Vietnam had now broken out, but the U.S. forces needed to win it were mostly gone.

Opening a second front, NVA troops attacked across the Cambodian border. An Loc, sixty miles north of Saigon, was taken under siege. Troops were pulled from IV Corps to bolster Saigon's defenses, and NVA and VC units then attacked in the delta.

In I Corps, the naval base at Cua Viet was overrun and permanently abandoned. On 1 May, Quang Tri City fell; the ruined provincial capital would not be retaken until 15 September. Hue was threatened, and an estimated 80 percent of its population fled to Danang.

The only thing that saved Vietnam and the American servicemen still in-country (there were 66,300 on 1 May) was U.S. air and sea power. On 6 April, Operation "Linebacker" unleashed the heaviest bombing and shore bombardment of NVA forces both above and below the DMZ since 1967. Six carriers operated in the Tonkin Gulf, and the Seventh Fleet's tempo of operations climbed higher than at any time in the war. B-52 bombers began blasting targets in the north. More significantly, President Nixon ordered an action the navy had been pleading for since at least 1963—the mining of Haiphong and North Vietnam's other major ports.

On 4 May 1972, Admiral Thomas H. Moorer, chairman of the Joint Chiefs of Staff, was attending a ceremony in which John Warner relieved John Chafee as secretary of the navy. Moorer was handed a note by a marine orderly, saying that President Nixon wanted to see him at the White House.

When Moorer was shown into the Oval Office, he saw that only one other person besides the president was there—former Texas Governor John Connally.

"How long," the president asked, "would it take to make a plan to mine Haiphong Harbor?"

"About three seconds or so," Moorer answered. The plan had been drawn eight years earlier, Moorer said, when he commanded the Seventh Fleet.[23] (Vice Admiral William P. Mack, in his reminiscences, says the plan actually was drawn up by his staff when he, Mack, was COMSEVENTHFLT and the mining order was received. It is likely, though, that the older plan was simply dusted off and updated.)

Nixon told Moorer he wanted to go on the air and tell the American people "the instant the first mine hits the water." The navy preferred to mine at 0900, Moorer said, because of visibility and so forth. With the twelve-hour time difference, this meant the president's address could begin at 2100—prime time. Nixon asked what was the latest he could give Moorer the go-ahead and have the mining conducted on the same day, and Moorer said about 1400 or so.

"Will it leak?" Nixon asked. "I can't do it if it's going to leak."

Moorer assured him that the navy was the only service that could conduct an operation like this without fear of leaking. "If there are any reporters on board we won't let them go ashore, and if there are any ashore we won't let them come out," he said.[24]

Four days later, on 8 May, the president told the nation that North Vietnamese ports were being mined. Foreign ships in these ports were given seventy-two hours to clear out before U.S. minefields became active. Further, he said, he had ordered the bombing of rail lines leading from China, and was taking other necessary steps to stem the flow of war material to North Vietnam. He would keep these measures in effect until (1) all U.S. POWs were released, and (2) an internationally supervised cease-fire was in effect in South Vietnam.

"At that time," Moorer said, "we were flying 1,000 sorties a day in all of Southeast Asia. We took . . . 26 airplanes, they were gone one and a half hours, and not one ship entered or left that harbor until we swept the mines up ourselves. . . . We had given them free gangway from 1963 until 1972. Not a person got hurt. And yet for eight years we had let their damned ships carry shells and means of killing American boys for free, and we let the Chinese trawlers steam right through the American fleet and go right in and offload, all because of 'we seek no wider war.' "[25]

There were twenty-six merchant ships, including several belonging to the Soviet Union, in Haiphong when U.S. mines were laid. None left until the channel was swept, more than a year later. According to Moorer, the North Vietnamese refused to furnish pilots for the ships' departure during the seventy-two-hour "grace" period given by Nixon.

The mining of North Vietnam's ports, just as the navy always had said it would, cut down decisively on the flow of war material to NVA divisions fighting in the south. North Vietnam was hammered by U.S. bombers. Naval gunfire rained down on enemy troop concentrations and armor. Slowly, the military situation in South Vietnam stabilized, and Hanoi's great offensive, meant to end the war, was rolled back.

North Vietnamese negotiators returned to the conference table in Paris with perhaps more serious intent than ever before. The "peace talks" were then in their fourth year. The parallel "secret" meetings between Henry Kissinger and North Vietnam's Le Duc Tho resumed.

In the meantime, Vietnamization of the naval war had proceeded apace, as if the Easter Offensive meant nothing. On 14 April 1972, the logistic support base at Danang was turned over to the VNN, completing the ACTOVLOG program. On 18 April, the headquarters of Naval Forces Vietnam was moved to the MACV compound at Tan Son Nhut. On 4 June, the AO of Tran Hung Dao IV (formerly Solid Anchor) was reduced to an area two kilometers wide on either side of the Cua Lon and Bo De rivers. On 30 June the last five yard craft scheduled for transfer to the VNN were turned over, bringing to a formal close the entire ACTOV program. In all, approximately thirteen hundred U.S. ships and craft had been transferred to the Vietnamese.

Salzer was relieved by Rear Admiral Price on the last day of June 1972, and left Vietnam one day after General Abrams did.

"I must say," Salzer said, "that I was not sorry to leave Vietnam for the second time. I felt we had done as much as we could with the pace of withdrawal. It had left us with, at best, a shaky foundation for the success of Vietnamization. . . . The Vietnamese had plenty of faults of their own, and they were being asked to undertake a super-human task of absorbing the full load of military defense of their country with sophisticated equipment (which they needed consider-ing what was coming down from the north) in far too short a time."[26]

Price served as COMNAVFORV for a little less than two months. He was relieved on 23 August by Rear Admiral James B. Wilson, who had been his logistics chief. Wilson was the last officer to serve as commander Naval Forces Vietnam.

The continuing draw-down of U.S. forces in-country (at the end of August 1972 there were only 39,000, and President Nixon had announced that 12,000 of these would be withdrawn by 1 December) seemed to stiffen the backs of North Vietnamese negotiators in Paris. They demanded an unconditional stop to the bombing and shelling of North Vietnam, the withdrawal of all U.S. military personnel (in-cluding advisors) from South Vietnam, and the ouster of South Viet-nam's President Nguyen Van Thieu. To Washington, this would have amounted to nothing less than humiliation for the United States.

U.S. negotiators wanted, first of all, the return of prisoners of war held in North Vietnam, and an accounting of the missing in action. They also wanted the withdrawal of NVA troops from South Vietnam, and an internationally supervised cease-fire.

As the talks dragged on, and domestic resistance to the war heightened in the United States, President Nixon grew increasingly frustrated. In December 1972 he summoned Admiral Moorer to Camp David for discussions concerning the military options left open to him.

"I told him," Moorer said, "that if we kept Vietnamization going, pretty soon the only Americans left in Vietnam would be the POWs."

"What shall we do?" Nixon asked.

"These people," Moorer said, "are just professional revolution-aries and they don't understand but one thing, Mr. President, and that's brute strength. I can get the POWs back."

"How?"

"Scare the hell out of them [the North Vietnamese]. If you let me, I know exactly how to get them back."

"What about the morality of the thing?"

"There is no morality involved in this, after they've tortured our people. The morality doesn't bother me a damn bit."

Nixon asked Moorer how many B-52s they would lose, and Moorer said about 2 percent of the sorties. (As it turned out, his estimate was right on the money: fifteen of the big bombers were lost in the Christmas bombing, and approximately seven hundred fifty sorties were flown.)

Beginning on 18 December, North Vietnam was subjected to the heaviest bombing of the war. Many targets previously declared "off-limits" were struck in the Hanoi-Haiphong area. North Vietnam's air defense system literally ran out of ammunition; its entire stock of surface-to-air missiles was expended. Afterwards, U.S. aircraft roamed almost at will.

The bombing, savage in its effect on North Vietnam, produced the results Moorer had predicted. On 30 December, President Nixon, responding to promising overtures from Hanoi, ordered a halt to bombing and naval shelling north of the 20th parallel. The secret peace talks between Kissinger and Le Duc Tho resumed, and on 23 January 1973 an agreement to end the war was initialed by the two in Paris.

On that date, President Nixon told the nation that the United States had "concluded an agreement to end the war and bring peace with honor in Vietnam and in Southeast Asia."

The agreement was formally signed in Paris on 27 January by U.S. Secretary of State William P. Rogers and North Vietnam's Minister for Foreign Affairs Nguyen Duy Trinh. A cease-fire was declared to be in effect as of 2400 that night. A banner headline in *Pacific Stars and Stripes* read, "It's All Over—Thieu Sends Thanks to America."[27] (In actuality, President Thieu had to be brow-beaten into accepting the agreement, and believed that he had been sold out by the Americans.) The Seventh Fleet began a well-deserved stand-down in West-Pac liberty ports.

When the cheering stopped, however, and men began to study the painstaking agreement hammered out by Kissinger and Le Duc Tho, it became evident that the United States had made some very large concessions to achieve "peace with honor" in Vietnam. The POWs, to be sure, were to be repatriated within sixty days (concurrent with the withdrawal of all U.S. military forces from Vietnam). North Vietnam, however, was not required to remove the estimated 150,000 troops it had in South Vietnam, and it in fact moved almost immediately to reinforce them.

It is likely the only concession Kissinger may have received was a promise that a "decent interval" would be observed between America's final withdrawal and North Vietnam's final solution to the problem of unification. Never did U.S. diplomacy achieve so little, at such great cost, and with so much acclaim. Kissinger and Le Duc Tho later were jointly awarded the Nobel Peace Prize. Kissinger accepted his; Le Duc Tho respectfully declined.

A protocol to the Paris peace agreement obligated the U.S. Navy to "clear all the mines placed in the territorial waters, ports, harbors, and waterways of the Democratic Republic of Vietnam. The mine clearing operation shall be accomplished by rendering the mines harmless, through removal, permanent deactivation, or destruction. With a view to ensuring lasting safety for the movement of people and watercraft and the protection of important installations, mines shall, on the request of the Democratic Republic of Vietnam, be removed or destroyed in the indicated areas; and whenever their removal or destruction is impossible, mines shall be permanently deactivated and their emplacement clearly marked."

This was an agreement that would have to be, and was, carried out largely by mirrors, for during the years of the Vietnam War the navy's mine-countermeasures capability had atrophied to the point of near absolute ineffectiveness.

Most surface minesweepers were decommissioned, and undue reliance had been placed on helicopter minesweeping, despite the failure to develop adequate minesweeping equipment that could be streamed and towed by helicopters.

(My own service background was heavily oriented to mine warfare, and as commander of a division of ocean minesweepers I had worked extensively with helicopter minesweepers. Once, on a visit to Washington, I asked a senior officer I had known in Vietnam, who was then on CNO's staff, what in the world was happening—didn't Admiral Zumwalt know what he was doing to the Mine Force? The reply was, "Well, we've got all these helicopters, and we think we can develop the gear they need to sweep mines. And if we can't, maybe we can fool the other guy [the Soviet Union] into thinking we've done it." Needless to say, I was appalled.)

Commander Mine Warfare Force, Rear Admiral Brian McCauley,

was alerted as early as July 1972 that sweeping U.S. minefields in North Vietnamese waters most likely would be a condition agreed to in the Paris peace negotiations.[28] Considerable time was provided, therefore, for planning. The type of mines, their settings, and their locations were known. Virtually all of the U.S. Navy's mine-counter-measures assets, and a large part of Seventh Fleet's Amphibious Force, was placed at McCauley's disposal when, as CTF-78, he was given command of Operation "End Sweep" and ordered to clear mines from North Vietnam's waters.

Two types of mines had been used to close North Vietnamese ports: Mk-52 magnetic mines designed to sterilize or go inactive after a pre-set period of time, and DST-36 "destructor" magnetic mines that self-detonated when their pre-set times expired.

The bottom line on End Sweep is that only one mine (believed to be a Mk-52) was swept, and two minesweeping helicopters were lost in accidents. Further, it is almost certain that a number of unexploded (though "sterile") mines remained in the Haiphong ship channel when the minesweeping operation came to a close and the channel was declared cleared. These would pose a hazard to dredges for years to come.

"Although End Sweep utilized all U.S. Navy airborne mine coun-termeasures assets and converted nearly twice that number of U.S. Marine Corps CH-53 helicopters for the minesweeping mission, plus using essentially all active U.S. Navy MSOs," McCauley said, "it still would have required from four to six months to sweep against two relatively simple magnetic mines of known settings and locations in the coastal waters of North Vietnam. If we had to go against un-known mines in sustained attrition minefields under adverse environ-mental conditions, we could not have done it with U.S. mine counter-measures resources that are currently available. Neither could we have simultaneously conducted End Sweep and any other single mine countermeasures commitment."[29]

End Sweep, delayed and suspended on several occasions when on-going negotiations with the North Vietnamese stalled, officially began on 6 February 1973. It ended on 18 July, well after the date when all mines were past their self-destruct or sterilization dates. In addition to Haiphong, the ports of Hon Gai, Cam Pha, Vinh, Quang Khe, Dong Hoi, and Than Hoa were "swept." Due to North Viet-namese intransigence, no sweeping of inland waters was conducted.

It is not likely the North Vietnamese were fooled by End Sweep. They, too, knew that in time the mines would either self-destruct or become inactive. Even before the U.S. Navy signaled an "all clear," merchant traffic began to move into and out of North Vietnam's ports.[30]

Meanwhile, in South Vietnam, the withdrawal of the remnants of Naval Forces Vietnam proceeded uneventfully. On 31 January 1973, the number of U.S. Navy personnel in Vietnam had declined to 1,413. On 28 February, there were only 575. On 26 March, Commander E. M. Barrett, the last U.S. woman naval officer to serve in Vietnam, went home. On 29 March, Naval Forces Vietnam/Naval Advisory Group, Military Assistance Command Vietnam was disestablished. Five navy captains, a commander, a marine colonel, a lieutenant colonel, and a major remained in the Defense Attaché's Office. Within a few months, some of these, too, would go home.

America's failed crusade in Vietnam was over.

Epilogue

On 29 March 1973, the last of 587 American prisoners of war were released and the last American soldiers left Vietnam. In June, Congress passed legislation blocking the expenditure of funds for U.S. military operations in Indochina. Despite President Nixon's written pledge to President Thieu, when the next great North Vietnamese offensive came, U.S. air and sea power did not oppose it. Nixon himself, of course, would be gone then, forced from office by the scandals of Watergate. He resigned the presidency on 9 August 1974.

Reflecting, almost certainly, the will of a strong majority of the American people, Congress slashed appropriations for military aid to South Vietnam. In fiscal year 1973, $2.8 billion, augmented, as has been shown, by transfers from U.S. military accounts, was given to support Vietnam's armed forces. Two years later, the appropriation was only $300 million. This drastic reduction in funding bewildered and embittered a South Vietnamese military schooled, during all the years of U.S. involvement, to expect more—more arms, more ships, more ammunition, more bombing, more naval gunfire support.

For the Vietnamese Navy, funding cutbacks led to huge reductions in strength—river forces were cut by 70 percent, sea forces by 30 percent.[1] It was ACTOV in reverse, a downward plunge on a roller coaster. Ammunition was rationed even in the face of an offensive-minded enemy. According to the last commander of the Fourth Riverine Area, he was allowed to expend no more than 20,000 rounds of .50-caliber ammunition a month—roughly 40 rounds per gun barrel.[2]

The VNN played almost no effective role in the final defense of South Vietnam. That part of the fleet that could still operate clustered around Saigon to facilitate the evacuation of senior military officers, their families, and their friends.

The end, when it came, came with dramatic suddenness. On 14 March 1975, President Thieu ordered the withdrawal of ARVN forces from the Central Highlands and northern provinces of I Corps. The retreat became a rout. Hundreds of thousands of refugees clogged escape routes. South Vietnamese soldiers threw away their weapons and their uniforms, and simply melted away.

On 25 March, Hue was abandoned. More than a million panic-stricken refugees converged on Danang. The U.S. Military Sealift Command sent all available ships, tugs, and barges to assist in a massive evacuation operation. (The U.S. Navy, out of respect for the Paris peace agreements, was forbidden to participate.)

More than thirty thousand refugees were carried south by MSC units in a four-day operation. Many hundreds of thousands more were left behind. Order in the city collapsed. ARVN and VNMC troops went on a rampage—shooting, looting, raping. The last planes took off with people clinging to their landing gear. The water-front became so thronged with desperate people that ships could not come in to load for fear of being swamped or commandeered by crazed soldiers. The First Coastal Zone commander, Commodore Thoai, escaped in a small junk—his ships had sailed without him.

"You could not control it," he said. "I believe there were 100,000 people [on the dock]. Who would go and who would stay? They pushed and killed themselves. Lots of babies fell into the sea. . . ."[3]

Almost miraculously, most VNN ships and many smaller craft escaped from Danang. On the voyage south, overloaded PBRs and PCFs slipped, one by one, beneath the waves in heavy seas.

Danang was occupied by the NVA on 29 March. In quick succession, Qui Nhon, Nha Trang, Cam Ranh Bay and all other ports north of Vung Tau fell. Most of the refugees embarked in Danang were eventually landed on Phu Quoc Island in the Gulf of Thailand, about as far from advancing Communist armies as it was then possible to go.

With upwards of seventeen NVA divisions marching on Saigon, President Thieu resigned on 21 April, fleeing the country four days

later. His successor, Vice President Tran Van Huong, transferred authority to General Duong Van ("Big") Minh on 28 April, believing
that Minh stood a better chance of negotiating with the Communists.
Minh promptly ordered all Americans to leave Vietnam within
twenty-four hours.

At 0630 on 29 April, Secretary of Defense James Schlesinger read
the following statement to newsmen at the Pentagon:

"Gentlemen, the president ordered the formal withdrawal of the
Americans from Vietnam at approximately 11 o'clock last night on
the advice of the ambassador and subsequent to the closing of Tan
Son Nhut, making it necessary to go to a helicopter lift. The first
helicopters touched down at approximately 3 a.m. this morning, our
time. Since that time we have lifted out approximately 4,000 people.
The lift is continuing as well as can be expected. At the DAO compound essentially all Americans and Vietnamese have now been removed and we're down to the ground security force. At the Embassy
the evacuation is proceeding more slowly, but it is proceeding expeditiously and we hope in some hours, if all goes well, that the evacuation will be completed."[4]

The scenes of that evacuation, helicopters hovering over the U.S.
Embassy roof while marine guards fought back with rifle butts
screaming masses of people hoping to escape, will hardly ever be
forgotten by Americans who served and sacrificed in Vietnam. Had
North Vietnam not given tacit consent to the helicopter lift, thousands of Americans, potential hostages all, would have been trapped
in Saigon.

Offshore, the scene was no less searing. A great armada of U.S.
Navy and Military Sealift Command ships had been assembled to
conduct the evacuation. Thirty-five major warships from the Seventh
Fleet participated. The operation was called "Frequent Wind" and it
was commanded by Rear Admiral Donald B. Whitmire, commander
of the Amphibious Task Force (TF-76). Proving that White House
"desk admirals and generals" had learned nothing from Vietnam, the
airwaves were filled with strange and often conflicting instructions
for the on-scene commander. To his credit, he appears to have tuned
most of them out and proceeded with the difficult and dangerous task
at hand.

Ships operating rescue helicopters had to contend with Vietnamese helicopters whose pilots refused to be waved off. Some of
these helicopters had to be jettisoned over the side. Other VN heli-

copters and small planes crash-landed at sea in the vicinity of U.S. ships. Passengers and crews were picked up by small boats.

The USNS *Greenville Victory* embarked approximately ten thousand refugees in the twenty-four-hour period ending at 2000 on 29 April. The refugees came out in boats that subsequently were abandoned and set adrift. The ship reported that at one time more than forty boats were clustered on its starboard side, and that a steady flow of boats of all sorts and descriptions was leaving Vung Tau, in a front that was at least three miles wide. The boats were stretched "as far as the eye could see."[5]

Ambassador Graham Martin's helicopter touched down on the task force flagship, the USS *Blue Ridge* (LCC 19), at 0547 on 30 April. Two hours later, the last eleven marines were lifted off the U.S. Embassy roof. At 1200, the South Vietnamese government unconditionally surrendered.

U.S. Navy and Military Sealift Command ships were ordered to move to seaward, out of sight of land, "to complete the refugee embarkation by the morning of 1 May." When Frequent Wind was declared ended, 51,888 people had been taken aboard U.S. ships.[6]

Some twenty-six VNN ships carrying perhaps seven thousand refugees ran "from the rivers to the sea" in the final hours of South Vietnam's agony. Escorted by a U.S. Navy destroyer and three tugs, the woeful remnants of "the world's fourteenth-largest navy" sailed for the Philippines. Rear Admiral Cang's flagship, an LST, broke down and had to be towed for half the voyage. An LSM lost propulsion and electrical power, took on water, and sank. A second LSM and a YOG had sunk earlier at Con Son Island, the VNN's offshore rendezvous point.[7]

When this pitiful fleet at last reached Subic Bay, a further indignity awaited it. Philippine President Ferdinand E. Marcos refused to permit its entry into port while flying the Republic of Vietnam flag. U.S. Navy officers were put on board each ship, and the ships entered port under the Stars and Stripes.

Admiral Zumwalt was not there to see how it ended. His own navy torn by drugs, "permissiveness," and the very racism he had courageously tried to stamp out, his senior officers in near open defiance of his controversial "Z-Gram" leadership style, he had been relieved on 1 July 1974 by Admiral James L. Holloway III and had passed into an embittered retirement.

In Saigon, Admiral Chon, his great patron gone, had retired too.

"Only the rivers and the memories remain."

Almost alone among the senior leadership of the Vietnamese Navy, Chon did not escape when Saigon fell. Perhaps he did not even try. Taken into custody, he would spend thirteen long years in a Communist "re-education camp."

During my January–February 1989 return visit to Saigon, I looked everywhere for vestiges of the Brown Water Navy. I saw only one: What I took to be one of our barracks barges was moored at the foot of Hai Ba Trung Street near the old Vietnamese Navy Headquarters.

The hull was painted blue with white stripes, and it was then a floating restaurant and café—the *My Ca'nh*. In the evening, Saigonese relaxed on its topside decks, enjoying the breeze off the river.

I wandered through that part of the below-decks area that still had working lights, through spaces filled with great, black, hanging cobwebs. A Vietnamese family lived aboard as caretakers and didn't seem to mind my looking around. I saw repair lockers, shops, a crew's washroom, a berthing space. I imagined the sights and sounds that filled these spaces many years before. I was swept by a feeling of unutterable sadness.

It was then the eve of Tet, and firecrackers were being set off in the streets of the city. When I first heard them, I thought: My God, haven't these people heard enough of that after so many years of war? The firecrackers sounded exactly like the rattle of small-arms fire.

All over Saigon there were signs, in English, wishing people "Happy New Year." Christmas trees were still up in many hotels and restaurants. Nguyen Hue, the "Street of Flowers," which earlier in the week had been a sea of color, was then swept clean, its great market closed.

At midnight, all hell broke loose. Ships in the river began sounding their sirens, red and green pop flares arched across the sky, parachute flares (no doubt left over from the war) lighted the waterfront. And the longest and loudest explosion of firecrackers I had ever heard tore through the city. From every street corner, from every house, from every apartment, from every balcony, great strings of firecrackers were lighted and tossed into the night. The whole city seemed to explode. It went on and on, for a half hour or so, and then, as if on signal, it ended.

The next morning, Miss Quan, the assistant guide for the little group of tourists I had joined (all American visitors had to join a tour then) was in the hotel lobby. Her eyes were shining.

"Last night," she exclaimed, "we set a new record. We set off more firecrackers than ever before! Vietnam a very rich country now!"

I smiled and walked out into the street for a final look around before leaving for the airport. A pretty Amerasian teen-ager walked by. She was wearing a T-shirt on which was emblazoned, "Made in America."

* * *

The Great Green Fleet of the Delta, the brave PBRs, the Swift boats, and the Brown Water Sailor himself all belong to the past. Only the rivers and the memories remain.

Notes

Chapter One. FROM EARLIEST TIMES TO THE INDOCHINA WAR

1. Quoted in Karnow, *Vietnam, A History,* p. 153.
2. Address of President Woodrow Wilson to the Congress of the United States, 8 January 1918. *Congressional Record,* 65th Cong., 2nd Sess., pp. 680–81.
3. "Declaration of Independence of the Democratic Republic of Vietnam," [2 September 1945]. *Southeast Asia, Documents of Political Development and Change,* edited by Roger M. Smith, pp. 313–15.
4. "Preliminary Franco-Vietnamese Agreement," [6 March 1946]. *Southeast Asia, Documents of Political Development and Change,* edited by Roger M. Smith, p. 316.

Chapter Two. THE INDOCHINA WAR, 1946–54

1. Quoted in Karnow, *Vietnam, A History,* p. 154.
2. Truong Chinh, "The Resistance Will Win," [1947]. *Southeast Asia, Documents of Political Development and Change,* edited by Roger M. Smith, pp. 321–22.
3. Quoted in Karnow, *Vietnam, A History,* p. 175.
4. For a full discussion, see *Containment, Concept and Policy,* edited by Terry L. Deibel and John Lewis Gaddis. Washington: National Defense University Press, 1986.
5. Vo Nguyen Giap, *People's War, People's Army,* p. 106.
6. Croizat, *The Brown Water Navy,* p. 111.
7. Statement of President Dwight D. Eisenhower, 21 July 1954. Department of State *Bulletin,* vol. 31 [2 August 1954], p. 163.
8. Ho Chi Minh, "Appeal on the Signing of the Geneva Agreement" [22

July 1954]. *Southeast Asia, Documents of Political Development and Change,* edited by Roger M. Smith, p. 326.

Chapter Three. THE ADVISORY PERIOD, 1954–64

1. "Agrarian Reform Law," [4 December 1953]. *Southeast Asia, Documents of Political Development and Change,* edited by Roger M. Smith, pp. 330–32.
2. Captain James D. Collette, oral history [15 December 1970]. Naval Historical Center, Washington, D.C.
3. *The New York Times,* 29 September 1955.
4. Karnow, *Vietnam, A History,* p. 224.
5. CINCPAC, "Counter-Insurgency Operations in South Vietnam and Laos," 26 April 1960.
6. *History of Naval Operations in Vietnam, 1946–1963,* Office of the Chief of Naval Operations, Naval History Division [June 1964], p. 197.
7. *United States–Vietnam Relations: 1945–1967.* U.S. Government Printing Office, Washington, 1971. Book 2, pp. 96–97.
8. CINCPAC message 152015Z November 1961.
9. Buckingham, *Operation Ranch Hand: The Air Force and Herbicides in Southeast Asia, 1961–1971,* pp. 14, 129.
10. Westmoreland, *A Soldier Reports,* p. 57.
11. "Vietnamese Navy's Role in the Counterinsurgency," June 1964, p. 8. NAVFORV Historical Files.
12. Captain Phillip H. Bucklew, oral history [10 July 1978], pp. 8, 11 of transcript. Naval Historical Center, Washington, D.C.

Chapter Four. THE READINESS OF THE NAVY FOR LIMITED WAR

1. Marolda and Fitzgerald, *The United States Navy and the Vietnam Conflict,* vol. 2, pp. 10, 14.
2. President John F. Kennedy, inaugural address, January 1961.
3. "Reminiscences of Vice Admiral Gerald E. Miller," p. 491 of transcript. U.S. Naval Institute Oral History Collection.
4. "Reminiscences of Admiral Alfred G. Ward," p. 262 of transcript. U.S. Naval Institute Oral History Collection.
5. Ibid., p. 263.
6. Marolda and Fitzgerald, *The United States Navy and the Vietnam Conflict,* vol. 2, p. 294.

Chapter Five. THE TONKIN GULF—BEYOND THE POINT OF NO RETURN

1. Captain Phillip H. Bucklew, oral history [10 July 1978], p. 8 of transcript. Naval Historical Center, Washington, D.C.
2. "Report of Recommendations Pertaining to Infiltration into South Vietnam of Viet Cong Personnel, Supporting Materials, Weapons and Am-

munition," [15 February 1964], p. 2. Vietnam Delta Infiltration Study Group.

3. Ibid., pp. 3, 13.

4. Westmoreland, *A Soldier Reports,* p. 109.

5. William E. Colby, taped interview, 9 June 1980. Naval Historical Center.

6. CTG-72.1 message 041727Z August 1964. Quoted in Marolda and Fitzgerald, *The United States Navy and the Vietnam Conflict,* vol. 2, p. 440.

7. Marolda and Fitzgerald, *The United States Navy and the Vietnam Conflict,* vol. 2, pp. 446–49.

8. Department of State, Publication 6446, *American Foreign Policy: Basic Documents, 1950–1955,* vol. 1, pp. 912–16.

9. Admiral Thomas H. Moorer, author's taped interview, 12 April 1988.

10. "Reminiscences of Admiral Horatio Rivero," pp. 439–41 of transcript. U.S. Naval Institute Oral History Collection.

11. Ibid.

12. "Reminiscences of Vice Admiral William P. Mack," vol. 1, p. 410 of transcript. U.S. Naval Institute Oral History Collection.

Chapter Six. 1965, THE ORIGINS OF MARKET TIME AND GAME WARDEN

1. *History of U.S. Naval Operations in Vietnam, 1964,* Office of the Chief of Naval Operations, Naval History Division [May 1969], pp. 175, 184.

2. Commodore Ho Van Ky Thoai, VNN, taped interview, 20 September 1975. Naval Historical Center.

3. Naval Advisory Group Activities, Historical Review, March 1965, p. 4.

4. Ibid., p. 5.

5. CINCPAC message 100023Z March 1965. Quoted in Marolda and Fitzgerald, *The United States Navy and the Vietnam Conflict,* vol. 2, p. 516.

6. Westmoreland, *A Soldier Reports,* p. 184.

7. Vice Admiral Paul P. Blackburn, taped interview, 26 November 1973. Naval Historical Center.

8. Ibid.

9. Lieutenant John Chidsey, taped interview, 1 December 1966. Naval Historical Center.

10. Chief, Naval Advisory Group Vietnam letter serial 00100-65 of 25 August 1965.

Chapter Seven. THE BUILDING OF NAVAL FORCES, VIETNAM—1966–67

1. NAVFORV, Monthly Historical Summary, May 1966.

2. NAVFORV, Monthly Historical Summary, June 1966.

3. NAVFORV, Monthly Historical Summary, August 1966.

4. PACFLT, Monthly Historical Summary, June 1968.
5. MACV, Command History, 1968, pp. 492–95.
6. CINCPAC message 200223Z July 1968.
7. NAVFORV, Monthly Historical Summary, December 1966.
8. NAVFORV, Monthly Historical Summary, December 1967.
9. "Counterinsurgency Lessons Learned No. 62: Salient Lessons Learned," MACV, 11 March 1967.
10. Westmoreland, *A Soldier Reports,* p. 208.
11. "Reminiscences of Vice Admiral Robert S. Salzer," p. 414 of transcript. U.S. Naval Institute Oral History Collection.
12. Ibid., pp. 415–16.
13. Ibid., pp. 417–18.

Chapter Eight. THE AIR WAR—CLIPPING THE WINGS OF EAGLES

1. "Reminiscences of Admiral U. S. Grant Sharp," vol. 2, p. 370 of transcript. U.S. Naval Institute Oral History Collection.
2. Ibid., pp. 335–36.
3. Vice Admiral Paul P. Blackburn, taped interview, 26 November 1973. Naval Historical Center.
4. "Reminiscences of Vice Admiral Raymond E. Peet," pp. 275–82 of transcript. U.S. Naval Institute Oral History Collection.
5. "Reminiscences of Rear Admiral Kenneth L. Veth," pp. 398–99 of transcript. U.S. Naval Institute Oral History Collection.
6. "Reminiscences of Admiral U. S. Grant Sharp," vol. 2, p. 341 of transcript. U.S. Naval Institute Oral History Collection.
7. Ibid., p. 343.
8. Ibid., p. 379.
9. Ibid., pp. 360–61.
10. Sharp, *Strategy for Defeat,* p. 94.
11. Ibid.
12. "Reminiscences of Admiral U. S. Grant Sharp," vol. 2, p. 368 of transcript. U.S. Naval Institute Oral History Collection.
13. Ibid., p. 405.
14. Ibid., pp. 411–12.
15. Ibid., p. 468.
16. Ibid., pp. 472–76.
17. Ibid., pp. 477–81.
18. Ibid., p. 481.

Chapter Nine. TET, 1968

1. Westmoreland, *A Soldier Reports,* p. 313.
2. "Reminiscences of Rear Admiral Kenneth L. Veth," p. 405 of transcript. U.S. Naval Institute Oral History Collection.
3. Captain F. F. Jewett II, letter of 13 November 1969 to COMNAVFORV.

4. Westmoreland, *A Soldier Reports,* p. 321.

5. "Reminiscences of Vice Admiral Robert S. Salzer," p. 398 of transcript. U.S. Naval Institute Oral History Collection.

6. Ibid., pp. 398–402.

7. Ibid., p. 403.

8. Ibid., p. 404.

9. Ibid., pp. 404–5.

10. Ibid., p. 701.

11. COMNAVFORV letter serial 0402, 5 July 1968.

12. Ibid.

13. MACV, Command History, 1968, pp. 461–62.

14. CTF Clearwater message 031400Z May 1968.

15. MACV, Command History, 1968, pp. 448–49.

Chapter Ten. SEA LORDS

1. Admiral Thomas H. Moorer, author's taped interview, 12 April 1988.

2. Captain Howard J. Kerr, taped interview, 22 September and 9 November 1972. Naval Historical Center.

3. Admiral Elmo R. Zumwalt, Jr., COMNAVFORV change of command remarks, 15 May 1970.

4. Admiral Thomas H. Moorer, author's taped interview, 12 April 1988.

5. COMNAVFORV, Monthly Strength Report, September 1968.

6. COMNAVFORV, Logistics Summary Report, October 1968.

7. "Reminiscences of Vice Admiral Robert S. Salzer," p. 476 of transcript. U.S. Naval Institute Oral History Collection.

8. Ibid., pp. 477–79.

9. Ibid., p. 490.

10. COMNAVFORV message 200211Z October 1968.

11. Ibid.

12. Ibid.

13. COMNAVFORV letter serial 0666, 29 October 1968.

14. First Sea Lord message 071330Z November 1968.

15. "Reminiscences of Vice Admiral Robert S. Salzer," pp. 488–90 of transcript. U.S. Naval Institute Oral History Collection.

16. COMNAVFORV message 130018Z November 1968.

17. Commander Coastal Division 11 message 161815Z November 1968.

18. NILO Ha Tien message 160845Z November 1968.

19. COMNAVFORV message 200134Z November 1968.

20. COMNAVFORV message 210258Z November 1968.

21. Ibid.

22. CTF-116 message 010815Z December 1968.

23. COMNAVFORV message 021131Z February 1969.

24. COMUSMACV, Weekly Intelligence Estimate Update, 25 January 1969.

25. COMNAVFORV message 260203Z December 1968.
26. COMNAVFORV message 021052Z December 1968.
27. Ibid.
28. "Reminiscences of Vice Admiral Robert S. Salzer," p. 487 of transcript. U.S. Naval Institute Oral History Collection.

Chapter Eleven. ACTOV

1. Captain Howard J. Kerr, taped interview, 22 September and 9 November 1972. Naval Historical Center.
2. Naval Advisory Group Activities, Historical Review, April 1965.
3. Naval Advisory Group Activities, Historical Review, May 1965.
4. NAVFORV, Monthly Historical Summary, November 1966.
5. Ibid.
6. Ibid.
7. NAVFORV, Monthly Historical Supplement, February 1968.
8. NAVFORV, Monthly Historical Summary, December 1966.
9. Lieutenant Commander James R. Seeley, end-of-tour report dated 29 June 1969.
10. Commander Dale W. Duncan, end-of-tour report dated 6 January 1969.
11. Lieutenant John F. Abel, end-of-tour report dated 15 November 1968.
12. Lieutenant John W. Richardson, end-of-tour report dated (?) September 1968.
13. Lieutenant (j.g.) William J. McNally III, end-of-tour report dated 16 December 1968.
14. Lieutenant Howard M. Cullen, end-of-tour report dated 20 August 1968.
15. Lieutenant J. C. Fritz, end-of-tour report dated 30 November 1968.
16. Lieutenant Richard A. Crooks, end-of-tour report dated 14 November 1968.
17. Lieutenant Commander Billie L. Price, end-of-tour report dated 26 November 1968.
18. Commander Raymond T. McDonald, end-of-tour report dated 19 August 1968.
19. Lieutenant Hugh R. Harris, end-of-tour report dated 27 September 1968.
20. Lieutenant Robert Peck (MSC), end-of-tour report dated 29 October 1968.
21. Commander William C. Filkins, end-of-tour report dated 5 November 1969.
22. Lieutenant (j.g.) Theodore J. Bowler, end-of-tour report dated 27 September 1968.

Chapter Twelve. GIANT SLINGSHOT AND BARRIER REEF

1. COMNAVFORV message 250047Z November 1968.
2. CTG-194.9 message 051544Z December 1968.

3. Ibid.

4. COMNAVFORV message 120510Z December 1968.

5. "Reminiscences of Rear Admiral Arthur W. Price, Jr.," pp. 469–70 of transcript. U.S. Naval Institute Oral History Collection.

6. COMUSMACV, Weekly Intelligence Estimate Update, 4 January 1969.

7. COMUSMACV, Weekly Intelligence Estimate Update, 18 January 1969.

8. COMUSMACV, Weekly Intelligence Estimate Update, 1 February 1969.

9. Senior Advisor Long An Province message 150930Z March 1969.

10. COMNAVFORV message 211409Z March 1969.

11. COMUSMACV, Weekly Intelligence Estimate Update, 5 April 1969.

12. COMNAVFORV message 290836Z March 1969.

13. COMUSMACV, Weekly Intelligence Estimate Update, 26 April 1969.

14. COMNAVFORV message 030826Z May 1969.

15. Ibid.

16. COMUSMACV, Weekly Intelligence Estimate Update, 28 June 1969.

17. COMUSMACV, Weekly Intelligence Estimate Update, 9 August 1969.

18. Commanding General II Field Forces Vietnam message 200845Z June 1969.

19. "Reminiscences of Vice Admiral Robert S. Salzer," p. 433 of transcript. U.S. Naval Institute Oral History Collection.

20. Ibid.

21. Commanding General II Field Forces Vietnam message 270525Z June 1969.

22. COMNAVFORV message 280644Z December 1968.

23. COMUSMACV message 311330Z January 1969.

24. COMUSMACV, Weekly Intelligence Estimate Update, 8 February 1969.

Chapter Thirteen. SAIGON, REDUCTIO AD ABSURDUM

1. General William C. Westmoreland, author's taped interview, 9 January 1988.

2. COMUSMACV message 030133Z December 1969.

Chapter Fourteen. SEA FLOAT/SOLID ANCHOR

1. CTG-194.2 message 220740Z December 1968.

2. COMUSMACV, Weekly Intelligence Estimate Update, 5 April 1969.

3. NAVFORV, Monthly Historical Summary, April 1969.

4. Ibid.

5. CTF-115 message 151415Z May 1969.

6. MACV, Command History, 1969, p. V–134.

7. CTG-115.7 message 170445Z July 1969.
8. COMUSMACV, Weekly Intelligence Estimate Update, 14 June 1969.
9. CTG-115.7 message 180337Z August 1969.
10. COMNAVFORV message 261330Z August 1969.
11. CTG-115.7 message 280101Z July 1969.
12. CTG-115.7 message 060314Z September 1969.
13. CTG-115.7 message 140730Z September 1969.
14. CTG-115.7 message 170555Z September 1969.
15. Senior Advisor An Xuyen Province message 291355Z September 1969.
16. COMUSMACV, Weekly Intelligence Estimate Update, 6 September 1969.
17. COMUSMACV, Weekly Intelligence Estimate Update, 25 October 1969.
18. CTG-115.7 message 211520Z October 1969.
19. CTG-115.7 message 220020Z October 1969.
20. COMUSMACV, Weekly Intelligence Estimate Update, 6 December 1969.
21. CTG-115.7 message 200114Z December 1969.
22. CTG-115.7 message 181506Z January 1970.
23. CTF-115 message 170707Z January 1970.
24. CTG-115.7 messages 151416Z and 161502Z January 1970.
25. CTG-115.7 message 220330Z January 1970.
26. CTG-115.7 message 242320Z February 1970.
27. NAVFORV, Monthly Historical Summary, January 1970.
28. CTG-115.7 messages 160406Z and 180016Z January 1970.
29. COMNAVFORV message 240544Z January 1970.
30. CTG-115.7 message 040610Z March 1970.
31. Commander NSA Saigon message 200104Z October 1970.
32. NAVFORV, Monthly Historical Summary, April 1970.
33. Ibid.
34. NAVFORV, Monthly Historical Summary, July 1970.
35. Ibid.
36. CTG-116.1 message 200940Z September 1970.
37. NAVFORV, Monthly Historical Summary, September 1970.
38. NAVFORV, Monthly Historical Summary, December 1970.
39. Ibid.
40. NAVFORV, Monthly Historical Summary, January 1971.

Chapter Fifteen. THE NAVAL WAR IN THE NORTH

1. CTF Clearwater message 041010Z October 1968.
2. MACV, Command History, 1968, p. 463.
3. NAVFORV, Monthly Historical Summary, November 1967.
4. NAVFORV, Monthly Historical Summary, November 1966.
5. Rear Admiral Thomas Weschler, letter to COMNAVFORV, 8 December 1969.
6. CTF Clearwater message 210857Z February 1969.

7. Captain Frederick F. Jewett II, letter to COMNAVFORV, 13 November 1969.
8. Commander S. A. Swartztrauber, letter to COMNAVFORV, 7 December 1969.
9. Ibid.
10. E.g., Commander Dong Ha River Security Group message 240616Z October 1968.
11. CTF Clearwater message 190755Z April 1969.
12. Commander NSA Danang message 300905Z January 1969.
13. CTF Clearwater message 091200Z January 1970.
14. CTF Clearwater message 092043Z January 1970.
15. CTF Clearwater message 021310Z September 1969.
16. COMNAVFORV message 260708Z November 1969.
17. Commanding General, XXIV Corps message 130635Z January 1970.
18. CTF Clearwater message 240922Z January 1970.
19. COMNAVFORV message 250103Z April 1969.
20. COMUSMACV, Weekly Intelligence Estimate Update, 20 April 1969.
21. CTU-115.1.0 message 260900Z May 1969.
22. CTU-115.1.0 message 200400Z June 1969.
23. CTF-115 message 240315Z May 1969.
24. Ibid.
25. Commander S. A. Swartztrauber, letter to COMNAVFORV, 7 December 1969.
26. CTU-115.1.0 message 080030Z October 1969.
27. CTF-115 message 220850Z November 1969.
28. NAVFORV, Naval Statistical Summary, 12 February 1970.
29. NAVFORV, Monthly Historical Summary, May 1971.
30. MACV, Command History, 1968, p. 495.
31. Ibid., p. 502.

Chapter Sixteen. A BOY NAMED CHOU

1. Lieutenant (j.g.) Wellington Maupin Westbrook III, personal history, recorded 26 February 1970 by Lieutenant Commander Forrest L. Edwards.
2. Ibid.
3. Ibid.

Chapter Seventeen. READY DECK

1. COMNAVFORV message 200632Z May 1969.
2. COMNAVFORV message 042301Z June 1969.
3. COMUSMACV, Weekly Intelligence Estimate Update, 5 July 1969.
4. COMUSMACV, Weekly Intelligence Estimate Update, 26 July 1969.
5. COMNAVFORV message 110001Z October 1969.
6. COMUSMACV, Weekly Intelligence Estimate Update, 3 January 1970.
7. MACV, Command History, 1971, p. V–19.

Chapter Eighteen. THE FOREST OF ASSASSINS

1. OINC, SEAL Team One, Detachment Golf, letter to COMNAV-FORV, serial 3000, dated 17 July 1968.
2. NAVFORV, Monthly Historical Summary, May 1966.
3. NAVFORV, Monthly Historical Summary, August 1966.
4. NAVFORV, Monthly Historical Summary, November 1966.
5. NAVFORV, Monthly Historical Summary, December 1966.
6. MACV, Command History, 1967, p. 472.
7. Ibid.
8. COMNAVFORV message 030321Z July 1969.
9. Senior Advisor, RSSZ message 301636Z September 1969.
10. COMNAVFORV message 030155Z February 1970.
11. Lieutenant Robert W. Champion, end-of-tour report dated 24 February 1970.

Chapter Twenty. BREEZY COVE

1. *Pacific Stars and Stripes,* 10 May 1970.
2. COMNAVFORV message 090316Z September 1969.
3. CTG-194.0 message 180716Z September 1969.
4. CTG-194.0 message 290408Z September 1969.
5. Ibid.
6. MACV, Command History, 1969, p. V–165.
7. CTG-194.2 message 281400Z November 1969.
8. MACV, Command History, 1969, pp. V–165–66.
9. Ibid.
10. COMUSMACV, Weekly Intelligence Estimate Update, 27 December 1969.
11. MACV, Command History, 1969, p. V–166.
12. Captain Cyrus R. Christensen, author's taped interview, 22 June 1990.
13. NAVFORV, Monthly Historical Summary, September 1970.
14. NAVFORV, Monthly Historical Summary, October 1970.
15. Captain Cyrus R. Christensen, author's taped interview, 22 June 1990.
16. NAVFORV, Monthly Historical Summary, October 1970.
17. Captain Cyrus R. Christensen, author's taped interview, 22 June 1990.
18. Ibid.
19. Ibid.
20. NAVFORV, Monthly Historical Summary, October 1970.
21. Captain Cyrus R. Christensen, author's taped interview, 22 June 1990.
22. NAVFORV, Monthly Historical Summary, October 1970.
23. Captain Cyrus R. Christensen, author's taped interview, 22 June 1990.

Chapter Twenty-One. THE UNRAVELING

1. NAVFORV, Monthly Historical Summary, May 1970.
2. Vice Admiral Jerome H. King, Jr., "Personal Memorandum for all NAVFORV Staff Officers," 29 May 1970.
3. NAVFORV, Naval Statistical Summary, 15 March 1970.
4. COMNAVFORV message 240718Z November 1968.
5. COMNAVFORV message 090308Z January 1969.
6. CINCPACFLT message 132018Z March 1969.
7. Quoted in JCS message 051928Z May 1969.
8. Speech by Commander Hop, VNN, commanding officer of the Vietnamese Naval Training Center, Cam Ranh Bay, given on 8 February 1969.
9. Internal NAVFORV staff memorandum for 004, 26 February 1969.
10. Internal NAVFORV staff memorandum for the senior naval advisor, 5 March 1969.
11. Mobile Training Team Weekly Report, 7 April 1969.
12. Mobile Training Team Final Report, 17-69VN.
13. NAVFORV, Monthly ACTOV Progress Reports.
14. COMNAVFORV message 310456Z March 1969.
15. NAVFORV, Monthly ACTOV Progress Reports.
16. COMNAVFORV message 130015Z October 1969.
17. COMNAVFORV message 160400Z April 1968.
18. NAVFORV, Monthly Historical Summary, May 1970.
19. NAVFORV, Monthly Historical Summary, June 1970.
20. Captain George G. Ryon (SC), end-of-tour report dated 8 September 1969.
21. Ibid.
22. Commander Coast Guard Activities Vietnam, Op-Plan 2-69, dated 1 February 1969.
23. COMNAVFORV message 280121Z January 1970.
24. COMNAVFORV, Briefing Memo, serial 031, dated 21 November 1969.
25. Captain Bui Huu Thu, VNN, taped interview, 14 August 1975, Naval Historical Center.
26. Commodore Hoang Co Minh, VNN, taped interview, 18 September 1975, Naval Historical Center.

Chapter Twenty-Two. THE NAVY'S HELPING HAND

1. Quoted in JCS message 291543Z July 1969.
2. COMUSMACV message 270420Z June 1969.
3. Admin COMNAVFORV message 210840Z October 1969.
4. COMNAVFORV message 111055Z October 1969.
5. NAVFORV, Monthly Historical Summary, March 1970.
6. NAVFORV, Monthly Historical Summary, September 1970.
7. NAVFORV, Monthly Historical Summary, April 1971.
8. Commodore Hoang Co Minh, VNN, taped interview, 18 September 1975, Naval Historical Center.

9. Commodore Ho Van Ky Thoai, VNN, taped interview, 20 September 1975, Naval Historical Center.

10. COMNAVFORV message 030618Z September 1969.

11. CTF-115 message 131330Z October 1969.

12. Third Coastal Zone Advisor message 120810Z January 1970.

13. COMRIVPATFLOT Five message 090700Z February 1970.

14. CTF-115 message 060730Z February 1970.

15. NAVFORV, Monthly Historical Summary, March 1970.

16. NAVFORV, Monthly Historical Summary, May 1970.

17. Commodore Ho Van Ky Thoai, VNN, taped interview, 20 September 1975. Naval Historical Center.

Chapter Twenty-Three. END GAME

1. NAVFORV, Monthly Historical Summary, February 1971.

2. Captain Bui Huu Thu, VNN, taped interview, 14 August 1975. Naval Historical Center.

3. "Reminiscences of Vice Admiral Robert S. Salzer," p. 532 of transcript. U.S. Naval Institute Oral History Collection.

4. NAVFORV, Monthly Historical Summary, April 1971.

5. "Reminiscences of Vice Admiral Robert S. Salzer," p. 544 of transcript. U.S. Naval Institute Oral History Collection.

6. Ibid., pp. 545–46.

7. Ibid., pp. 550–51.

8. Ibid., pp. 552–54.

9. NAVFORV, Monthly Historical Summary, May 1971.

10. "Reminiscences of Vice Admiral Robert S. Salzer," pp. 559–61 of transcript. U.S. Naval Institute Oral History Collection.

11. Ibid., pp. 562–64.

12. NAVFORV, Monthly Historical Summary, July 1971.

13. NAVFORV, Monthly Historical Summary, September 1971.

14. "Reminiscences of Vice Admiral Robert S. Salzer," p. 571 of transcript. U.S. Naval Institute Oral History Collection.

15. Ibid., pp. 572–73.

16. NAVFORV, Monthly Historical Summary, September 1971.

17. "Reminiscences of Vice Admiral Robert S. Salzer," pp. 596–98 of transcript. U.S. Naval Institute Oral History Collection.

18. Ibid., pp. 607–9.

19. "Reminiscences of Rear Admiral Arthur W. Price, Jr.," p. 578 of transcript. U.S. Naval Institute Oral History Collection.

20. "Reminiscences of Vice Admiral Robert S. Salzer," pp. 620–21 of transcript. U.S. Naval Institute Oral History Collection.

21. Captain Cyrus R. Christensen, author's taped interview, 22 June 1990.

22. "Reminiscences of Vice Admiral Robert S. Salzer," p. 626 of transcript. U.S. Naval Institute Oral History Collection.

23. Admiral Thomas H. Moorer, author's taped interview, 12 April 1988.

24. Ibid.

25. Ibid.

26. "Reminiscences of Vice Admiral Robert S. Salzer," p. 638 of transcript. U.S. Naval Institute Oral History Collection.

27. *Pacific Stars and Stripes,* 29 June 1973.

28. Rear Admiral Brian McCauley, "Operation End Sweep," U.S. Naval Institute *Proceedings,* March 1974.

29. CTG-78 letter to COMSEVENTHFLT, serial 51010 of 3 July 1973.

30. Ibid.

EPILOGUE

1. Commodore Hoang Co Minh, VNN, taped interview, 18 September 1975, Naval Historical Center.

2. Commodore Bang Cao Thang, VNN, taped interview, 21 August 1975, Naval Historical Center.

3. Commodore Ho Van Ky Thoai, VNN, taped interview, 20 September 1975, Naval Historical Center.

4. Quoted in CINCPAC Command History, 1975.

5. Ibid.

6. Ibid.

7. Rear Admiral Chung Tan Cang, VNN, taped interview, 31 July 1975, Naval Historical Center.

Bibliography

BOOKS

Barron, John, and Anthony Paul. *Murder of a Gentle Land*. New York: Reader's Digest Press, 1977.

Berman, Larry. *Lyndon Johnson's War*. New York, London: W. W. Norton & Company, 1989.

Bouscaren, Anthony T. *All Quiet on the Eastern Front*. Old Greenwich, Conn.: The Devin-Adair Company, 1977.

Buckingham, William A., Jr. *Operation Ranch Hand: The Air Force and Herbicides in Southeast Asia, 1961–1971*. Washington, D.C.: United States Government Printing Office, 1982.

Butler, David. *The Fall of Saigon*. New York: Simon and Schuster, 1985.

Caputo, Philip. *A Rumor of War*. New York: Holt, Rinehart and Winston, 1977.

Containment, Concept and Policy. Edited by Terry L. Deibel and John Lewis Gaddis. Washington: National Defense University Press, 1986.

Croizat, Victor. *The Brown Water Navy: The River and Coastal War in Indo-China and Vietnam, 1940–1972*. Dorset, United Kingdom: Blandford Press, 1984.

Cutler, Thomas J. *Brown Water, Black Berets*. Annapolis, Md.: Naval Institute Press, 1988.

Du Berrier, Hillaire. *Background to Betrayal: The Tragedy of Vietnam*. Belmont, Mass.: Western Islands, 1965.

Emerson, Gloria. *Winners & Losers: Battles, Retreats, Gains, Losses and Ruins from a Long War*. New York: Random House, 1976.

Fall, Bernard B. *Street Without Joy*. New York: Schocken Books, 1972.

Gardner, Lloyd C. *Approaching Vietnam: From World War II through Dienbienphu*. New York, London: W. W. Norton & Company, 1988.

Giap, Vo Nguyen. *People's War, People's Army*. New York: Frederick A. Praeger, 1962.

Hammel, Eric. *Khe Sanh: Siege in the Clouds, An Oral History.* New York: Crown Publishers, Inc., 1989.

Herring, George C. *America's Longest War.* 2d ed. New York: Alfred A. Knopf, 1986.

Hooper, Vice Admiral Edwin Bickford. *Mobility, Support, Endurance: A Story of Naval Operational Logistics in the Vietnam War, 1965–1968.* Washington, D.C.: United States Government Printing Office, 1972.

Hooper, Edwin Bickford; Dean C. Allard; and Oscar Fitzgerald. *The United States Navy and the Vietnam Conflict, Vol. I.* Washington, D.C.: United States Government Printing Office, 1976.

Isaacs, Arnold R. *Without Honor.* Baltimore and London: The Johns Hopkins University Press, 1983.

Karnow, Stanley. *Vietnam, A History.* New York: Viking Press, 1983.

Levinson, Jeffrey L. *Alpha Strike Vietnam: The Navy's Air War, 1964–1973.* Novato, Calif.: Presidio Press, 1989.

Maclear, Michael. *The Ten Thousand Day War: Vietnam 1945–1975.* New York: St. Martin's Press, 1981.

Marolda, Edward J. *Carrier Operations.* New York: Bantam Books, 1987.

Marolda, Edward J., and G. Wesley Pryce III. *A Short History of the United States Navy and the Vietnam Conflict, 1950–1975.* Washington, D.C.: Naval Historical Center, Department of the Navy, 1984.

Marolda, Edward J., and Oscar P. Fitzgerald. *The United States Navy and the Vietnam Conflict, Vol. II.* Washington, D.C.: United States Government Printing Office, 1986.

McCloud, Bill. *What Should We Tell Our Children About Vietnam?* Norman, Okla.: University of Oklahoma Press, 1989.

Miller, John Grider. *The Bridge at Dong Ha.* Annapolis, Md.: Naval Institute Press, 1989.

Nixon, Richard. *No More Vietnams.* New York: Arbor House, 1985.

Nixon, Richard. *Real Peace: A Strategy for the West.* New York: author's private edition, 1983.

Parker, F. Charles IV. *Vietnam, Strategy for a Stalemate.* New York: Paragon House, 1989.

Second Indochina War Symposium. Edited by John Schlight. Washington, D.C.: United States Government Printing Office, 1986.

Sharp, Admiral U. S. Grant. *Strategy for Defeat: Vietnam in Retrospect.* Novato, Calif.: Presidio Press, 1978.

Sheehan, Neil. *A Bright Shining Lie: John Paul Vann and America in Vietnam.* New York: Random House, 1989.

Sheehan, Neil, et al. *The Pentagon Papers.* New York: Bantam Books, 1971.

Snepp, Frank. *Decent Interval.* New York: Random House, 1977.

Southeast Asia, Documents of Political Development and Change. Edited by Roger M. Smith. Ithaca, N.Y., and London: Cornell University Press, 1974.

Spector, Ronald H. *Advice and Support: The Early Years of the U.S. Army in Vietnam, 1941–1960.* New York: The Free Press, 1985.

Summers, Harry G., Jr. *On Strategy: The Vietnam War in Context.* Washington, D.C.: United States Government Printing Office, 1981.

Terzani, Tiziano. *Giai Phong! The Fall and Liberation of Saigon.* New York: St. Martin's Press, 1976.

The Pentagon Papers, as published by *The New York Times.* Toronto, New York, & London: Bantam Books, 1971.

United States Navy and Marine Corps Bases, Overseas, edited by Paolo E. Coletta. Westport, Conn., and London, England: Greenwood Press, 1985.

Vien, General Cao Van. *The Final Collapse.* Washington, D.C.: United States Government Printing Office, 1983.

Viet Cong Tet Offensive, 1968. Edited by Lieutenant Colonel Pham Van Son, ARVN. Saigon: Printing and Publications Center of the Joint General Staff, RVNAF, 1968.

Vietnam, The Naval Story. Edited by Frank Uhlig, Jr. Annapolis, Md.: Naval Institute Press, 1986.

Westmoreland, General William C. *A Soldier Reports.* New York: Doubleday & Company, 1976.

World Almanac of the Vietnam War. Edited by John S. Bowman. New York: Bison Books, 1985.

Zumwalt, Admiral Elmo, Jr., and Lieutenant Elmo Zumwalt III, with John Pekkanen. *My Father, My Son.* New York: Macmillan Company, 1986.

Zumwalt, Admiral Elmo R., Jr. *On Watch.* New York: Quadrangle/The New York Times Book Company, 1976.

Unpublished Documents

"Compendium of Lessons Learned in the Naval War in Vietnam." Saigon: Commander Naval Forces Vietnam, 1970.

"The Naval War in Vietnam." Saigon: Commander Naval Forces Vietnam, 1970.

Oral Histories

Blackburn, Vice Admiral Paul P. Naval Historical Center, 26 November 1973.

Bucklew, Captain Phillip H. Naval Historical Center, 10 July 1978.

Cang, Rear Admiral Chung Tan, VNN. Naval Historical Center, 31 July 1975.

Chidsey, Lieutenant John. Naval Historical Center, 1 December 1966.

Collett, Captain James D. Naval Historical Center, 15 December 1970.

Ellingson, Lieutenant (j.g.) Luther J. Recorded by Lieutenant Commander Forrest L. Edwards on 5 March 1970.

Felt, Admiral Harry D. U.S. Naval Institute Oral History Collection. Based on four interviews in March 1972.

Kerr, Captain Howard J. Naval Historical Center, 22 September and 9 November 1972.

Mack, Vice Admiral William P. U.S. Naval Institute Oral History Collection. Based on twelve interviews from February through May 1979.

Miller, Vice Admiral Gerald E. U.S. Naval Institute Oral History Collection. Based on nine interviews from January through October 1976.

Minh, Commodore Hoang Co., VNN. Naval Historical Center, 18 September 1975.

Peet, Vice Admiral Raymond E. U. S. Naval Institute Oral History Collection. Based on seven interviews from May through July 1978.

Price, Rear Admiral Arthur W., Jr. U.S. Naval Institute Oral History Collection. Based on four interviews from May through July 1978.

Rivero, Admiral Horatio, Jr. U.S. Naval Institute Oral History Collection. Based on six interviews from May through November 1975.

Salzer, Vice Admiral Robert S. U.S. Naval Institute Oral History Collection. Based on fifteen interviews from February through November 1977.

Sharp, Admiral U. S. Grant, Jr. U.S. Naval Institute Oral History Collection. Based on eleven interviews from September 1969 through June 1970.

Thang, Commodore Bang Cao, VNN. Naval Historical Center, 21 August 1975.

Thoai, Commodore Ho Van Ky, VNN. Naval Historical Center, 20 September 1975.

Thu, Captain Bui Huu, VNN. Naval Historical Center, 14 August 1975.

Veth, Rear Admiral Kenneth L. U.S. Naval Institute Oral History Collection. Based on seven interviews in July and August 1977.

Ward, Admiral Alfred G. U.S. Naval Institute Oral History Collection. Based on eleven interviews from August 1970 through December 1971.

Westbrook, Lieutenant (j.g.) Wellington Maupin III. Recorded by Lieutenant Commander Forrest L. Edwards on 26 February 1970.

Author's Taped Interviews

Christensen, Captain Cyrus R. 22 June 1990.
Moorer, Admiral Thomas H. 12 April 1988.
Westmoreland, General William C. 9 January 1988.

Index

About the Author

R. L. Schreadley enlisted in the navy in 1949 and saw service during the Korean War on the aircraft carrier *Leyte* (CV 32). In 1955 he graduated from Dickinson College with a degree in English Literature, and that year was commissioned as an ensign in the naval reserve. Augmenting into the regular navy, he was promoted through the ranks and achieved the grade of commander in 1969 while serving on the staff of Commander Naval Forces Vietnam as director of COMNAVFORV's special history project. His naval assignments included three commands at sea—USS *Sturdy* (MSO 494), Mine Division 24, and USS *Blakely* (DE 1072). He retired from the navy on 1 November 1973.

From 1967 to 1969 he attended, under navy sponsorship, the Fletcher School of Law and Diplomacy, receiving the master of arts degree in 1968, and the master of arts, law, and diplomacy degree in 1969. In 1972, Fletcher awarded him the degree of doctor of philosophy.

In June 1974 he joined *The News and Courier* in Charleston, South Carolina, as a reporter. In February 1975 he became an editorial writer for *The Evening Post* in that city, and progressed rapidly to become associate editor, editorial page editor, and, on 1 January 1978, editor of the *Post*. On 1 September 1981 he was promoted to executive editor of both the *Post* and *The News and Courier*. Some eight years later, in June 1989, he retired from the newspapers to pursue other interests as a writer.

The **Naval Institute Press** is the book-publishing arm of the U.S. Naval Institute, a private, nonprofit professional society for members of the sea services and civilians who share an interest in naval and maritime affairs. Established in 1873 at the U.S. Naval Academy in Annapolis, Maryland, where its offices remain today, the Naval Institute has more than 100,000 members worldwide.

Members of the Naval Institute receive the influential monthly magazine *Proceedings* and discounts on fine nautical prints, ship and aircraft photos, and subscriptions to the quarterly *Naval History* magazine. They also have access to the transcripts of the Institute's Oral History Program and get discounted admission to any of the Institute-sponsored seminars offered around the country.

The Naval Institute's book-publishing program, begun in 1898 with basic guides to naval practices, has broadened its scope in recent years to include books of more general interest. Now the Naval Institute Press publishes more than sixty titles each year, ranging from how-to books on boating and navigation to battle histories, biographies, ship and aircraft guides, and novels. Institute members receive discounts on the Press's nearly 400 books in print.

Full-time students are eligible for special half-price membership rates. Life memberships are also available.

For a free catalog describing the Naval Institute Press books currently available, and for further information about U.S. Naval Institute membership, please write to:

Membership & Communications Department
U.S. Naval Institute
118 Maryland Avenue
Annapolis, Maryland 21402-5035

Or call, toll-free, (800) 233-8764.

THE NAVAL INSTITUTE PRESS

FROM THE RIVERS TO THE SEA
The U.S. Navy in Vietnam

Designed by Karen L. White

Set in Sabon and ITC Fenice
by BG Composition
Baltimore, Maryland

Printed on 50-lb. Sebago Eggshell Creme and 70-lb. Glatco Gloss
and bound in Holliston Kingston Natural
by The Maple-Vail Book Manufacturing Group
York, Pennsylvania